Flying Dragons

Flying Dragons

The South Vietnamese Air Force

Robert C. Mikesh

Schiffer Military History
Atglen, PA

Dedication

Dedicated to those who served the South Vietnamese Air Force

Three Northrop F-5A Freedom Fighters of the 522nd Fighter Squadron from Bien Hoa AB on an air strike over South Vietnam in March 1970. *RG 342- 93279 USAF*

Cover artwork by Steve Ferguson, Colorado Springs, CO.
BLACK BIRDS OF DISTINCTION
Highlighted on the cover is a strike by VNAF A-1 Skyraiders of the 514 Fighter Squadron "Blackbirds" led by VNAF CO Nuyen Kao-Ky against North Vietnam targets late in 1964. In April of the following year, the 514th Blackbirds would be the sole VNAF unit to be awarded a Presidential Unit Citation by American President Johnson for the preceding year's missions flown in the ever intensifying civil war.

Book Design by Ian Robertson.

Library of Congress Control Number: 2004117804

Printed in China.
ISBN: 0-7643-2158-7

We are interested in hearing from authors with book ideas on related topics.

Published by Schiffer Publishing Ltd.
4880 Lower Valley Road
Atglen, PA 19310
Phone: (610) 593-1777
FAX: (610) 593-2002
E-mail: Info@schifferbooks.com.
Visit our web site at: www.schifferbooks.com
Please write for a free catalog.
This book may be purchased from the publisher.
Please include $3.95 postage.
Try your bookstore first.

In Europe, Schiffer books are distributed by:
Bushwood Books
6 Marksbury Avenue
Kew Gardens
Surrey TW9 4JF
England
Phone: 44 (0) 20 8392-8585
FAX: 44 (0) 20 8392-9876
E-mail: Info@bushwoodbooks.co.uk.
Free postage in the UK. Europe: air mail at cost.
Try your bookstore first.

Contents

Foreword

The 20 year existence of the South Vietnamese Air Force could be viewed in various ways; like a 20 year old man, it was in the prime of life when it came to an untimely end. To others, a mere two decades have other meanings of time. By comparison, it was only a young air force with outside support, like that needed by any small nation. It had great potential to grow and develop, thus fulfilling its mission to safeguard its country.

The South Vietnamese Air Force was rooted in the traditions of the French Air Force. The senior leaders were still nearly all French trained, and were more fluent in French than English—even after a 20 year break. The men who later entered the Air Force were younger and of a different kind. They were U.S. trained, and often did not speak French at all. Their techniques, learned from a different kind of training, were in contrast to those of their more elderly leaders, yet these younger men became the muscle of the VNAF. Only a few of the pilots that remained at the end had flown VNAF aircraft from the F8F Bearcat through the more advanced F-5 jet fighter.

It might be assumed that the VNAF was a U.S. Air Force transplant. It was not; it merely used many of the same aircraft, procedures, and techniques—even the language to a large degree. But there the resemblance ended. The realities of Asian economics and Asian background took over. What seemed viable and natural to the Western mind would often prove to be the opposite for them. However, Vietnamese solutions were often very good. With more time and material, the men and women of the VNAF might well have developed their Air Force into one of the most formidable in the world, and might have been able to assist neighboring Asian countries with similar ideologies and backgrounds to do likewise in protecting themselves.

I am often asked to advise leaders of other developing countries as to the ways and means in creating their air forces. I believe that the contents of this book about our own experiences within the VNAF will often be referred to as a basis upon which to assess the weaknesses and strengths of the VNAF's short but proud service to its country, the Republic of Vietnam.

In conclusion; I wish to express my appreciation and gratitude to all the American fliers who assisted the VNAF in our years of struggle against the enemy. The experiences shared have created a permanent, mutual bond that neither politics nor time can erode nor erase.

Nguyen-Cao-Ky

Air Vice Marshal Nguyen-cao-Ky, Commander in Chief of VNAF, 1963-1967.
RG 342-172960 USAF

Nguyen-cao-Ky

Although he was once the Prime Minister of the Republic of Vietnam, Nguyen-cao-Ky proudly refers to his profession in life as that of a pilot. Born on 8 September 1930 in Son Tay, a town near Hanoi, he first joined the army when of age, and became a platoon leader in the jungle warfare against Communist guerrillas. When accepted for pilot training, he was sent to Marrakech, Morocco, and later to France for two years at Avord Air Base for advanced training, and on to Algeria for five months of tactical flight training. He graduated as a pilot in 1954, and before long was participating in and leading daring air raids against the enemy that later were carried well into North Vietnam. Ky's leadership qualities accelerated his rise to become Commander of the Air Force from 1963 to 1967, then Prime Minister from 11 June 1965, and Vice-President of Vietnam 3 September 1967. In the last three years of the war he was technically a civilian, but highly regarded as an advisor and looked upon for his guidance in matters of state. Now in exile, Mr. Ky resides in the United States.

Acknowledgments

This is the second book written by this author about the former South Vjetnamese Air Force with the hope of keeping its history alive. The first book, also titled *Flying Dragons*, was published by Osprey Publishing Ltd, London, in 1988. Schiffer Publishing, Inc., and this author convey our thanks for their permission to again use this material in this new publication by the same name.

No book is ever written without sacrifices by some and help from many. My greatest debt is owed to Ramona, my wife, who encouraged me from the beginning and unstintingly gave up her own claims upon my time. I am deeply indebted to three other people as well for the contents of this book and their constant encouragement. Pham-quang-Khiem, a former VNAF pilot, was a continual source of help when the Vietnamese language became troublesome. A historian of the VNAF and collector in his own right, he freely gave from his collections and experiences for inclusion in this book. Offering endless technical assistance was Lt Col Robert J. Mills, Jr., USAF (Ret). At one time Bob, along with Ralph B Young, planned to write this history, but after learning of my interests in doing the same, both stepped aside and graciously passed their material to me and offered endless assistance. Ralph turned over his extensive collection of catalogued VNAF photographs to this project, which formed an excellent foundation for initial photo research and selection. These three share much in the credit for the accomplishment and completeness of the original book.

With limited resource material to draw upon, former VNAF members were crucial to the success of this book, particularly those who had been members of the VNAF from the beginning to the very end. Those that gave willingly of their time to help me with this history, and for which I am deeply grateful, are former VNAF Brig. General Nguyen-ngoc-Oanh, Commander for many years of the Air Training Center, and former Colonel Vu-van-Uoc, at one time the Commander of the 62nd Tactical Wing, and later Commander of Air Operations Command. Their personal knowledge and experience in the VNAF from its beginning was invaluable. Other former VNAF senior officers contributing to this history were Nguyen-cao-Ky and Tran-van-Minh, both of whom had been Commanding Generals of the VNAF: Nguyen-huu-Tan, former Commanding General of the VNAF 4th Air Division; and Duong-thieu-Hung, commanding officer for the 23rd and 33rd Wings. Another previous VNAF officer that I could always depend upon was Vinh-Ahn, past president of the Vietnamese Air Force Veteran's Association of Central California. He mustered members, friends, and colleagues to find answers to the many and difficult questions that I would ask. Visibly included in this group were Nguyen-van-Chuyen and Tran-van-Ngoc, yet there were many, many others that I did not meet personally who have contributed with their knowledge to enrich this effort.

A number of other persons made significant contributions to this effort. Included are Major William H. Austin, Chief of the USAF Magazines and Books Division, and William C. Heimdahl, Air Force History Program, both of whom made it possible to declassify files that could be included in this history about the VNAF. Brig. General Mary A. Marsh, USAF, told of the part that women contributed to the VNAF based upon her experience in being involved at the start of that program. Vice Admiral Ken Moranville, USN (Ret.), when still a junior officer was the first U.S. Navy pilot to serve in Vietnam to aid the VNAF. He conveyed valuable information about the early days in modernizing that Air Force with new equipment. Dr. Ira E. Chart at Northrop Corporation was very helpful in providing data on the F-5 aircraft. Reference sources in France were identified by Stephane Nicolaou of the Musee de l'Air. Leon Wohlert and his VNAF 51-75 website drew in additional details not otherwise available.

The list of contributors for the many photographs and uniform device illustrations are too numerous to mention here. I only hope that the credit line with their valued illustrations that made this book possible will be compensation to some degree for recognition. I owe them a debt of gratitude. Among the photographs, those identified with a RG (Record Group) prefix can be found in the National Archives at College Park, Maryland.

My regret is that time and circumstances did not permit me to talk at length with many more former VNAF officers and men whose lives are part of this story. But I salute them, and hope that this book will revive the memories of their own proud days when serving in their Air Force for the freedom of their country.

Robert C. Mikesh
Washington, D.C.

Introduction

The history of the independent South Vietnamese Air Force, or *Flying Dragons*, as its insignia portrays, in many ways is an American story. It was organized, trained, equipped, and attained its maximum size under the tutelage of the U.S. military. As France disengaged from its failed attempt to retain its former colonies in Indochina in the mid-1950s, U.S. military advisors began an association with airmen of the fledgling Vietnamese Air Force (VNAF) that was to outlive the existence of a nation. By the end of the 1950s the VNAF began to adopt the basic organization of its U.S. benefactors; it flew American built airplanes, received its training from the Americans, and the two nations often swapped air crews between these two air forces. The comaraderie and working relationships that developed between the thousands of American aviators, aircrew, and aviation support and service personnel that served in Vietnam and their VNAF counterparts created a strong bond that is still felt but not seen.

This is not a political history of the Vietnam war; rather, it is the story of the transition of the VNAF from an under-trained and ill-equipped French Air Force auxiliary unit to the fourth largest air force in the world. As American military assistance, involvement, and influence grew, it reshaped and structured the VNAF to the point that it appeared as a miniature facsimile of the American system. Lightly armed hand-me-down, World War II vintage training aircraft gave way to more advanced American types. By the time U.S. involvement ended, the South Vietnamese Air Force had grown from four squadrons of obsolete propeller-driven observation and transport aircraft to a tactical air strike force comprising more than 60 flying units, most of them equipped with jet aircraft.

When the U.S. Congress voted to cut off all further military assistance (including aviation fuel) in August 1973, Vietnam was militarily isolated, and its immediate demise seemed certain. Contributing to this bleak outlook was the fact that the VNAF's original cadre of French-trained mechanics, who had learned to make do with little outside support, were gone. Their successors had never been trained, nor had the need to improvise. Now, the seemingly bottomless well of parts and equipment was dry. American-trained Vietnamese mechanics could remove and replace an aircraft engine, but the new generation of mechanics had to learn to diagnose mechanical problems and improvise to correct them. Many hardly knew where to begin. Despite these problems the South Vietnamese Air Force was able to provide hundreds of missions a day had sufficient fuel stocks been available.

This history is necessarily incomplete: the fall of the Republic of South Vietnam in April 1975 ended, for the foreseeable future, any opportunity to examine official histories and other germane source documents. It is likely that some information was irretrievably lost when destroyed by fleeing members of the South Vietnamese government. Some day Vietnam's present rulers may permit access to any remaining official files of the former South Vietnamese government; until then, the primary records are those from various U.S. official sources and from former VNAF members now living in the United States. Many official records remain classified; some of this material was declassified and appears for the first time in this work. Many former VNAF officers consented to interviews and volunteered valuable information. Such memories are understandably subjective and incomplete due to the passing of time, yet are far better than no accounting at all. Others preferred to remain silent, keeping their contribution to this history to themselves.

The author hopes that this account will not only record such memories of the VNAF fairly and impartially, but that it will inspire others, especially former VNAF members, to add to these accounts to improve and embellish the story of the 20 years at war—and not a single moment of peace—that was the background of the entire life span of the South Vietnamese Air Force.

Note: The spelling of geographical locations, such as cities and provinces, is in the form of the American language usage, while other Vietnamese words, including names of people, appear in this book in the Vietnamese language format.

Preface

I felt an uneasiness from the moment I woke up that morning—a feeling of waiting for something unexpected to happen. It was my day off from squadron duties, which was about our only break from the war that had enveloped my country for all my lifetime. Wandering around downtown Da Nang, I greeted friends and dropped into the Fang-Hang Restaurant for a mid-day *com dia* (dish of rice) and a glass of *ice café*. I had hardly begun to eat when my friend Than-xuan-Tho spotted me and rushed over to me. I could tell by the expression on his face that something traumatic *had* happened.

'Van, have you heard that Dung was shot down this morning and was killed?'

I was stunned! This could not be! He was too good a pilot to have let this happen to him. There was some mistake!

I left the restaurant immediately and rode my Honda motor scooter to my squadron as quickly as I could to learn what had happened. My fears were realized, however, when Major Nguyen-anh-Toan, the operations officer, told me the details. While on a medevac mission, the entire cockpit of Dung's Huey[1] was blown away by an artillery shell, killing both pilots, but the two medics on board, Sergeant Ky and Sergeant Hoa, though badly injured, survived. They went down while approaching a landing zone (LZ) in an area in northern I Corps, an area off limits to most aircraft because of the intense enemy antiaircraft fire.

'Van, we must evacuate the wounded medics as quickly as possible,' Major Toan continued as he looked at me questioningly.

I knew that he was asking me to volunteer to take the mission, but was hesitant in putting it into words. As an unmarried pilot, I was often asked by others to take their place during holidays and special occasions, so they could be with their families. This had been no problem for me, and I was always willing to take their place. If I refused this mission, however, someone else on duty that day would have to do it. I knew that Major Toan would not ask me directly, but it was my friend that had been killed, and I felt that it was up to me to recover the rest of his downed crew. I agreed to make the pick-up.

Grabbing my flight helmet, I proceeded to the Huey that was assigned to me. Sloshing through the rain-filled depressions of the flight line, I was flanked by the pilots of the two gun ships that were to accompany me. We exchanged a few words regarding the procedures we would use on this mission, while all the time my mind was on Dung and his sudden death that morning. How would his wife, who was five months pregnant, be able to cope with this loss? I felt that I should be comforting her right now, but the mission ahead was almost a way of escaping from that very unpleasant situation. I do not think the full impact of his loss had yet hit me.

From Da Nang Air Base we flew along Route 1 to the north past Hue and on to Dong Ha, our destination. A light rain was falling, hampering forward visibility through the glass bubble windshield, but the landmarks clearly visible on either side through the open windows were very familiar to me.

As we approached the pick-up area I made contact with the Marine Detachment that was at the LZ. They briefed me on the ground situation at that moment and what I might expect as I approached. They told me nothing that I wanted to hear—the situation sounded almost impossible. The LZ was on top of a hill, with a cleared area barely large enough for one helicopter. In that location, anything on top of the hill, especially my helicopter, was a perfectly silhouetted target against the sky. If only there was a reason to turn back, aside from my pure fear of the situation, I would have done so.

Skimming the tree tops to avoid enemy fire, I visually homed in on the raised point of ground that was the LZ. Red smoke was ignited as a prearranged signal that the area was still in friendly hands. I could hear ground fire as I slowed down for the landing. Without looking directly, I could see through my left window the twisted remains of a Huey's rotor blades, obviously the ones blown away from Dung's helicopter. That made me aware of the wreckage of the fuselage to my right, laying on its side, minus the nose section. This sight, coupled with the chatter of small arms fire around me, caused the sweat on the back of my flying suit to feel like ice water, literally giving me proverbial 'cold feet.' I wanted to turn and run. Instead, I became mesmerized by the touch down point in the small clearing and continued in. I raised the pitch control and eased back on the stick to slow my forward speed, then dropped the Huey into the LZ.

Bell UH-1H gun ships of the VNAF depart on an escort mission. *RG 342- 107438 USAF*

No sooner was I on the ground than incoming artillery rounds began exploding all around the LZ. The concussions were deafening, making the sound of my engine almost inaudible. A Marine raced frantically toward me, flailing his arms to signal me to leave the area. Now at the side of my window, he shouted above the noise to 'get out of here, or you will get us all killed!'

Responding immediately to his order, I 'pulled torque' somewhere past the red line of the instrument gauge as I blasted the Huey out of there—fast. Once again in the air, every gun in the area seemed to be pointed at me and firing hot lead. My gunships were in hot pursuit above the trees as the rain seemed to intensify. We landed at Hue Phu Bai, our closest safe haven, for our mission was not complete and we would have to go back again.

I could not sleep well that night. The monsoon rain on the roof served as a background to the thoughts that raced through my mind all that night. I kept thinking of Dung's wife and their unborn child, now fatherless. Thoughts of my mother lay heavily on my heart, yet she had died when I was very young. What would the future hold for my younger brother, who was about to finish in the army training school? I had joined the Air Force in the hope of having a better life than that of a foot soldier, but now the question remained as to what was ahead of me when morning came.

Before daylight my fellow crew members and I were up, fumbling in the dark for our clothes as we dressed. We could not help but waken the others that were sleeping in the open bay, but they knew what our mission was for that morning, and did not give us the usual hard time for being too noisy. They must have been relieved that it was not they who were preparing for this extraction in an area where no one wished to go.

The early morning sky was just beginning to reflect its light on the ground through a heavy cloud cover as we approached the LZ. Our plan was to get into the LZ and out again before the enemy would expect us and have a chance to shoot. Once again I was in contact with the Marine detachment at the LZ. This time I asked that no marking smoke be used so as not to alert the enemy.

As my chopper hit the landing spot, we were suddenly engulfed by white smoke that caught all of us by surprise. At first I was confused, then realized that it had been initiated to conceal us from the enemy. Friendly forces emerged through the smoke, rushing the wounded toward my aircraft to place them on board. The wounded were a pathetic sight, trying very hard to hide their pain and discomfort. Two motionless bodies were set on the floor last. I knew that one of them had to be my good friend Dung.

Within seconds after landing I popped up out of the smoke and into a heavy barrage of gunfire that opened up on us. I felt a sickening thud as something struck and exploded at the rear of the helicopter. In a voice of obvious panic, the flight engineer shouted to me that our tail was half shot away. I thought we would go out of control any second and fall on to the ground as my dead buddies had done, but the Huey continued to respond to my controls and gained as much forward speed as the load and the straining engine would allow. The gunships were now on both sides of me as increasing distance from the LZ allowed us to breathe a little more comfortably. I gained more altitude above the trees and continued on to Da Nang without stopping. Coming around the mountain to the north of Da Nang and catching sight of the base, I could not help but wonder if we were coming back from the dead ourselves, or if it was true that we actually accomplished the mission we had set out to do.

Successfully accomplished or not, I was not exuberant over the results. I do not remember much about what happened as we landed back at Da Nang, except that I felt sick to my stomach and wanted to be alone. At base, I found an unoccupied room and slumped into a corner, trembling out of control. I wished I could cry, but tears would not come. The realization had just set in that I had lost another of my many friends in this war which seemed to have no end. I had not lived in a land where there was peace for one moment in my whole life. Where was this all to lead? Would I be the next one for whom someone would have to risk his life to come for me—whether I be dead or alive? Would there ever be a peaceful future for my war-torn country?

A Bell UH-1H Huey of the VNAF buzzes the landing zone while preparing to land near enemy territory.

1

Where it Began

Following World War II, France attempted to reassert her authority over her Indochina colonies, which included Vietnam and the kingdoms of Laos and Cambodia. Communist and Nationalist Viet Minh forces attacked French outposts across a wide front, supported by many people who had only one purpose—national independence. So began the costly eight year Indochina war that ended at a Geneva conference table in July 1954 with a superficial division that created a North and a South Vietnam. In one of many attempts to gain the support of the people, the French incorporated a token force of indigenous personnel into the French armed services as auxiliaries beginning in the early 1950s. Thus began the first semblance of Vietnam's military service.

Cadet Vu-van-Uoc was too busy to enjoy his solo training mission, his mind filled with mental commands to practice steep turns: 'Keep the ball centered! Hold that 45 degree bank angle! Back on the stick to hold the turn!' In two more months he would be graduating in the first class of Vietnamese military pilots to be trained at Nha Trang, in their own country. That graduation date of July 1952 still seemed a long way away, and that flying...BLAM!

A shivering crash and violent impact interrupted his thoughts as he caught sight of what seemed like a torching missile that streaked past after hitting his right wing. Regaining his senses, Uoc found his Morane-Saulnier MS.500 Criquet trainer in an accelerated spin. Two turns went by, and the spinning green earth below was filling the windshield. The long-winged Criquet was not to be intentionally spun, but recovery techniques were taught, just in case. They worked, and at about 150 ft (46 m) above the ground the airplane was level once again. Tremendous control forces were needed to hold the aircraft level. Uoc surveyed the damage: half of the right leading edge was gone, and the outermost wing ribs flailed in the air, creating an awesome racket and shaking the aircraft. Full left rudder and full left aileron maintained some control over the airplane, although the Criquet remained flying in a 10 degree right wing—what was left of it—low attitude and a pronounced slip.

Vietnamese Air Force cadets march past the gate at Nha Trang Air Base identified by the name in Vietnamese, which reads "Air Training Center." *RG 342-K 24835 USAF*

Would he be able to get the airplane back to Nha Trang? This thought filled Uoc's mind. Grasping the hand-held microphone to report his emergency was a difficult task under these conditions, for controlling the damaged airplane took everything he had. He was cleared to make a straight-in approach to runway 12.

After what seemed an eternity, the Cricket's long-legged landing gear touched the ground, bounced, and then stabilized on the runway. The crisis was over. The crash trucks were waiting at the end of the runway, but Uoc taxied the battered airplane to its assigned parking spot. As the propeller came to a stop Captain Fatio, French commander of the Training Center, was at the cabin door to see if Uoc was OK, and to learn what had happened. At his side was RAF-trained Sgt Beck, his flight instructor. Relieved he was safe, they inspected the mutilated airplane: 60 percent of the right wing was damaged, and the wing tip missing.

Who collided with Cadet Uoc's Criquet? A search effort was begun, and before long, the smoldering remains of a crashed Criquet were found. Only the tail, with its brightly painted yellow Vietnamese flag and the plane's serial number remained intact. The missing student was

A formation of Morane-Saulnier 500 Criquets buzz the field at the Nha Trang Air Training Center. *Courtesy of E.C.P.Armees #52112 n16.*

This MS.500 was the type of primary trainer, observation, and communications airplane used extensively in the early years of Vietnamese aviation, generally seen in these French markings. *Courtesy of E.C.P.Armees #INA 1030.*

Nguyen-tam-Dang, now remembered as the first airman to give his life in the newly-formed Vietnamese Air Force.

The next day the fallen airman's casket was draped with the Vietnamese flag, with nearly the entire base in attendance to bid him farewell. Heading the ceremonies was French Maj Chaussin, Commander of the Flying School *(Ecole de Pilotage)* at Nha Trang. Overhead, a formation of Criquets gave a final salute in the form of one aircraft sharply breaking away from the formation to fly alone 'toward an uncertain horizon.'

The graduation of this first class of 14 pilots[2] in the South Vietnamese Air Force marked another milestone on the road to independence. They were not yet independent of French influence; however, with the graduation of this first class of pilots trained in Vietnam, national sovereignty seemed much closer.

(The background of Vu-van-Uoc is described on page (97). He went on to become a Colonel, having his last assignment as commander of the Air Operations Command (OAC), VNAF.)

The Criquets

The sound of the Criquet was common at Nha Trang in the early 1950s. These were not sounds from insects, however, but reverberations from the exhaust ports of the 240 hp Argus engines of the Morane-Saulnier built version of the 1936 German designed Fieseler Fi 156 Storch, which the French called "Criquet." Casual observers of flying operations at Nha Trang Air Base were used to seeing the familiar red, white, and blue French roundels on the fuselage sides and wings of these dark blue aircraft. Occasionally, an aircraft was observed with an unfamiliar orange-yellow circle with three concentric red stripes. These aircraft were part of a small number of MS.500s that France transferred to the Vietnamese government, and were the embryo of what one day would become the South Vietnamese Air Force.

Basic flight training in Vietnam began and ended at Nha Trang in these early days, flying these two-seat Criquets. The dual-controlled tandem seat Criquets proved to be excellent pilot trainers, although considered by some to be too easy to fly. They could be flown under full control as slowly as 28 knots (51 km/h; 32 mph)

This is the first class of VNAF Aviation Cadets in 1951-52 at Nha Trang. All graduated and later filled responsible positions except Dang, third from top left, who was killed in a flight training accident.. Four student officers were also graduated from this first class. Six cadets from this graduating class of 10 cadets were killed in action. *Courtesy of Vu-van-Uoc.*

The workhorse of the early VNAF were the Morane-Saulnier 500 Criquets. These French-built aircraft were of the Fieseler Fi 156 Storch design that were used extensively by the Germans during World War II. The French supplied these aircraft for VNAF for training, reconnaissance, and liaison duties. *Courtesy of E.C.P. Armees #A52-112 R15.*

The MS.500 Criquet was the airplane most representative of the Vietnamese air power in its formative days. These observation/training aircraft were readily identifiable by their long gangly landing gear. This Criquet crosses the coast line near Nha Trang, an area noted for its beauty. *Courtesy of Armor Force History #4.*

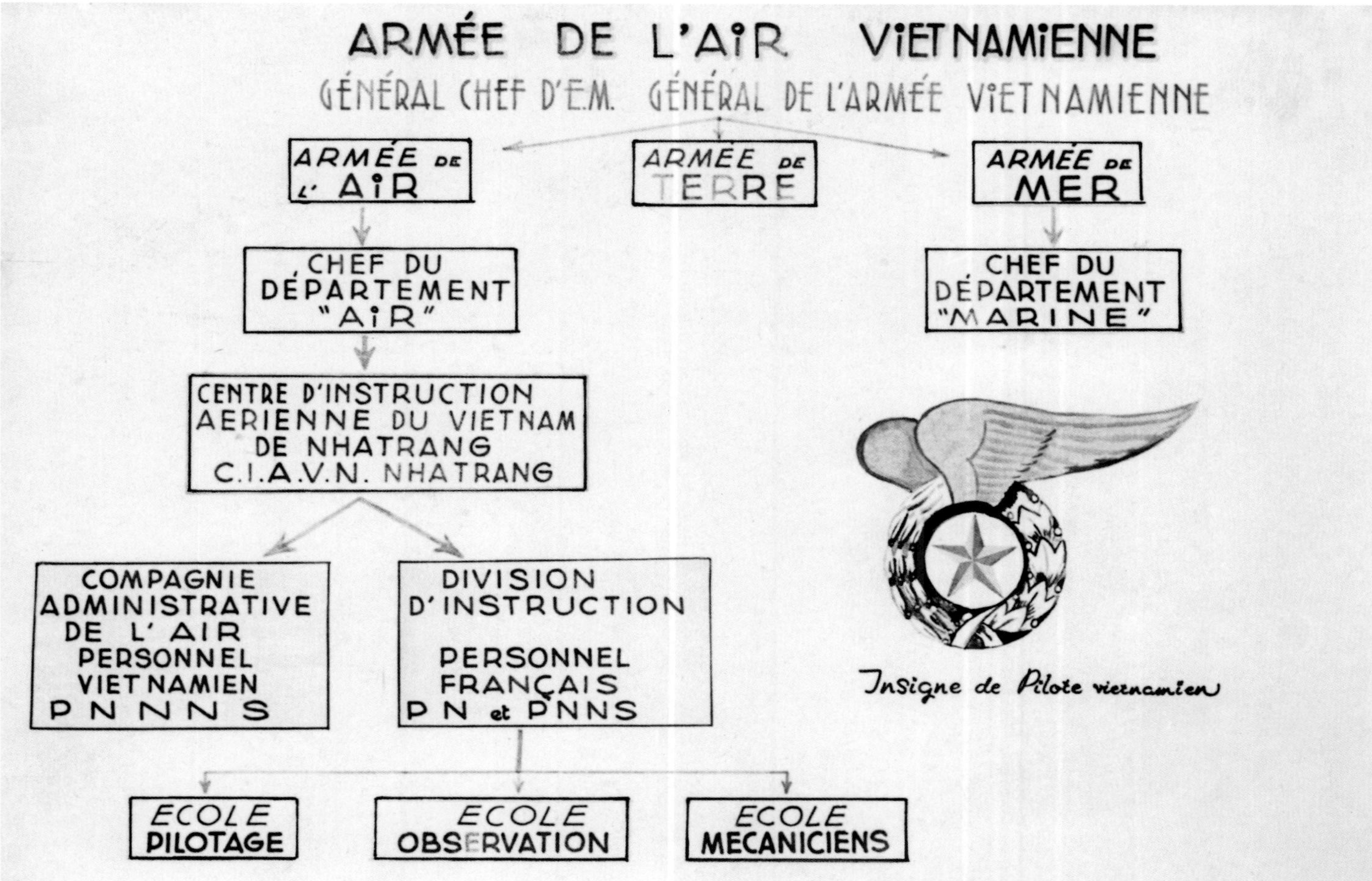

Above: This chart found on file at the French Army Headquarters, Paris, represents the first known organization structure that includes air units of the Vietnamese armed services in May 1951. It shows the relationship of the ATC with the other military services at that early time. *Courtesy of E.C.P.Armees #R 0967*. Below: Organizational chart of 1951 shows air units within the RVNAF when that Vietnamese military service was initially formed under French control.

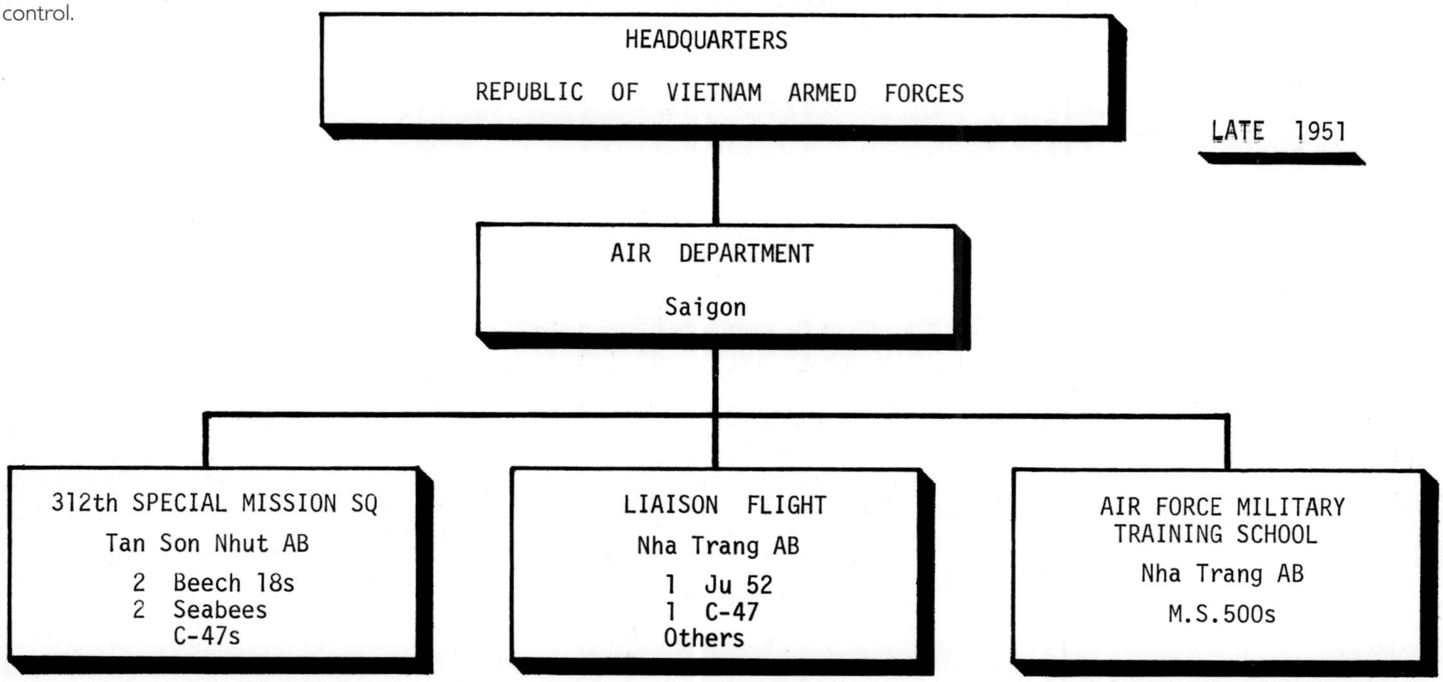

To help counter outside aggression, the French agreed to include Vietnamese in the military role of protecting their own country. They remained only in small numbers and never in positions of leadership. Seen here are French C-47s moving troops at Na San Air Field in northwest Vietnam, during military operations against the Viet Minh in 1953. *Courtesy of Musee de l'Air.*

because of their many high lift devices along the wing. In experienced hands they could be landed in less than 60 ft (18 m) in still air. Their long-stroke landing gear was designed to absorb the impact of high vertical descent rates for these short field landings.

The Criquet was the most commonly observed aircraft in the skies around Nha Trang, and other parts of the country, as well. Because of their presence, this slow, docile aircraft became a symbol of the Vietnamese Air Force during this early period. The diminutive observation plane was hardly a show of force or power, but it was a start.

By mid-summer 1951 the air arm of the Vietnamese Army was limited to a few dozen Criquets, which formed one liaison flight (less than squadron strength). During this period a program of building small air strips was begun to aid military and government officials in their efforts to gain access to even the most remote villages in the country. Most strips were dirt paths, but they were more than adequate for the Criquets and their short takeoff and landing (STOL) characteristics. Vietnamese pilots and their Criquets played a major role in nation-building by providing air liaison for internal communication.

The French Period

The French Air Force established Nha Trang in 1949 and, by 1 June 1951, it opened an Air Training Center there to train Vietnamese Air Force personnel. In small numbers at first they began to learn about aircraft maintenance, communications, and other required technical skills, most of which were directed toward maintaining aircraft no more complicated than these fabric-covered Criquets.

Earlier Vietnamese pilots and aircrews received flight training in the French schools at such places in France as Salon Air Base (AF Academy) and Avord AB (transports), and in Morocco there were Marrakech and Meknes ABs (fighters) and Blida AB in Algeria. Other not-to-be-forgotten bases for the Vietnamese were Rochefort and Chamberry ABs in France for mechanics training, and Auxerre AB for communications training. Fez and Khouribga ABs in Morrocco housed the air navigation and fighter gunnery schools, respectively.[3]

In March 1952 French instructors at Nha Trang began to train small numbers of pilots and observers. There was little evidence as yet to suggest the making of an independent Vietnamese Air Force. The Vietnamese served merely as supplemental personnel in the French Air Force, having no air units of their own.

This hesitant start in establishing an air force stemmed not from the Vietnamese people themselves, but from French unwillingness to transfer any form of power to the people over whom they wished to maintain colonial control. Only through outside pressure on the French Government, when the loss of all of Indochina appeared likely, was a concession made to allow the Vietnamese people to play a larger part in determining their own destiny.

The emergence of this Air Force did not occur easily, nor did it happen without an aggressive will to excel. Its beginning can be traced to the French effort against the Communist and Nationalist Viet Minh[4] forces in Southeast Asia after World War II. Its initial roles were restricted to observation and liaison work in support of the French. Although Vietnamese nationals entered the French Air

Aviation Cadet Duong-thieu-Hung of the first pilot class in 1952 prepares to start the engine of this MS.500 for a training mission. Hung was later the 23rd Tactical Wing Commander. *Courtesy of E.C.P. Armees #R 0991.*

Control tower procedures are demonstrated at Nha Trang AB by this French instructor to Nguyen-ngoc-Oanh, who later commanded this Air Training Center through its formative years. *Courtesy of E.C.P. Armees #R 0975.*

Force ranks beginning in 1949, another six years would pass before Vietnam would gain its own air arm.

Events leading to its ultimate formation can be linked to the concerns of the western world over the emergence of Communist China in 1949. This was viewed as an extension of Soviet power that threatened to spread throughout all of Asia. The United States had commercial and strategic interests in that part of the world, and the victory of the Chinese Communists spurred the United States Congress to pass the Mutual Defense Assistance Act, which was designed to deal with this theater of the newly-termed "Cold War." The President was empowered to dispense funds to various nations, including the general area of China, which was extended to cover Southeast Asia, and specifically, Vietnam.

With the appearance of Chinese Communist troops at the northern frontier of Vietnam at the beginning of 1950, and formal recognition of Ho-chi-Minh's Democratic Republic of Vietnam by Communist China and the Soviet Union in January 1950, the United States government acted promptly by rendering assistance to southeast Asian countries to check further communist encroachment. On 7 February 1950 the United States extended diplomatic recognition to the French controlled State of Vietnam, as well as to the kingdoms of Cambodia and Laos, as a statement of America's supportive position.

Nine days later, France requested American economic and military assistance to continue prosecuting the war in Indochina. Without American aid, France considered withdrawing from the region

Training in Morse code is headed by this French instructor for cadets of the first pilot class in 1952. In front row are Vo-Dinh, Tu-bo-Cam, and Nguyen-the-Anh. In the last row are Vu-van-Uoc and Nguyen-ngoc-Oanh, all of whom figured prominently in the future leadership of the young air force. *Courtesy of E.C.P. Armees #R 0963.*

This student pilot with instructor is discussing an air route for a training flight cross-country. Aspirant (Warrant Officer) Duong-thieu-Hung at left listens intently to his instructor Lt Le-minh-Luan at right. This picture was taken at Da Nang in 1953, early in the life of VNAF, when French aircraft began taking on the new yellow and red circled national insignia. *Courtesy of Albert Grandolini.*

if Ho-chi-Minh received increased resources from China and the Soviet Union. What the French needed in Vietnam were immediate supplies and replacements for their obsolete aircraft. The problem was exacerbated because few fully-trained military maintenance technicians were on hand. There was even a general shortage in France itself, where the French Air Force depended to a large degree on contract aircraft maintenance.

American policy makers, opposed to losing Southeast Asia to Communism, provided $164 million in military aid to France for use in Indochina. In parallel with this action the United States encouraged France to give "greater reality" to Vietnamese nationalistic aspirations, and thereby deny to the Viet Minh their sole claim of struggling for independence. With the Vietnamese people thus allowed a greater stake in their own destiny, the French had to place more reliance on indigenous military forces, requiring better equipment and training facilities. Another underlying factor was that this action would allow the French to direct more of their effort to the needed support of NATO[5] defenses in Europe.

The French were almost forced to agree to this request. Not only were factions outside the country encouraging Vietnamese involvement, but the voices of the Vietnamese themselves were beginning to be heard through their native leader, Emperor Bao-Dai. Bao-Dai was the last of the Vietnamese royal family, but was only a puppet leader under France. Yet he was able to obtain French agreement that Vietnamese personnel would be included in the military forces to aid in the protection of their country.

Through this agreement, the French authorized the formation of the Republic of Vietnam Armed Forces (RVNAF) in 1950. But this organization would remain under the strict control of the French, who continued to govern Vietnam. Military equipment for the newly formed army included the first airplanes to be recognized as belonging to the Vietnamese. These were a small number of Morane Saulnier 500 Criquet light observation aircraft that increased in number over the years.

The French established the 312th Special Mission Squadron for the Vietnamese at Nha Trang on 1 August 1951, and moved it the next year to the commercial airport at Saigon, better known as Tan Son Nhut Airport. This squadron was equipped mostly with French-supplied Douglas C-47s and three Beechcraft 18s for carrying high priority passengers and cargo hauling missions. Two Republic Seabees were included. The mission of the squadron was mainly to support the meager forces at Nha Trang, 200 air miles northeast of Saigon.

Republic RC-3 Seabees, acquired in limited numbers, did not fill the need for coastal and river patrol as intended *Courtesy M.C. Roberts.*

The earliest use of the French-built Morane-Saulnier M.S. 500 Criquet when in VNAF colors was that of flight trainers.

Three Beech D-18Ss were introduced into Vietnam in the early 1950s for light transport duties as part of the 312th Special Mission Squadron at Tan Son Nhut.

Douglas C-47s were seen only using this style of Vietnamese national insignia, supposedly for better recognition when flown out of country.

By 1954, twin-engine Marcel Dassault MD-315 Flamants were added to the RVNAF's Esquadrille of Liaison (ELA), a mixed-mission squadron with a variety of aircraft at Nha Trang. There were three versions of the Flamant: one for liaison duties; a transport version for carrying up to 16 troops; and a few that were bomber versions, with exterior bomb racks and glazed nose for a bombardier, enabling them to be used for limited ground support operations.

To manage the aircraft of the Armed Forces of Republic of Vietnam, the first VNAF office was established on 1 July 1951. This was located in one office room with the military headquarters of the Vietnamese Army, and situated on Than-hung-Dao Boulevard in Saigon. It was initially called "Aviation Vietnamese," a harmless enough title for the ruling French military leaders to accept. The French in Indochina were very cautious in relinquishing any control to the local people, especially when it pertained to military matters. Thus, while gaining some official status on this date, the "Aviation Vietnamese"—soon called the "Department Air"—still functioned as an auxiliary of the French Air Force.

Before the formation of this headquarters, National Amendment Number 9, dated 25 June 1951, mandated by the French, had already authorized the establishment of a Vietnamese Air Training Center at what was then French Air Base Number 194, at Nha Trang. Before the country was divided into North and South by the 1954 Geneva Accords, Nha Trang was the only military air base located in the southern part of the country. This was logical, as most of Vietnam's air activities were concentrated in the north, adjacent to Communist China, and in particular, in the area of the capital city of Hanoi. On 15 December 1952 the facility was given greater status when it was officially redesignated as the "Air Instruction Center," and widened its scope of instruction. As the young Air Force grew, all aviation training within Vietnam was undertaken at Nha Trang. Graduates, intentionally or not, retained a kinship-type allegiance to the Air Instruction Center, whose influence contributed greatly to the overall development of the Vietnamese Air Force.

Dien Bien Phu

The relentless battle against the guerrilla activities of Ho-chi-Minh and his communist followers was a constant threat to those French and the Vietnamese that opposed communist influence and takeover of their country. This situation prevailed for months following World War II. The freedom of movement by the enemy of its forces and supplies was the greatest problem to the French in combating these forces.

In an effort to block Viet Minh incursions into the fertile plains of Dien Bien Phu, in northwest Tonkin, from across the Laotian border, the French intended to maintain a fortification to control the main road between the two regions. In 1953 French General Henri Eugene Navarre concentrated his forces on the plain of Dien Bien Phu to establish such a stronghold to block the Viet Minh supply movement. Supporting the French and Vietnamese effort was American backing in the form of equipment, aircraft, and supplies.

Beginning on 10 March 1954, the Viet Minh mounted massed assaults against the French outposts and two airfields with devastating effect. This led to the tragic and humiliating defeat of the French on 7 May when Viet Minh forces overran their last fortification and ended the costliest battles the French ever fought in Vietnam. World attention was focused on this fierce battle in Vietnam as never before.

The Viet Minh victory at Dien Bien Phu allowed the communists to move troops and weapons toward the perimeters of Hanoi, the most important city of northern Vietnam, together with its port, Haiphong. The safety of its Expeditionary Corps in Vietnam being the prime consideration at this point, the French Government directed the French forces to withdraw to the south. They stabilized at the 18th Parallel, with the intent of safeguarding the southern part of Vietnam.

A cease fire ensued, and peace negotiations began in Geneva. After two months of deliberations a settlement was reached with the signing of the Geneva Accords by French and Viet Minh mili-

Dessault MD-315 Flamanats were part of Vietnam's military forces in the early years while still under French control. *Courtesy of Stephane Nicolaou.*

The Criquet also served as a Medivac aircraft with stretcher provisions behind the second seat. Shown here are Lt Do-khac-Mai in rear and Lt Nguyen-the-Anh in the front at Nha Trang. Anh was killed in a A-1E accident at Bien Hoa in 1967. The PDQS insignia is of the Observation Squadron. *Courtesy of Albert Grandolini.*

A formal parade is in progress at this training facility. Lined behind are Dessault MD-315 Flamanats that were also used as crew trainers. *Courtesy of Albert Grandolini.*

tary representatives on 21 July 1954. The Accords established two states separated at the 17th parallel of latitude, a demilitarized zone on each side of the line, and the withdrawal of French troops from the North and of Viet Minh forces from the South. These Accords prohibited the introduction of fresh troops, arms, and ammunition, as well as building new military bases in Vietnam. Initially, these restrictions influenced the type of new aircraft and air base expansion for Vietnam's air force. Finally, under the Geneva Accords, there were to be, by July 1956, elections throughout Vietnam to unify the country, but these never took place. In the 12 months that followed the signing of this agreement, and before the Viet Minh stopped the migration, about 880,000 Vietnamese fled from the North to the South. In the years that followed, it was not uncommon to find many South Vietnam Air Force personnel among the loyal number that fled from the north.

Ho-chi-Minh made no secret of his determination to extend his control over all of Vietnam. Immediately after the Geneva agreements he called for a "long and arduous struggle" to win the south, which he described as "territories of ours." He soon sent cadres—known then as the Viet Minh, prior to being regular North Vietnamese Army troops—across the 17th Parallel. They expanded the communist network in the south, prepared for future infiltration of men from the north, and worked for eventual unification under Hanoi through subversion, as well as open conflict.

The French regrouped in the south in an attempt to maintain control over their shrinking holdings in that part of Asia. For a while, very little was done to improve the status of the Vietnamese air arm, which they still controlled. In 1953 the RVNAF Criquets had been formed into two GAO units (squadrons), and a year later the ELA (light Combat Liaison-Tactical Squadron) was formed and equipped with French Dassault MD-315 Flamants, along with a variety of other aircraft. Some of these Flamants had wing-mounted bomb racks that gave the Vietnamese a token bombing capability. This total air strength was solely Vietnamese.

Although the flight training program was in progress, it yielded only a small number of Vietnamese liaison pilots and observers. Many more were needed. Those already in flying service had combat experience under French control as early as late 1952. These Vietnamese officers and pilots became the nucleus of the future expansion of the Vietnamese Air Force. In the period 1951 to 1955, however, the total Vietnamese air strength barely exceeded 300 men.

For logistics support, the French used the main depot at Hanoi until it was evacuated and the materials were moved to Bien Hoa Air Base, where a depot was activated on 1 June 1955. By that date, the Vietnamese Air Force remained essentially a small auxiliary air arm, entirely under the control of the French, with limited training capability and observation duties. Few Vietnamese held high rank; most were inexperienced, and the French did not encourage, much less grant, leadership responsibilities. Desertions of enlisted men were common and damaging to the French image. Outside observers pointed out that the French practiced an arrogant colonial policy that alienated native loyalties to such a point as to render the planning of military strategy almost impossible. Nevertheless, after the fall of Dien Bien Phu and adoption of the Geneva Accords, which led to the eventual military withdrawal of French forces from all of Southeast Asia, the stage was set for the emergence of an independent Vietnamese Air Force free of French Air Force control.

2

Time of Transition

In the early 1950s, Communist influence was very visibly expanding everywhere. U.S. Secretary of State John Foster Dulles described the now-famous Domino Theory in a nationwide broadcast:

"If they (the Soviets) could get this peninsula of Indochina, Siam, Burma, Malaya, they would have what is called the rice bowl of Asia...And you can see that if the Soviet Union had control of the rice bowl of Asia that would be another weapon which would tend to expand their control into Japan and into India.'"

The exact moment cannot be drawn between the time when French influence and control over the Vietnamese Air Force ended and American aid and advice prevailed. While French influence prevailed in Indochina, the United States had provided assistance to Cambodia, Laos, and Vietnam in varying degrees since 1950—long before the fall of Dien Bien Phu in May 1955—in an effort to stave off the influence of a communist takeover. The United States promoted its hard line against the spread of communism, as well as to protect its interests in Asia, and was compelled to assist both the French and the Vietnamese in this cause.

But, as though deliberately timed by the Communists, this assistance had to be severely diluted when Communist troops crossed from North Korea into South Korea in June 1950. American forces were committed to assist the United Nations with both men and equipment in defending South Korea in a war that lasted until July 1953. Throughout that three year period, American assistance in support of French holdings in Indochina was, by necessity, only in the form of supplying materiel.

MAAG and MAP

To administer this materiel aid, the United States established a Military Assistance Advisory Group (MAAG) in August 1950, with headquarters in Saigon. To enable these goods to be transferred, the U.S. signed a Mutual Defense Assistance Agreement on 23 December 1950 with France, Vietnam, and neighboring Cambodia and

Somewhere in the northern part of yet-to-be-divided Vietnam, these French pilots race to their Grumman F6F Hellcats to fly missions against enemy insurgents. *Courtesy of E.C.P.Armees #COC 51.25 R06*

Laos. This agreement allowed for indirect American military aid to the three countries. Although the Americans hoped to work directly with the Vietnamese as well as with the French, the French regarded the Bao-Dai government and its military forces to be incapable of dealing with assistance matters. French troops were carrying the burdens of the war, and the few Vietnamese units in existence had limited capability, except as auxiliaries. Following requests from the French, MAAG transferred Military Assistance Program (MAP) materiel to them, and tried to ensure the proper use of the items supplied. Subsequently, much of the military aid (C-47s in particular) went to reinforce French forces instead of going directly to Vietnamese air units. Eventually these aircraft reached the South Vietnamese, but only when the French units departed.

In October 1950 a French aircraft carrier docked in Saigon with 40 F6F Hellcats, complete with French markings, destined to replace the aging Mk IX Spitfires. The few Vietnamese pilots serving as auxiliaries to the French were reconciled to the fact that these sporty Hellcats would be flown by French pilots only.

The French had also requested Bell P-63 Kingcobras from the Americans, primarily because French pilots liked the nose-firing 37 mm. cannon. Three *Armee de l'Air* squadrons with 63 Kingcobras had previously served in Indochina. Spare parts and ammunition for these obsolete WWII Kingcobras were not available; accordingly, 80 Grumman F8F Bearcat fighters were offered. The Bearcats arrived in Vietnam during February and March 1951. These airplanes were transferred to the French under the supervision of the USAF 13th Air Force, headquartered in the nearby Philippines. Hong Kong Aircraft Engineering in Hong Kong refurbished the Bearcats and modified some in order that all the aircraft would be to the 20 mm equipped F8F-1B configuration equipped with 4 x 20 mm cannon.. To support the Bearcats through the war, Lockheed-Singapore subsequently received a contract to perform scheduled maintenance and repair battle damage during the period 1953-58. Some of these Bearcats would eventually be flown by Vietnamese pilots, but that would be well into the future.

Built in 1945, the Bearcats had missed air operations with the U.S. Navy in the Pacific War by only a few months. During the Korean War the Corsair was favored because it was better equipped for the air-to-ground support role than the Bearcat, which was designed as an air superiority fighter. Because of the Bearcat's availability in 1951, the French eagerly accepted this newer equipment to replace their Spitfires and Hellcats. After the Korean War, 26 of

To support the French and the Vietnamese Government, the United States supplied military equipment during the time of their own war effort in Korea. Seen here at Na San Air Field, near Diem Bien Phu, an Armee de l'Air Douglas B-26 returns from a bombing mission while a C-47 of 2/62 FRANCHE-COMTE waits for takeoff. Both types were supplied from USAF resources. *RG 342-47820 USAF.*

French pilots in Indochina liked the Bell P-63 Kingcobra and their nose firing 37 mm cannon. Limited U.S. supplies of this already obsolete equipment restricted their use. *Courtesy of E.C.P. Armees #IN.A R 1038.*

the F4U Corsairs (actually AU-1s) joined the French in Vietnam in April 1954. With French pilots, both the Bearcats and the Corsairs served gallantly in many operations, including the battle of Dien Bien Phu.

A substantial number of Douglas B-26 Invaders and C-47 transports were transferred to the French in the early 1950s. Despite the higher American priorities in Korea, U.S. materiel dispatched to Vietnam helped the French combat major Viet Minh offensives. Further French victories in May 1951 compelled the Viet Minh to abandon open combat in favor of low-key guerrilla operations of harassment and ambush. Consequently, the war reached a stalemate, this situation prevailing for several years. The attempt to block Viet Minh incursion between northwest Tonkin and the nearby border of Laos resulted in the French stand at Dien Bien Phu in 1954. In consequence of their resulting defeat, and the division of Vietnam into two countries, the French played a far less active role than before in maintaining the stability of the country. American influence grew because of this increasing vacuum of leadership and suppressed Vietnamese authority.

In order to rectify the situation, the U.S. Military Assistance Advisory Group identified one problem area as being the urgent need for Vietnam to have a real air force of its own. While extraordinary priority was given by the French to develop the Vietnamese army, scant attention had been accorded to Vietnamese aviation units. These minor units were incapable of assisting in large SEATO[6] operations in the Southeast Asian theater. SEATO, sponsored by the United States in 1954, consisted of eight nations to provide mutual protection over Laos, Cambodia, and "the free territory under the jurisdiction of the State of Vietnam." Ratified on 1 February 1955, it supported President Eisenhower's "domino theory" that all of Southeast Asia would fall under Communist rule if Ho-chi-Minh's government was able to control all of Vietnam. Having SEATO

The U.S. Navy released 80 Grumman F8F Bearcats to the French in 1951 to bolster their fighter-bomber requirements in Indochina. *Courtesy of E.C.P. Armees #33119 R8.*

Effective weapons carried by these French-piloted Bearcats were five inch rockets, along with their four 20 mm cannon. *ECPA 53119 R10*

forces at hand for air support in the event of further outside aggression, South Vietnam could focus chiefly on the expansion of its Vietnamese army.

To support this plan to increase Vietnamese military air activity, the Vietnamese Army was authorized 3,000 men in January 1955, to be organized into two air liaison squadrons and one air transport squadron. It was thought that this number would be adequate to deal with minor operations, mainly to give tactical support to ground activities in the country through airlift, paradrops, visual and photo reconnaissance, and medical evacuation. Yet, by the time Vietnam's Air Force was formed six months later, it had gained less than half its authorized strength.

At this stage USAF advisors were hardly needed to fill many MAAG positions, because the French were retained to organize and train those Vietnamese required to operate this relatively small air unit. Consequently, the small number of USAF officers initially assigned to MAAG had few duties, though they received some specialist training in the United States to undertake advisory roles. They advised when requested, and tried to stay abreast of the Vietnamese military programs as best they could. It was difficult enough for the American advisors, but the Vietnamese personnel had two very different military doctrines and languages to adjust to—French and American—plus Asian customs of their own. It was not an easy period for the Vietnamese airmen.

As Vietnamese-marked aircraft began to be associated with Vietnamese manned air units and squadrons, their importance was beginning to be realized. Their services were increasing, yet they were a difficult organization for Army commanders to manage while looking after what they felt to be the more important ground role of the Army. Aviation units were showing their worth, but direct Army management was another matter.

Another American airplane that served the French Air Force in Indochina were Vought Corsairs. These became available to the French in 1954 when the war in Korea ended. These French Corsairs saw action in the battle over Dien Bien Phu.

The French Air Force in Indochina made effective use of U.S. supplied Douglas B-26 Invaders. This particular Invader of CB 1/19 GASCOGNE carried 14 forward firing 50 Cal machine-guns, plus four more in two turrets. *Courtesy of Musee de l'Air.*

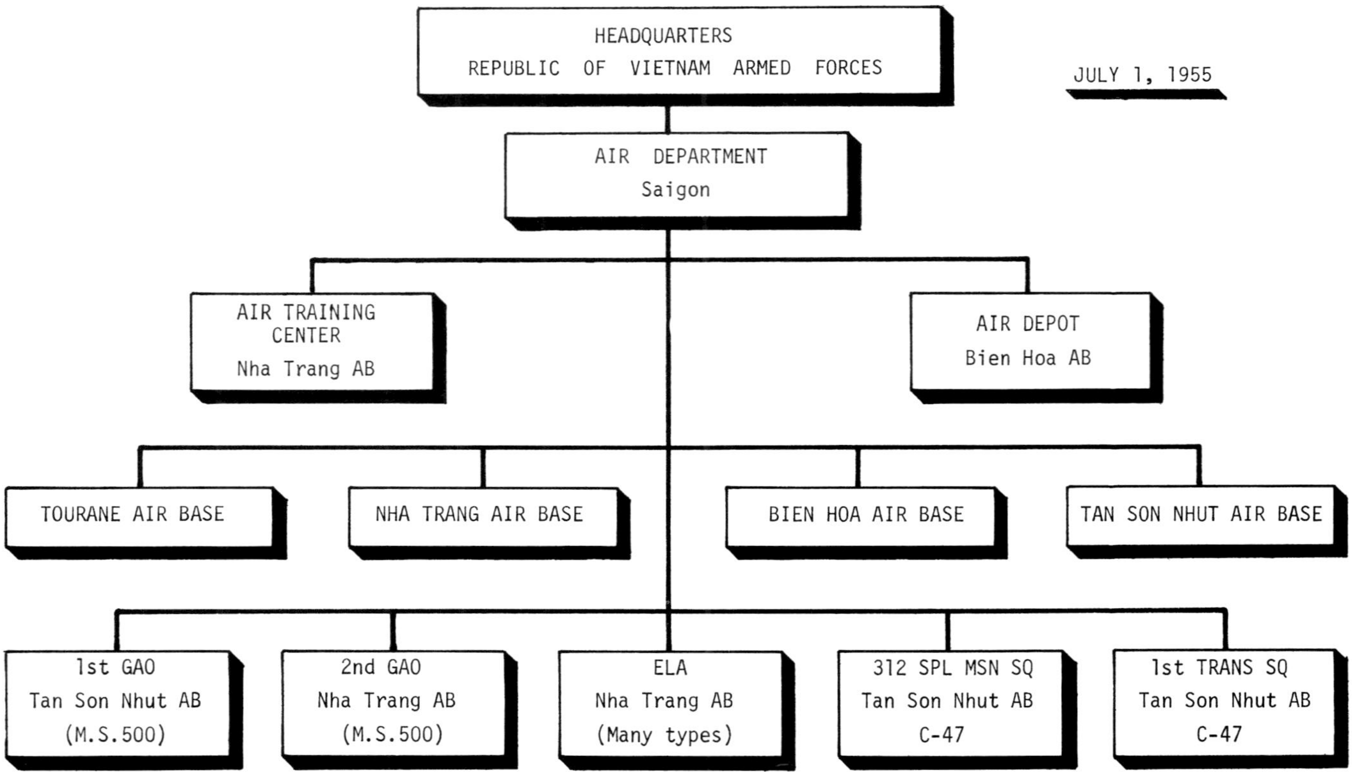

GAO: Group Artillery Observation
ELA: Esquadrille of Liaison, (Combat Liaison Tactical Sq.)

Organizational Chart of July 1, 1955, showing the units of VNAF on the day it was formed as an independent branch of military service.

Air to ground communications between the airborne observer (later Forward Air Controller) and field commanders was essential. This hand carried radio is of the type used to communicate with the observer carried in the M.S. 500 Criquet aircraft. Courtesy of *E.C.P. Armees 34.4 R22.*

This photograph taken on October 1, 1953, shows French Captain Cottet passing his command of the 1st GAO (Group, Artillery Observation) to Lt. Nguyen-ngoc-Oanh (right) at Tan Son Nhut Airport. This was one of the very early command positions transferred to the Vietnamese. The French officer is wearing Vietnamese pilot wings. *Courtesy of E.C.P. Armees SC 54.4 R 10.*

Birth of the VNAF

With parade ceremonies at Saigon and Nha Trang, on 1 July 1955 the South Vietnamese Air Force (VNAF) was established as a separate and distinct military unit; it was not only separated from the Vietnamese Army, of which it was formerly a part, but from the French Air Force. This date was subsequently observed each year with much pride by the people of the Republic of Vietnam. Perhaps no other milestone in the Vietnamese struggle for independence had greater meaning than the birth of its own air force.

The designation VNAF for this new air force was popularly used. In command of the newly formed Vietnamese Air Force was Than-van-Ho, one of the first four Vietnamese officers to receive flight training in France. Prime Minister Ngo-dinh-Diem made his selection from the four candidates, and having a commander native to the South greatly influenced his decision. Ho was advanced immediately from the rank of 1st Lt to Major upon his appointment.

While this was the most noted command position allocated to the VNAF, some of the first command transfers from the French to

Vietnamese airmen served as auxiliaries to the French Air Force prior to the establishment of their own air force. They assisted in such missions as shown here of this French C-47 moving refugees and bringing reinforcements. *Courtesy of P Dampier.*

Two Bearcats of the French Air Force in Indochina stand ready for combat armed with napalm tanks when being flown by the French during their struggle in French Indochina. Their operational days were numbered, however, for they were all but worn out. Excessive oil consumption limited their range. *Courtesy of Musee de l'Air CMA 1738.*

the Vietnamese officers of the Air Department took place two years earlier. In 1953, command of the 1st GAO (Group Artillery Observer) at Tan Son Nhut was transferred from French Air Force Captain Cottet to that of Vietnamese 1st Lt Nguyen-ngoc-Oanh. At the same time, French Capt Blanchard relinquished command of the 2nd GAO to 1st Lt Vo-Dinh at Nha Trang AB. Placing these two Criquet units under the command of Vietnamese officers at that time was a major boost for Vietnamese pride.

When the VNAF was formed in mid-1955, its only assets were the training base at Nha Trang and the air depot at Bien Hoa, all air bases to the north of the 17th parallel having been incorporated in the territory of North Vietnam. VNAF air units consisted of the reassignment to the 1st GAO, which had moved from Tan Son Nhut to Hue Citadel Airport, then to Da Nang, and 2nd GAO at Nha Trang, along with the ELA (Esquadrille of Liaison, or Combat Liaison Tactical Squadron) at Tan Son Nhut, having a large variety of aircraft, but probably without its Flamants. There was also a transport squadron of C-47s. The record is not clear, but this C-47 unit was probably the 312th Special Missions Squadron based at Tan Son Nhut. The major portion of the airport occupied by RVNAF[7] took on the status of an air base in 1953.

On the day of the VNAF's inauguration the 1st Transport Squadron was formed, which gave the VNAF 32 C-47s in their two squadrons. These transports were part of the early Mutual Defense Assis-

These poor quality photos are historic in nature, because they show these Bearcats in operational service with VNAF. These rare photographs show the Bearcats marked with their newly acquired star and bar VNAF insignia around 1956/57. *Courtesy of Albert Grandolini.*

Bearcats became the pride of the VNAF after the French turned their war weary F8F-1Bs over to the Vietnamese. Seen here are two of these fighters breaking off as they return from a mission. Note the four 20 mm cannon barrels at the wing leading edge. *Courtesy of Albert Grandolini.*

tance Program, reassigned from French units. The C-47s were not unfamiliar to the Vietnamese, for they had been in their country for many years, though flying in French markings. The Gooney Birds allocated to the 1st Transport Squadron, commanded by Major Nguyen-cao-Ky, came from the French GT2/63 Semega at Tan Son Nhut which, according to French sources, were officially transferred to the VNAF on 1 July 1955. Initially, there were 35 VNAF pilots for these C-47s, but only four were qualified for instrument flying.

On induction, the VNAF consisted of 58 aircraft and approximately 1,345 personnel, this modest strength hardly meriting the term "air force." The French had made no effort to expand the VNAF to a force able to assume a significant role in support of its country, the emphasis placed not on the delivery of fire power, but on routine aerial surveillance and limited movements of small bodies of troops, primarily platoons, by C-47s. At this stage no formalized structure existed for the coordination of the Army of the Republic of Vietnam (ARVN) and VNAF activities; nor was there a central system for directing the combined force. Though vital, such meager resources did not merit the need for a central system. However, it did eventually emerge.

As the Bearcats neared the end of their operational service life with VNAF, this one was prepared for static display showing the ordnance that could be carried. Note the insignia of the 415th Fighter Squadron on the cowling. *RG 342-K-26995 USAF*

In May 1956, by agreement with the Vietnamese government and the VNAF, the USAF openly assumed some of the training and organizational responsibilities of the VNAF. Thus, when the French turned over the depot at Bien Hoa to the Vietnamese and suddenly withdrew their supply advisors, American personnel informally filled the vacuum. To ease this transition, teams came from the USAF Southern Air Materiel Area, Pacific, based at Clark AB in the Philippines during 1957-58, began to convert the VNAF from French to USAF procedures. Transition from French to American control occurred between 1955 to 1957.

On 1 June 1957 French training contracts expired, and the United States took over the role of tutor to the VNAF. Diem worsened the VNAF's personnel situation in August 1959 when he terminated additional contracts with French air crews and service technicians who operated the Air Viet Nam commercial airline. He replaced them with military flight crews and mechanics, making this commercial operation ostensibly a part of the VNAF.

An outward manifestation of the new arrangement was the VNAF's adoption of the USAF's unit organizational system and unit designations. The introduction of U.S. aircraft simplified both the support system and the standardization of operational procedures, including training of personnel. The former "Air Department" was renamed the "Air Force Department" in 1956, and had moved to a new location at 110 Than-qui-Cap, a quiet tree-shaded street in another part of downtown Saigon. On 3 October 1957 it was redes-

This Bearcat lived on long after the type was removed from operational service. This F8F was photographed as late as Feb/March 1963, kept flyable almost as a private enterprise until the powers-to-be found out about it and grounded the airplane. It became a gate guard. *Courtesy of Frank Baldwin.*

The VNAF insignia is proudly displayed on the wing of this Bearcat that was almost retained under clandestine conditions. This picture taken as late as 1966 gives the impression that this airplane was still in airworthy condition. *Courtesy of Terry Love.*

ignated "Headquarters Vietnamese Air Force" and moved to Tan Son Nhut Airport, where it remained.

It did not take American advisors long to discover that Vietnamese aviators were good pilots, although young and relatively inexperienced. Few had tactical training, and even less had command experience. This situation was exacerbated by the fact that Vietnamese Army officers were permitted to transfer to high-level Air Force posts in preference to flying officers. Thus, the Vietnamese Army officers dominated not only the Joint General Staff,[8] the governing body of the VNAF, but also the VNAF, a situation that prevailed throughout its lifetime. This is an important point to note when following the growth and disposition of VNAF. Its effect was far more evident in later years when the USAF's presence was no longer felt.

President Diem himself often took an active part in military operations and directed air strikes. Diem preferred the use of airborne troops rather than tactical air strikes; in the latter case, positive identification of targets presented problems. Diem's preference for infantry operations unintentionally slowed the VNAF's development. While under French control, the VNAF's pilots had increased to 92 pilots in the two years from the date of its inception on 1 July 1955. Despite the difficulties in recruiting qualified Vietnamese, the VNAF began to take on the recognizable form of an independent military organization.

Beginning in August 1955, U.S. aircraft deliveries were made directly to Vietnam under the Mutual Defense Assistance Program (MDAP). Sixty Cessna L-19 (O-1) Bird Dogs were among the first aircraft to be received through MDAP channels in January 1956, although there is evidence that Bird Dogs may have reached the VNAF the year before through some other source. These all-metal aircraft were issued to the 1st and 2nd GAOs (Group, Artillery Observation) at Da Nang and Nha Trang, respectively, replacing by 1957 the almost depleted inventory of obsolete MS.500 Criquets. The MD-315 Flamants were totally phased out of Vietnam by this time.

In June 1956 the 2nd Transport Squadron was formed at Tan Son Nhut. This led to the creation of the 1st Air Transport Group, consisting of the 1st and 2nd Transport Squadrons. The Douglas transports of the two squadrons, and many more that followed, remained the mainstay of the VNAF fixed wing airlift until the end of the war, even though they were later augmented by newer transport types.

The activities of the French-established 312th Special Missions Squadron of C-47s are obscure. This unit was either deactivated during the transitional period, or reorganized as the 314th Special Missions Squadron. The aircraft assigned to this squadron included one Aero Commander (used at times by President Diem and other government officials), three VC-47s for VIP missions, and three Beechcraft 18 twin-engined light transports.

The Bearcats

As the French presence declined, the VNAF still lacked an offensive capability. To rectify this, the French left behind 22 of the 80 Grumman F8F-1B Bearcats that they had received five years before.[9] These aircraft gave the VNAF "fighting guns." However, the once potent Bearcats were now decidedly tired aircraft. The Vietnamese possessed limited maintenance skills, and spare parts were in short supply.

The French established an F8F transition school on the airfield at Cap Saint-Jacques, better known by its Vietnamese name, Vung Tau. This was the Vietnamese equivalent to the French Riviera, located at the mouth of Ganh Rai Bay, southeast of Saigon. Pilots selected to fly the Bearcats had previously flown the MD-315 Flamant twin-engine aircraft, by now withdrawn from VNAF service. When these pilots became proficient with these 2400 horsepower fighters, they flew them to Bien Hoa Air Base, where they formed the 1st Fighter Squadron on 1 June 1956.

The Bearcat's range and speed permitted it, in theory, to reach almost any part of South Vietnam to provide immediate air support

Alouette III was a modern helicopter for its time in 1955 when introduced into Vietnam service by the French. Three of these helicopters were used for VIP transportation duties from Tan Son Nhut Airport at Saigon, as seen here in February 1963. *Courtesy of Roger Baker.*

when required. Few air fields in South Vietnam were capable of supporting F8F operations; most Bearcat sorties were flown in the area around Saigon and the Mekong Delta, flying out of Bien Hoa almost exclusively. Because of their age and less than ideal maintenance, excessive engine oil consumption limited tactical missions to about one and a quarter hours. Nevertheless, their impressive speed and spectacular maneuverability gave the impression of a strong Air Force and reassurance to observers in the Saigon area.

The high performance of the Bearcats and the flying skill demanded to make them an effective weapon gave the Vietnamese crews the opportunity to prove that they were excellent pilots. The results of their missions and the reports of the observers flying with them confirmed this. They had to create tactical skills not only to match the airplane's special capabilities and performance, but to reconcile these with the type of targets to be attacked.

A typical mission started early in the morning. They were mostly preplanned missions upon known Communist insurgent points, or upon concentration areas where weapons and food were known to be stored. Because leaflet drops were made a day or two before, telling of the impending strike, friendly civilians had time to evacuate the area. Before dawn on the day of attack, a L-19 Bird Dog would takeoff from the lighted runway at Tan Son Nhut and be over the target area at first light to spot any enemy activity. At daybreak, the Bearcats would take off from their unlighted runway at Bien Hoa and rendezvous with the Bird Dog, whose pilot would then identify the target with a smoke-spotting charge.

The attack was usually made by four Bearcats in two sections of two aircraft each. One napalm tank from the center line rack was normally the first of the ordnance to be dropped. This was accomplished by the first aircraft in the attack firing its 20 mm cannon from almost out of range toward the target, then push-over for a dive toward the ground, short of the target. On pulling out near the ground, it would be on a level approach to the target while the 20 mm rounds already fired were exploding on or near the target. A second burst from the cannon was fired at this point, both bursts keeping ground defenses under cover. The wing man in number two position fired and dropped simultaneously with the leader.

Just as the initial smoke and flame from the first pair of fighters subsided, the second set of fighters, already preparing to move in at a 45 degree angle to that of the first, reinforced the attack before defensive fire could resume. After the napalm drops, the six wing-mounted 5-inch HVAR rockets would be fired in single or multiple attacks, followed by two 500 lb (454 kg) general purpose bombs from each aircraft. This method of ground attack provided pinpoint accuracy, and the Vietnamese used it very effectively in neutralizing enemy positions. For a time, however, attacks of this nature were with only rockets due to shortages of bombs.

The 1st Helicopter Squadron of the Vietnamese was formed at Tan Son Nhut in 1956. Using French equipment only, they later acquired Sikorsky H-19s turned over to them as the French departed the country. This photo was taken at Bien Hoa AB in September 1962. *RG 342-96616 USAF.*

Training at the Nha Trang Air Training Center continued to expand, not only in pilot training, but in many ground support and technical skills as well. This later picture of Aviation Cadets in summer khaki uniform was taken in 1970. *RG 342- 107452 USAF.*

The Vietnamese pilots liked the Bearcat during the three years it was in squadron service. In late 1960 one tragic incident, however, discredited the aircraft, casting doubts on its structural strength, and thereby lessening its effectiveness. The accident took the life of their revered squadron commander, Captain Luu-van-Duc. He was leading an attack like the one just described. On this first pass, the 20 mm cannons did not fire as they should have. Following the pull-out from the dive, the guns should have fired a second time, but again, they did not. Nor did the wing man fire, firing and dropping of ordnance being done on cue with the lead aircraft. Just as the napalm was released the right wing of the lead aircraft came off, and Captain Duc crashed upside down into the target area and was killed.

VNAF officials listed two probable causes of the crash, one being structural failure of the aging aircraft, and the other the possibility that one of the 20 mm cannon jammed and exploded, tearing off the wing. Others based their opinion on the report made by the wing man, who believed he had seen a rocket fired at them from the target which may have struck the wing of Captain Duc's Bearcat. When observers went into the target area after the attack they found a hand-held bazooka rocket launcher in the hands of a charred body, along with sufficient parts of the aircraft to reinforce their opinion that Duc's Bearcat had been hit by a rocket, and that his death was not due to aircraft structural failure. Before making these attacks the 20 mm cannon were not test fired, and Duc's cannon were quite probably jammed or inoperative at the time of his first attack. He and his wing man were thus directly vulnerable to unimpeded defensive fire during this attack. The cause of the crash, however, was never fully established.

After this loss, Bearcats were restricted from combat missions for the next month. Although A-1s were already on site and took up the air-to-ground role, this provided the motivation for requesting jet fighter-bomber aircraft.

More Planes and Facilities

Fixed-wing aircraft were not the only equipment used by the VNAF during these early years. Helicopters played a vital part throughout the entire war period. In April 1956 the 1st Helicopter Squadron was established without helicopters at Tan Son Nhut. It was manned initially by four pilots and 25 enlisted men, flying with a French unit that served the International Control Commission. The Commission was composed of personnel from Canada, India, and Poland who supervised the armistice and reported violations. In time the VNAF crews received and operated a few of the outdated Bell

This poor quality photo of a North American T-6G Texan is a very rare picture of this airplane in VNAF service. These yellow WWII advance trainers were used for several years at Nha Trang until all VNAF flight training was moved to the United States, where larger numbers of aviation cadets could be managed. Serial number appears to be 49-3471. *Courtesy of internet: http://vnaf.net*

This landmark at Da Nang Air Base was a memorial dedicated to Vietnam's fighting men. These pointed stylized wings were the symbol used for the 41st Tactical Wing, headquartered at Da Nang. "Elementary school" is the sign to the right.

H-13 Sioux helicopters. As the French systematically began to leave Vietnam, 10 Sikorsky H-19 Chickasaws, previously acquired from the U.S., were returned to American control in April 1958. The U.S., in turn, transferred these helicopters to the Vietnamese Government, to be used by the 1st Helicopter Squadron, VNAF, for airlift and air rescue missions.[10]

The Air Instruction Center located at Nha Trang Air Base was one of the greatest assets acquired by the VNAF from the French. The VNAF took control of this facility on 7 July 1955, one week after it became independent from the French. Full withdrawal by the French was completed by the following November. As American influence increased, Cessna L-19 Bird Dogs, painted bright yellow overall, replaced the French-built Criquets as primary trainers for the VNAF pilots. North American T-6G trainers, also in the standard yellow color, arrived at Nha Trang to serve as advanced trainers.

Recognizing the ever increasing American influence upon the VNAF and RVNAF in general, the Armed Forces Language School was established in 1956 as an English-language school. Its courses were designed to give officers and enlisted men a working knowledge of English before they entered foreign military courses or engaged in advanced training with United States military units.

Tan Son Nhut airport, which served the capital city of Saigon, grew into a major military base, and by mid-1956 a 7,200 ft (2200 m) runway was built with American aid. Air traffic continued to increase at this airport, which became an international hub for this corner of Southeast Asia. A 10,000 ft (3000 m) parallel concrete runway was soon added, this time funded by the U.S. International Cooperation Administration.

At Tourane—later to be well known as Da Nang Air Base—the French had laid down a NATO standard 7,800 ft (2400 m) asphalt runway in 1953-54 to improve the base for the Douglas B-26 Invader operations of two and sometimes three French bomber squadrons. Because the war in Indochina was primarily a daylight affair, Tourane did not have runway lights or permanent maintenance buildings while in French hands. Not until the VNAF began developing this airfield as Air Force Support Base 4 on 1 November 1957 were further improvements made.

When the French moved their air depot from Hanoi to Bien Hoa in June 1955 they provided permanent warehouses and hangars, but did not improve its pierced-steel planking (PSP) runways. The French had also operated from a 5,900 ft (1800 m) PSP runway at Cap Saint-Jacques (Vung Tau). When the Vietnamese pilots finished their F8F Bearcat transition, the French stripped the airfield of its major installations, and from that point onward, Vung Tau failed to develop as a major airfield in South Vietnam, although it could accommodate transport resupply aircraft. The fledgling Vietnamese Air Force had to rely on the Vietnamese Army for air base maintenance, ordnance, quartermaster, communications, and other specialized support.

It was a meager beginning, but these bases and many others would continue to grow to unbelievable proportions. More and more U.S. forces and VNAF units would move in, causing massive expansion, and transforming the base facilities from their humble existence in the early 1960s.

3

Coming of Age

Hanoi leaders formed the National Liberation Front for South Vietnam in December 1960, which the Saigon regime dubbed the "Viet Cong," meaning Communist Vietnamese. Infiltration from the North was intensified. South Vietnamese army units unsuccessfully attempted to overthrow President Diem, who seemed unresponsive to the worsening war situation. After several other attempts, Diem and his brother were murdered following their surrender in November 1963. A counterinsurgency plan was endorsed by President Kennedy that provided more U.S. advisers and equipment for South Vietnam. By the end of 1963, 15,000 American advisers were in South Vietnam as the Communists stepped up their operations to take over the South.

In the 1960s the Vietnamese Air Force came into its own. It was a time for re-equipping established squadrons, creating new units, and acquiring new types of aircraft. It was a period in which the VNAF eventually came into the jet age.

None of this happened without disappointments and setbacks, however. In September 1959, President Diem made a very strong attempt to acquire jets for his Air Force. He focused his attention on the aging condition of the F8F Bearcat; he restricted them in combat and asked for jets to replace them, citing the U.S. jets given to nearby Thailand and the Philippines. Lockheed F-80s were considered, but the lessons learned in Korea by the United States Air Force when first deploying the Shooting Star showed that propeller-driven aircraft were far more effective as fighter-bombers against ground targets than the new jet aircraft. Initial steps were taken, however, to honor Diem's request, and two T-33 trainers and four RT-33 photoreconnaissance aircraft were added to the military assistance program to be delivered in late 1960. These would be the beginning of a jet as well as a reconnaissance force. But the planes, while remaining pledged, were never delivered, because the Geneva Accords prohibited introduction of new type military hardware into Vietnam.

To replace the Grumman Bearcats, only propeller driven aircraft could be considered. One early candidate was the faithful and heavily worked twin-engined Douglas B-26 Invader. These bombers already had seen long service in Vietnam when flown by three French squadrons. While Invaders were to be introduced once again

Imagine this picture if it were in color, with silver Bearcats of the new VNAF against the rich blue sky, streaming red and yellow smoke, the national colors of South Vietnam. *Courtesy of Kenneth E. Moranville.*

This welcome sign to Base Operations carries the names of the key players when taken in February 1967. *Courtesy Terry Love.*

into the air war in Vietnam through the USAF "Farm Gate" program—to be covered later—they were neither owned nor operated by the VNAF.

As early as October 1958, consideration was given to introducing North American T-28 Trojan two-seat trainers, armed for the ground attack role. This brought sheer disappointment to members of the VNAF, who were hoping for a more modern and higher performance aircraft. At this early time, however, VNAF mechanics possessed limited maintenance skills and related experience on more sophisticated equipment. The 1st Fighter squadron was spared these earlier fears of having to transition from the mighty Bearcats to the lesser powered T-28. The VNAF would have T-28s, but these would come later.

Skyraiders

Bearcat replacements were still a priority issue, however. Someone in military planning who had a substantial knowledge of the capabilities of existing aircraft influenced the sound decision to replace the aircraft with Douglas Skyraiders. The aircraft was to become the steadfast standard bearer of the VNAF as a fighter-bomber to the end of the war, although newer equipment would follow.

When Navy Skyraiders were first considered for Vietnam, it was suggested that they be flown by aviators "on leave" from the U.S. Navy under an AVG (Allied Volunteer Group) arrangement, *a la* General Claire Chennault's Flying Tigers of World War II fame. This did not materialize, and Vietnamese pilots flew them instead. It was often repeated, but seldom fully understood, that the Vietnamese wished only to fight and win their own war. All they needed was American equipment and political backing.

The single-seat AD-4 was first considered to be the ideal Skyraider model and was available from Navy stocks. The Navy, however, could not guarantee continued supplies for these obsolete planes. Thus, the program was changed in early 1960 to include AD-6 aircraft still operational in the U.S. Fleet, but due to be phased out of service. Before the aircraft could be introduced into the VNAF, both air and ground crews had to be trained on this new aircraft.

Under sponsorship of the Military Assistance Program (MAP), six selected pilots[11] from the 1st Fighter Squadron were sent to Aviation Training Unit 301 (ATU 301) at Naval Air Station Corpus Christi, Texas, where the Navy had its AD Skyraider training program. Each of these handpicked pilots met the requirements: having between 800 and 1200 flying hours in the Bearcat, and able to speak good English. The Bearcat was, for its day, a high performance aircraft, but looking up from the ground to the huge robust Skyraider for the first time, the pilots realized that this was a *big* aircraft. It may have had only one engine, but from the ground to its cockpit was like climbing into a second story window after reaching the front porch roof.

ATU 301 was the training site for the Vietnamese and other Skyraider pilots. They were given 40 hours in the Skyraider, which included several tactical and bombing practice missions. Again, the Vietnamese proved themselves to be good pilots, but they had one major problem with the Skyraider—the ability to give full rudder travel. This was essential in flying the Skyraider, which the unsuspecting soon discovered on their first encounter. The Vietnamese,

Tan Son Nhut Airport was quite tranquil and under-developed in the early days of 1962. This view looks north across the Base Operations hangar at the left and the ramp of VNAF's 1st GAO L-19s and U-6s, with one USAF C-118 (right) and C-123Bs of Project Mule Train in support of South Vietnamese armed forces. *RG 342-98070 USAF.*

Nha Trang Air Base was the oldest military flying field in South Vietnam. Primarily a VNAF training base that later became the Headquarters for the 2nd Air Division, its expansion was restricted by the city of Nha Trang, which surrounded it. This view looks down runway 12 to the southeast, and the island-sheltered coastline. (K & KE 19702 USAF)

Replacements for VNAF's aging Bearcats were the Douglas AD-6 Skyraiders, shown here in a tactical exercise in support of Vietnamese tanks. This 1963 photograph shows the colorful fuselage bands used by the 1st Fighter Squadron. *RG 342-99222 USAF*

This group picture taken at NAS Corpus Christi, Texas, in mid-1960 shows the first six VNAF pilots to be qualified in the AD-6 Skyraider. With their Navy flight instructor Lieut Ken Moranville (white uniform), they are (L to R) Capt Huy, 1/Lt Nguyen-ngoc-Bien, 1/Lt Nguyen-van-Chan, Capt Pham-phu-Quoc, Capt Nguyen-quang-Tri, and 1/Lt Nguyen-van-Long. *Courtesy of Kenneth .E. Moranville.*

being short in stature, had to use a large number of pillows in order to move them closer to the rudder pedals. This was solved somewhat by switching to seat back parachutes, an arrangement for which the Skyraider was not designed. The problem was further resolved by fabricating a filler block for the seat where the seat pack chute was normally placed. More than one Skyraider was eventually lost on takeoff or landing due to insufficient rudder travel on the part of the pilot.

Following training at Corpus Christi, the Vietnamese pilots went to Attack Squadron 122 (VA-122) at NAS LeMoore, San Diego, for 40 more flying hours with the RAG (Replacement Air Group) for tactical training, then proceeded back to Bien Hoa, their home base, to await delivery of their new aircraft.

While the first six of these Skyraiders were aboard a jeep aircraft carrier bound for Saigon, one U.S. Navy pilot was selected to oversee the Skyraider's introduction into VNAF service. The assignment was to ensure that the transition would be a smooth one from the time the AD-6s arrived until they were in operational squadron service. Navy Lieutenant Kenneth E Moranville was selected for the assignment from more than 40 volunteers at Corpus Christi.

In the early morning hours this Douglas AD-5 is towed from its transporting ship through the streets of Saigon to Tan Son Nhut. There it will be readied for flight to one of the awaiting VNAF fighter squadrons. RG 428N-*1113984-D USN.*

Heading for a pre-planned mission is this Douglas AD-5 loaded with 12 canisters containing 7 2.75 folding fin rockets each. The AD, later redesignated A-1, was an excellent and stable platform for air-to-ground attack missions. *RG 342- 94555 USAF.*

He was the first operational U.S. Naval officer to be assigned to wartime Vietnam. The six Vietnamese pilots whom he had already trained at Corpus Christi met him upon his arrival. They held a deep respect for this man who towered above them, knowing that he had taught them well about the many secrets that made the AD-6 a good fighting machine. Though Moranville was assigned administratively to the MAAG in Saigon, he and his team of four chiefs and two first class petty officers worked almost independently at Bien Hoa. When the first six of the initial 25 AD-6 Skyraiders arrived on 23 September 1960, the Navy party was there to meet them. Once off-loaded, they were gingerly towed through the streets of Saigon on their way to Tan Son Nhut, the city's airport. Their next destination was a ferry flight to nearby Bien Hoa AB, where spare engines, spare parts, and ground support equipment were already in place.

Demonstrating its versatile load carrying capability, this AD-6 Skyraider is loaded with a variety of weapons, ranging from 5 inch HAVR rockets and 28 pound fragmentation cluster bombs to 750 lb. napalm tanks. *RG 342-96797 USAF.*

At first, the Skyraiders did not look too impressive because of the preservatives they had been coated with for the long ocean voyage. Once this coating was removed, they were beautiful birds! In their newly repainted standard U.S. Navy light gull gray and white color scheme, they glistened in the tropical sun. On the four wing positions and sides of the fuselage were the star and bar insignia of Vietnam, with the yellow and red flag on the tail. Finally, on the engine cowl was the insignia of the 1st Fighter Squadron, already placed there by the Americans. They had arrived directly from the rework facility at Naval Air Station Quonset Point, Rhode Island, where they were "zero-timed" and just like new.

As each AD-6 was readied for flight, Moranville made the functional check flight and ferried the Skyraider to its new home at Bien Hoa Air Base. The day the first one was demonstrated was a big event at their home base. Many VIPs turned out to see this new airplane that was to carry the war to the enemy. Among those in attendance was the VNAF Chief of Staff, Nguyen-xuan-Vinh, holding that service's highest rank at that time (Lieutenant Colonel). Lieutenant Moranville took advantage of this opportunity to demonstrate the AD-6's awesome capabilities. His performance clearly impressed the Vietnamese. Many years later, when Vice Admiral, Commander of the Third Fleet, Pearl Harbor, Hawaii, Moranville remembered the occasion:

This September 1963 photo of Douglas A-1H Skyraiders is the earliest record of fuselage waist bands on VNAF aircraft. Shown here are three of the four designs used by the 1st Fighter Squadron at Bien Hoa. Their significance cannot be determined, but are thought to be flight leaders. Only one squadron of AD-6s existed at the time. *RG 342-966615 USAF.*

"It may well have been the day that I demonstrated the AD's firepower before a group of military leaders one day not long after arriving at Bien Hoa. I carried a full load of rockets and bombs. I took off and made a few runs at a simulated target on the field. On one of the deliveries I simultaneously fired eight pods full of rockets, 152 in all. They completely obliterated the target. When all the ordnance was gone I flew a tight loop to a landing, taxied up to the line of VIPs in the style like that of an ice skater skidding to a stop, shut down the engine, and jumped out of the cockpit—all smiles. In my youth, I couldn't help showing off a bit, and must admit I got a kick out of seeing the guests with their jaws agape in awe of the Skyraider's capabilities."

Assisting the Vietnamese pilots, Moranville established a brief refamiliarization program at Bien Hoa. Since the AD-6 was a single-place aircraft, he flew on their wing in either a squadron Bearcat—of which only eight remained—or an AD-6, whichever was available. Ordnance was carried on the aircraft to enable them to perform air strikes when required. A typical ordnance load for the Skyraiders included two napalm tanks, some 500 lb general purpose bombs, and LAU 22 pods with 19 x 2.75 inch (70 mm) folding fin rockets. That was an impressive load for any aircraft, especially one with only a single engine. Simplicity and effectiveness is what made the Skyraider the ideal aircraft in air to ground tactics.

Once assured that the 1st Fighter Squadron was doing well with their new airplanes, Moranville left Vietnam at the end of 1960. Nine years later he returned to the Gulf of Tonkin as executive officer of a carrier-based A-7 Corsair II squadron.

"In 1969," Moranville recalls, "as best as I could determine, only one of the 28 Vietnamese pilots I flew with was still alive. While I was at Bien Hoa, our only loss was the C.O. in the Bearcat. Those guys surely must have logged a lot of combat missions over the years.'

When VNAF was being re-equipped in 1963, this picture of a T-28 with a joint American/Vietnamese crew shows the variety of air to ground weapons it could carry. In the background is an AD-6 of the 514th Fighter Squadron, and B-26s of the USAF Operation Farm Gate unit. *RG 342-96579 USAF.*

A Douglas B-26 Invader of the USAF "Farm Gate" project begins to taxi at Bien Hoa AB for a combat mission. A Vietnamese observer was always carried as a crew member to make this a joint effort. When this picture was taken in January 1962, the T-6G trainers in the background were being returned to the Unites States, since VNAF pilot training was moved to the U.S. *RG 342-98671 USAF.*

What the Vietnamese Air Force achieved with this one Squadron of AD-6 Skyraiders made an impressive accounting. In January 1962 records showed that the VNAF flew a total of 251 combat sorties with this one Skyraider squadron in its first year with their new airplane. In startling contrast, April 1963 figures for combat missions showed a total of more than 1,500 offensive sorties flown against Viet Cong personnel and emplacements, which by this time was divided among three fighter-bomber squadrons. The 1962 tabulations for Viet Cong killed and wounded in action show almost 4,000 troops in these two categories, the majority in the KIA group. More than 11,500 structures belonging to the insurgents were destroyed or damaged by the VNAF air strikes, and more than 1,500 boats were sunk by VNAF aircraft. The latter accomplishment may seem somewhat inconsequential, but in the Mekong River delta region of Vietnam boats represent virtually the only means of transportation in an area that has few roads, even fewer bridges, and literally thousands of canals and other waterways.

As the VNAF continued to gain in stature and capability, more Skyraider squadrons were added. The 1st Fighter Squadron—redesignated the 514th effective 1 January 1963—was the first to have Skyraiders. The 516th Fighter Squadron at Da Nang, first outfitted with T-28 fighter-bombers in December 1961, was replaced by May 1964 with AD-6s, now redesignated A-1Hs. In the meantime, the 518th was formed at Bien Hoa on 15 October 1963 with A-1s. The 520th at Bien Hoa and 522nd at Tan Son Nhut, both with A-1s, came into being on 16 June 1964 and 1 June 1965, respectively. Subsequent additions to the VNAF's growing force of Douglas Skyraiders created the 524th at Nha Trang on 15 September 1965.

The A-1 Skyraider maintained its status as the main attack aircraft of the VNAF in its early years. As the war continued and the VNAF expanded more rapidly, more fighter units and Skyraiders were added. The next two squadrons were the 526th and 528th, but were formed with jet A-37s. The ability of the A-1s could not be ignored, and the next successive fighter unit, the 530th, was acti-

North American T-28s of the 2nd Fighter Squadron search for targets of opportunity in the northern portion of South Vietnam in October 1962. As the war continued to escalate, the T-28s were replaced with more combat advanced equipment, and only this one VNAF squadron used the Nomads. *RG 342-92963 USAF.*

North American T-28 fighter-bombers are off-loaded from the USNS *Breton* at Saigon in February 1962. These airplanes equipped the 2nd Fighter Squadron at Nha Trang AB, the only VNAF unit so equipped. *RG 342-K 21712 USAF.*

When the 2nd Fighter Squadron became combat ready in their T-28 Nomads, they moved to Da Nang AB in January 1963 and were renumbered the 514th FS. The USAF Farm Gate forces used them as well; both units finding them to be good weapons delivery aircraft, but only in a permissive environment. *RG 111-SC 610133 US Army.*

vated at Pleiku in 1970 with more Skyraiders. While some of the earlier squadrons, and all later squadrons converted to newer type aircraft, such as F-5s and A-37s, the greatest number of Skyraider units at any one time was six, which was in the late 1960s. The total number of recorded A-1s assigned to the VNAF over the years was 308. This says a lot for the value placed upon the Skyraider by both the VNAF and the USAF, who also used them.

The VNAF and USAF Farm Gate

The introduction of Douglas AD-6s (later A-1H) to the 1st Fighter Squadron in 1960 marked the beginning toward the further expansion of the VNAF. This would prove to be slow, but at this point there was but a very small foundation upon which to build. Other types of aircraft were brought into the country during this period. Douglas B-26s and North American T-28Ds, sporting the Vietnamese insignia, appeared in the skies over Vietnam in 1961. Though not VNAF aircraft, they are worthy of inclusion here because of VNAF personnel involvement.

In Florida the USAF had established a special air unit, nicknamed "Jungle Jim," which was designed to fight guerrilla wars in any part of the world. As an effort to teach members of the VNAF the art of this type of operation, a Jungle Jim detachment deployed to Bien Hoa Air Base on 4 November 1961. This operation, designated Farm Gate, initially consisted of 151 officers and men, eight T-28Ds, four SC-47s, and four RB-26s. In time, these numbers increased.

In these aircraft, USAF pilots flew "combat training" missions closely associated with members of the VNAF AD-6 squadron, which was also at Bien Hoa. This airbase was not adequately equipped for night flying operations; therefore, VNAF pilots were only proficient in daytime flight. Frequently inoperable flight instruments prevented pilots from gaining experience in night and

As the 2nd Fighter Squadron matured, they proudly applied their squadron insignia to the fin of their aircraft. The unit code letter appeared as well, that being a "L," prefix to the aircraft letter; in this case "T." Note the gun pod on the wing pylons. *RG 342-92964 USAF.*

The flight line of the 2nd Fighter Squadron at the southeast end of Nha Trang AB in January 1962. Their T-28s start engines in preparation for a combat mission. *RG 342-98060 USAF.*

The Douglas A-1 Skyraider was symbolic of VNAF airpower for many years. Although they were not the jet aircraft that the South Vietnamese government had hoped for, the VNAF pilots used them very well in the air-to-ground weapons delivery role, for which the airplane was well suited. M1A2 cluster bombs are on the outboard stations of this 1st Fighter Squadron Skyraider. *RG 342-96693 USAF.*

This VNAF pilot, Lt. Duy Chanh, runs from the jeep on a hot scramble at Binh Hoa Air Base, where the 514th Fighter Squadron was based. Under the wings are 260 lb fragmentation bombs and rocket pod. This view, taken 23 November 1963, shows two American RB-26 Invaders of the "Farm Gate" project in the background. *RG 342-99250 USAF.*

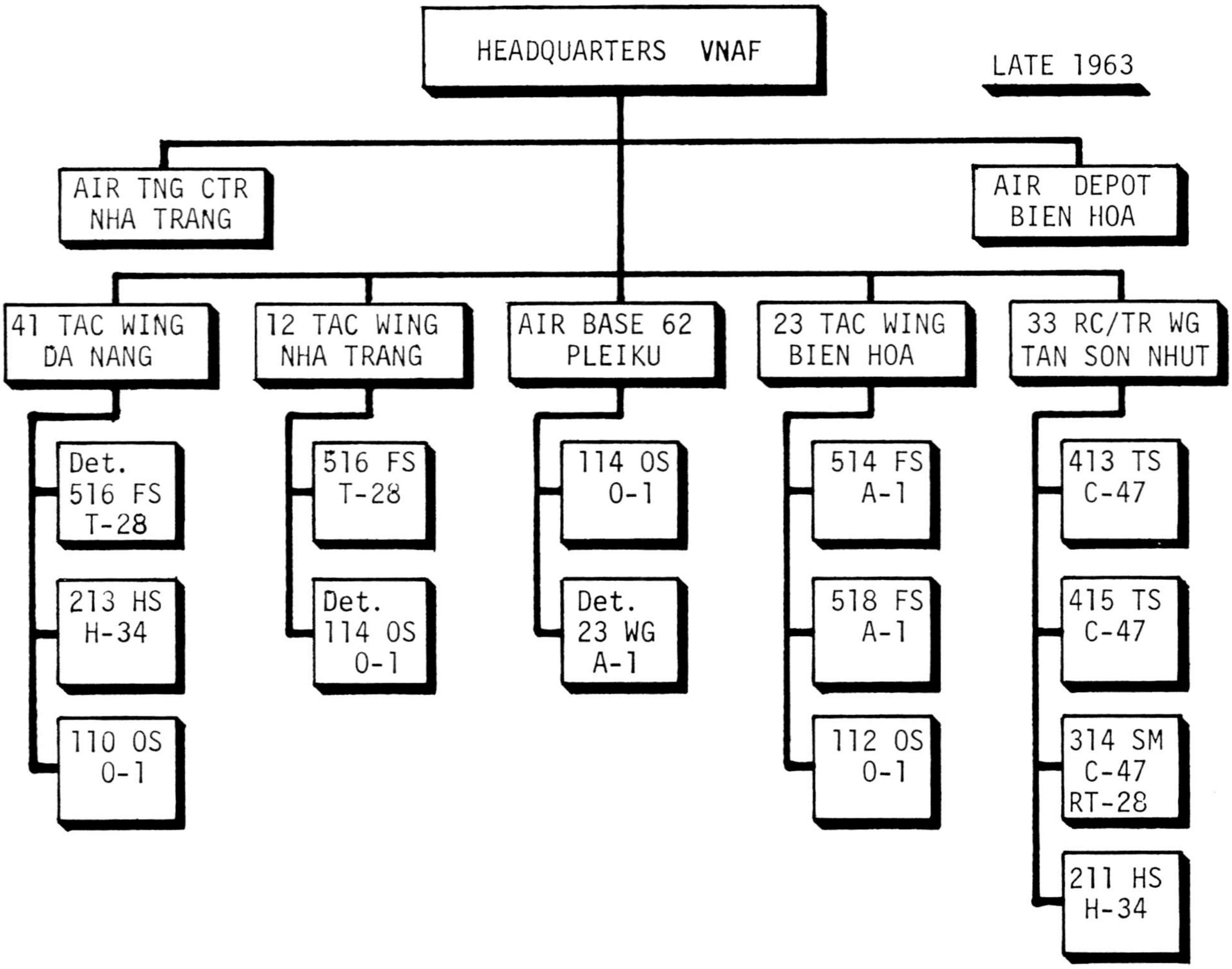

Organizational chart of 1963 that reflects the first significant growth in air units of the VNAF.

Covert operations into North Vietnam were flown as early as 1961 with C-47s drawn from one of the two VNAF transport squadrons. These were night, low-level missions for dropping saboteurs and their supplies into the heartland of North Vietnam. This C-47 of the 1st TS was photographed at Clark AB in January 1959. *Courtesy of David Menard.*

all-weather flying, even though the Viet Cong operated mostly during the hours of darkness.

Training for this type of mission, and that of providing cover for the Americans engaging in combat sorties, was undertaken by AD-6 pilots of the 1st Fighter Squadron, who often served as observer crew members on B-26s and T-28s, particularly on night missions, under flare light furnished by the Farm Gate SC-47 "Gooney Birds." No one liked flying in the rear seat of a T-28, particularly rated pilots, but the VNAF pilots could not take over the front seat on combat missions until they were fully qualified. This eliminated any need for a Farm Gate instructor to fly in the rear seat with a VNAF pilot in the front. Back seat combat training was more political than practical, but the requirement prevailed to have a VNAF crew member on board for either training or as an observer.

This set the stage for the establishment of the VNAF's 2nd Fighter Squadron, which was formed at Nha Trang AB in December 1961. To equip this new unit, more T-28Ds came from the United States. Since Nha Trang was the VNAF Air Training Center, it was the ideal location for the overall upgrading program on this new aircraft. Along with the pilot transition program, maintenance crews trained while supporting the flight operations, and supply procedures were also tailored to the new equipment. Most, if not all pilots assigned to the 2nd Fighter Squadron received earlier pilot training on T-28s in the United States.

In January 1962 USAF personnel assigned to a Farm Gate detachment sent four of their pilots to the 2nd Fighter Squadron to assist in training 25 VNAF pilots in tactical operations on the T-28 fighter-bombers at Nha Trang. The Americans served as instructors for day and night bombing, rocketry, and gunnery, and helped the

To better equip the 83rd Special Operations Group for their clandestine missions, three C-123Bs were used between 1964 and 1966. This rare picture of these gray, VNAF-marked airplanes show one parked in front of Base Operations at Nha Trang in 1965. *Courtesy of Pham Quang Khiem.*

While assigned to the 83rd SOG, none of the 522nd Fighter Squadron carried the national insignia. In its place on each side of the fuselage was the Kamikaze unit insignia of the 83rd seen in this photo taken in November 1966. *Courtesy of Terry Love.*

The highly publicized 522nd Fighter Squadron, with its Douglas A-1Hs, was the aggressive element force for the 83rd SOG when penetrating North Vietnam territory. These were the first aircraft in VNAF, as well as in this war zone, to have a multi-color disruptive-pattern type camouflage. Note the yellow nose marking *Cuu-Sach*, meaning "The Better." *Courtesy of the Talmantz Collection.*

unit to become combat ready. Before long, a detachment of six T-28s were assigned to Da Nang, and by mid-1962, the 2nd Fighter Squadron became fully operational. In January 1963 the 2nd was redesignated the 516th Fighter Squadron, and by February the next year the squadron and its T-28s joined its detachment at Da Nang, where it remained.

At Bien Hoa the Farm Gate Program continued to operate, with VNAF members on each operational mission as observers. As the AD-6 Skyraider pilots completed their training with Farm Gate, VNAF Aviation Cadets awaiting travel to the United States for flight training—including 15 noncommissioned officers—generally took their place as in-flight observers. Although this association created personal friendships, neither the Americans nor the Vietnamese liked the Program, which was seemingly cosmetic. Fortunately for all concerned, the Program was relatively short-lived.

On 8 July 1963 the Farm Gate Program became the 1st Air Commando Squadron (Composite), a regular PACAF organization. Although PACAF wanted the code name *Farm Gate* dropped, Air Force Headquarters disapproved because various logistic facilities supporting Farm Gate were familiar with the name and all it implied.

Farm Gate had two strike sections: the first with 10 B-26s and two RB-26s with 23 crews; and the second had 13 T-28s with two crew members per aircraft. In addition, there were two support sec-

Newly painted A-1Hs had a sinister look about them in this camouflage scheme, along with the absence of national markings. On the fuselage side is the unit insignia of the 83rd Special Operations Group, and on the rudder are the colors and representation of the South Vietnamese flag. Photo taken at Tan Son Nhut, September 1966. *Courtesy of Terry Love.*

Insignia of the 83rd Special Operations Group.

When painting these all gray A-1s with camouflage, the area of the U.S. Navy BuNo was masked over to avoid having to paint again. The "U" was the identifier for the 522nd fighter Squadron, followed by an individual aircraft letter. *Courtesy of David Menard.*

When first formed in 1965, the 522nd Fighter Squadron used this parking ramp at Tan Son Nhut in their country's capital city. This was the pride of VNAF, showing a new and more aggressive Air Force in the making. *Courtesy of Terry Love.*

tions, one with four psychological warfare Helio U-10s, and the other with six C-47s. The remaining eight B-26s were in detachments at Pleiku and Soc Trang. With the exception of logistical support and reconnaissance aircraft, this was the extent of strike power that the U.S. had in Vietnam in mid-1963. The remainder of the strike capability was in the hands of the VNAF.

The equipment used in the air war drastically changed in early 1964 with the crash of two B-26s caused by structural fatigue. This led to the final withdrawal from the theater of all B-26s and RB-26s, which had been visible in the skies over Vietnam from the early 1950s, when first flown by the French. On 8 April 1964 the last of the B-26s and RB-26s were ferried to Clark Air Base for salvage. This remote association between the VNAF and the B-26 operation should clarify the point that B-26 Invaders were never part of the VNAF, even though they carried the VNAF insignia, as did the Farm Gate-assigned T-28s. However, VNAF expansion plans in October and November 1962 envisaged the formation of one VNAF squadron of 25 B-26s and two RB-26 aircraft, but this never materialized.

After the first eight years since the VNAF gained independence it had achieved only modest combat capability: a squadron of Douglas AD-6 Skyraiders located at Bien Hoa, and a squadron of T-28 fighter-bombers stationed at Da Nang. This was to change, as training was accelerated across all the many functions required for maintaining and operating a larger air force. The VNAF's expansion became evident when its new squadrons of A-1s were strategically deployed throughout its Corps Areas in support of ARVN forces.

The Kamikazes

During wartime, certain combat units emerge above all others, either through their exploits or media publicity. One of these units was the VNAF's 83rd Special Operations Group (SOG). Its fame was due not only to its combat record, but also by the air of mystery that surrounded this clandestine organization, a circumstance that is always certain to draw special attention.

Air missions for the 522nd and its A-1H Skyraiders, when assigned to the 83rd SOG, were that of escorting Vietnamese patrol boats back from waters off North Vietnam after picking up RVN agents planted behind enemy lines several nights before. *RG 342-K18921 USAF.*

This A-1H carries nose markings of "*Cuu-Sach*," meaning "The Better," found in a game of *Bat*. Personalized markings were not uncommon in the early 1960s for VNAF aircraft. *Courtesy of David Menard.*

This new form of camouflage carried over to the next squadrons as they acquired Skyraiders. This A-1H of the 516th Fighter Squadron at Da Nang in September 1966 shows their tiger head insignia on the cowl and the blue 41st Tactical Wing fuselage stripe. These colors for camouflage quickly changed to those used by the USAF when the standard three-color SEA scheme was adopted. *Courtesy of Neal Schweider.*

The war in South Vietnam was one of constant battle against infiltration from the North. As early as April 1961, and lasting for more than a year, there were a series of VNAF C-47 night missions over the area of Hanoi to drop sabotage teams tasked with blowing up roads, bridges, and power plants. As these clandestine operations continued, it was natural that this small group of VNAF volunteers from the 1st and 2nd Transport Squadrons, Tan Son Nhut Air Base, would increasingly become a separate unit as mission requirements increased. This group, yet to have an identity, was formed in 1962 during the regime of President Ngo-dinh-Diem. As with most of the covert operations of this type in Southeast Asia at that time, the CIA is rumored to have been involved.

When an insurgent air drop mission was called for, C-47s assigned to the project would depart Tan Son Nhut for Nha Trang, where personnel were briefed for the mission while their aircraft were being loaded for the drop. Nha Trang became the headquarters for these Special Forces. Taking off in the late afternoon, the single or small number of Gooney Birds would head west, cross the southern border of Laos, and land at an isolated site, where they were refueled and the crews given a final briefing. Take-off was normally about midnight, and the flights headed north at low level through the valleys of the Truong-Son mountains toward North Vietnam. The most common drop zones for infiltration were the high ground in the Cao-Bang, Lang-Son, and Phat-Diem areas. These operations were not without danger; three C-47s and all crew were lost during these harrowing, ground-hugging night missions.

Within this special organization was one pilot who gained prominence by volunteering for most of these early missions, Major Nguyen-cao-Ky. By 1964 Ky had risen to the rank of Colonel and was the Commander of the Vietnamese Air Force. This permitted him to gain greater public recognition and greater logistical support for this clandestine organization. Now with unit status, it was called "Biet Doan 83," which translates to Special 83 Squadron. This was later advanced to group status, and were known as the 83rd SOG. This group was under the direct control of VNAF Headquarters, i.e., Ky's direct control. Symbolizing the elite status members of this Unit held, each person wore neatly tailored black flying suits, emblazoned with the usual colorful insignia patches of their unit and Air Force, punctuated with a purple neck scarf with small white polka dots.

As the Unit's operational demands increased, the need arose for newer equipment. In 1964 five crews were sent to the Unites States for training in the Fairchild C-123B combat support transport. When they returned to their parent unit, three of these twin-engine Provider aircraft were on hand for their use, but remained assigned to the USAF, whose maintenance crews also serviced these aircraft. Outwardly these light gray painted C-123Bs were unusual in having South Vietnamese insignia, yet retained their USAF serial numbers. They were readily identifiable through radio communication, however, by their call sign "Co Trang," which meant "White Crane." Though they fulfilled their requirements, by 1966 the C-123s were phased out of this VNAF organization.

In addition to the C-47s and C-123s, the 83rd SOG used one U-17 Skywagon, more commonly referred to by the VNAF crews as the Cessna 185, from which the military version was derived.

At this time the 83rd SOG lacked the strike power necessary to support these special air operations. On 1 April 1965 a new fighter squadron, the 522nd, was formed to be part of the 83rd. Two months later, aircraft and crews were selected by the Air Force Chief of Staff (Col Ky) from existing Douglas A-1H fighter units. This newly formed squadron was readily recognizable by its uniquely camouflaged and marked aircraft, the first of a pattern-type camouflage to appear on aircraft involved in this war. Instead of carrying the South Vietnamese national insignia, these Skyraiders defiantly carried only the insignia of their group painted on both sides of the fuselage. With this blue and gold insignia was the inscription *Than-Phong*. Directly translated this means "God of Wind," but literally its meaning was *Kamikaze*, meaning the "Divine Wind," said to have been the typhoon that saved Japan from the Chinese invasion in the 13th century.

Their purpose was—as one might suspect—very special. If any mission could be called routine, they may have been when flying escort to C-47s and H-34s on insertion missions. They were often called upon for special strikes on enemy camps outside their borders, or to provide ground support for special forces operating along the border, or into North Vietnam.

Although many types of combat missions were flown by the 522nd Fighter Squadron, its most important mission was providing air cover for Vietnamese Navy patrol boats withdrawing from North Vietnamese waters in early morning hours—which lasted well into daylight. As related by their former Operations Officer, Nguyen-ngoc-Khoa, during the night hours, the patrol boats would pick up South Vietnamese agents dropped by air, well above the DMZ. When they had completed their mission, at a pre-arranged time and day the agents would move to the shore to be picked up by boat. The Skyraiders would then ensure the safety of the boats as they sped southward to their own waters. This became quite routine to some,

Opposite: This nose art seen on the right side of some of the A-1s of the 522nd Fighter Squadron when assigned to the 83rd SOG depicts the four characters used on the highest cards in the Vietnamese game of *Co-Bai-Bat*, in short called *Bat*, and pronounced "*Buk*." They are the nine cards (a lucky number to the Vietnamese), of which in this game there are four levels, and therefore four different characters. The Chinese figure 9 is incorporated at the right of each. Presumably all four figures were used, although photographic evidence shows only the 1st and 3rd designs, which were applied to at least two airplanes each. *Bat* was a Vietnamese game played in the North, and only those who fled to the South were familiar with this meaning.

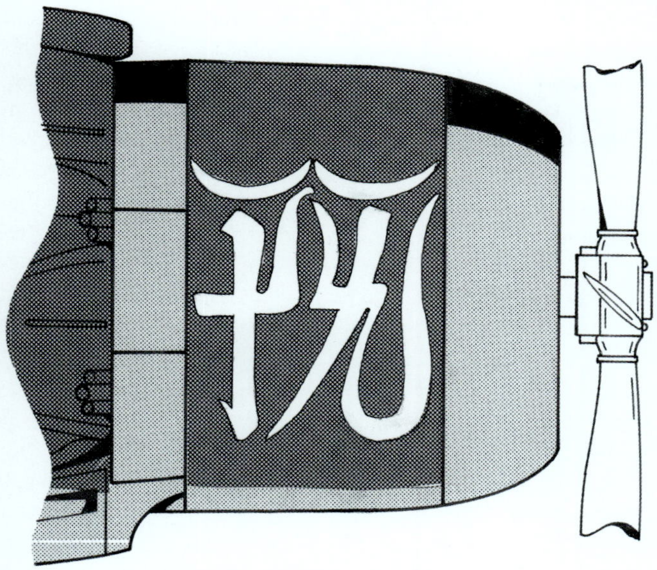

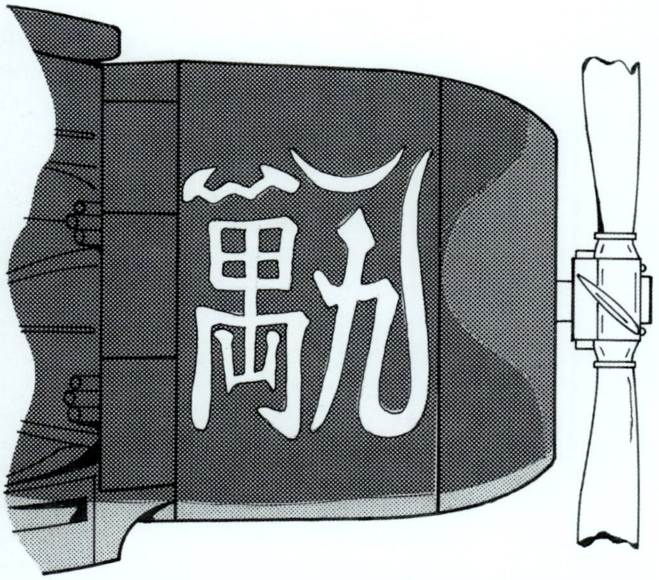

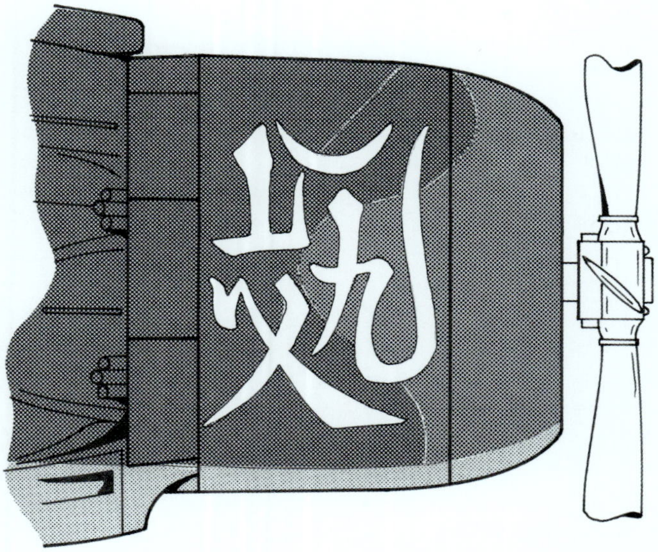

CỬU-XÙNG

(Nine-Xùng)

The Best of the Best.

CỬU-SÁCH

(Nine-Sách)

The Better.

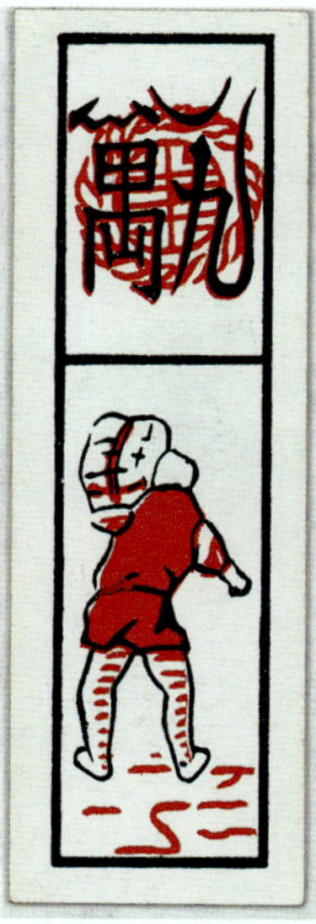

CỬU-VẠN

(Nine-Vạn)

The Best.

CỬU-VĂN

(Nine-Văn)

The Good.

Proudly displaying their national colors, this flight of five Douglas Skyraiders stream smoke of red and yellow to form the Vietnamese flag in the sky. This display was frequently done in the early 1960s to bring attention to the increasing effectiveness of the VNAF. *RG 342-K23297 USAF.*

who reported that it was almost an every Tuesday and Thursday morning event.

The national elections in late 1967 placed Maj. Gen. Nguyen-van-Thieu as the new Chief of State, and Ky, retaining his military rank of Air Vice Marshal, was now the Vice President. These two South Vietnamese leaders did not always agree on government matters. Thieu feared that Ky would use the 83rd SOG in a coup to remove him from office, as Ky had effectively used air power against President Diem, and to suppress another coup before that. To prevent political use of this unique force, President Thieu ordered that the 83rd SOG be disbanded in January 1968. Upon inactivation crews were dispersed, and the 522nd Fighter Squadron moved to Bien Hoa to become part of the 23rd Tactical Wing. To further dilute the prestige of the 83rd, black flying suits were made regular issue to all VNAF aircrew members. Only the unit's legend remained.

Creating the Pilots

Who were the men that flew the airplanes of the VNAF? For the most part they were from the better educated and affluent families of Vietnam that were in good physical condition. In the earlier years, most came from Dalat and Thu Duc Military Schools, as well as civilian universities and colleges. As the VNAF required greater numbers of pilots, these unwritten prerequisites slowly eroded, and all applicants were screened to select the best officer and flight training candidates. Throughout its entire existence the VNAF remained an all volunteer force.

In the VNAF's early years under American guidance, it became obvious that the number of aircrews had to be appreciably increased in order to create an effective Air Force. Training the large numbers of VNAF personnel would logically be accomplished by American instructors in Vietnam, but the Geneva Accords limited the number of advisors assigned to the MAAG at 342 officers and men, greatly restricting the creation of a new program of flight training. While the Accords were in force, the solution was to send prospective VNAF pilots to the United States to receive this training.

Pilot training in the United States was not always relished by the Vietnamese. The serviceman's absence for a period of approximately nine months left many uncertainties in their minds about the safety of their families and loved ones left behind in war-torn Vietnam. This affected their concentration on what was a demanding flight training course, but few let it show. To make matters more difficult, the young Vietnamese student pilots were confronted with a totally alien culture in the United States, as well as a new language.

Some of the first Vietnamese to receive pilot training in the United States took place between 1957 and 1959. Most pilots were already rated pilots, and only received upgrade or transition training at those bases where the required aircraft types were based. To train new pilots for the Vietnamese Air Force, a concentrated flight training program began at Graham Air Base, a civilian contract course at Marianna, Florida, on 17 July 1958. Seven Vietnamese students received their USAF pilot wings that year. The course was designed for students who would not continue on to fast jets, since the VNAF had only propeller-driven aircraft.

Before American instructors could effectively train Vietnamese personnel, the Vietnamese had to acquire a command of the English language. Most were trained at the Defense Language Institute at Lackland AFB, Texas. Others were trained at the Republic of Vietnam Armed Forces Language Institute in Saigon. The training lasted nine weeks; however, if a student still had difficulty with the language, he was detained and sent through the course again. Too much time was lost if a student could not comprehend the language used in flight instruction.

The throaty roar of the R-3350s that power these Skyraiders as they streaked in trail formation over these pilot candidates would quicken the blood of any young man wanting to fly. These graduating officer candidates are at ceremonies at Dalat Military Academy. *Courtesy of Pham-Quang-Khiem.*

When pilot training was again accomplished in South Vietnam it took place at the Air Training Center, Nha Trang AB. As a basic trainer, Cessna U-17s were used like the one shown here. The airfield was located near the shore at the top left of this picture. *RG 342-101534 USAF.*

Learning to fly while mastering a foreign language is a challenging task. Former VNAF Lieutenant Pham-quang-Khiem remembers one incident while he was a student pilot at Keesler AFB:

"I know now that the instructor was demonstrating a series of stalls[12] to me. He would bring the nose of the aircraft up high, it would shudder, then at some point he would lower the nose and resume level flight. If the instructor explained the purpose of this maneuver and what was going on, I missed it at some point. I tried to imitate what he had demonstrated, but I certainly was not pleasing him. I would even count to myself the time period from when he pulled the nose up to pushing it forward, but that did not work when it came my turn. The 'monkey see, monkey do' technique just did not work for me.

For those of us in training in the United States, the theory of 'work together, graduate together' had a positive effect. Every night after training we would gather in a buddy's room and all talk about the day's experiences. We learned well from each other. I expressed my problem with the 'stall series' and learned from my friends what this was all about and what was to be learned. The next day in the air—no problem!"

Vietnamese undergraduate pilot students in the late 1950s received their flight training at Randolph AFB, Texas. The entire nine month course was flown in the T-28, and they received about 200 flying hours of instruction. During 1961 the Vietnamese were trained in two types of aircraft, beginning with 30 hours in the lighter T-34, followed by 170 hours in the heavier T-28. Eighteen Vietnamese students graduated from this course. After 1961 the training reverted to the single airplane concept, with the full 200 hours in the T-28. Basic flight training conducted by the USAF remained this way through the 1960s, when just over 400 VNAF pilot officers were graduated.

The flight training program was accelerated at Nha Trang so that all the pilot training would not have to be conducted in the United States. There was a language advantage for the students when learning from Vietnamese instructors. This U-17 departs with student and instructor. *RG 342-K32503 USAF.*

Three flight students with instructor make a walk-around inspection of the Cessna U-17 used for flight training. Note the insignia of the Air Training Center. *RG 342-K 32496 USAF.*

Vietnamization included flight training conducted by VNAF personnel themselves. Here 2nd Lt. Nguyen-huu-Phuc briefs a student on instrument interpretation in a Cessna U-17 prior to flight instruction at Nha Trang AB in July 1970. *RG 342-107465 USAF.*

An essential part of the training program for VNAF members was English language training. Seen here is T/Sgt Riley Seevers conducting a class at the Air Training Center at Nha Trang AB in December 1966. *RG 342-100589 USAF.*

Although the basic course did not change very much over the years, bases of assignment and training did. In January 1961 the flight training program was moved to Graham Air Base, a civilian contract base that closed soon after, causing the program to transfer to Moody AFB, at Valdosta, Georgia. The program remained there until the summer of 1963, when it moved again, this time back to Randolph AFB. A few years later, to make room for Randolph's new USAF Undergraduate Pilot Training (UPT) mission, the course moved during the winter of 1966-1967 to Keesler AFB, Biloxi, Mississippi. VNAF fixed wing pilot training changed little until the introduction of jet aircraft (to be dealt with later in this book).

Helicopters were also a vital part of the VNAF, and the training of pilots for these aircraft became critical. In late 1962 the VNAF was expecting to receive 30 Sikorsky UH-34 Choctaw helicopters by mid-1963, with 18 more the following year. Up to this time, the VNAF had but a handful of H-13s and Korean War vintage H-19s in various states of operational condition. This was the 1st Helicopter Squadron at Tan Son Nhut, redesignated the 211th Helicopter Squadron in January 1963. Given the new influx of UH-34s with the rather low ratio of five pilots for every four helicopters, the VNAF expected to be 51 pilots short by mid-1964 through lack of training. The VNAF's early helicopter pilots had been trained by the U.S. Army in the United States, but inherent travel delays, often caused by last-minute security checks, brought about unacceptable slippages in training.

A study was made to consider ways of training the VNAF helicopter pilots in Vietnam. While there were advantages and disadvantages, pilots could be trained in greater numbers if the problems of international travel could be eliminated. It was also felt that the Vietnamese might be able to train their pilots quicker if it was held in Vietnam.

In February 1963 training was conducted in eight H-19B helicopters at Tan Son Nhut, pending the arrival of the UH-34s. Three H-19Bs were available at Tan Son Nhut, while the remaining five were in flyable storage at the VNAF Bien Hoa Depot. This first pilot training class, designated 63A, consisted of 15 VNAF cadets, each accumulating 75 hours of flying time. All 15 graduated and were swiftly assigned to VNAF helicopter squadrons for upgrade and operational training.

Helicopter mechanics also trained with air crews. The first class began in July 1963 with 30 Vietnamese students, and training consisted of classroom instruction and practical experience. Each student was assigned to a crew chief or specialist that assisted him in the daily maintenance of the helicopter. One Air Training Command report stated that:

> "The student mechanic displays much elation at the prospect of actually working on mission aircraft and is desirous of proving himself to his flight line supervisor."

Similar statements were repeatedly made in American instructors' reports on their VNAF students, a lasting tribute to the men of the VNAF.

The success led to another program that enabled the VNAF to overcome its shortage of fixed wing pilots. In 1963 the USAF pro-

The use of a training aid size E-6B navigational computer, familiar to all pilots of that period, is explained by a VNAF 1st Lt. instructor to three Aviation Cadets at the Air Training Center in April 1968. *RG 342-103933 USAF.*

cured the aircraft needed for the program—25 single-engined Cessna 185 Skywagons, later designated the U-17A. These were "off-the-shelf" aircraft, readily available, and Cessna supplied the technical assistance and training to support them.

This specially-designed 16-week course, involving 50 Vietnamese student pilots per class and USAF instructors, began in September 1963 at the VNAF's Air Training Center at Nha Trang. After four weeks of classroom theory, each student received at least 80 hours of flying time in the remaining 12 weeks. This training involved the teaching of Vietnamese students under the guidance and advice of USAF instructors in a "practice teaching" situation. By the time the fourth class began training in June 1964, all of the VNAF instructor pilots and maintenance instructors had completed their training. Unlike the previous three, the fourth and subsequent classes were taught in the Vietnamese language, eliminating the language barrier which had hitherto posed difficulties for the Vietnamese students.

Having trained 117 pilots and 32 maintenance personnel during the first year, the Americans turned the training program over completely to the Vietnamese.

A quick engine change is made of this A-1H in the hangar of the 514th Fighter Squadron at Bien Hoa in 1965. A USAF M/Sgt. helps with on the job training, as was the case for much of the VNAF training after completing a technical school course. *RG 342-KE17497 USAF.*

4

The Expansion Period

In March 1961, the SEATO Council noted with concern the violation of the Geneva accords by an armed minority attempting to destroy the government of South Vietnam and declared its resolve not to acquiesce to any takeover of South Vietnam. In addition, the two governments of South Vietnam and the United States issued a joint communique underlining an agreement on an eight-point program for military and economic aid to Vietnam. In the United States, however, focus was on President Kennedy as he forced the Soviets to withdraw missiles from Cuba in October 1962.

During this period, the VNAF stood virtually alone against North Vietnamese aggression. The decision in July 1962 by the United States Secretary of Defense, Robert S. McNamara, to expand the VNAF over the next three year period was a turning point in its history, and was based on two fundamental considerations: a balanced air arm to complement the Republic of Vietnam's Armed Forces (RVNAF); and, more importantly, contain the growing Communist threat of South Vietnam.

Two VNAF pilots of the 514th Fighter Squadron, Dam-thuong-Vu and Le-quoc-Hung, discuss the mission that they have just conducted against the Viet Cong in 1965. Vu, left, became the first squadron commander of F-5s, and Hung commanded the 518th FS until 1972. *RG 342-94782 USAF.*

From the beginning, air operations were a joint planning effort, with the VNAF, USAF, U.S. Navy, and other forces involved. For the most part, this was USAF sponsored and controlled. This is the Tactical Air Control Center at USAF 2nd Air Division Headquarters, TSN, March 1962. *RG 342-98132 USAF.*

Squadrons, Planes, and Men

The VNAF, unlike other air forces, had no distinct chain of command. Wings and squadrons, having been created haphazardly, worked independently of each other. It was at this time that the question arose of how best to utilize its assets: this problem was to plague the VNAF throughout its entire existence.

The U.S. Army stated that it should be responsible for command of all air unit engagements, since it was the responsible Service for counter-insurgency, arguing that counter-insurgency was primarily a ground force operation. Thus, all deployed USAF forces, along with Army forces, should be placed under the operational control of the Senior U.S. Army Advisor to the ARVN Corps Commander. Likewise, it was argued that the VNAF units should be placed under the command and control of the ARVN Corps Commander.

On the other hand, the USAF advisers to the VNAF held that all air units should be centralized under the control of the Senior USAF Air Commander to take advantage of air power's inherent flexibility, and best concentrate the fire power of the finite number of U.S. and VNAF units, based upon the level of combat demanded.

This interesting view taken in 1966 of C-47s belonging to the 413th Transport Squadron gives some perspective of the crowded conditions that grew continually at Tan Son Nhut. These C-47s were being prepared to carry ARVN forces to Da Nang to suppress a serious civil disorder that year. *RG 342-K20980 USAF.*

Distinctive markings for observation and fighter squadrons were assigned to each of the four Corps areas. This O-1 carries the black and yellow fuselage band of the 23rd Tactical Wing headquartered at Bien Hoa. The "D" tail code identifies the 112th Observation Squadron. *RG 342-K46185 USAF.*

As VNAF began its rapid expansion in the mid-1960s, each Corps area had an A-1 squadron assigned. Shown here in early camouflage unique to VNAF is an A-1H of the 516th Fighter Squadron at Da Nang. As part of the 41st Tactical Wing, it carries the fuselage band of blue with white stars.

Transport and reconnaissance squadrons were reorganized with most assigned to the 33rd Tactical Wing located at Tan Son Nhut. This C-47 carries the 33rd insignia on its nose. The small "M" in the tail marking identifies this as an R/E.C.-47 reconnaissance aircraft seen at Pleiku in December 1967.

There simply were not enough units, both U.S. and Vietnamese, to assign to Corps Commanders, and doing so diluted the impact of air power, tying them to specific geographic areas. These restrictions created an imbalance of military activity from area to area. The VNAF believed that it should not be divided up and placed under the control of each of the ARVN Corps Commanders. Initially, the whole of South Vietnam was covered by three Corps: I Corps covering the northern part of the country; II Corps, the central highlands; and III Corps, the area surrounding Saigon and the southern Mekong Delta region. After November 1962 these became known as Corps Tactical Zones, and III Corps was divided, adding IV Corps to cover the Mekong Delta region. As a result of limited air resources to cover all of South Vietnam at that time, the argument about command of air units abated. The USAF and the VNAF came under the command and control of the representative Senior Air Commanders—the USAF 2nd Air Division, in the case of USAF units—and the VNAF remained under Commanding General of the Vietnamese Air Force. Both commanders worked nearly side by side at their respective headquarters at Tan Son Nhut Air Base.

On the surface, this is how the system was programmed to work. In actual practice, however, each Corps commander wielded virtually absolute control over all civilian and military activities within his boundaries, including air power. No air strike; preplanned or immediate, could take place without his approval. It was not uncommon for Corps commanders to cancel air missions in order to avoid political repercussions should noncombatants be accidentally killed or wounded. As they were often away from their headquarters, it was usually impossible to fill requests from the field for immediate air support. Further, the Joint General Staff required no advance notice from them on operations being planned and executed in their area, unless the commander wanted more aircraft from other resources. Given these working and planning conditions, a well-coordinated country-wide air campaign against the Viet Cong was inconceivable.

As the VNAF continued to expanded, its air strength was reorganized and redistributed. In 1963 air units were restructured by assigning a tactical wing to each of the four geographical Corps areas: the 41st Tactical Wing (I Corps) at Da Nang; 12th Tactical Wing (II Corps) at Nha Trang: and the 23rd Tactical Wing (III Corps) at Bien Hoa. In April 1964 the 74th Tactical Wing formed at Can Tho, and was later moved to Binh Thuy (IV Corps). (The last digit in the wing designation corresponded to the corps area, and the first digit was the sequence in which it was formed. The VNAF squadrons were also renumbered, all now having a three digit number. *See* Appendix C.)

Continued expansion called for the formation of the 33rd Tactical Wing; a reconnaissance and transport wing assigned at Tan Son Nhut, followed by a logistic and support wing at Bien Hoa, while the Air Training Center remained at Nha Trang. The 62nd Tactical

This air view of the ramp at Nha Trang AB shows Douglas A-1Es and Hs of the 524th Fighter Squadron in September 1966. This was a time of transition from the all gray scheme to SEA camouflage. The H-34 helicopters may not have been assigned at Nha Trang at this early time. *Courtesy of Terry Love.*

The control of VNAF was always, either directly or indirectly, that of the Army and the Joint General Staff. In this November 1965 photograph at Bien Hoa AB, Commander of the VNAF Air Vice Marshal Ky (hatless) discusses conditions with Army Lt. General Cao-van-Vien, Chief of JGS. With briefcase is Captain Phan-dam-Lieu, and extreme right is Lt Col Vo-xuan-Lanh. *RG 342-95122 USAF.*

Wing was expanded from the 62nd Air Base Group at Pleiku in March 1964. To make room at Pleiku for the newly formed 72nd Tactical Wing, the 62nd moved to Nha Trang in January 1965, together with the 114th Observation Squadron. The 12th Tactical Wing at Nha Trang was then deactivated. In subsequent years further wings were formed. Assigned to these units were teams from the USAF Advisory Group to assist the expansion of the VNAF.

Between early 1962 and July 1963 the VNAF grew from approximately 4,000 to 7,711 officers and airmen; and by the end of 1965 VNAF strength totaled 12,976 officers and airmen. It was significant that by 1965 each Corps areas had an A-1H Skyraider squadron for quick response to ground operations, including H-34 helicopter squadrons for heliborne missions.

The VNAF's rapid expansion meant that leadership and management skills were far from adequate. Leadership was a major problem because of the limited service and flying experience of the emerging senior officers; the most senior pilot officers had a maximum military experience of only 10 years' service.

It was in the 1963-1966 period that the most capable and dynamic VNAF leaders emerged. Without doubt, the most important figure in the VNAF during this period was Nguyen-cao-Ky. His rise to national importance, both military and political, was mete-

North American RT-28s, which served as reconnaissance aircraft for the VNAF, remained in service until April 1965, long after the fighter-bomber version was phased out. The tail insignia is that of the 314th Special Missions Squadron at Tan Son Nhut. *RG 342-93251 USAF.*

Douglas C-47s were the main air carrier for VNAF in support of the ARVN mobility force. Many of these were passed down from French squadrons when they left Indochina. These Gooney Birds were maintained in immaculate condition, as seen by this one at Da Nang AB. *Courtesy of Robert J. Mills.*

Many attempts were made to improve the Psychological warfare program during the Vietnam war. This VNAF Cessna U-17 was equipped with a speaker system, just aft of the door on the left side of the fuselage. Sound was directed very effectively to the ground when in a left turn around the desired contact area. The lower opening aft of the speaker is the leaflet drop chute. *RG 342-K33746 USAF.*

oric. He was appointed VNAF Commander in December 1963 at the age of 33 following a *coup d'etat* in November. He remained loyal to Army Major General Nguyen-duc-Khanh in the bloodless coup of 30 January 1964. Between the first political rebellion in November 1963 and 5 March 1964, Ky's loyalty was rewarded with promotions from the position of a Lieutenant Colonel commanding the VNAF's 33rd Tactical Group to that of a full Colonel commanding the VNAF. In his military career he attained the rank of Major General, but he was most frequently addressed as Air Vice-Marshal, an honorary distinction awarded in 1964. AVM Ky became increasingly involved in politics, attaining the position of Prime Minister of South Vietnam in June 1965.[13] He carried with him the loyalty of the VNAF, which he simultaneously headed—an important element in determining the political course of the nation.

The attempted *coup d'etat* of dissident army generals on 13-14 September 1964 serves to illustrate the rise of Air Vice-Marshal Ky and the VNAF simultaneously to positions of political importance. Without bloodshed, Ky demonstrated the use of airpower as a political bargaining instrument against the rebellious army officers. When the coup began, the VNAF established a command post at their Tan Son Nhut headquarters. Ky, who was at Bien Hoa, 17 miles away, immediately came to Tan Son Nhut and took charge of the situation. He ordered the 23rd Tactical Wing's A-1H aircraft to be armed with rockets, and aerial patrols over Saigon to begin as a

Truck and train convoys, as well as heliborne assaults, became far safer with the presence of an airborne FAC in a Cessna O-1 Bird Dog. When an ambush was spotted, the FAC would call for an air strike on the enemy position. This operation in May 1962, 60 miles west of Saigon, was shepherded by an O-1 from the 112th Observation Squadron. *RG 342-98779 USAF.*

DeHavilland U-6A Beavers entered Vietnamese military service beginning in 1958. More were added in the 1960s for special missions, such as psychological warfare, by having a speaker system for propaganda messages. This Beaver is assigned to the 314th Special Missions Squadron at Tan Son Nhut. *RG 342-KE40077 USAF.*

visible show of force. This encouraged support from other units at Da Nang and Bien Hoa to consolidate his resistance.

Instead of going to the rebellious generals, Ky held out at Tan Son Nhut and made the leaders come to him on 14 September. With that move the rebellion collapsed. Air Vice Marshal Ky's leadership and use of the loyal VNAF were the decisive elements in breaking the back of this attempt to overthrow the government in September 1964. He rallied the forces of opposition at a critical point, sent his armed fighter aircraft on low-level passes to harass and frighten his opponents, mustered VNAF C-47s to bring in outlying forces to support the nucleus of his personnel at Tan Son Nhut, used his observation aircraft to drop leaflets and make broadcasts to rebel elements to undermine their unity, and even stopped a convoy of troops *en route* to Saigon in one case. His cool leadership qualities, organizational ability, understanding of the total problem, and willingness to use the VNAF were decisive elements not only in defeating the *coup d'etat*, but in enhancing his own prestige.

The incident marked the emergence of the VNAF in the political activities of the nation, and some of its lesser leaders would be appointed to political positions following Ky's success, thus draining VNAF of some of its better-trained and more experienced leaders.

Equipping the VNAF with Sikorsky H-34 helicopters vastly improved the ARVN's capability of moving troops, and eliminated having to have many in ready reserve units. *RG-111-SC 601512 USA.*

This H-34 Choctaw of the 219th Helicopter Squadron comes in low and fast at Da Nang or Nha Trang. Note the unusual camouflage. The bright color applied behind the main rotor aided the FAC in knowing VNAF from U.S. forces. These colors sometimes varied between units. *Courtesy of Pham Quang Khiem.*

This unusual color scheme for a H-34 in Vietnam identified these as "King Bee" aircraft, most likely assigned to special operations. Note the top identifying color behind the main rotor as being the light color of the camouflage. *Courtesy of Bob Chenoweth.*

More Aircraft and Increased Missions

The manpower expansion of the VNAF and the emergence of recognized leaders in the years from 1962 to 1965 were accompanied by a similar rapid growth in the numbers and types of aircraft assigned. Between December 1961 and December 1965 the VNAF's aircraft inventory grew from 70 to 393 aircraft. In 1965 alone it added 108 (an increase of 38 percent). That no other air force had a similar experience of rapid expansion would be an understatement, and it would become even more startling in the years to come.

With this surge of aircraft came an acute shortage of pilots to man these planes. To alleviate the problem, the U.S. Air Force assigned 30 of its own pilots to the two transport squadrons at Tan Son Nhut. The "Dirty Thirty," as the USAF contingent became known, served as C-47 co-pilots for the Vietnamese to relieve a like number of trained VNAF pilots to tactical operations in T-28s. These Americans soon appreciated the flying skills of their VNAF counterparts and accepted their own role as co-pilot. Some at first criticized the informality of Vietnamese flying methods, but all came to agree that these were often the safest, given the difficult flying environment in Vietnam.

It is interesting to look at the distribution of types and numbers of aircraft at this point, as the VNAF began its change in appearance with more modern aircraft. At the beginning of 1964 VNAF still had the one squadron at Da Nang with its 29 T-28s, but this converted to Douglas A-1s in May. To give the VNAF a more sophisticated capability of aerial surveillance, the 314th Special Missions Squadron at Tan Son Nhut received 18 RT-28s for reconnaissance duties. In addition to the squadron of 22 A-1 Skyraiders al-

The attrition rate for aircraft in Vietnam was not always caused by combat. Damage to this O-1 was the result of a landing accident and a resultant ground loop. This occurred at Quang Ngai AB with one of the 110th Observation Squadron aircraft. *Courtesy of George Pfromm.*

Since the O-1 had been out of production for many years, the next suitable aircraft that was in production was Cessna's 185, designated by the USAF as the U-17. These not only served training and transport duties, but as FAC aircraft in the absence of O-1s. Note the 110th Observation Squadron insignia. *RG 342-KE42000.*

Spirits were high for the anticipated air strikes into North Vietnam being made by these VNAF pilots. This photo shows Col Vu-van-Uoc (left) and Col Nguyen-huy-Anh (right) just prior to going to their A-1s for strikes against the radar station at Vinh-Linh in 1965. *Courtesy of Vu Van Uoc.*

Armorers raise a 500 lb general purpose low-drag bomb to the pylon of this Douglas A-1H of the 518th Fighter Squadron. The nose fuse of the bomb was not installed until the bomb was in place. *RG 342-107326 USAF.*

ready at Bien Hoa, now redesignated the 514th, a second squadron, the 518th, converted to Skyraiders during February and March of that year. There were, in addition, two squadrons of H-34 helicopters, comprising 24 aircraft each, the two squadrons of C-47s remained unchanged, and 48 Cessna L-19 (now redesignated O-1) Bird Dog aircraft equipped three observation squadrons.

In the spring of 1964 psychological air warfare operations were often the sole swift means of communications between the government and remote rural peoples. Since part of President Khanh's weakness stemmed from loss of contact with the hinterland, it was proposed to expand the training of Vietnamese in psychological operations.

To support the Vietnamese armed forces in political warfare, the Vietnamese Air Force set up a general political warfare directorate with headquarters at Tan Son Nhut and officers at each wing. Ten single-engine utility aircraft, consisting of six de Havilland U-6A Beavers and four Cessna U-17A Skywagons, were delivered to the VNAF for psychological warfare duty. These aircraft were modified to carry a tape recorded public address system with fuselage-mounted speaker. As the airplane circled a populated area, prerecorded tapes or direct speaking was broadcast to the people below.

Caught in VNAF's conversion to fighter aircraft, however, the Vietnamese paid scant attention to psychological warfare. The four U-17s were used in and around Saigon as planned, yet only one U-

Skyraiders from many VNAF squadrons start their engines in preparation for a raid upon North Vietnam on March 14, 1965. Targets included a Naval Radar establishment on the Tiger Islands just north of the 17th parallel. VNAF's first raid into the north was on February 8, 1965.

Not all landings are graceful, yet all depend upon conditions. This A-1H, piloted by 2nd Lt. Bui-dinh-Giang of the 514th Fighter Squadron, landed wheels-up at Bien Hoa AB after being hit by enemy ground fire in June 1966. *RG 342-97914 USAF.*

6 was modified due to the complications in installing speakers. This method of pursuing psychological warfare was kept active, however, both with VNAF and the USAF in varying degrees throughout the war. Well-prepared tapes of supernatural wailing messages from supposed departed loved ones, together with frightening background noises played at night to those VC hiding in the jungle had a terrifying effect and caused many to surrender.

There were other sides, as well. The author recalls two consecutive days during the Christmas season when carols, including Bing Crosby's *White Christmas*, came from the USAF psy-war aircraft that circled for hours in the sun-baked sky above Pleiku Air Base, directing these melodies to those of us on the sweltering ground below. A negative or positive effect is still in question!

Expansion in numbers and the addition of new aircraft types was still a major characteristic of VNAF during 1965. The number of A-1 Skyraider squadrons grew with two more in 1965, bringing the total to six squadrons assigned to five major air bases throughout South Vietnam. The number of A-1s assigned increased from 89 at the beginning of 1965 to 146 after all six squadrons were operational by the end of the year. Furthermore, the observation fleet increased considerably over the same period. The Cessna O-1A inventory more than doubled in size (37 in January to 84 in December), all of which were taken from the active inventory of the USAF and U.S. Army units. Since the O-1 was long out of production, replacements for more of these observation planes were made through the purchase of additional side-by-side U-17A (Cessna 185) Skywagons—less effective for aerial observation, but nevertheless they augmented the O-1 units and fulfilled their requirements. Their number grew from the initial 25 to 46 during 1965. With these, the VNAF now had four observation squadrons, a flying school squadron at Nha Trang using Cessna U-17As, plus a detachment of U-6A Beaver special missions airplanes. Helicopter squadrons of H-34s numbered four; one each in the four corps areas, and the two troop carrier squadrons of C-47s assigned at Tan Son Nhut. With these units the force was more than double the VNAF aircraft inventory of July 1962, when the United States first became openly committed to the rapid build-up of forces in Vietnam.

Low clouds and rain dampen Da Nang Air Base during the typical monsoon season. Two A-1s of the 516th Fighter Squadron are ready for a mission when this picture was taken in 1964. Weather like this hampered air missions in support of ARVN troops in contact. *RG 342-K29933 USAF.*

The VNAF had only a few of the multi-place A-1E Skyraiders compared to the single place models. The "P" on the fin identifies this as an A-1E assigned to the 516th Fighter Squadron at Da Nang. The blue fuselage band is that of the 41st Tactical Wing. *Courtesy of Neal Schneider.*

Combat Effectiveness

The role of these forces was naturally to give the Vietnamese more air combat capability for countering insurgent forces. Slow in asserting this role at the beginning due to necessary expansion and combat training, it was not long before VNAF was making its mark in aerial combat. Since no two or more air sorties were ever flown the same, nor the results predictable, it was difficult to describe VNAF air operations other than by statistics. This was the measure of all air operations flown over Vietnam, therefore, it is only proper and fair to record some of them here.

Before the USAF-manned aircraft arrived in Vietnam, the VNAF performed all combat, observation, and forward air control duties themselves, averaging about 2,200 sorties[14] per month to the beginning months of 1963, with the exception of the USAF Operation Farm Gate. When this operation began in late 1961 to assist VNAF and improve their operational capability, joint VNAF-USAF

This photo was taken from the lead Skyraider of a three ship formation of the 520th Fighter Squadron based at Binh Thuy. Note the hinge line for the speed boards just forward of the fuselage insignia. These were wired off and not functional at this late time of the A-1H's service life. *Courtesy of Charles Long via Phan-Quang Khiem.*

With jets added to VNAF in its latter periods, the Douglas A-1 Skyraider remained the dependable workhorse for air to ground weapons delivery. These former U.S. Navy attack bombers were being phased out of U.S. service, only to enter an all new air force and 10 years of combat. This A-1H was assigned to the 516th Fighter Squadron at Da Nang, October 1964. *Courtesy of David Menard.*

The distinctive water tower landmark at Bien Hoa AB identifies the location of this Douglas A-1H of the 514th Fighter Squadron. These multi-place aircraft served a number of missions other than purely air-to-ground ordnance delivery. *Courtesy of David Menard.*

combat sorties amounted to 2500 out of a total of 7000 overall missions (35 percent) during the first six months of 1962. Of these missions, 1900 interdiction missions were flown by the VNAF.

Other examples of joint USAF-VNAF air operations were very apparent in May and September 1962. Using Douglas B-26s, along with AD-6 and North American T-28 aircraft, they flew 28 napalm and other strike sorties in the southern portion of I Corps, destroying a Viet Cong assembly area and an active radio installation. In September, 10 VNAF T-28s and an equal number of H-34s participated in another joint search and destroy operation with the USAF in I Corps. A total of 79 sorties were flown in this combined operation. Joint exercises flown during operation Farm Gate accounted for about 38 percent of the Viet Cong killed in the first eight months of 1963.

During 1963 VNAF C-47s joined USAF Fairchild C-123 Provider aircraft for flare illumination missions every night, beginning in June. Also that year, VNAF-USAF units flew 2388 escort missions for railroad trains. The simple presence of the unarmed O-1 often broke up an ambush. On 3 August two O-1s spotted 200 guerrillas lying in wait between Quang Ngai and Da Nang for an ammunition train headed north. When the planes appeared the Viet Cong fled. Later that month an O-1 stopped the lead vehicle of a convoy it was escorting just short of an explosive charge set in the road by the VC.

In contrast to the 32 requests for convoy escort from January to July 1962, there were 506 requests between August and October that year, emphasizing the importance ground commanders were placing on air support. Doing most of the train and truck convoy escort, O-1s flew ahead of the units and searched for signs of ambush and radioed for ground and air reinforcement as required. Except for compulsory combat air cover for high-priority cargo, tactical aircraft selected for escort duties usually stayed on ground alert. The combination of aircraft assigned to these duties constituted of about 10 percent of the total tactical air effort. For several months from July 1962 no train or convoy escorted by air ran into an ambush.

The number of combat sorties and total flying hours also showed a dramatic increase, especially toward the end of December 1963; important indications as to the operational performance of the VNAF during its expansion. In 1964, for example, VNAF fighter pilots flew 14,251 sorties for a total of 24,139 operational flying hours, an average of 281 hours and 166 sorties for each pilot during that year. Considering that the average sortie lasted only 1.7 hours for these relatively short-range missions this was a considerable achievement, especially as many of these pilots also had administrative responsibilities. This amounts to sorties actually flown on two of every three days during the year. This increase was accomplished during the period when the VNAF was having problems training enough A-1 pilots to meet the expansion and conversion of its tactical wings. This training began in May 1964, yet the number of A-1 sorties increased from 145 in June to 324 in December, while flying hours increased from 1616 to 3278.

Although there were problems in other areas, especially for the helicopter pilots converting from the H-19 to the more advanced H-34, the VNAF managed to fulfill its operational commitments.

By 1965, the VNAF had flown a grand total of 118,120 operational sorties, and its monthly flying hours increased from 14,142 in January 1965 to 19,564 in December of that year.

An example of the massive air strikes flown by the Vietnamese was that which took place toward the end of April 1964. Seventeen Vietnamese A-1Hs were combat loaded and deployed from Bien Hoa to Da Nang. The mission proved to be the start of a seven-battalion search-and-clear heliborne sweep in the sector of II Corps. During the five day operation between 27 April and 31 May, the sorties flown by the VNAF totaled 266 O-1 and U-6A, 420 A-1H and T-28, and 102 H-34 helicopter flights. The helicopters were tasked with psychological warfare, medical evacuation, resupply, and crop destruction. A daily average of 10 A-1Hs were stationed at Da Nang, and the 516th Fighter Squadron kept five T-28s at Quang Ngai airfield on combat readiness.

The operation apparently caught the Viet Cong by surprise. Not only were many automatic weapons captured and destroyed, but enemy installations were neutralized, and when the fighting was over, the plan to leave three irregular companies behind for mopping up actions was revoked, as the VC had been scattered. Nonetheless, this example of well-coordinated combat aviation gave everyone confidence that Vietnamese air power was clearly on the upswing.

North Bound

In 1965, as the Viet Cong guerrilla war against South Vietnam was intensifying, President Johnson sent his national security advisor, McGeorge Bundy, to assess the situation. He arrived in Saigon for briefing on 4 February. Three days later the Viet Cong made a deliberate attack against American installations in South Vietnam, sparking President Johnson's decision to counter-attack with a plan called Flaming Dart, which allowed American air raids against North Vietnam. These strikes began immediately.

Not to be outdone, the VNAF responded in the same manner the very next day, 8 February 1965. From the outset, U.S. technicians were apprehensive that the upgrading of Vietnamese-manned aircraft to a capability of making attacks north of the 17th Parallel would enable the VNAF to make retaliatory attacks against North Vietnam and take control out of American hands for trying to prevent escalation of the war. With U.S. forces taking the initiative with retaliatory strikes, there was little doubt that the Vietnamese Air Force would do likewise.

The Douglas A-1H was an aircraft capable of this type of strike, and now that VNAF had sufficient numbers of these Skyraiders the attack was feasible. With Air Vice Marshal Ky in command of the strike, this was the first VNAF multi-aircraft bombing attack on North Vietnam.

Between April 1961 and July 1962 Ky had similarly led a series of C-47 night missions over Hanoi to drop sabotage teams charged with blowing up roads, bridges, and power plants. Now, in early 1965, he flew one of the lead A-1H Skyraiders. He had with him a total of 24 aircraft, all A-1s "borrowed" in small numbers from other VNAF A-1 squadrons. Flying each aircraft was a very experienced pilot, hand picked or approved by Ky himself to ensure the effectiveness of the operation.

On the afternoon of 8 February the six four-ship flights of A-1s departed from Da Nang and flew a northerly course until sufficiently out over the South China Sea. Staying low to the water and well away from the coast they turned northwest, and flew parallel with the coast, hoping to avoid detection by enemy radar.

The 125 mile (201 km) flight to their target in the Vinh Linh-Chap Le area took just under one hour before the formation broke off into separate elements to attack supply and troop concentration areas to the rear of the demilitarized zone. Results of the raid were very effective, reportedly destroying 90 percent of the military establishments at Vinh Linh. Although heavy anti-aircraft fire was encountered on the strike and each of the 24 planes was hit at least once, only one Skyraider failed to return to Da Nang. Lt Col Duong-thieu-Hung was forced to bail out of his stricken aircraft over the water on the return flight, but he was subsequently rescued by a helicopter that was standing by.

All landings are not necessarily happy ones. This A-1E Skyraider, photographed 1 July 1966, apparently made a wheels up landing at Bien Hoa AB. How embarrassing at a strange filed, since this is a 524th Fighter Squadron airplane from Nha Trang. *Courtesy of Earl L. Otto.*

This significant military operation by VNAF aircraft, coming only five months after Ky had thwarted the political *coup d'etat* by rebellious Army generals, certainly enhanced his prestige, and set the scene militarily for his assumption of the role of Prime Minister the following June. In addition, the daring strike over enemy territory with such relatively little loss to the VNAF forces must have contributed to the *esprit de corps* of the VNAF, and certainly its unswerving loyalty to its leader. The spirits of the loyal Vietnamese throughout the south were heightened immensely.

On 11 February a second air strike by VNAF aircraft in consort with USAF and Navy aircraft was launched against North Vietnamese barracks at Chanh Hoa and Vit Thu Lu. This was in retaliation for an enemy attack against U.S. installations at Qui Nhon that killed more than 20 Americans.

American leaders watched intently, hoping that the VNAF would not carry the air war outside the bounds of their own country for fear of the international implications that could be aroused at this relatively early stage of the escalating war. But the attacks across the Northern border continued with U.S. sanction. The VNAF flew approximately 30 of these missions over the next year in combined operations with the U.S. 7th Fleet. With extensive bombing missions being flown by U.S. aircraft, the VNAF's operations were accomplished with little outside attention.

In recognition of the VNAF's air combat performance, the 514th Fighter Squadron, VNAF, was awarded the Presidential Unit Citation of the United States in April 1965. This was rewarded to the squadron for its heroism and outstanding performance of duty against the enemy over the 13 month period from January 1964 through February 1965. It was this squadron at Bien Hoa, originally known as the 1st Fighter Squadron, and then flying F8F Bearcats, that was the first to be equipped with Douglas Skyraiders. This award was an act of singular importance in the history of the VNAF, for it enhanced the young service's prestige, and demonstrated that its operational capabilities were fully recognized by the United States after nearly nine years of continuous military assistance.

5

VNAF and Jets

North Vietnamese patrol boats attacked the American destroyer USS *Maddox* in the Tonkon Gulf 2 August 1964. Reprisal attacks were made against North Vietnamese targets, and the U.S. Congress gave President Johnson extraordinary power to act in Southeast Asia. The Viet Cong attacked Bien Hoa AB 1 November 1964 and destroyed 5 USAF B-57s, damaged 15 others, and destroyed or damaged 4 VNAF A-1Hs. Four deaths resulted and 72 were wounded. Political unrest in the Saigon government caused numerous coup d'etat that resulted in changes in leadership and forms of government, creating an uneasy situation with the United States. The air war accelerated as U.S. pilots sighted Soviet MiG jet aircraft for the first time on 3 April 1965.

The B-57 Canberras

B-57 Bombers For VNAF were the front page headlines of the Saigon Sunday Post for 1 August 1965. This first public announcement stated that "The Vietnamese Air Force would soon have its first jet aircraft," and that "four B-57 twin-jet Canberra bombers will soon be turned over to them."

Up until this time the United States was reluctant to equip VNAF with jet airplanes because it was against the 1956 Geneva Accords. With constant violations of these Accords by North Vietnam, the need for the South to honor them no longer existed. This being the case, some American planners felt that VNAF might escalate the war by making strikes to the North. These reasons being

A VNAF Martin B-57B moves along the taxiway at Da Nang in preparation for a strike mission in 1965. Four aircraft were assigned for VNAF use from active USAF Canberra units, but were often flown by a mixed crew of USAF/VNAF members. *RG 342-97427 USAF.*

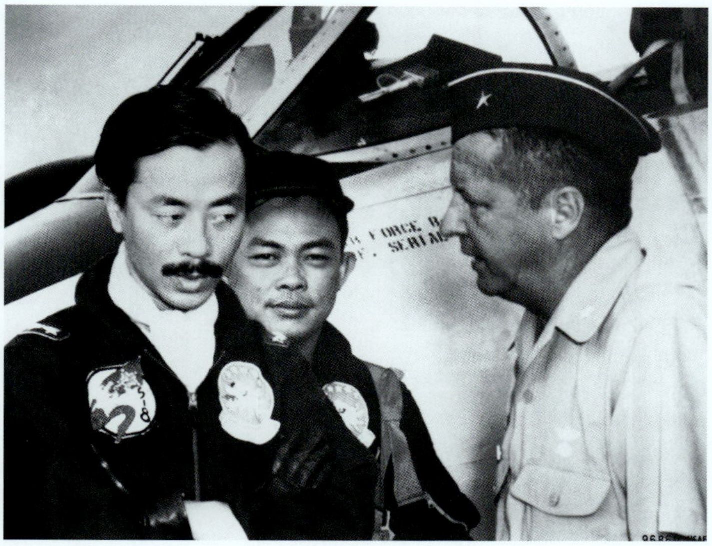

During formal delivery of B-57s to the VNAF at Tan Son Nhut on August 9, 1965, Nguyen-cao-Ky, left, then Prime Minister of the Republic of Vietnam and Commander of the VNAF talks with B/Gen Albert W. Schinz, MACV Advisor. Capt Nguyen-van-Tuong, pilot of another B-57, looks on. Both wear 518th and 83rd patches. *RG 342-96860 USAF.*

After Vietnamese crew members became proficient with the Canberras, pilots and navigators were teamed as a VNAF crew. They remained under the operational control of the USAF 8th and 13th Bomb Squadrons, whichever were stationed at Da Nang at the time. *Courtesy of Douglas J. Beggerly.*

no longer valid, and with continual reminders from Saigon that they had equipped other friendly nations with jets, the U.S. was forced to reassess the situation. The Vietnamese people, too, needed a boost in morale, for the lengthy war was no longer stagnant but, in fact, escalating.

The program had already begun, however, as early as May 1964, only one month after B-57s with USAF units stationed in Japan moved to Clark AB, Philippines. After unusual diplomatic arrangements were made between the Vietnamese and Philippines governments, three VNAF officers arrived at Clark for this training. They were Major Nguyen-ngoc-Bien and Captains Nguyen-van-Tuong and Nguyen-van-Long. Instructors of the 8th and 13th Bomb Squadrons were relieved to learn that all three had extensive pilot experience, but what they knew of jet flying remained to be seen.

Heading this training program was Captain Don Nation, USAF, who recalls that, after the initial problem of converting from the A-1 tail-dragging Skyraider to a twin-engine jet with tricycle landing gear, these officers were excellent pilots. They completed their conversion to the Canberra without problems.

Training for the next three officers proved to be very interesting also. Unlike the first group of three, this training—which the directive message referred to as "Familiarization Training"—was to be accomplished at Tan Son Nhut instead of Clark AB. It soon became obvious why, for these students were none other than Nguyen-cao-Ky, now the Commander of VNAF (and yet to be Prime Minister the following year 1965 until 1967), Col Nguyen-ngoc-Loan, later General and Chief of National Police for Ky, and Major Van, Chief of the VNAF Command Post. With the help of other

While the USAF B-57s were assigned at Da Nang, this VNAF marked Canberra appears loaded and ready for its next mission. In the early months that VNAF officially had B-57s they flew with mixed crews of one USAF and one VNAF member.

The first VNAF crew members assigned to the B-57 program handled the airplane very well. As the program progressed there became less interest in the airplane by later arrivals, and after nine months the program ended. *Courtesy of Douglas J. Beggerly.*

Specific Canberras were not assigned to VNAF. To maintain a promised quantity, insignia were frequently exchanged when periodic maintenance would take one out of service. In this case 52-1532 is wearing VNAF markings and a newly painted camouflage scheme. *Courtesy of David Menard.*

USAF instructors and a few more dual-control B-57Cs, the training of these three was completed in the prescribed 30-day period, woven into the officers' busy schedules.

More than a year passed before the announcement was made that the VNAF would receive jet bombers, and a formal presentation ceremony to the Vietnamese Government was arranged for 9 August 1965. Positioned in front of the crowd when they arrived was one B-57, void of USAF markings and already painted with the VNAF insignia. On the ground in front for the dignitaries to inspect were the various ordnance loads that the B-57 could carry. This had some of the appearance of a trade show and the need to "sell" the aircraft to prospective customers.

Prior to the event, three B-57C Canberras took off from Tan Son Nhut in preparation for the flyover as part of the presentation of the four Canberras. In the front seats of each aircraft were Ky, now Prime Minister, yet retaining command of VNAF, and VNAF Captains Tuong and Long. With the passing of time these pilots had lost their proficiency in B-57s, so the back seats of these dual-control models were occupied by American instructor pilots who had previously trained them. In the lead aircraft was Gen Ky, with Capt Don Nation in the back seat. Ky was an excellent pilot, but since he was unable to participate in the practice fly-bys preceding this event, Capt Nation took over to land the aircraft. His humorous comments about the event are worth repeating here:

"As we neared the far end of the runway I pulled up in a steep climb with a half-roll and reverse for what I thought would make an interesting entry onto the downwind for landing. We still had a good head of speed, but I fudged a bit and got the gear down at not too excessive an airspeed at about the time I turned on base leg. While doing everything possible to slow down to flap extension speed, yet keep the pattern in tight, I started talking to myself over

When the USAF Project Skoshi Tiger was completed in the combat evaluation of the F-5 Freedom Fighter, these and other airplanes were turned over to the VNAF to re-equip the 522nd Fighter Squadron at Bien Hoa AB in April 1967.

A two-seat F-5D joins other A models at Da Nang AB in April 1968. Stationed at Bien Hoa, the 522nd deployed to many air bases throughout South Vietnam as a display of force when the airplanes were new to VNAF. Nose art of a girl's head was on a number of F-5s.

Sand filled revetment walls protect these F-5s from the frequent mortar attacks against airfields. This is the 522nd Fighter Squadron area at Bien Hoa, seen in October 1967. Note the one F-5D two seat version. *Courtesy of Terry Love.*

This weapons delivery display at Da Nang AB shows a combat loaded F-5 with a typical load, compared to the A-1 Skyraider, which has a variety of ordnance packages. When photographed in April 1968 the F-5 was still new to the VNAF inventory.

the hot-mike for the benefit of the General in the front seat, hoping this would reassure him (and myself) that everything was still under control! 'Slow down—you (s.o.b.)—s-l-o-w d-o-w-n!,' I expounded, not knowing that my death grip on the throttles, attempting to get the engines to idle even slower, was also keying the mike button, and my comments were being transmitted. Moments later, as I rolled out on final, a very calm American voice from the tower responded to my comments, 'Dragon One,[15] if you have your aircraft slowed down sufficiently—you are cleared to land.' This transmission, which identified General Ky as being on board by his personal VNAF call sign, made it clear that I had boo-booed!"

All three B-57s got on the runway in spectacular form to the delight of the audience (and aircrews). At the far end of the runway, out of sight of spectators, the canopies raised, and the three American pilots slid out of the back seats and on to the ground. The Vietnamese pilots taxied the ships to the reviewing area, knowing that their solo appearance would have a prestigious effect upon the press—which it did.

Ky, looking very dapper as always in his distinctive black tailored flying suit, climbed from the cockpit amidst reporters and flashing cameras. He had insisted that the three American pilots, despite their baggy, sweat soaked flying suits, join him at the champagne reception that followed the speech making. As festivities continued, three more B-57Bs at Tan Son Nhut were painted in Vietnamese markings and exchanged for the dual-control "Cs" that left the next morning for Clark AB to resume their training role.

Shortly after the presentation day, a transition and weapons delivery school for Vietnamese pilots was established at Clark AB. Six additional pilots were selected, which soon increased to 12,

Armorers make a final check in the arming area of this F-5 before taking off on a strike mission. Other checks include any leaking fluids that may point to mechanical problems. This Northrop F-5 of the 522nd FS, shown here in January 1968, is in the west arming area at Bien Hoa AB. The 50 ft dirt pile has the appearance of a mountain. *Courtesy of Terry Love.*

The pilot of this F-5A displays his seat pin just pulled from the now-armed ejection seat, indicating to the ground crewman to remove the wheel chocks. The airplane is armed with 500 lb low drag general purpose bombs. *RG 342-K28824 USAF.*

This VNAF F-5A taxies past the photographer on his was to the runway at Bien Hoa AB for a strike mission in January 1973. The presence of the F-5s brought a threat to the NVA and Viet Cong of affective airpower, often directed at the frequently changing ground situation to neutralize the enemy's effectiveness. *Courtesy of Robert J. Mills.*

Secure from ground launched weapons by the Viet Cong, ground crews prepare this F-5 for its next strike. Small in size and close ground clearance made the F-5 an easy airplane to service without stands and ladders. This view at Bien Hoa AB was taken in October 1967. *Courtesy of Terry Love.*

together with 12 navigators and very eager VNAF maintenance personnel. The new program began on 20 September 1965 when Maj Bien returned for a refresher course and weapon delivery training, together with Capt Lan and Lts. Ty and Vu. Each new pilot to be upgraded was to receive 70 hours flying experience, with no less than 40 training sorties before being considered qualified in the Canberra.

From here, training moved into the combat weapons delivery phase; apart from the aircraft type, this was nothing new to the VNAF pilots. Don Nation reflects:

"Because of their many years of combat experience already behind them, I think they ended up teaching us in this final phase of their training. They were very good with ordnance delivery. As I recall, it was Capt. Long that literally drove Harry Zahn 'up the wall' with his dive bombing technique. His first bomb was invariably 250 to 350 feet short, then the next ones would be right down the pipe! When questioned about this apparent consistent miscalculation, Long's confident-sounding explanation for this was to 'scare the enemy into the target area—then really zap 'em.'"

The VNAF's navigator training for the B-57 began in October 1965. This training was to familiarize them with the systems they would operate in the back seat of the Canberra, and to generally transition their thinking from reciprocating engine aircraft speeds to that of jets. As the crews assigned to the 615th Flight completed their training, they went to Da Nang and flew their B-57 combat missions with either the 8th or 13th Bomb Squadrons, USAF, whichever was currently on rotation from Clark AB. To gain combat experience in the B-57, each new crew member flew with an American pilot or navigator, whichever the case may be. Eventually, VNAF crew members were teamed together and flew in VNAF-marked

In the early months that VNAF operated the F-5 they made themselves very visible in the skies over Vietnam. Although the F-5 was not a new design, it was considered a very new fighter for the VNAF. *RG 342-107697 USAF.*

This flight of two F-5s is ready at the departure end of the runway for a formation takeoff. This is the view seen by the lead's wing man. The two GE J85-13 jet engines with 4080 lb (1850 kg) thrust with afterburner gave these Tiger II fighters a snappy takeoff performance. *Courtesy of Terry Love.*

VNAF F-5s were often deployed to different jet-capable air bases, not only to support other Corps commanders than the III Corps, where they were stationed at Bien Hoa AB, but to show the flexibility of VNAF's growing airpower. Shown here in their early service is a flight of F-5s deployed to Da Nang in April 1968.

B-57s, their combat missions remaining under USAF operational control. There were usually a few B-57s in VNAF markings at Da Nang for these crews, a figure that seldom exceeded four, but these aircraft and their insignia were changed frequently with those of the USAF bomber squadrons in order to meet maintenance schedules for down times.

However, the VNAF B-57 program was not making the impact that the Vietnamese Government felt it should, for reasons of morale. An appropriate time to rectify this situation came on the Vietnamese Armed Forces Day, which was 29 October 1965. To highlight the occasion, five B-57s at Da Nang were painted in VNAF insignia and each was armed with 13 500 lb GP bombs and fully

Upgrade pilot training for the F-5 was accomplished at Williams AFB, Arizona. VNAF pilots selected as outstanding in March 1967 showing their trophies are (l. to r.): 1st Lt. Nguyen-dam-Thuyen, Top Gun Trophy; and 1st Lt. Nguyen-tan-Dung, 2nd Lt. Nguyen-van-Ghi, and 1st Lt. Truong-cong-Chanh, Academic Trophies. They wear overseas blue uniforms. *RG 342-103511 USAF.*

Left: Preparing for a mission in the F-5, Lt. Le-Hai reviews the AF Form 781 for prior discrepancies. He wears a partial anti-G suit. *RG 342-103513 USAF.*

Acquiring the Cessna A-37 Dragonfly for the VNAF was a major step forward for modernizing their weapons delivery capability. The A-37 carried a heavy load for its small size, and was a stable platform for weapons delivery. This A-37B photographed in 1971 was from the 516th Fighter Squadron at Da Nang.

This flight of two Dragonflys of the 516th Fighter Squadron at Da Nang AB are in the arming area, just prior to takeoff on a bombing mission. Armorers have nose hatches open as they arm the weapons in the arming area at the north end of the runway at Da Nang. *RG 342-KE41409 USAF.*

VNAF pilots liked the handling characteristics of these nimble Northrop fighters. Four VNAF squadrons were eventually activated with F-5s, all within the 23rd Tactical Wing. Serial number of the lead aircraft is among those originally allocated to the Korean AF. *Courtesy of Pacific Stars and Stripes Photo #10271-B.*

Three squadrons of A-37s were assigned at Binh Thuy, which had elaborate color schemes for identifying squadrons. It is believed that each squadron had four color combinations to identify flights. This A-37 was assigned to the 546th Fighter Squadron. *Courtesy of Pham Quang Khiem.*

This Binh Thuy based A-37 of the 526th Fighter Squadron was photographed at Bien Hoa in January 1973. Of note is the MATS C-133 in the background. The A-37 is being armed for a strike mission on the return to Binh Thuy. *Courtesy of Robert J. Mills.*

Another example of colorfully marked A-37s is this Dragonfly of the Binh Thuy squadrons. Only these colors and designs distinguished one A-37 squadron from another, since tail code letters were not used on A-37s. *Courtesy of Greg Gatewood.*

This A-37B waits patiently for its crew, fully loaded for an air-to-ground strike mission. Aside from its nose-firing gatling gun, it carries six M82 low drag GP bombs. Colorful markings indicate that this airplane belongs to the 524th Fighter Squadron based at Nha Trang. This photo was taken 10 September 1969, possibly after the squadron was moved to Pham Rang AB. *RG 342-K33749 USAF.*

loaded guns. En route to Saigon, these Canberras conducted a preplanned air strike on a suspected VC stronghold, making the presence of VNAF bombers known before landing at Tan Son Nhut. After being turned around, the Canberras joined other Vietnamese aircraft in a tight V-formation fly-by over the capital city at a low 300 ft, ripping along at 300 kts down the main street of Saigon and over the Presidential Palace. This jet bomber force was visually part of VNAF, and even more impressive to onlookers was the announcement that just a few hours before they engaged the enemy in combat, the first B-57s in VNAF markings to have done so. Much to the displeasure of VNAF personnel, however, these Canberras were manned exclusively by American crews.

By the end of January 1966 the crews' enthusiasm for the VNAF B-57 program began to wane. In addition, a training accident that occurred that month when VNAF Lt Lom, along with an instructor pilot, lost control on touchdown when making transition landings at NAS Cubi Point in the Philippines. The airplane was a total write-off. This accident served to lower the morale of the Vietnamese further. Some flatly stated that they could not physically perform the maneuvers required in this heavy and fully manually controlled B-57.

Before a solution to the problem could be found, however, another accident occurred, to the detriment of the VNAF crews, and especially the program. It occurred in February 1966 when a VNAF-

For camouflaged aircraft, the A-37s of the 62nd Tactical Wing at Nha Trang were quite colorful. The fuselage band and insignia on the fin is that of the 524th Fighter Squadron. On the right side of the fin was the 62nd Tactical Wing insignia. Photo taken in May 1969. *Courtesy of Ralph Young.*

Maintenance technicians of the VNAF begin a landing gear retraction test on a Cessna A-37 during periodic inspection. All maintenance procedures were patterned after the USAF system, and the Vietnamese learned them rapidly. *RG 342-107162 USAF.*

Vietnamese Armorers cock this left wing station in preparation to attaching a bomb, usually a M82 low drag. The A-37 normally carried six of these weapons, along with having a mini-gatling gun in the nose. VC and NVA had a high regard for these airplanes.

marked B-57, crewed by two Vietnamese—the pilot being Maj N N Bien—ran into bad weather at Da Nang while on a strake mission. Because of hung ordnance and inadequate fuel, Bien elected to recover to Pleiku Air Base. They disarmed, but because the Vietnamese ground crew were inexperienced on the type they were unable to start the engines. They decided to push the aircraft by hand, Bien remaining in the cockpit to guide the aircraft with wheel brakes. But hydraulic pressure had not been built up beforehand, and as the heavy airplane began to roll down a slight grade, it became uncontrollable and rolled off the side of the taxiway. In a freak accident Bien jumped from the cockpit, stumbled, and fell in front of the left main gear, which rolled over him, causing fatal injuries.

His death stunned all who knew him, for he was well-liked and highly respected by both Vietnamese and Americans. Maj Bien had been a driving force and dynamic leader of the VNAF B-57 program. With his loss there seemed to be no incentive on the part of Vietnamese crews to stay with the Canberra, and few, if any, went to Da Nang to fly the B-57s. With the concurrence of the USAF 13th Air Force, the VNAF B-57 operation was terminated on 20 April 1966.

Freedom Fighter

Vietnam proved to be an excellent location for the USAF to evaluate the combat capability of the Northrop F-5A Freedom Fighter, which in 1966 was in the suitability stage of development. This

Bringing jet aircraft in greater numbers into VNAF was a boost in overall morale of this air force. Up to 248 A-37 Dragonflys joined the VNAF fleet. Despite the fact that the A-37 was a development of the T-37 Tweedy Bird basic trainer, this fighter-bomber version provided a very practical weapons delivery system. This A- 37B photographed November 1970 was from the 526th Fighter Squadron, Binh Thuy. *RG 342-107609 USAF.*

A standard practice among U.S. and Vietnamese pilots when aircraft were carrying live ordnance was for the pilot to place both hands upon the windshield frame. This assures armorers (under wing) that none of the armament switches will be activated while they are arming bombs, rockets, and guns. These two Dragonflys are of the 516th Fighter Squadron at Da Nang AB. *RG 342-KE41405 USAF.*

aircraft was a lightweight, all-purpose fighter developed for the Military Assistance Program for export to countries with a requirement for an agile, supersonic fighter. In order to determine the best of a number of ordnance configurations, 12 F-5As arrived at Bien Hoa in 1966 for the USAF Project Skoshi Tiger,[16] for which the 10th Fighter Squadron, Commando, was formed. This test program proved the F-5 a reliable aircraft in a combat environment, although less in sheer ordnance weight lifting than larger USAF fighters. When the project was completed, most of these and other F-5As were designated for VNAF operation, beginning 17 April 1967.

To further modernize VNAF, U.S. Secretary of Defense Robert S. McNamara approved the conversion of six VNAF A-1 Skyraider squadrons to two squadrons of F-5As and four squadrons of A-37s on 13 July 1966. This occurred about the time the F-5As were becoming available for USAF use in Vietnam. The first squadron selected for F-5A conversion was the 522nd at Bien Hoa. This squadron stood down in the first week in September 1966, in order to send some of their maintenance personnel to Clark Air Base in the Philippines for training on the new aircraft. In August 33 pilots left Vietnam for the United States for flight training on the F-5A, and to serve as a cadre for this initial squadron of jet fighters. Already very experienced with the Douglas A-1 in combat operations, an upgrading program was all that was needed, and only nine pilots required the nine weeks' language training before entering the program. Arriving at Williams AFB, Chandler, Arizona, for the advanced jet training of 88 flying hours, they first flew the T-38 Talon trainer, which was very similar to the F-5A. Once proficient in this introduction to jet flying students were then transferred to the F-5A. Course duration was from three and a half to four months, with courses starting every six or seven weeks. Though uncommon, one or two VNAF students did drop out before graduating.

Under belly details are apparent in this view taken from another Cessna A-37 while on the way to the target. Note the two M-82s outboard of each external fuel tank. *Courtesy of Charles Hammack via Pham-Quang Khiem.*

The combat crew training program was completed by 29 May 1967, and pilots began returning to their squadron at Bien Hoa that spring. By this time there were 27 operationally ready crews. Although some sorties had already been flown, the VNAF did not officially accept the F-5As until Armed Forces Day, 19 June 1967, at a formal ceremony held at Bien Hoa.

Now emblazoned with the familiar yellow and black checkerboard fuselage band of the 23rd Tactical Wing, these F-5As of the 522nd Fighter Squadron, commanded by Lt Col Duong-thien-Hung, deployed to those bases in Vietnam that could temporarily accommodate them. As the new jet fighter force belonging to the South Vietnamese Air Force their performance was spectacular and impressive, and they were frequently seen departing from their temporary air bases to make strikes against the enemy.

In the first official month of operation in June 1967, the 20 F-5A Freedom Fighters accomplished 388 sorties, amassing 443 flying hours, and in the month that followed 436 sorties, 477 flying hours. By December 1967 they flew 527 sorties and amassed 556 flying hours, their highest utilization month of that year. Pilot manning was 1.5 per aircraft for the newly equipped fighter squadron.

The formation of the second squadron of F-5As was delayed because it became apparent to the Air Force that the F-5A's air-to-ground weapons delivery system did not meet their specifications. Consequently, further jet upgrading was completed on the Cessna A-37 Dragonfly. It was not until 1974 (seven years later) that the second squadron of F-5As was formed, followed by others. However, the withdrawal by the United States from the conflict led to a re-appraisal of the F-5A by the VNAF to fill the vacant air defense role.

The VNAF was now the largest user of the Northrop F-5A Freedom Fighter in the world. Northrop records show that by January 1975 160 F-5As had been acquired, suffering 54 subsequent losses, 6 F-5Bs with one loss, and 10 RF-5As with six losses. For the F-5Es delivered there are no accurate records. After early 1975 aircraft accountability became unreliable.

Dragonfly

It was not until the late-1960s that the Cessna A-37 Dragonfly entered VNAF squadron service. Being the third and final jet aircraft type to enter VNAF service, it is appropriate to mention it in conjunction with the previous two types.

The Air Force's plans for modernizing the VNAF called for the eventual conversion of four VNAF A-1 fighter squadrons to Cessna A-37 jets. The introduction of the aircraft into VNAF service resembled that of the F-5A Freedom Fighter, but it did not come up to unit strength until early 1969. As the A-37 was an unproven combat aircraft, yet with seemingly great potential for counter-insurgency operations, the USAF conducted a combat suitability test in Vietnam.

Beginning in August 1967, about 10 of these ground attack aircraft were deployed from the United States to Bien Hoa and Pleiku for evaluation by the USAF 604th Special Operations Squadron under the project name Combat Dragon. Since the aircraft were already designated for Vietnamese Air Force use, one wonders if the project name was ascribed to the VNAF, the *flying dragon* being its insignia? The same question could apply to the aircraft's name, "Dragonfly."

Commander of the VNAF's Air Operations Center at Tan Son Nhut, Colonel Vu-van-Uoc, describes the command and control system for close air support. The ARVN corps commanders controlled the VNAF resources within their area, but all strikes were coordinated through the AOC. *RG 342-107641 USAF.*

While the USAF test program was underway in 1967, the Vietnamese Air Force assigned 103 pilots to the three squadrons scheduled to receive the A-37s. On 1 January 1968 the first Skyraider fighter squadron designated to receive the A-37, the 524th at Nha Trang, stood down for training and conversion. The following month the first 18 pilots departed for the United States to begin T-37 conversion at England AFB, Louisiana. In May an A-37 mobile training detachment arrived at Nha Trang to begin maintenance training. During this conversion period the squadron's 14 A-1Hs were distributed to other Skyraider units to replenish the losses they had incurred over the years: three went to the 516th at Da Nang; 10 to the 518th at Bien Hoa; and one to 520th at Binh Thuy.

Squadron conversion began in November 1968 with delivery of the first A-37 jets from the United States. These included some 39 T-37s taken from the USAF Air Training Command inventory, modified into A-37s. By May 1969 a complement of 54 A-37B jets were assigned to the 524th, 520th, and 516th Fighter Squadrons. The first A-37 jet squadron was declared operational in March 1969, the last in July, but others would follow. On 23 July 1971 a UPT course began at Sheppard AFB, Wichita Falls, Texas, under the auspices of the 363rd PTS. After 30 hours experience on the T-41 Mescalero, the VNAF pilots received further training in the T-37 under the A-37 program.

The VNAF's personnel adapted willingly and readily, but conversion was not easy and did not go smoothly. It suffered its share of setbacks and subsequent high cost. A report[17] prepared in October 1968 by the USAF to evaluate the early conversion to jet aircraft prior to A-37 arrivals stated:

> "Although the VNAF showed the ability to convert to the F-5 and maintain it during the modernization period, it still could not handle its own maintenance load in critical periods, and therefore sought U.S. assistance. The depot at Bien Hoa could not handle crash and battle damage on occasion, and it experienced many logistical problems. Since the United States Military Assistance Program for the VNAF had increased from $5.3 million in 1965 to 98.4 million in 1966, and to 264.0 million by 1967, the VNAF supply depot had trouble coping with this huge growth....
>
> These problems should not obscure the fact that VNAF's achievements were many during this first stage of its modernization program. Stressing professionalism at all levels and having developed a high esprit de corps, the VNAF became a well-organized, well-led air arm with considerable combat experience, in addition to other aerial roles. It aided greatly in the defense of the Republic of Vietnam...."

Managing the Force

Having an air force is one thing, but being able to employ it effectively in combat is another issue. The VNAF's system of command and control developed over the years with the assistance of the USAF. The system handled the flow of aircraft from take-off to target area, and return to base. Known as the Tactical Air Control System (TACS), it assured positive radar control in all areas where significant combat operations were indicated. Without this system,

DEPLOYMENT OF FORCES

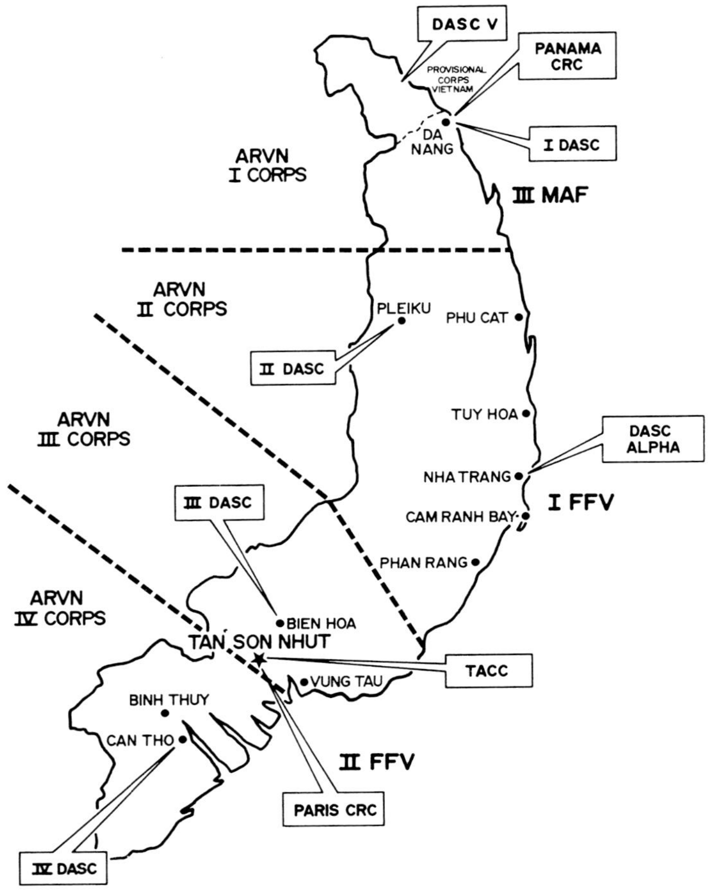

TACTICAL AIR CONTROL SYSTEM

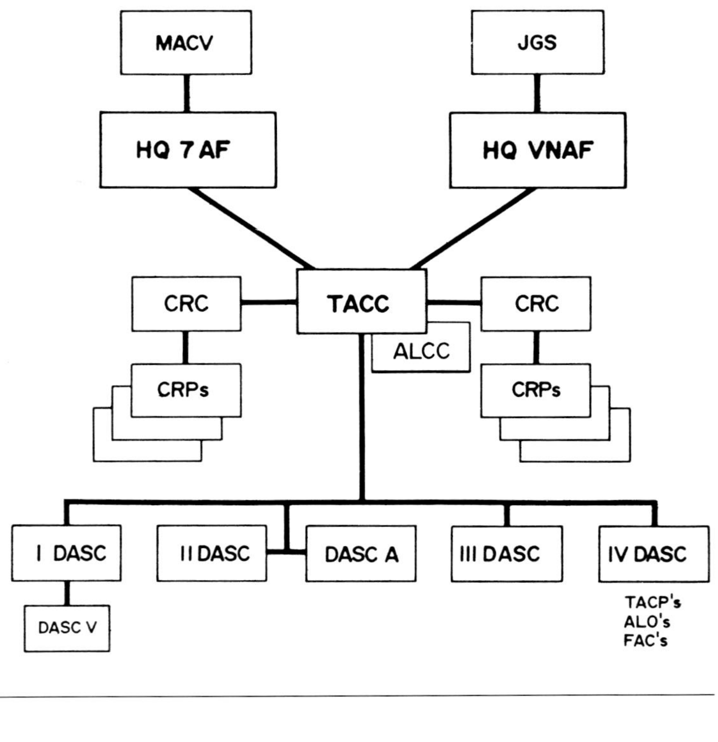

it would not have been possible to deploy the force between areas of combat.

For example, a strike aircraft scheduled for a pre-planned mission in the section of I Corps could be diverted with a minimum of disruption to that of II Corps. On arrival in the assigned area, the strike aircraft would be instructed to contact a Forward Air Controller (FAC), often flying a Cessna O-1 Bird Dog, over the action area. These were assigned to observation squadrons, the term *liaison* being discontinued soon after the VNAF was formed. The FAC would describe the precise target to the strike aircraft, often mark it with a smoke rocket or grenade, and the attack would begin. Given the ground situation in Vietnam, flexibility of air operations during periods where troops were in contact was essential for the VNAF's operations to have maximum effect.

The Tactical Air Control Center, located at Tan Son Nhut, became the major hub of the system that eventually developed. It was in close proximity to the headquarters for both VNAF and USAF, and the commanders of both Air Forces utilized its facilities. Known as TACC, it was from here that air operations were planned, coordinated, executed, and monitored. Subordinate to the TACC were outlying Direct Air Support Centers (DASC) assigned to each of the Corps Headquarters, with a direct line communication to the TACC. DASCs were responsible for the deployment of aircraft located within their sector, often in support of ground operations. They reacted quickly to any change in the enemy threat, diverting aircraft from a preplanned target to an immediate threat. Operating under each DASC were numerous Tactical Air Control Parties (TACPs), manned by one or more VNAF/USAF personnel positioned with forces such as corps, field divisions, battalions, and other units, including the airborne Forward Air Controllers. A communication network linked all three levels of command and control, giving TACC overall control of the air situation at all times. Additional control and information was provided by a radar network that covered all of South Vietnam and beyond, monitoring all strike aircraft. This gave real-time information for controlling the air operation.

The VNAF struggled from the very beginning to achieve control of its air resources (*see* Chapter 4), and to have the prerogative to respond to requests made by respective ARVN Corps Commanders, rather than have its aircraft assigned to them directly. The USAF-proven Tactical Air Support System evolved, providing the control for the VNAF as well as the USAF, resulting in a common operating system in South Vietnam.

In the early years, the VNAF's air-ground coordination system contained some elements of the French system. For example, the Army Division would initiate requests for air support to the Army Corps Tactical Operations Center (TOC), where a VNAF Air Liaison Officer subsequently advised on optimum deployment. However, in the early years these officers held little rank and were insufficiently trained to advise on such important matters.

As a first step to effecting a more centralized control for coordinating air-ground operations, the Air Tactical Command was formed at Tan Son Nhut, but was ineffective. Thinking a change in title would improve the situation, it was redesignated the "Air Operations Control Center" on 1 February 1956. Not until the introduction, in 1961, of the battle-proven U.S. air-ground operations system was an improvement seen in even the elementary coordination between the South Vietnamese Army and Air Force.

One of only two UH-1Bs that carried the VNAF insignia. This one was a gift to Air Marshal Ky from the United States government when he was Commander of the VNAF. Ky was helicopter and jet qualified. Photograph taken at Tan Son Nhut, September 1966. After service with Ky this Huey went to the Wisconsin National Guard, then was sent to Honduras in 1982. *Courtesy of Terry Love.*

One of the most difficult things to develop in a theater of operations is an air-ground operations system, because it must be based upon mutual respect and communication between air and ground forces. To do the job well, both forces had to willingly accept the fact that, at times, decisions made by the overall commander could be contrary to the desires of one or the other.

In the Vietnamese armed forces, no overall commander of combat (theater) operations existed; ARVN General Cao-van-Vien, Chief of the Joint General Staff, came closest. Previously, corps commanders were almost autonomous, reporting directly to the President on all civil matters in their area, and received direction from the President on critical military matters, although they were technically responsible to the Chief of the General Staff. Each corps commander had a great deal of authority, and acted almost independently of his counterparts. This arrangement made the Joint General Staff relatively weak, and as a result hampered the close coordination of corps activities, and in particular priority determination of strike aircraft deployment.

When a request for air support was approved by a corps commander, it was sent to the Joint General Staff in Saigon. The operational element of the Army-dominated JGS was the Joint Operations Center, staffed by VNAF and later USAF officers holding junior positions. The JOC determined the number of aircraft, armament, time, and target for attack. It then passed the approved mission to the Air Operations Center, a VNAF facility with a USAF officer acting as deputy director to the VNAF director. The AOC then executed the mission, the JOC notifying the corps that the mission would go ahead. If an urgent request developed, aircraft were diverted from a planned target to the more critical area.

This was the situation when the VNAF's total strike force consisted of one squadron of Skyraiders operational and one squadron of T-28s in the process of formation. The system was too slow, and inadequate air representation made it difficult to make a proper assessment as to the suitability of the mission. As USAF airpower was introduced into the conflict in 1961, the system needed to be changed to conform with USAF-accepted air-ground system practices. There was initial opposition by the ARVN to the U.S. system, as it meant that centralized control of the air strike force would not allow corps commanders to have the final say on aircraft deployment within their sectors.

As these changes were discussed, the question as to the control of U.S. Army helicopters arose. It was evident that much closer coordination was needed for the routing of helicopters, suppression of enemy fire in the target area, and diversion of other areas if the situation dictated. The USAF took the view that the Air Operations Center was the proper agency to exercise this control, not the Joint Operations Center, and to have senior Army officers assigned there to advise and assist in the coordination of Army activities. As the VNAF was deploying helicopters to transport ARVN forces, their problem was the same.

The arguments in favor of this control system were overwhelming because of the operational flexibility it would provide. The decision was made to develop this method of controlling the forces in Vietnam, and the USAF would train the VNAF to operate the system. Although the VNAF was nominally responsible for the system, the USAF in fact operated the TACS from the outset.

In 1961, to get the new system working, the heaviest radar was installed at Tan Son Nhut, establishing a Control and Reporting Center (CRC)—radio call sign *Paris Control*. Likewise, a similar radar facility was positioned at Da Nang *(Panama)*, and at Pleiku *(Peacock)*. By April 1962 USAF Air Liaison Officers (ALOs) and Forward Air Controllers (FACs) had been assigned to Army Corps and Divisions to serve as air advisors until the VNAF could provide its own personnel.

By the end of 1962 the skeleton of a control system was in place, permitting USAF/VNAF commanders at Tan Son Nhut to control and manage air operations to meet the steadily increasing air support requirements of the ARVN and U.S. Special Forces. From this grew the Tactical Air Control Center described earlier, as the basic control system was augmented by the deployment of U.S. combat units and increased air activity for both the VNAF and the USAF.

Although the VNAF's command and control structure was established, the ARVN still had a say in its activities—as will be covered in greater detail later—Corps commanders influencing decisions regarding the deployment of VNAF units within respective Corps areas. Often, these decisions were not coordinated through the centralized system. From the writer's experience as a USAF FAC in I Corps, it was not uncommon to be directing a pre-planned strike on a target and see a VNAF FAC directing a separate strike on other targets in very close proximity. It was as if two wars were going on independently within the same air space.

6

Turn of the First Decade

On 8 March 1965 two U.S. Marine battalions landed to defend Da Nang AB, the first American combat troops in Vietnam. The South Vietnamese Government became more stable, as Air Vice Marshal Nguyen-cao-Ky took over as prime minister of a military regime in Saigon 11 June 1965. He declared a formal state of war against North Vietnam, an extension of Saigon's curfew, and price controls. On 18 June American B-52s made their first attack of the war in an attempt to dislodge Communist troops north of Saigon. By now, the enemy had nearly isolated the Central Highlands of South Vietnam. President Johnson authorized Gen Westmoreland to employ American troops in fighting the enemy. By the end of 1965 American ground forces in Vietnam reached nearly 200,000.

The year 1965 not only marked the midpoint of its life as an independent Vietnamese Air Force, but was also an important transition period for the VNAF. The turn of its first decade envisaged the advent of the three types of jet aircraft described in the previous chapter, and also marked the end of its phenomenal expansion phase and the beginning of a modernization and professionalization program. This was to dominate all aspects of the VNAF, including men, money, and materials. Controlled expansion became a facet of modernization, which affected every aspect of the maturing air service. Major reconstruction and rehabilitation of the overworked and over-saturated bases was completed in late 1966.

Although expansion of the VNAF had been underway for the previous three years, certain targets had already been met, and new problems had also arisen. "VNAF is a healthy child that needs to mature..." was how the U.S. commander of the USAF Advisory Group, Brig. Gen. Albert W. Schinz, described it at the time. He further emphasized that it suffered from growing pains, and that in spite of its problems, the potential was there, "...for it to become one of the most efficient and effective Air Forces in the Far East." Modernization over the next few years was an ambitious attempt, but it was successful because of training and joint VNAF/USAF use of bases; together with U.S. support, these factors would prove beneficial to the VNAF in the future.

Nevertheless, the VNAF continued to experience personnel, organization, and leadership problems. By 1965 the service was still being run at squadron level. Higher levels of command were not functioning properly; there was little coordination between headquarters and squadrons; there were no command posts at wing and

Throughout the Vietnam War the Skyraider remained the primary fighter-bomber for VNAF. Shown here are two A-1Hs on the break for landing with all there ordnance expended. The gray pods are probably smoke generators. These A-1Hs belong to the 514th and 518th Fighter Squadrons, respectively. *RG 342-K20229 USAF*

Skyraiders of the 514th Fighter Squadron are at rest in their squadron area on the west ramp at Bien Hoa in October 1967. Components in gray color are replacement parts that have yet to be matched to their surrounding camouflage colors. *Courtesy of Terry Love.*

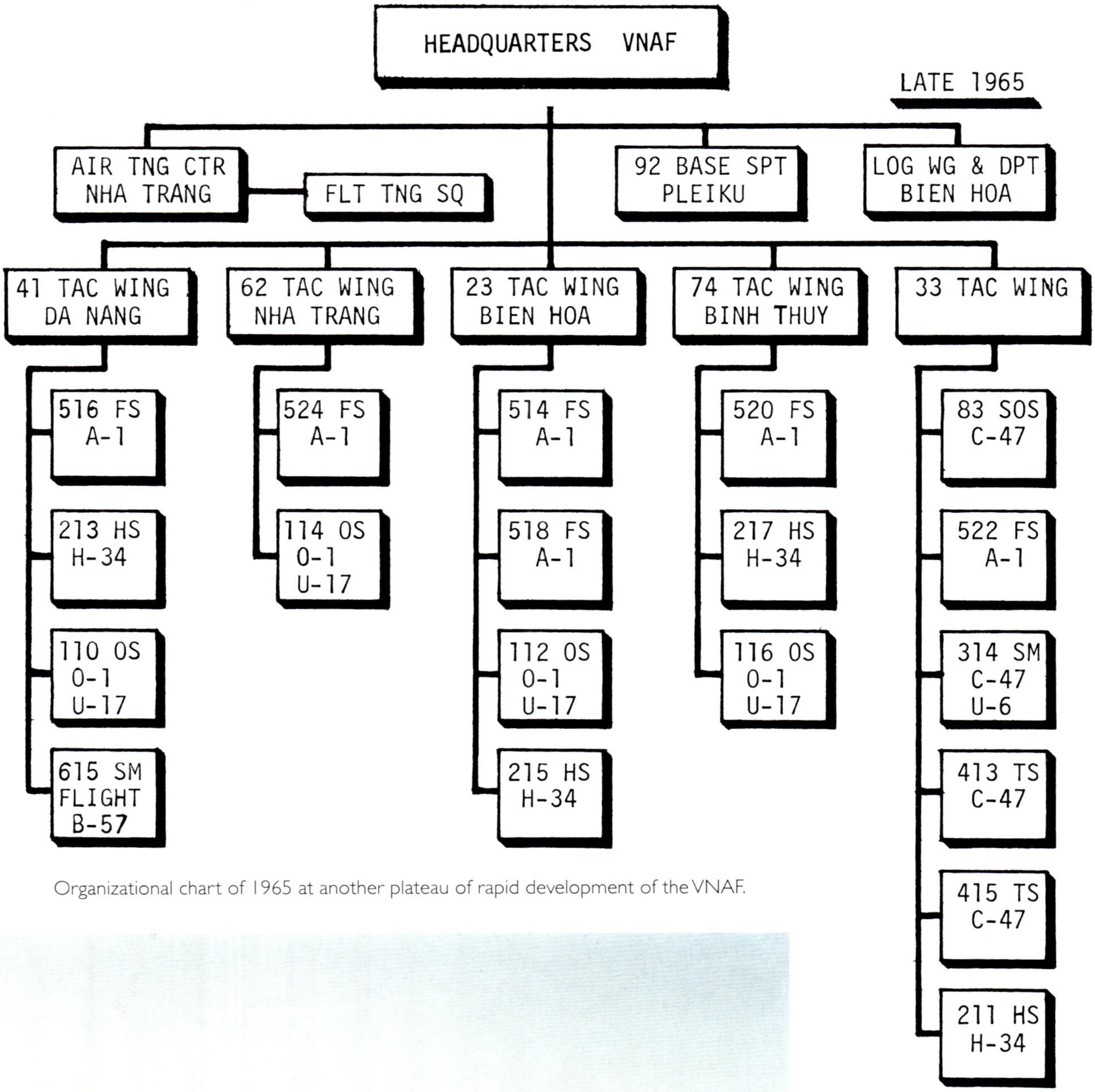

Organizational chart of 1965 at another plateau of rapid development of the VNAF.

The lack of any national or unit markings on this Douglas A-1H makes this a curious photo taken in February 1967. However, this was not unusual for aircraft of the Vietnam war. The folding wing capability for these former Navy shipboard aircraft was advantageous when it came to the usual congested parking ramps, such as were found at Tan Son Nhut. *Courtesy of Terry Love.*

Ground crew escape from the hot sun under this Douglas A-1E of the 524th Fighter Squadron at Nha Trang. This model of Skyraider had side-by-side seating arraignments for two pilots and caverness space in the rear for many uses. It has been said that 17 Vietnamese have been evacuated in one of these aircraft. *Courtesy of Terry Love.*

Battle scars can be seen as patches on the nose of this CH-34 at Binh Thuy AB. Dark olive drab shows it came from U.S. Army resources. In VNAF markings it was assigned to the 217th HS, as identified by its unit code "R" prefix and the red fin with black starts.

headquarter echelons, and the rapid expansion of the force had left management skills dangerously thin. The problem of leadership was accentuated after June 1965, when it was noted by American observers that the VNAF seemed to suffer from a lack of positive direction, since the VNAF Commander-in-Chief, Air Vice Marshal Ky, simultaneously holding the position of Prime Minister, was "preoccupied with politics." However, there was the promise of good future leadership among the advancing field grade officer ranks.

The number of qualified pilots continued to increase despite severe losses in combat. Between July 1965 and September 1966 there was an increase of 144 newly trained pilots, which brought the total to 805 assigned—yet 943 were needed. In spite of this increase in the 15-month period, the VNAF lost 46 pilots killed, missing in action, or accident victims.

Modernizing with Airplanes

One of the most notable areas in the VNAF's improvement between 1965 and 1968 was the modernization of its aircraft inventory. While higher performance in both fixed and rotary wing aircraft was the objective, the greatest improvements were seen in the increase of helicopters and better trained units.

At the end of 1965 the VNAF inventory consisted, essentially, of A-1G and A-1H aircraft, H-34 helicopters, C-47 transports, and miscellaneous reconnaissance and liaison aircraft, such as RC-47s, O-1As, U-6As, and U-17As. By 30 November 1966 there were 131 A-1 Skyraiders, 36 C/RC-47s, 65 H-34s, 79 O-1As, seven U-6As, and 45 U-17s still in the VNAF, but changes had already been planned and approved as part of the modernization program.

Fighters were given special attention; the initial plan called for the conversion of two Skyraider squadrons at Bien Hoa AB to the Northrop F-5s to provide quick response, either to the north or south,

A fleet of 30 EC-47s were transferred to the VNAF by late 1974 to improve their electronics surveillance of enemy ground radio activity. This EC-47 of the 314th Special Missions Squadron has considerable enemy rocket damage along the top and rear of the fuselage. *Courtesy of David Menard.*

Cessna O-1s were the most commonly seen fixed wing aircraft in South Vietnam throughout the 1960s. The yellow rudder identifies this Bird Dog as belonging to the 116th OS. Tops of wings were normally white so that they could be seen better from above by attack aircraft they were directing.

When Cessna O-1 Bird Dogs were in short supply as replacements the Cessna 185 became a suitable substitute. As military aircraft these were U-17s. This one was assigned to the 110th Observation Squadron with their detachment at Hue Citadel Airport, inside that ancient walled city.

De Havilland U-6 Beavers were acquired in small numbers by VNAF. Based at Tan Son Nhut in the 314th Special Missions Squadron, they were configured for psy warfare activities by having a battery of speakers on the left side of the fuselage for sending tape recorded propaganda messages to the enemy below. They often warned civilians of impending air strikes so they could move to safety.

for close air support or other tactical missions. The VNAF could also assume air defense roles should the USAF support be withdrawn. The expansion plan at this time was to have four A-1H Skyraider squadrons—one assigned to each of the four Corps areas. Though implemented, the plan for the future was soon changed when the overall fighter capability was re-evaluated. Consequently, it was finally decided to have one F-5 squadron, the 522nd at Bien Hoa, which became operational in June 1967, and convert three of the A-1 squadrons to A-37 jet attack aircraft. Tests conducted by the USAF with the F-5 and the A-37 in actual combat conditions in Vietnam showed the latter to be far more effective in the ground support role than the F-5. Further revisions to the expansion plan delayed conversion of three squadrons to A-37s until 1969.

Determined to get the most out of the Skyraider, the VNAF made a novel modification to some of their A-1Gs. Beginning in 1966, and known as Operation Blackeye, these multi-seat aircraft were fitted with belly windows to allow an observer to lie on the floor on visual/armed reconnaissance missions. Seeing targets of opportunity far more readily in this fashion, the observer was then able to describe the target to the pilot so that he could begin the attack. Continuous reconnaissance of this nature was provided until May 1966, when it was interrupted because of political turmoil in the city of Da Nang. The VNAF's 522nd Fighter Squadron at Tan Son Nhut was deployed to Da Nang to assist the 516th Fighter Squadron, which was flying airborne alert missions instead of Blackeye operations. After 400 dissident ARVN troops finally surrendered at Da Nang, the 516th Squadron resumed its Blackeye operations in June, flying 237 of these classified reconnaissance missions before the operations were suspended later that month.

Helicopters, transports, and reconnaissance aircraft took on a new look and perspective. The four H-34 helicopter squadrons, each assigned to a Corps area in 1965, were to convert to Bell UH-1 Iroquois over the next four years, and a new squadron was added. This would give greater flexibility for ARVN ground troops in search-and-clear operations. By March 1968, 39 pilots had indigenously completed their training in the new helicopter. Further groups of 15 entered training every 90 days.

The second decade of the VNAF was marked by the introduction of jet aircraft into their inventory. The VNAF made these nimble F-5 Freedom Fighters visible throughout South Vietnam, not only to the enemy, but their own people as well, which boosted their morale. *RG 342-93268 USAF.*

Great promise was felt when VNAF first received the F-5A Tiger II, but for an air to ground attack aircraft, it was not among the best aircraft types. By 1974 there were four squadrons of F-5As and three squadrons of F-5Es. Shown here is an F-5A of the 522nd Fighter Squadron at Bien Hoa. *Courtesy of E.K. Wasscroft via R.J. Mills.*

The Cessna A-37 Dragonfly proved to be a very effective air-to-ground support aircraft within the VNAF inventory. They were light, and easy to maintain and fly. VNAF eventually had 10 squadrons of these aircraft. Shown here is a Dragonfly landing at its home base of Binh Thuy, where three of these squadrons were based. *Courtesy of Greg Gatewood via R.J. Mills.*

The 83rd Special Operations Squadron, described earlier as the "Kamikazes," was upgraded to group level, remaining under the 33rd Tactical Wing at Tan Son Nhut. Redesignated the 83rd Tactical Group (Special Missions), it was activated on 1 January 1966 to fly special missions in support of the Joint General Staff (JGS). With 370 persons, it had 34 aircraft available from other squadrons that included six A-1Gs, 10 H-34s, and eight specially-equipped U-6As.

Some transport squadrons were not only upgraded with new aircraft, but also allocated new roles. Up to this point only the USAF was providing air base protection, employing Douglas AC-47 Spooky gun ships' orbiting flares, which they dropped at night while firing at base infiltrators. The 817th Attack Squadron at Tan Son Nhut was the first VNAF squadron to be formed to perform these duties, receiving its AC-47s from the deactivated USAF 4th Air Commando/Special Operations Squadron.

The 413th Transport Squadron, which operated C-47s before the VNAF became a separate armed service, gave up its Gooney Birds (many of which were received from the French) for the C-119G Flying Box Cars. These crews had undergone training at Ellington AFB, Texas, and its maintenance personnel had been trained both in the United States and at Tan Son Nhut by the USAF. By March 1968 there were 16 C-119Gs assigned to the 33rd Wing—one previously having been damaged beyond repair in the Viet Cong mortar attack on the base on 18 February 1968.

The best of the 413th's aging C-47s augmented the sister organization, the 415th Transport Squadron's C-47s at Tan Son Nhut.

Two A-1H Skyraiders on their way to a target in support of ARVN ground troops. They have just departed Bien Hoa AB with external stores and centerline fuel tank under the wings. Being void of all unit and national markings was not unusual for operations in Southeast Asia.

Although newer types of transports became part of the VNAF, the reliable Douglas C-47 remained from the beginning to the end. The unit identity code H is hardly discernable on this camouflaged Gooney Bird, 43-48801, of the 417th Transport Squadron at Tan Son Nhut as seen in 1970. *Courtesy of Norman E. Taylor.*

The 716th Composite Reconnaissance Squadron was redesignated, dropping the "Composite" on 1 July 1966. Its three newly assigned RC-47s had improved infrared photo systems that could locate the enemy by heat source imagery. These were used for photographic reconnaissance in III and IV Corps sectors with two crews permanently assigned. EC-47s, which could plot the location of a 10 watt radio transmitter within one degree at a range of 25 nautical miles, were introduced later. These could give lines of position to an enemy transmitter, regardless of the aircraft's heading. This squadron also received eight U-6As for special missions.

Aircraft conversion and the expansion of the VNAF were not the only aspects of the modernization program. Proficiency was also emphasized at all levels. This included extensive training throughout the VNAF, publication of manuals for all aircraft operations, formalization of command post procedures, development of instrument flying capability, and construction of adequate communications and electronics facilities. As the VNAF's rapid expansion during the three years prior to 1965 had diluted the numbers of available skilled leaders and technicians to meet increased demands, an energetic proficiency program was undertaken. This included such vital areas as the establishment of a more effective command and control system, leadership training in management and disciplinary responsibilities, and increased technical capabilities to produce the skill levels needed by a modern air force.

The People of VNAF

Members of the South Vietnamese Air Force were proud of their service, and it remained an all-volunteer service to the very end. Since Vietnam drafted young men to fill Army quotas, conscription provided an incentive to be a member of this more elite group. Qualifications for joining the service were similar to those required of an American joining his or her own Air Force. As a matter of comparison, some of the details are worth examining.

Recruits reported to any one of the four recruiting centers: Can Tho in the Delta region; Tan Son Nhut at Saigon; the Training Center at Nha Trang; or Da Nang, in the northern part of the country. A screening test was required, followed by the usual physical examinations. Basic requirements for service in the VNAF in 1968 were:

The 413th Transport Squadron turned in their C-47s for replacement with Fairchild C-119Gs beginning in 1968. The "Gs" were intended for coastal patrol, but sensing equipment never arrived, so this model was also used for transport duties. This Flying Boxcar 53-3161 was photographed at Da Nang in February 1971. *Courtesy of Norman E. Taylor.*

The landing gear wheel well doors are closing as this A-1H Skyraider of the 524th Fighter Squadron skims the runway on departure from Pleiku AB in November 1966. *RG 342-102996 USAF.*

Vietnamese citizenship.
Minimum age of 17 for airmen, 18 for cadet candidates.
Maximum age of 25 for flying training, and 30 for non-flying.
No criminal record.
A certificate of completion for high school (9th grade equivalent to U.S. high school) for airmen; a Baccalaureate I degree (11th grade) for those going to pilot training; and a Baccalaureate II (12th grade) for non-rated officer training.

If these qualifications were met the recruit was sent to basic training. This was conducted at an ARVN training base located at Lam Son, 15 miles (24 km) NNW of Nha Trang, up until the early 1960s, when the VNAF handled its own basic training at the Air Training Center at Nha Trang. Some training of NCOs and airmen was also conducted at Bien Hoa under the guidance of the ATC. After two months of basic training (four months for aviation cadets) the recruit airman was given an aptitude test and progressed to a specified technical training program. From there he was sent to one of the VNAF wings, where he gained practical experience, enabling him to complete and increase his skills.

Aviation cadets pursued one of three courses upon completing their four months of basic training. Some entered for observer or observation pilot training at the ATC; others were sent to the United States for a more advanced pilot training (about 70 percent of the

The crescent design on the yellow tail rotor fin of this UH-1D identifies the 217th Helicopter Squadron from Soc Trang. They carried members of the 14th Regiment, 9th ARVN Division to a new area of operations in the Mekong Delta in March 1970. *RG 111CC-65446 US Army.*

Ground troops on a search and clear mission in the Delta can be seen in the background of this VNAF UH-1 Iroquois. The tail color and markings identify a particular flight of the 217th Helicopter Squadron. *RG 111CC 65440 US Army*

Douglas AC-47 Gun ships were used effectively at night for airfield perimeter and outpost defense. Beginning in 1968 the VNAF began absorbing some of this responsibility from the USAF. The 817th Attack Squadron was formed at Nha Trang AB with former USAF AC-47s. *Courtesy of Greg Gatewood via R.J. Mills.*

The mission of the VNAF was primarily to support ground forces. This brought about continual controversy as to what branch of service should have overall command authority. This 23rd Tactical Wing Skyraider has just released a 250 lb bomb on a concentration of enemy forces in South Vietnam. *RG 342-102109 USAF.*

By 1965 each of the four corps areas had a squadron of Sikorsky H-34s assigned for heliborne operations. This H-34 of the 211th Helicopter Squadron prepares to land at a remote camp in November 1966. Note the caribou outside the fenced in landing zone. *RG 342-100928 USAF.*

total in the mid-l960s); and others pursued technical training in preparation for some non-flying assignment. All courses lasted about nine months, whereupon the cadet served in an operational unit for about a year before receiving a commission as a second lieutenant.

The VNAF had two methods by which Non-Commissioned Officers were recruited. One was by promotion from the lower grades, having the necessary skills to make them eligible for NCO training at the ARVN NCO Academy at Dong De, Nha Trang Province. This was a seven week course, followed by two weeks of VNAF orientation at Tan Son Nhut Air Base. The other method was somewhat unorthodox—NCOs being recruited directly because of their special qualifications. This was not prevalent though, only 40 being recruited from early 1967 through 1968.

Seen here at Tan Son Nhut are some of the C-119G aircraft that replaced C-47s of the 413th transport Squadron beginning in early 1968. Two other squadrons of these Flying Box Cars were formed later: the 819th Attack Squadron with AC-119Gs, and the 821st Attack Squadron with AC-119Ks. *RG 342-KKE31611 USAF.*

Women also proudly served in the Vietnamese Air Force. As early as 1954, about five women received French training and served as air traffic controllers for the military, but in a semi-civilian capacity. To augment the RVNAF, the Women's Armed Forces Corps (WAFC) was formed to fill selected non-combat duties beginning in December 1965. Some of them served on detached duty, assigned to the VNAF, and initially held very minor positions. By 1968 their status had increased, and about 100 of these women were assigned to the air service with a female Second Lieutenant in command. Although not technically an official body of the VNAF (WAFC was under the control of the Joint General Staff), they were assigned to VNAF wings, Headquarters, the Air Logistical Wing, and to ATC, performing administrative duties as personnel specialists, secretaries, and telephone operators.

In 1970, the first class of 12 WAFC warrant officers (referred to as Waf-C) went to Incarnate Word College in San Antonio, Texas, for four years to receive a BS degree in nursing, followed by an officer commission. New classes began each year thereafter to fill the need for floor head nurses in VNAF Air Division hospitals.

Also in the 1970s, some members of WAFC entered the operational field as load masters on transport aircraft, undertaking flight attendant duties on 314th's VIP missions when required. It is interesting to note that beginning in 1968, the WAFC was proud to be headed by a Lieutenant Colonel who was also the mother of seven children.

Military pay was low, even by Vietnamese standards. Family allowances varied according to the number of dependents, and a cost-of-living allowance varied from district to district. Some representative average pay scales for VNAF personnel, computed in U.S. dollars, for 1968 are shown below. For comparison purposes, the monthly pay for USAF members having two dependents as of 1 July 1968 is shown in parenthesis.

Grade	Base Pay	Family Alt	Cost of Living	Total Pay	Flight Pay
Lt Col	$77.30 ($1,120.00)	$12.46 ($157.50)	$48.87 ($47.88)	$134.63 ($1,325.38)	$26.08 ($145.00)
Capt	56.44 (753.00)	11.82 (130.05)	46.22 (47.88)	114.48 (931.38)	26.08 (185.00)
1st Lt.	48.02 (589.00)	7.27 (110.10)	39.53 (47.88)	92.82 (746.98)	28.46 (150.00)
Tech Sgt	24.97 (417.00)	12.76 (110.10)	48.80 (33.00)	86.53 (560.10)	13.53 (100.00)
Airman 1/C	18.98 (272.00)	9.02 (105.00)	38.02 (33.00)	66.02 (410.00)	10.89 (70.00)
Amn Basic	12.60 (102.00)	1.29 (83.10)	17.07 (33.00)	30.96 (218.10)	3.58 (50.00)

(Exchange rate in 1968 was approximately $1.00 to 168-175 Vietnamese piasters.)

While it is understood that lifestyles were very different, the wide difference between VNAF and USAF salaries did create problems for the Vietnamese. For example, a camera purchased on a military base by an American could also be bought by a Vietnamese at the same price through his own exchange, but generally he couldn't afford it. This naturally caused some resentment. The situation was not quite as severe for VNAF personnel as it was for those of the ARVN: VNAF personnel had better housing, flight pay, and the use of many USAF facilities.

Leadership is a predominant issue in any military service, and the same was true for the VNAF. As a result of the explosive growth of the VNAF during 1962-1963, a major leadership problem was evident by the mid-1960s. The USAF was very concerned about this. To survive, the VNAF needed strong internal leadership.

A study of potential VNAF leaders was conducted by the USAF in 1968, and the following forms part of their final report:[18]

H-34 helicopter crews depart their operations building of the 211th Helicopter Squadron at Tan Son Nhut in November 1966. Among them is Lt Nguyen-thanh-Tung at left. Their squadron name "Divine Mace" is on their insignia. *RG 342-100923 USAF.*

To improve the VNAF's helicopter capability, Bell UH-1 Iroquois were introduced into their squadrons beginning in the late 1960s. This Huey of the 211th Helicopter Squadron is leading a search and clear operation on 18 July 1970. *RG 342-107266 USAF.*

"Biographical data had been compiled for many of these senior officers in an effort to determine the overall patterns of emerging leaders' backgrounds. In this analysis, data has been compiled for the Air Vice Marshal (Ky), two Major Generals, 11 Colonels, nine Lieutenant Colonels, 20 Majors, and five Captains, all occupying key positions in VNAF. In general, these officers serving in responsible positions were born during the early 1930s, some of them in what is today North Vietnam. Presently (1968) 35 to 40 years of age, these officers have had extensive training and widely diversified assignments, including command assignments of major units at a very early age. Most are rated pilots or observers and obtained their flying training in France and Morocco. In addition, many have attended either the Squadron Officer's Course or the Air Command and Staff School of the USAF at Maxwell AFB, Alabama. Usually they have had both command and staff experience (mostly in the operations field) before being promoted to the rank of Colonel and above.

With rifles and water jugs in hand and packs on their backs, these ARVN soldiers prepare to board the VNAF's Binh Thuy based 217th Helicopter Squadron's UH-1s for an air assault against North Vietnamese Army units operating in the Mekong River Delta in 1970. *RG 111-SC 655138 US Army*

Timeout from the war lead some to become involved in hobbies. A VNAF helicopter pilot at Hue Citadel Airport adjusts his control line model airplane before flight in 1967. USAF Lt Col Richard L Brown, an ALO to the ARVN 1st Infantry Division, gives unofficial technical advice.

It is worthwhile to take a fleeting glance at the careers of some of the VNAF leaders today (1968). This is particularly true of Air Vice Marshal Ky, the former Commander of VNAF, Major General Tran-van-Minh (VNAF Commander), some of the wing commanders, and a few Colonels in key positions. Therefore, a short summary of highlights for each of these selected individuals follows:[19]

"Air Vice Marshal Nguyen-cao-Ky

Born 8 September 1930 in a town about 15 miles from Hanoi. Married. Rated pilot. Qualified as C-47 transport pilot and A-1H fighter pilot. Came in military service in 1951 and commissioned in infantry in 1952. Fought with French and sent to pilot training at Marrakech, Morocco, and Avord and Blida in Algeria during 1954. Graduate of Thu Duc Reserve Officers' School, Air Command and Staff School (U.S.). Wide variety of assignments before becoming VNAF Commander in 1963. Despite his political concentration since 1965, Ky remained loyal to the VNAF. (Became Prime Minister and Vice-President of South Vietnam. Resides in southern California.)

Two-thirds of the Lieutenant Colonels considered in this study were born in the 1929-1932 era, indicating that they are about the same age as the Colonels above them. Over half of them are rated as pilots or observers, but liaison pilots predominate. Two-thirds of these officers also attended French pilot training, and nearly half went to the Air Command and Staff School in the United States. Sixty percent of the Majors examined are rated pilots with fighter, liaison, transport, and helicopter pilots included in that quantitative order. Eighty percent of these officers were born in the period 1931-1934. Only about 45 percent of them received their flying training in France, while 41 percent had pilot training in the United States. These officers also have had more opportunity to attend technical courses, many in non-rated specialties, in the Philippine Islands, at Okinawa, or in the Continental United States. Of the five Captains reviewed, three were pilots, primarily in the liaison and fighter aircraft. Eighty percent of them were born in the 1932-1934 period. Only 40 percent had flying training in France, and an equal number did so in the United States.

From the above data, some general conclusions may be tentatively established. Age is not a factor in determining ultimate grade of the individual officer in the VNAF. An overwhelming majority of officers was born in the 1929-1934 time period, and this is true of all grades. A pilot rating is a definite factor in the emergence of today's top leaders. Major Generals, Colonels, and Lieutenant Colonels have progressed largely because of French pilot training early in their careers, attendance at U.S. professional schools, and service in a wide variety of responsible, and principally operational, positions. Majors are the transitional officers in the overall structure at present. They have mixed backgrounds—some with French pilot training, some with U.S. experience in this regard. Obviously, as younger officers progress upward in the overall rank structure of the VNAF, the officer corps will be more dependent on those trained in the United States or in the Air Training Center at Nha Trang than upon French experience, as the senior officers now reflect.

Vietnamese airmen learn the operation of an aircraft landing gear system in December 1966 at the Air Technical Training Center, Nha Trang AB. Efforts were continually made to improve VNAF's self sufficiency, but its rapid growth made this very difficult. *RG 342-100594 USAF*

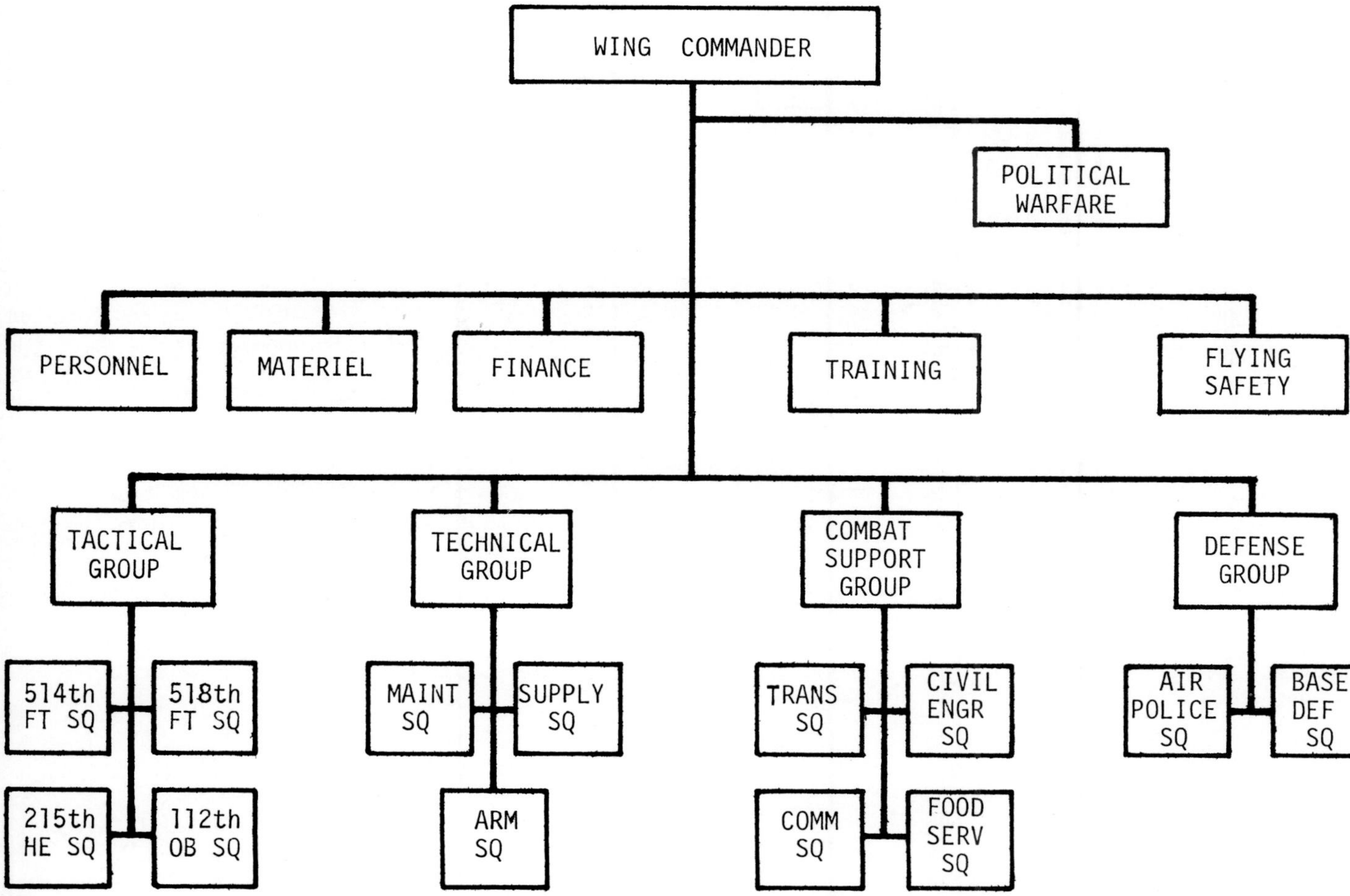

Above: Organizational chart of 1965 at another plateau of rapid development of the VNAF.

Right: Women had a part in the operation of the VNAF as well. USAF advisor Captain (later B/Gen) Mary A Marsh is briefing members of the Women's Armed Forces Corps, assigned to the VNAF in June 1968. From front to back are 2nd Lt Do-thi-Dong-Thao, and Junior NCOs Luc-thi Hoa and Ly-tri-Oanh. *RG 342-103950 USAF.*

The Tet Offensive at the end of January 1968 called upon all the resources of the VNAF. In the three day period, A-1s and F-5s of the VNAF flew a total of 268 sorties. This A-1H of the 516th fighter Squadron at Da Nang AB departs on such a mission. *USAF*

Major General Tran-van-Minh

Commander, VNAF. Born 21 July 1932 in South Vietnam. Single. Rated pilot. Graduate of Thu Duc Reserve Officers' School in 1952, Observer Training at Nha Trang ATC in 1953, Air Command and Staff School (1962), Advanced Management Seminar in VNAF Headquarters. Commander 74th Fighter Wing, 62nd Fighter Wing; Assistant Chief of Operations Division; Chief of Air Battle Staff; Vice Commander of VNAF, 1965-1967. He is a professional officer, sincere and dedicated, yet does not express any interest in politics. (Remained in command of VNAF to the end and became a Lt. General. He passed away 27 August 1997 in San Jose, California.)

Major General Nguyen-ngoc-Loan

Former Director General of the National Police (Detached from the VNAF itself). Born 11 December 1930. Married. Pilot, qualified in fighters. Attended Thu Duc Reserve Officers' School, graduate from French Air Force Academy in Salon de Provence, France, French

Air attacks by VNAF had results such as this. Four ammunition trucks are shown burning on a trail just south of the demilitarized zone in February 1968. Just seconds after this photograph was taken, the trucks exploded. *USAF*

All aircraft losses were not caused during air operations. This Cessna O-1A of the 110th Observation Squadron became a sieve at Da Nang AB on the night of 9-10 January 1968, caused by a VC rocket attack. The airplane had to be scrapped. Fin and rudder acquired by the author hangs in the Airpower Museum, Blakesburg, Iowa.

pilot training, and United States Squadron Officer's Course. Has been Commander of TACC, Deputy Commander of VNAF, and Chief of Staff. Shot and wounded in Cholon during May 1968 offensive with long recuperation periods. (Resided in the Washington, D.C. area, died 1996.)

Colonel Nguyen-huy-Anh
Commander, 74th Wing. Born 12 July 1934. Married. Rated pilot, qualified as both fighter and helicopter pilot. Attended French pilot training and Squadron Officer's Course in United States. Has commanded 1st Helicopter Squadron, 211th Squadron, and 62nd Wing before present assignment. (Became a Brig. General and was later killed in a helicopter crash, Can Tho, 1971.)

Colonel Vo-xuan-Lanh
Chief of Staff. Born 15 March 1931. Single. Pilot with qualification in fighter aircraft. Attended Thu Duc Reserve Officers' School, Nha Trang pilot training, United States pilot training, and Squadron Officer's Course. Deputy Commander of TACC (tactical air control center), Commander of 514th Fighter Squadron, and Commander of 23rd Wing before present assignment. (Became Major General. Died 1978 in the United States.)

Colonel Duong-thieu-Hung
Commander, 33rd Wing. Born 15 September 1930 at Hanoi. Married. Pilot with qualification in fighter aircraft. Attended Nha Trang pilot training (first class there in 1952) and French advanced pilot training. Has been Commander of 1st Fighter and Observation Squadron, Deputy Commander and Commander of 41st Wing before Present assignment. (Became commanding officer of 522nd FS (F-5s), 23rd Wing Commanding Officer. Resides in Severn, Maryland, USA)

Colonel Nguyen-ngoc-Oanh
Commander, Air Training Center. Born 10 June 1925. Married. Pilot with qualifications in liaison and transport aircraft. Also had observer rating. Graduate of Dalat Military Academy, Nha Trang pilot training (first class there in 1952), advanced pilot training in France, and Air Command and Staff School in the United States. Commander of 1st Observation Squadron, Chief of Inspection Section, DCS/Personnel, and twice Commander of ATC. (Became Brig. General and now resides in Glendale, California.)

Colonel Vu-van-Uoc
Commander 62nd Wing. Born 18 February 1930. Married. Pilot, qualified as liaison pilot. Graduate of Nha Trang pilot training school

Another victim of Viet Cong rocket and mortar attacks against air bases in South Vietnam was this VNAF C-47 of the 415th Transport Squadron stationed at Tan Son Nhut. This loss occurred on 18 February 1968. *RG 111-SC644716 US Army*

This photograph, taken in the vicinity of Dong Hoi, is illustrative of the continuous flow of traffic detected along this key north/south artery known as Route 1A. Thirteen empty vehicles can be seen headed north, and seven loaded vehicles are moving south. *RG 342-100101 USAF.*

(first class there in 1952) and Squadron Officer's School in the United States. Deputy Commander of the ATC, Deputy Commander of 41st Wing, and DCS/Operations before present assignment. (Later became jet qualified in 1967 in A-37, Commander of 62nd Tactical Wing, Commander of 2nd Air Division 1967-70, then Commander of Air Operations Command 1970-75. (Resides in Santa Ana, California, and remains active in the Vietnamese Air Force Veteran's Association of Central California.)

The above senior officers are only a few selected cases to illustrate the backgrounds of some of the emerging leaders of the VNAF. Four other rated pilots are detached from the VNAF at present—Colonels Ha-xuan-Vinh, Tran-van-Ho, Pham-ngoc-Sang, and Le-trung-Truc—to serve in a detached status for political positions in the RVN government, or with the Joint General Staff. Others are occupying key staff positions at Headquarters, VNAF, Tan Son Nhut Air Base."

Tet Offensive

While the Tet offensive in February 1968 can be viewed in a number of perspectives, it also had tremendous influence on the future of the VNAF. It was not the battles, but the political implications that followed, which affected the destiny of the Vietnamese Air Force.

The war in Vietnam was largely a five days a week war by unwritten mutual agreement between the opposing forces, although this was not the case with the foreign military services involved. Holidays were also respected, and the Lunar New Year of Tet in 1968 seemed to be no exception. A build-up by the NVA/Viet Cong was very obvious, however, and some type of offensive during the quiet period of the holidays was expected. In fact, from interrogations of Viet Cong prisoners, it was learned that the enemy were to attack the major cities of South Vietnam in an attempt to embarrass the Republic of Vietnam's government by holding strategic positions within these cities for several days to a week before withdrawing. In the past, the Viet Cong could only launch limited at-

Although not a combat airplane, this Pazmany PL-2 was a VNAF aircraft. This was a home-built, with its major components built at three bases and final assembly at Tan Son Nhut. More were to be built as VNAF trainers, but the concept did not progress beyond this one aircraft.

A casualty of the Tet Offensive in 1968 was this Cessna O-1A Bird Dog of the 110th Observation Squadron detachment at Hue Citadel Airport. When disassembled, it was airlifted from Hue to Da Nang by this H-34 of the 213th Helicopter Squadron. *USAF*

This single example of the Aero Commander resided at Tan Son Nhut with the 314th Special Missions Squadron as a VIP aircraft. As a pilot, President Ky used the aircraft occasionally, while the earlier President Diem said it was too noisy. Its use remained rather obscure. *Courtesy of N. Weeks via David Menard.*

tacks, and were then compelled to fall back into Cambodia and Laotian sanctuaries to rest, recuperate, restock, and prepare for another attack.

If these planned attacks during Tet would have any degree of success, they would have to be of a relatively short duration and have an effect on the U.S. political home front, which was showing signs of weariness and discontent with many of the war's aspects. Alternatively—according to those interrogated prisoners—if the enemy forces failed appreciably, the North Vietnamese would sue for a cease fire agreement, this ultimately being the objective of South Vietnam and American forces. This point received little, if any, publicity, being overshadowed by more tangible events. The enemy failed to achieve its objectives, yet the unrest in the U.S. negated the positive effects of this joint victory by South Vietnamese, Allied, and American forces.

The attacks began in the early hours of 30 January with a greater severity than anyone expected. A countrywide offensive was mounted against all the major cities and provincial capitals of South Vietnam. From the quality of the first assaults, it seemed that the enemy were seeking a political rather than a military victory. This was supported by the fact that most of the regular troops were held back in reserve and would only be committed if the situation dictated a decisive military victory. The opportunity never arose, owing to superior opposition. The primary objective of the enemy was to convey to the American people the illusion that the U.S. was not winning the war, and that the people of South Vietnam were anxious for the North Vietnamese to liberate them.

Despite the intense fighting and heavy loss of life, the Viet Cong forces were repelled much sooner than they had planned. No major cities, with the exception of Hue, were held for more than three days by the enemy. It was now a matter of waiting for the expected overture from the North to discuss the long-awaited cease fire arrangement.

But something else happened in the meantime. The Tet Offensive had failed, and Hanoi's dream of the collapse of the South Vietnamese Government and her armed forces failed to materialize. But the American people—who had only recently been assured that the Allies were winning the war—were shocked by news reports of the enemy strikes throughout South Vietnam, even to the gates of the American Embassy in Saigon. News accounts, particularly television films showing the devastation (although isolated) wrought by the enemy, created negative public opinion and seriously damaged support of the war effort. This dramatic point became very clear to the North Vietnamese leaders, who reasoned that American interests in the war could diminish to such a degree as to give North Vietnam's forces the upper hand. They were right. The Tet Offensive of 1968 was the turning point for American support for a war which was still being won at the fighting front, but was now lost in the United States.

Because of the Tet Offensive's political results, which led to the controlled withdrawal of American aid, the effectiveness of the fighting that took place during that time is often overlooked. In order that it will not be forgotten, a review is made here of the air operations undertaken by the Vietnamese Air Force. For air operations alone, more than 3,100 close air support sorties were flown during the first week of the assault. This drastically restricted ground movement for the enemy and closed off many of their resupply lines, resulting in their withdrawal.

When the enemy attack began on 30 January, 57 percent of the total VNAF force were on leave to be with their families over the Lunar New Year. Immediate recall was initiated, but it was difficult for VNAF personnel to get to their bases from scattered parts of the country because of the heavy fighting, many men being cut-off by enemy penetrations. Within 72 hours, however, 90 percent of VNAF were on duty.

The VNAF's strike capability at the time was limited to its 69 operational Skyraiders at four bases: Da Nang, Nha Trang, Bien Hoa, and Binh Thuy, together with 17 F-5s at Bien Hoa. In response to ARVN requests for air support against the gathering enemy forces, VNAF fighter pilots flew 211 missions on 29 January, and increased this pace to 258 on the first day of the assault. On the last day of January they flew 368 missions, an increase of approximately 50 percent on the previous day. In the three-day period at the end of January, the VNAF's A-1s and F-5s flew a total of 268 sorties, H-34s flew 215 missions, reconnaissance aircraft completed 196 sorties, and cargo planes accomplished 158 sorties overall. For those readers not acquainted with the situation at that time, these figures reflect a high degree of aggressiveness on the part of South Vietnam's forces.

This increased rate of flying continued into February, as the enemy effort intensified and the average number of daily strike sorties reached 78, in contrast to a normal figure of 65.5 before the Tet Offensive. The average rate of one combat sortie per assigned strike aircraft per day was maintained throughout the first two weeks of February 1968, despite the fact that there was little increase in aircraft maintenance capability. In all, VNAF flew over 1,300 strike sorties during the 17-day operation: 30 percent for close air sup-

This Douglas DC-6B was one of a kind, owned by the South Vietnamese Government, but maintained and operated by the 314th Special Mission Squadron at Tan Son Nhut.

port; 57 percent for interdiction; and 13 percent for escort of helicopters and truck convoys.

VNAF aircraft bombed and strafed Viet Cong positions throughout the RVN, killing nearly 600 of the enemy and destroying or damaging approximately 1000 structures. Transports from Tan Son Nhut's 33rd Wing dropped 14,400 flares in 12 nights, compared with the monthly average of only 10,000 for night illumination. On the night of 2 February alone, VNAF aircraft dropped 1447 flares on Saigon, the highest total in the entire war to that point. The helicopter fleet hauled ARVN troops, supplied them, and conducted medical air evacuation missions, flying 50 percent more than their average monthly sorties with 16 fewer aircraft—the result of combat losses and enemy-inflicted damage. Observation aircraft completed 656 reconnaissance sorties, VNAF pilots flying O-1 Bird Dogs and U-17 Skywagons.

During the Tet Offensive the VNAF lost 17 planes; 10 on the ground and seven in the air. Those lost in the air were five A-1s, one C-47, and one U-17, while five H-34s, four O-1s, and one U-17 were ground losses.

There was little doubt that the VNAF had effectively contributed towards the defense of the RVN during the Tet Offensive. It took the offense to the enemy, supported ARVN ground units capably, and achieved higher levels of strike performance, in terms of sorties flown and ordnance dropped, than previously. Despite the problems of getting personnel back to their units during the attacks, and continual maintenance problems, the VNAF's forces responded well to the tasks allocated during this emergency.

7

Preparing to Go it Alone

In the United States, vivid media coverage of the Tet Offensive implied that the South Vietnamese and Americans were losing the war in Vietnam. The occasional release or escape of American prisoners revealed inhuman treatment by the enemy of hundreds of detained POWs. Fearing that American bombs may kill American POWs, bombing in the Hanoi area became very restrictive. Prisoner exchange and visits by Red Cross teams were refused by the North Vietnamese, causing increased American frustration. The Hanoi Government made it clear that POWs would not be released until the United States withdrew from the war. Demonstrations in the United States increased the pressure upon the U.S. government to disengage from the war.

American involvement in the Vietnam War took on a different approach after the Tet Offensive in February 1968. Emphasis was placed on making the South Vietnamese capable of taking over the offensive role as American involvement would slowly diminish. However, this did not happen immediately. Gen Westmoreland, Army Chief of Staff, acquired 206,000 additional American troops to help win the war and bring the conflict to a speedy conclusion. Washington advisors disagreed, however. By now, Secretary of Defense McNamara had been replaced by Clark Clifford, who rejected this proposal for further American aid. This new policy received support from prominent peace movement groups through their frequent antiwar demonstrations.

By the end of March 1968, U.S. President Johnson ordered a cessation of hostilities in North Vietnam, except for the area immediately north of the DMZ. By de-escalating the war, he hoped that the North Vietnam Government would negotiate a peace. However, this did not happen, and the war in South Vietnam dragged on.

In Paris, discussions for a peaceful settlement included representatives of the Saigon Government, as well as those of the Viet Cong, by mid-May 1968. The Viet Cong delegates emphatically stated that they did not want interference in the conflict. In an effort to appease the enemy, Mr. Nixon announced—shortly after becom-

Smoke belches from this coughing Skyraider's 2,700 hp engine as it comes to life for a combat mission in July 1969 at Bien Hoa AB. Under its wings are 10, 500 lb general purpose low drag bombs, allowing the A-1H to make repeated attacks on the enemy. *RG 342-104632 USAF*

This high angle view from a helicopter shows this A-1H of the 23rd Tactical Wing taxiing out for takeoff with a full load of bombs for a strike mission in November 1967. Although later aircraft for strike missions came into the VNAF inventory starting at this time, the A-1s stayed in large numbers until the very end. *Courtesy of Terry Love.*

ing President in January 1969—that one of the primary goals of his administration would be to end U.S. combat in Southeast Asia, while simultaneously strengthening South Vietnam's ability to defend itself. Secretary of Defense in the new administration was Melvin R. Laird who, after visiting officials in Saigon in March, ordered the acceleration of the program to transfer combat operations to the South Vietnamese. The term "Vietnamization" came from the orderly withdrawal of American troops, the increase in their materiel aid, and better training for the South Vietnamese, enabling them to carry on the fight alone. For their part, the South Vietnamese people had longed for the day when their armed forces would be able to fight and win the war for themselves.

President Nixon met Prime Minister Ky's successor, President Nguyen-van-Thieu, on Midway Island on 8 June 1969 to discuss this transfer of responsibility. With Thieu's approval, President Nixon announced plans to begin the withdrawal of 25,000 U.S. forces from Southeast Asia, beginning the very next month.

Vietnamization

Vietnamization became U.S. national policy. To the Americans in the United States, who were showing more and more public discontent with the war, it came to mean American disengagement. To the Vietnamese, it brought accelerated training by the Americans for the day when they had to "go it alone." By the end of 1969, American troop strength in Vietnam had been reduced to 60,000, in contrast to 540,000 at the beginning of the year.

Though it had now come to mean the eventual withdrawal of U.S. forces from Vietnam, the term Vietnamization was not a new one to the American people. It was first used more than 20 years earlier when the Americans trained and equipped the Vietnamese, but their involvement gradually changed over the years as their combat forces entered the country and joined in the fighting.

The U.S. continued to provide air and naval support for an indefinite period, as U.S. ground forces were withdrawn on a specific schedule. The war would be fought by the South Vietnamese, and the U.S. would continue to provide military and economic assistance. When the South Vietnamese demonstrated a capability to combat the North Vietnamese U.S. air units would be withdrawn,

Vietnamization was popular with the Vietnamese, as it was for the Americans, but for different reasons. To the Vietnamese, they became better trained and therefore more self confident. Student mechanics study a cutaway engine for an A-1 at the Air Training Center in 1967. *RG 342-101366 USAF*

The English language remained an essential tool to learning, maintaining, and operating American equipment supplied to their military forces. Vietnamese Air Force personnel study English at Nha Trang in April 1968. RG 342-*103932 USAF*

After attending a U.S. Air Force technical school at Keesler AFB, Mississippi, SSgt Le-duy-Bao intently checks the working order of ground control approach (GCA) radar equipment at Nha Trang Air Base in May 1969. *RG 342-100075 USAF.*

New to VNAF in May 1969 were the turbo-powered Bell UH-1 helicopters. These eventually replaced all the older H-34 Choctaws. This VNAF crew chief prepares his "Huey" gun ship of the 217th Helicopter Squadron for a mission at Binh Thuy AB in April 1970. *RG 342-107440 USAF*

and the task of close air support would be undertaken by the VNAF. As a result of the decision to turn the war over to the Vietnamese as rapidly as possible, the VNAF was expanded at an unprecedented rate. This rate of expansion under the Vietnamization program. was willingly accepted by the Vietnamese, but was far more than the VNAF could cope with.

In this expansion process, a VNAF "first" occurred when a helicopter squadron completed conversion to the more modern, turbo-powered Bell UH-1H Huey helicopters in May 1969. Three more helicopter squadrons converted from the H-34s to Hueys during that year. By the end of 1969 about 70 Hueys were being flown by the VNAF on airmobile-combat, combat-support operations, and on medical-evacuation missions in all parts of South Vietnam.

At Tan Son Nhut, on the last day of June 1969, five Douglas AC-47 Spooky gunships were allocated to the newly formed 817th Attack Squadron, VNAF, for night air-base defense. This was part of the USAF-developed Improvement and Modernization (I & M) program, which became official in 1970. Vietnamese control of ground support facilities was a key part of the I & M Program; as VNAF proficiency increased, its personnel undertook air-traffic control, control-tower operation, weather forecasting, fuel-facility operation, and other essential support activities previously under American management. By summer of that year, the VNAF assumed full operational control of the Direct Air Support Center (DASC) in IV Corps, which then controlled all direct air strikes in the Mekong Delta.

This striking photo is typical of the Douglas A-1H Skyraider fleet of VNAF. Although jet aircraft were introduced into VNAF from 1968, the Skyraider remained the dominant attack aircraft to the very end. This view shows a loaded Skyraider on the way to a target in May 1966. RG 342-*K20735 USAF*

New striking power was transferred to the VNAF in the form of many Cessna A-37 Dragonfly light attack-bombers. The first squadron so equipped was the 524th Fighter Squadron at Nha Trang AB in April 1969. Major Dang-duy-Lac, squadron commander of the 524th "buttons-up", prior to flight. *RG 342-K33576 USAF*

In August 1969 Secretary Laird ordered the U.S. services to devise greater plans and programs that would increase the South Vietnamese capability to counter combined attacks made by the Viet Cong and North Vietnamese armies. One of the Program's first visible improvements took place 19 April 1969 at Nha Trang Air Base, when 20 Cessna A-37A light jet fighter-bombers were ceremoniously handed over to the VNAF's first Dragonfly squadron (524th Fighter Squadron), replacing their propeller-driven A-1 Skyraiders. The pilots had already received months of conversion training, and many had combat sorties to their credit. Before the end of 1969 two more A-37 squadrons (526th and 528th) were added, and more were promised.

This brightly marked Dragonfly pauses in the arming area at Binh Thuy AB prior to take off on a strike mission. Note armorers on the far side of the aircraft. Since A-37 squadrons did not use tail letter codes, only these colors distinguished one squadron from another. These squadron colors are believed to have been of the 526th Fighter Squadron. *Courtesy of Greg Gatewood via R.J. Mills.*

An interesting innovation was introduced in 1970 when the Air Force realized that certain VNAF airmen would be completing C-123 combat crew training in the United States about six months before activation of the first VNAF C-123 squadron. To maintain VNAF pilot proficiency in the interim these VNAF crews, both pilots and load masters, flew with USAF C-123 units after their return to Vietnam, pending transfer of these aircraft to the VNAF. This was a classic reversal of the 1962 assignment of 30 U.S. Air force pilots, the Dirty Thirty, who were supplemental crewmen flying with VNAF C-47 transport units. The ensuing practical training by USAF C-123 crews gave Vietnamese pilots current operational experience, reduced the need to train all of them in the United States, and also reduced Air Force C-123 pilot requirements in South Vietnam.

When the 421st Air Transport Squadron was formed in May 1971 at Tan Son Nhut with newly assigned C-123Ks, VNAF crews were ready to man these airplanes. During the Squadron's first two months, four USAF C-123K instructor pilots of the 19th Tactical Airlift Squadron, Tan Son Nhut, flew with the VNAF crews as temporary aircraft commanders. With 16 aircraft and eight VNAF crews initially, the Squadron was able to fly airlift missions immediately. Four months later a second C-123K squadron, the 423rd, was formed with an initial strength of 16 crews.

To ensure successful operations of any type, thorough training was an absolute necessity. As part of the Vietnamization Program, a method of practical training in many skills was adopted whereby VNAF officers and airmen worked within USAF units. This be-

On its way to the target is this Cessna A-37 preparing to attach VC positions at Ba-To, near Da Nang, on 5 October 1972. These simplistic and agile attack aircraft were ideal for this confined war, which had no air opposition. Ground fire eventually took air superiority away from VNAF, as well as American airpower. *Courtesy of Pham-Quang-Khiem.*

In 1971 the VNAF formed three squadrons of C-123Ks at Tan Son Nhut AB from aircraft transferred from departing USAF units. This aircraft, 55-4565, was assigned to the 421st Transport Squadron, identified by the Q on the tail. These C-123Ks were replaced by C-130As in the background. *RG 342-KKE65211 USAF.*

came common practice throughout South Vietnam from 1970, particularly at those bases where Vietnamese and American air units were co-located under the Vietnamization program. Conventional OJT methods were used, with courses tailored to VNAF requirements. Special emphasis was placed on training the Vietnamese in base support operations, a subject not previously given high priority. Airmen were trained in civil engineering, security, fire protection, weather, communications, and air-traffic control. Individual skill upgrading resulted from this integrated program, which was designed primarily to achieve VNAF self-sufficiency as soon as possible. By the end of January 1970 more than 900 trainees were in this integrated training program. By the middle of that year more than 1240 officers and airmen were being taught more than 30 different specialties at Tan Son Nhut, Bien Hoa, Binh Thuy, Da Nang, Nha Trang, and Pleiku Air Bases.

To further the course to VNAF independency, 243 Vietnamese technicians were sent to the United States in 1970 to be trained as instructors to serve at the Nha Trang Training Center. This training consisted of a basic mechanics course tailored to their specific needs, instructor training, and subsequent training with field training detachments sent from the USAF Air Training Command. The first instructor course began in March 1970. By mid-1971 more than

This C-123K of the 423rd Transport Squadron is one of two aircraft on a resupply mission in support of the 1st ARVN Division taking place in January 1972. These are four engine aircraft, having two jet engines in pods beneath the wings. *Courtesy of Pham Quang Khiem.*

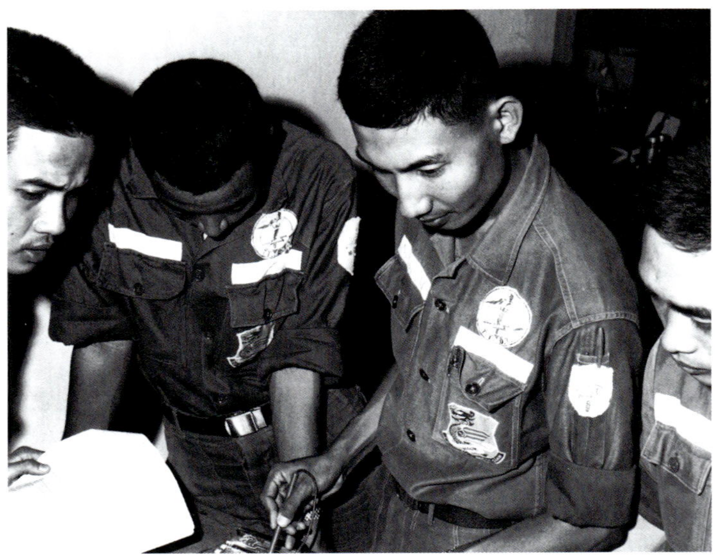

High quality training was essential for the expanding VNAF. Because of increasing numbers, training had to be shifted back from the United States to Vietnam to be conducted by qualified Vietnamese instructors. Note the VNAF, Air Training Center, and Electronics Center (T.T.D.T.) patches that are worn. *RG 342-101368 USAF*

This uncluttered view shows a C-123K of the 421st Transport Squadron at rest at Tan Son Nhut AB, 17 July 1971. VNAF had three squadrons of C-123 Providers for nearly a year and a half, during which 10 aircraft were lost, four of them due to ground fire. *Courtesy of Norman E. Taylor.*

5500 Vietnamese instructors had graduated and returned to Vietnam, while another 1330 remained in training in the United States. In addition to this program, USAF mobile training teams were sent to Nha Trang to teach 37 specialized skills. The Air Force Advisory Group also provided teams at each VNAF base to assist the Vietnamization program in any way possible.

Operations continued toward making the Vietnamese responsible for their own training within Vietnam, and most training accomplished in the United States was phased out. As part of this plan, the Air Force began translating technical orders into Vietnamese and building training aids. Additional training teams were sent from the United States equipped with specially designed training aids to expedite the learning programs.

As training capabilities improved the VNAF continued to expand. By 1970 VNAF strength was brought to 35,786 officers and airmen. To accommodate this major expansion, the Vietnamese Air Force was restructured again, in 1970, to included five air divisions, one for each of the four military regions, and a fifth one at Tan Son Nhut. The air divisions commanded 10 tactical wings, five maintenance and supply wings, and seven air base wings. The VNAF Air Logistics Wing became Air Logistics Command, equipped with a modern computer and made responsible for all VNAF inventory items. With the continued help of the USAF Air Training Command, the Vietnamese expanded their Nha Trang Training Center even further. It was now the location for six military schools and the English Language School for Tan Son Nhut, and all instructors were Vietnamese.

The VNAF had a solid corps of battle-hardened pilots to fill the air support role, which included a number from the senior ranks who had served with the French in the fifties, and others who had received training in the United States in the early sixties. These pilots were extremely good. Many had logged an incredible number of combat flying hours over the years, most in A-1s, up until about 1968. With the introduction of more sophisticated aircraft like the A-37 and F-5s, as well as AC-47 and AC-119, specialized training was required. This meant either withdrawing older pilots from combat duty to train in these new aircraft or starting from scratch with new recruits. The solution was a balance of both.

But all was not going as smoothly as the USAF and VNAF would have liked. Despite the increase in personnel by 1970, the VNAF was experiencing problems in manning its 22 squadrons. The main problem areas were maintenance and supply. The air depot at Bien Hoa was a prime example. Over the years, the USAF had placed teams at the depot to put it back on a sound basis, only to see it slip back into trouble a few months after they had gone. All developing air forces have found it difficult to resolve these problem areas.

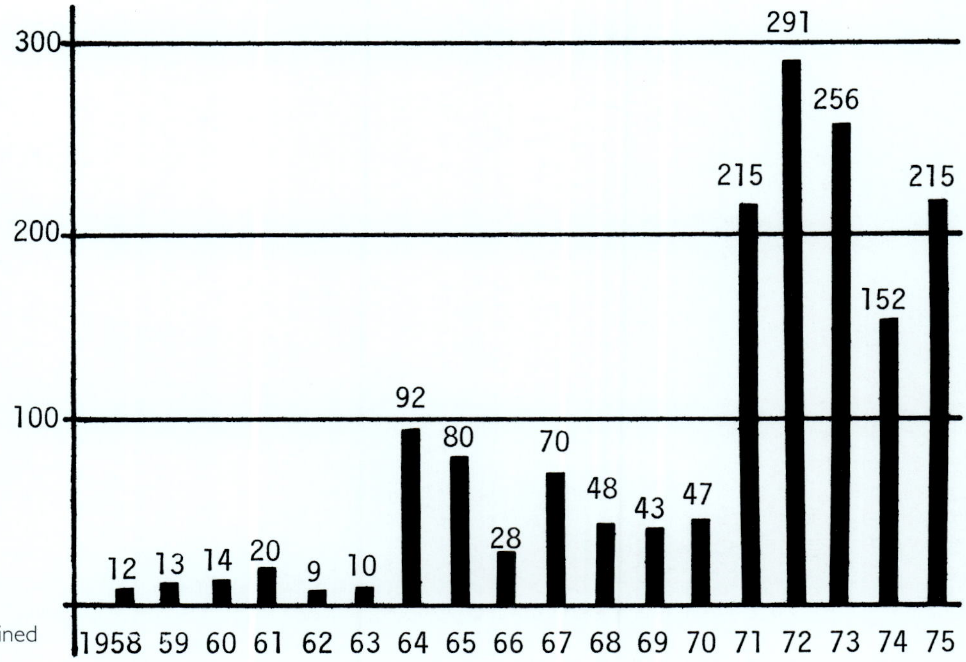

VNAF Undergraduate Pilot Training Graduates trained in the United States.

A flight instructor demonstrates a maneuver with a training aid to Aviation Cadets at Nha Trang. Initial flight training conducted in their own language with Vietnamese instructors proved very satisfactory, but English language was essential for advanced phases in the United States. *RG 342-103934 USAF*

In the cockpit of a U-17 Skywagon at the Air Training Center at Nha Trang in April 1967, 1st Lt Nguyen-trung-Hien, flight instructor (right seat), explains the functions of certain flight instruments to an aviation cadet (left seat). Note the type of headset used during this period. *RG 342-101362 USAF*

The South Vietnamese flag passes in review during graduation ceremonies at Nha Trang AB in November 1968 as U-17 Skywagons used for flight training fly a salute overhead. *RG 342-104792 USAF*

Graduation was a big moment in the lives of aviation cadets. At this graduation ceremony in November 1968, Maj Gen Tran-van-Minh (left), Commander of VNAF, presents pilot wings to honor graduate Nguyen-van-Thiet. Colonel Nguyen-ngoc-Oanh (right), later B/Gen, was commander of the Air Training Center for 12 years. *RG 342-104796 USAF*

In 1970 the VNAF transport fleet was increased to five squadrons, as American units leaving the country transferred their aircraft and unit support equipment to the VNAF. They included three squadrons of C-123s—the 421st, 423rd, and 425th. Three more C-119 aircraft were also added to the 16 already being flown by the Vietnamese in the 413th Transport Squadron at Tan Son Shut. The dependable 415th, with its trusty C-47 Gooney Birds, operated until around 1973.

Another type of transport aircraft was introduced into VNAF service in early 1971. As USAF units phased out, de Havilland C-7A Caribous were transferred to the newly formed 427th Transport Squadron at Phu Cat. As the inventory of Caribous was increased in mid-1972, a second C-7A squadron was activated at Phu Cat. A third C-7A squadron (431st) was formed a month later at Phu Cat, and as a result, the 427th and 429th transferred to Da Nang. In March 1973 the 429th and 431st were eventually relocated at Tan Son Nhut.

In November the VNAF took control of the three DASCs at Bien Hoa, Da Nang, and Pleiku. By the end of 1971 the Vietnamese were solely responsible for operating air navigation facilities at eight major air bases.

By early 1970 the VNAF was able to undertake most of the flying operations in IV Corps, and a larger share in the other three corps. On balance, however, the VNAF did a fair job in supporting ARVN operations, although there was a lack of experienced pilots

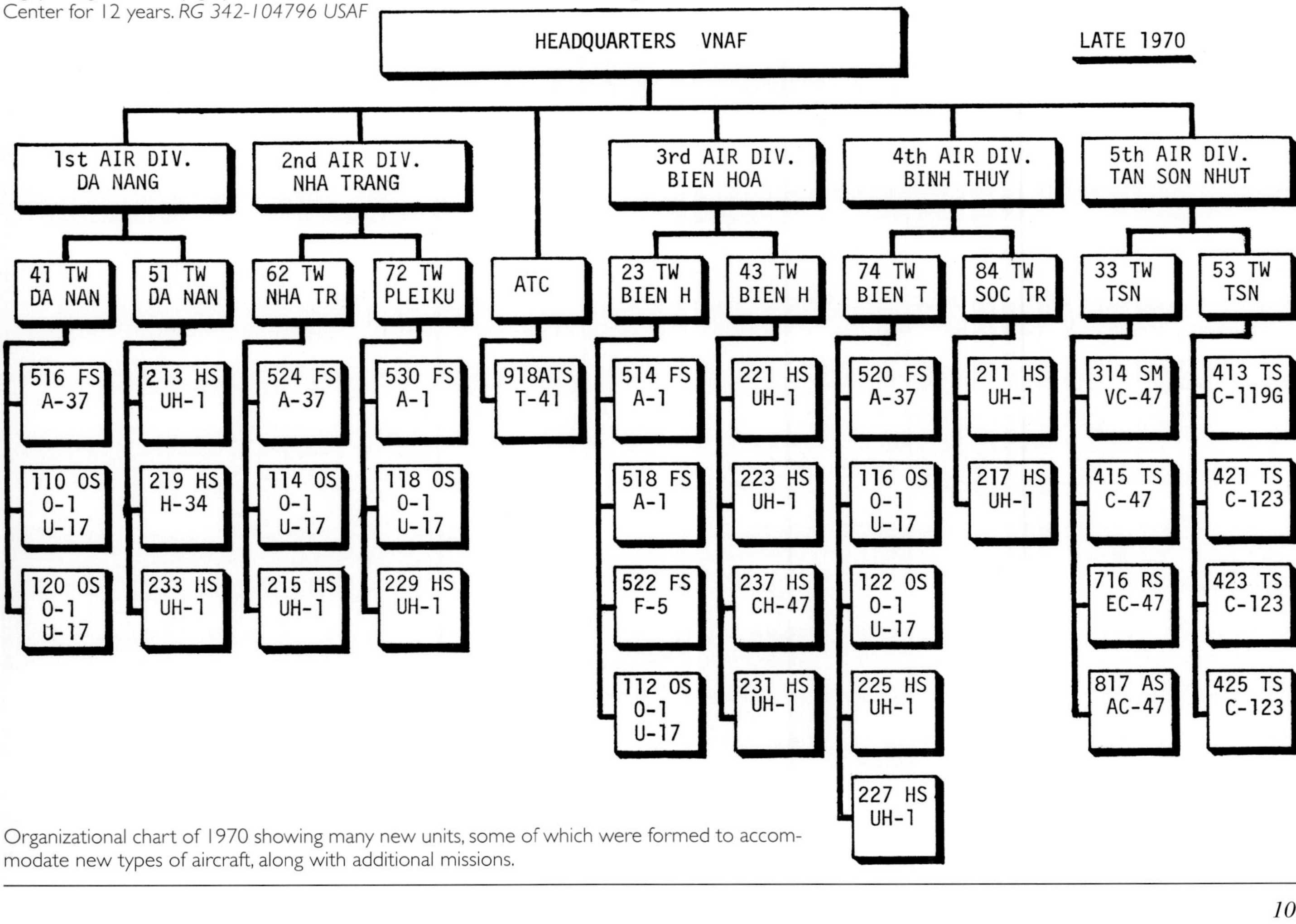

Organizational chart of 1970 showing many new units, some of which were formed to accommodate new types of aircraft, along with additional missions.

This Fairchild C-119G makes a brief stop at Da Nang in August 1968 soon after this type entered VNAF service. These Fairchild Flying Boxcars re-equipped the 413th Transport Squadron beginning in early 1968.

Headquarters for the ARVN II Corps was at Pleiku. Here at the air base near that headquarters is the C-47 assigned to the Corps Commander. The name "Plei-me" commemorates a significant battle for the South Vietnamese.

for the expanded air-ground operation system. The VNAF were unable to provide trained FACs at battalion level, essential for effective coordinated air strikes on confined targets. Consequently, the effectiveness of close air support was restrained throughout the country. The VNAF did exceptionally well in the areas where there were trained ALOs at Division level to control close air support. There were times when VNAF FACs in O-1s directed USAF and Australian Canberra strikes.

By 1971 the VNAF was making noticeable progress in improving its air operations. The VNAF flew more combat sorties in Vietnam than all the U.S. air arms combined: 63 percent of the total missions flown, and a 69.8 percent increase on 1970 operations. In September 1971 the Americans transferred a second C-119 squadron to the VNAF; the 819th Attack Squadron formed at Tan Son Nhut with AC-119G gunships.

The Spring Offensive, 1972

On land the war reached a critical stage when the North Vietnamese launched a major offensive into South Vietnam on 30 March 1972, all efforts to contain the enemy above the Demilitarized Zone having failed. This Communist "Spring Offensive, 1972" became a critical point in the survival of South Vietnam. Because eventual cease-fire negotiations would result in each side keeping the territory it held at the time; the North Vietnamese wanted to establish a strong foothold across existing borders. The invasion began with enemy forces rolling directly across the DMZ into I Corps, while others penetrated into II Corps from Laos. All were supported by considerable numbers of tanks and other armored vehicles. From the thrust of the invasion, it appeared that the enemy was seeking to cut off the northern two provinces and, but for the massive and concentrated use of airpower, both Quang Tri and Thua Thien provinces would have fallen immediately. U.S. air power, plus a strengthened Vietnamese Air force, had responded fiercely to the battle.

This overt enemy aggression led to further U.S. bombing in the north on 15 April, when President Nixon authorized attacks near the areas of Hanoi and the harbor of Haiphong. But it brought little respite to ARVN ground operations in the south; by 1 May the city of Quang Tri, in the northern province of South Vietnam, was occupied by North Vietnamese forces. A week later, after years of threatening, the U.S. mined the harbor at Haiphong and intensified their bombing of North Vietnam. Although mining the harbor had been advocated as early as the mid-1960s to speed the end of this war, it now proved to be ineffectual.

It became very difficult for the VNAF to conduct air operations within I Corps. Heavy anti-aircraft weapons had been moved to the south, across the borders of North Vietnam and Laos. The SAM envelope had spread south from Vinh, north of the DMZ, and covered the northern sectors of South Vietnam, now Communist-held, in preparation for further invasion of South Vietnam. Aircraft not equipped with missile detection devices could not survive. For the first time, helicopters and other low-performance aircraft, such as Cessna O-1 and O-2A FAC aircraft, were subjected to the heavy

The control tower at Pleiku AB, and the often clear blue sky of the high ground area in western Vietnam serves as a background for this VC-47D. There were many C-47s like this one of the 413th Transport Squadron that were detached to various locations for immediate transportation for field and headquarters commanders.

enemy antiaircraft defenses in South Vietnam, which took a major toll of these slow flying aircraft. Because of the SAM threat, the USAF's escorting AC-130 gunships were forced into the less heavily defended areas, which caused a reduction in their effectiveness. An instance occurred one night in March 1972 when one of the USAF's AC-130 gunships went down over Tchepone, an indication as to how far the enemy had spread into South Vietnam. During April, May, and June 10 U.S. and six VNAF aircraft fell victim to SA-7 missiles in the two northern provinces of the country. A new threat to aircraft, the Soviet-built surface-to-air-missile was called the Stela. Only 4.5 ft (1.4 m) long and 2.75 in (7 cm) in diameter, the SA-7 could be fired from the shoulder like a bazooka, making it extremely mobile and easy to conceal.

The buildup of the South Vietnamese forces continued, and the success of the Vietnamization program was ably demonstrated by the VNAF during this 1972 Spring Offensive. Responding to the enemy attack, the VNAF flew the first of more than 20,000 strike sorties—150 close air support sorties per day—which helped to stem the North Vietnamese advance. In the first month of the offensive its transports ferried more than 40,000 troops and delivered nearly 4000 tons of supplies throughout the country. Gunships and helicopters provided close air support to ARVN ground forces.

Lockheed C-130s were introduced into the VNAF when the 435th and 437th Transport Squadrons were formed at Tan Son Nhut in January 1973. The first VNAF C-130 instructor aircrew took its final test in December 1972, enabling the VNAF to train its own future Hercules pilots. To facilitate this conversion and reduce the drain upon VNAF resources, the C-123s of the 421st, 423rd, and 425th were returned to the USAF, and the three units were inactivated.

As the presence of U.S. forces continued to dwindle throughout 1972, more training programs became the responsibility of the VNAF, English language training included. In May 1972 the VNAF established a Communications and Electronics School at Bien Hoa to supplement the one at Nha Trang. Also, with the aid of USAF training teams, the VNAF took over maintenance training for C-130s, T-37Bs, and their support systems. An AC-119K training team from the USAF started cross-training VNAF AC-119G and C-119G air and maintenance crews on the gunship version of the Flying Boxcars.

Enhance and Enhance Plus

Signals from the Paris Peace talks in October 1972 gave encouraging signs that a settlement was in the offing. So encouraging, that 10 November 1972 was set as the date when all American transactions with the South Vietnamese Government would cease. This brought about one of the most rapid and wholesale transfers of military equipment ever, taking place in the closing month of 1972.

This operation was known as Project Enhance, which was a very appropriate title. The project was not solely directed toward

Departing USAF squadrons of C-7A Caribous left their aircraft behind for inclusion into the VNAF. They equipped three squadrons, but proved very difficult to maintain under the existing circumstances. This Caribou departs the muddy air strip at Tra Bong, in I Corps. *RG 342-KE36123 USAF*

the VNAF, but also toward equipping and improving the combat capabilities of South Vietnam's armed forces (RVNAF) in general. The operation could be implemented quickly, because it used the base of a force structure that had been developed four years earlier. In May 1968 the Military Assistance Command Vietnam (MACV) drew up a plan titled Consolidated RVNAF Improvement and Modernization Program, or in short—CRIMP. CRIMP was intended to provide a better balance in the combat forces and increase the fire power, mobility, and logistics of the RVNAF. This plan became a vital part in the initial phase of the Vietnamization program.

From the initial concept, CRIMP was expected to add just over a million men to the armed forces by mid-1971, and 1,100,000 more a year later. Included would be the equipment needed for such a force. Though Vietnam had the manpower resources, the critical factor was maintenance, equipment, and training costs.

The Spring Offensive of 1972 brought about a modification of the CRIMP resupply program (Project Enhance). This modified program compensated for the heavy loss of materiel during the campaign by delivering replacements before the expected cease-fire conditions could curtail those deliveries. It not only provided equipment, but also activated and manned new units for South Vietnam's Army, Navy, and Air Force.

In addition, Project Enhance supplied the VNAF with a large number and variety of aircraft. These aircraft supplemented some of the existing units and created new units with others. With the establishment of new units came the introduction of Fairchild AC-119K gunships to form the 821st at Tan Soon Nhut, with a detachment at Da Nang. C-119G aircraft destined for the 720th Reconnaissance Squadron for maritime patrol operated solely as transports. Two squadrons of CH-47 helicopters arrived, which probably formed the last of four CH-47 helicopter squadrons—the 247th and the 249th.

This rare aerial photograph taken in January 1972 shows formations of C-123Ks from the 53rd Tactical Wing and C-47s below from the 33rd Tactical Wing, both at Tan Son Nhut. This marked the 1st anniversary of the 5th Air Division. *Courtesy of Pham Quang Khiem.*

Before the conclusion of Project Enhance a supplemental project, called Enhance Plus, was added to further augment and modernize the VNAF. New aircraft types were introduced into newly formed squadrons, and exchanges for other aircraft types were also made. On a one-for-one basis, 35 twin-engined O-2A FAC aircraft replaced the single-engine O-1 Bird Dogs, although it is probable that these exchanged O-1s never left the country. Also exchanged were 37 C-123s for 32 C-130A transports, all of which were allocated to the 435th and 437th Transport Squadrons.

The following breakdown shows the aircraft delivered under both projects.

ARVN troops line up to board awaiting UH-1H helicopters for an assault attack against enemy forces. Helicopters gave the ARVN this flexibility of ground forces, but in time the lack of supplies kept many on the ground. *RG 342-107488 USAF.*

AIRCRAFT DELIVERIES TO VNAF IN PROJECT ENHANCE AND ENHANCE PLUS
(23 October 1972 to 12 December 1972)

Aircraft Type	Enhance	Enhance Plus	Project Totals	Grand Totals
A-37	(2 Sq)	(3 Sq)	90	249
AC-119K***	(1 Sq)		22	
C-119G	(1 Sq)			
C-7A	(1 Sq)			
C-130A		(2 Sq)*	32	
RC-47	12			
EC-47		10	23	33
F-5A/B	5	(2 Sq)	118	153
F-5E		(3 Sq)		
A-1			28	
O-2A			35**	
T-37			24	
UH-1	32	(3 Sq) = 21 Sq	(286)	
CH-47	(2 Sq)		23	

* C-130s replaced all 37 C-123s.
** O-2As were exchanged 1 for 1 with O-1s.
*** Must have meant C-119G. No transport model Ks were in RVN.
(All C-119K (sic) and C-47 transports were returned to U.S.)
Source: MACV Official History.

Shipments under these projects were delivered to all South Vietnamese services by sea and air during a remarkably short period of time. Larger aircraft destined for the VNAF were ferried by air, while others were disassembled and airlifted aboard seemingly endless flights of C-5As bringing aircraft and equipment direct from depots in the United States. The first cargo aircraft under this project arrived at Tan Son Nhut on 23 October 1972, and the last shipment arrived by surface at Newport, near Saigon, on 12 December. In just seven weeks nearly 5000 short tons came by air and 100,000 short tons by sea. Excluding aircraft gained under Project Enhance, the VNAF received 618 additional aircraft under Project Enhance Plus alone. It was a round-the-clock operation to build up the reserves felt necessary for South Vietnam to maintain superior strength over its enemy in order to deter further aggression.

However, this build up of military strength was not one sided. Closely monitoring the situation was Col William E Le Gro, U.S. Army, Chief Intelligence Officer at the U.S. Defense Attache Office in Saigon. In his detailed reports, Col Le Gro stated that, while the United States was rushing equipment to Vietnam to avoid the constraints expected to be imposed by the cease-fire agreement, the Communists were also moving great quantities of materiel down the roads into South Vietnam. Uninhibited now by American B-52s and fighter-bomber interdiction strikes, they freely moved field guns, tanks, antiaircraft weapons—including SA-2 air defense missiles—on their way to Khe Sanh in Quang Tri Province. As later demonstrated, the Communists were not concerned about any restrictions a cease-fire might impose on shipments to South Vietnam; the surge of shipments was in response to the heavy losses that the NVA suffered during the Spring Offensive, 1972, and the ARVN counter-offensive.

Based upon what Col Le Gro felt was clearly reliable data, MACV estimated that North Vietnam sent nearly 148,000 replacements into South Vietnam during 1972. This estimate included individual replacements to make up for the staggering losses incurred during the campaign, but not the organized divisions, regiments, and battalions sent to join the offensive. Although the estimates of enemy losses are based on less reliable information, the NVA probably lost over 190,000 men during 1972. Of these, about 132,000 were killed in action, another 46,000 probably died of wounds or

New airlift muscle was given to the VNAF in the form of Lockheed C-130As in January 1973. Two squadrons were formed, replacing the C-123Ks so that maintenance capabilities could be concentrated. These airplanes were already 17 years old with inherent age problems when received. Smiling with pride over the new airplanes is the flight engineer (left) and Lt Pham-quang-Khiem, pilot. *Courtesy of Pham Quang Khiem.*

Pilot training formerly given to Vietnamese candidates in the United States was moved to Nha Trang AB and other bases in Vietnam. To accomplish this, Cessna T- 41Bs were transferred to VNAF in the early 1970s. This T-41 taxies by at Tan Son Nhut in December 1970. *Courtesy of Norman E. Taylor.*

were permanently disabled, 2500 were prisoners of war, and 10,000 turned themselves in to South Vietnamese authorities. In the case of materiel shipments, the North Vietnamese showed no urgency in transporting replacements prior to the cease-fire. These replacements methodically crossed the border from Laos and the Demilitarized Zone (DMZ) without inspection or control, a condition that existed until the end.

These large figures for enemy losses seem impressive, yet since the preparation of the report, and as the picture of the Vietnam War becomes more clear, there is evidence that these figures were not always correct.

"ARVN claims of numbers of enemy troops killed in battle should be viewed with the utmost skepticism," warned an attache assessment made shortly after. The report went on to substantiate that "Commanders are virtually obligated to report success. To do otherwise could bring anything from verbal abuse to relief of command to, in some cases, court martial and imprisonment. When commanders experience failure they must make it appear to be success. A unit ambushed and sustaining heavy casualties almost always reports much higher enemy casualties, showing that they gave better than they received."

Military and civilian authorities in Vietnam were, understandably, under pressure to maximize success and minimize failure. However, misleading intelligence reports of this nature, to serve parochial purposes or viewpoints, were detrimental to the proper assessment of, and making the appropriate plans to cope with the situation.

Further upgrading in pilot training was accomplished in Cessna T-37B Tweedy Birds of the 920th Training Squadron at Pham Rang. Small numbers of these trainers were acquired late in the war for initial jet training for VNAF pilots. Proudly standing in front of this airplane is Aviation Cadet Tran-minh-Quan. *Courtesy of Pham Quang Khiem.*

Project Enhance brought a surge of equipment to Vietnam in late 1972 in anticipation of a cease fire. This C-5A disgorges an F-5A at Bien Hoa AB to supplement those already in the VNAF. *Courtesy of USAF.*

Newly acquired F-5s from USAF resources are in fully assembled condition, and appear to be ready for service after a change of national markings. Each of these revetments hold three of these tiny fighters. Note two camouflaged aircraft fins. *Courtesy of USAF.*

Project Enhance and Enhance Plus saw the delivery of 118 F-5s to Vietnam, bringing their total strength to 153. Many F-5s like these were replacement aircraft that were never called upon. Some were acquired for the VNAF from South Korea, Iran, and Taiwan resources. *Courtesy of Pham Quang Khiem.*

This F-5A nears completion of reassembly and repainting to join an active squadron. The VNAF had, at one time, five active F-5 squadrons, with equipment for several more. The lack of replacement parts and fuel with which to fly them were major problems for the VNAF. *Courtesy of USAF.*

While Project Enhance and Enhance Plus was in progress, equipment and supplies were added to the RVNAF's inventory at a very high rate. As part of this program, arrangements were made for the ground facilities under American control to be transferred back to the South Vietnamese Government; particularly, the air bases from which the VNAF needed to operate. It was clearly essential that these assets had to be legally in the hands of the South Vietnamese Government and operating at the time of any cease-fire agreement, or they would have to remain neutral.

Planning for the anticipated cease-fire at the headquarters of Military Assistance Command, Vietnam, took into consideration the fact that MACV and all American and third country forces had to be withdrawn within 60 days of the cease-fire date. The arbitrary date of 10 November 1972 was also to be the completion date for all base transfers. To meet this deadline, all U.S. installations changed hands *en masse* on 6 November 1972, except for Tan Son Nhut Air Base. This was to be the last air facility to be transferred, scheduled to take place on 10 November. But, since a cease-fire date was still being negotiated in Paris with no schedule set, the transfer agreement allowed U.S. personnel to occupy transferred facilities until no longer required. This also gave the U.S. re-entry rights to Tan Son Nhut, Bien Hoa, and Da Nang Air Bases.

This agreement turned out to be prudent, for the peace talks in Paris dragged on week by week, past the anticipated October date. Finally, on 27 January 1973, the cease-fire agreement was signed by all parties. Unfortunately, there was little faith that it would last, but there were no other alternatives.

With the war now totally in the hands of the Vietnamese, they were left with a tremendous arsenal to manage. Although the VNAF was programmed and authorized to have 1852 aircraft, it now had 2075 aircraft of 25 different types and models, the maximum number ever possessed. It had reached a strength of 65 squadrons and 61,147 personnel. It was obvious that the VNAF could not operate this size Air Force with so many different types of aircraft. The rationale for such a large force was based on the supposition that, given time, the VNAF would eventually develop the ability to handle such a large force, and because of the provisions of the cease fire agreement (that no additional equipment could be introduced after the cease fire) only replacements on a one-for-one basis were authorized. Thus, regardless of the validity of the request for such large amounts of equipment, these requests were honored; an important factor in persuading President Thieu to agree to a cease-fire.

On view of its numbers of aircraft, the South Vietnamese Air Force emerged as the fourth largest Air Force in the world—behind Communist China, the United States, and the Soviet Union.

As impressive as this size may sound, it was comparable to an over-stuffed dragon, so large that it was almost incapable of moving. Up until Project Enhance and Enhance Plus, every attempt was

Boeing-Vertol CH-47 Chinooks formed four squadrons as medium-lift helicopters, one for each of the four Corps areas. Formerly with U.S. Marine HMH 462, this Chinook may never have been placed in VNAF service and remained in storage. *Courtesy of Donald Mohr.*

made to expand the VNAF only at a rate for which it could handle. But apart from the sudden surge, which was somewhat justified, the growth rate of the VNAF had been rapid and controlled; the VNAF continually improving over the previous years of its service life.

In June 1974 the VNAF made a decision to put 224 surplus aircraft in storage. Among them were 52 C-7A cargo transports, 34 C-47 and AC-119 gunships, all 31 Cessna O-2A FAC aircraft, 31 UH-1 helicopters, and all remaining 61 A-1 Skyraiders stored at various airfields. The condition of these war weary Skyraiders was such that their life expectancy was nearly exhausted. They were old and had been flying combat with a "three G" restriction for some time. Their instruments had deteriorated to the point where they only flew good-weather day sorties. However, without American supplies, the VNAF found the modern aircraft more difficult to maintain, and units like the 514th Fighter Squadron at Bien Hoa, though trained to operate the A-37s, continued to fly the less maintenance-demanding Douglas Skyraiders to the very end.

Even though about 500 people were devoted to the inspection of storage aircraft, there was still an increase in the number of airworthy aircraft. Since there had been no replacements for aircraft lost since the cease-fire, the VNAF, by the end of December 1974, had approximately 1484 aircraft. A total of 299 aircraft had been lost in combat, through accidents or transfers. (These totals, gains, and losses do not tally in some cases, as the figures were taken from various reports. Exact time periods, and often counting combat and support aircraft separately or together, cause discrepancies in these figures.)

While the numbers of available aircraft was no problem, a nonexistent supply line became a major one. Supplies of critical items, however small, were often exhausted, and had to be robbed from stored aircraft. Missions normally flown with four bombs were flown with two. Fuel tanks were filled to the half-way mark so that fuel could be used for other aircraft, and for additional missions that otherwise may not have been flown. This was the situation not long after the Americans withdrew. The flow of supplies and spare parts trickled, then soon stopped. The South Vietnamese were truly "going it alone!"

The USAF brought the Cessna O-2A into the conflict to supplement the O-1 Bird Dog by having twin engine reliability in mountainous areas of Vietnam and Laos. Project Enhance and Enhance Plus passed 35 of these FAC airplanes on to two VNAF squadrons, but were soon placed in storage to reduce demands upon maintenance. (Digitized modified image.) *Courtesy Pham-Quang-Khiem.*

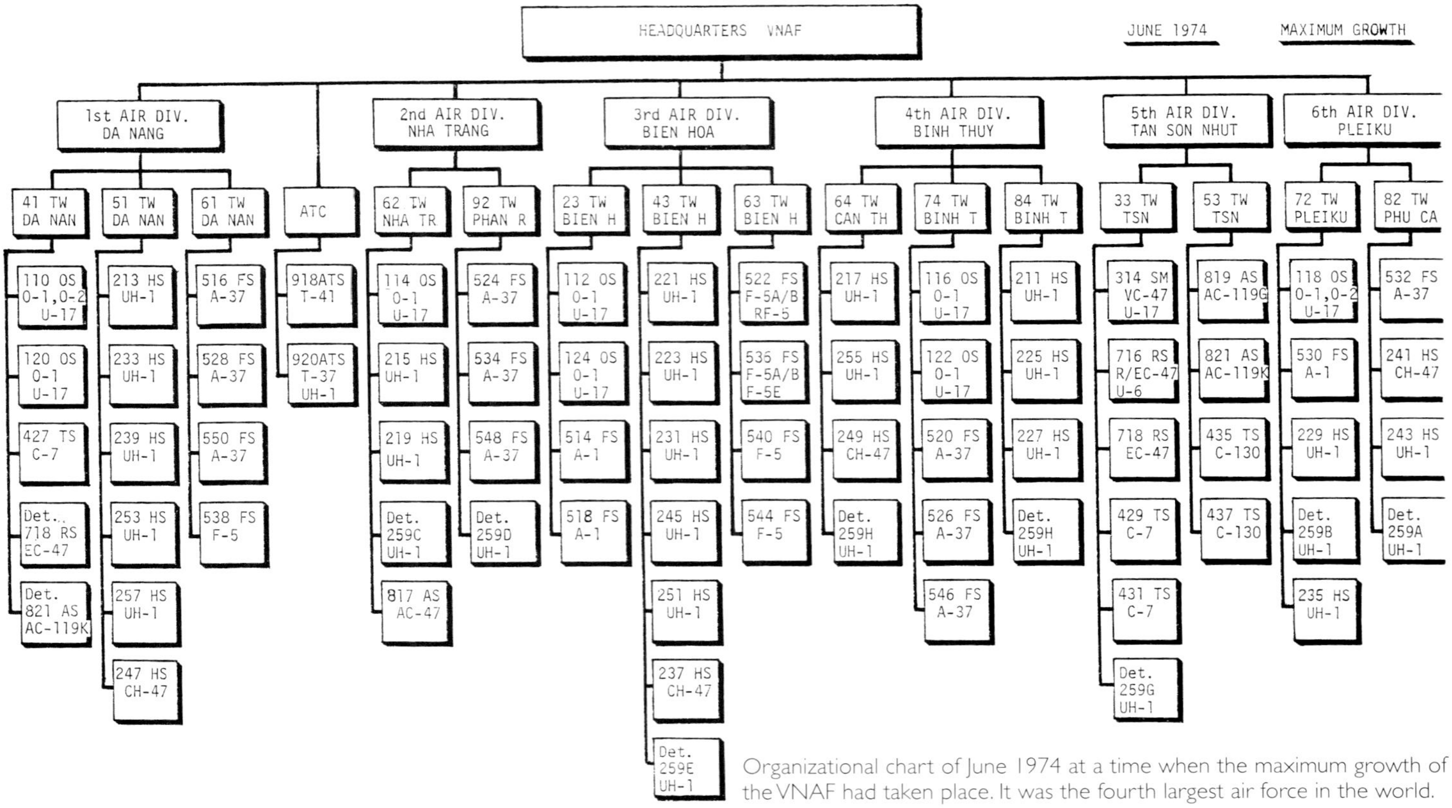

Organizational chart of June 1974 at a time when the maximum growth of the VNAF had taken place. It was the fourth largest air force in the world.

A squadron of these C-119Gs was accepted by VNAF to form the 720th Reconnaissance Squadron for maritime patrol. Surveillance equipment failed to arrive, so these Flying Box Cars were used solely as air transports. This C-119G, 53-7873, has just arrived at Tan Son Nhut on delivery 8 February 1968. *RG 342-KKE 31611 USAF.*

This C-130A, 57-0460, now resides in the National Air and Space Museum in Washington, DC, because of its historic and operational background. Having served the USAF in Vietnam, it later was transferred to VNAF. A C-130 crew with family members escaped the collapse of Vietnam by following a well thought through plan, yet with many obstacles, and reached safety in Singapore. This airplane then served U.S. Air National Guard units until retired to the museum. *Courtesy of Pham Quang Khiem.*

8

The Cease-Fire

The cease-fire agreements were formally signed in Paris on 27 January 1973. On that day, the USAF B-52 force (ARC LIGHT), which had conducted air strikes in South Vietnam continuously since June 1965, ceased strike operations in all areas of Southeast Asia, except Laos. The last American troops left Vietnam on 29 March, leaving only a Defense Attache Office and administrative support elements in Saigon and outlying bases.

Throughout the war, the North Vietnamese main priority during negotiations had been to bring an end to the bombing of their country. Towards this end, and in the hope of ending the war, bombing above the 20th Parallel ceased on 1 April 1968. The bombing was significant to the U.S., since it was the only way that they could force the North Vietnamese to come to an acceptable agreement. The ground war in the South was controlled by the North Vietnamese, who had the tactical flexibility to fight when the situation was favorable or withdraw when combat conditions were too disadvantageous. In the air, it was quite the opposite: the United States had the initiative, and the North Vietnamese could not stop the attacks.

The risk of moving additional forces and weapons to South Vietnam was minimal, provided that bombing was halted, or there were only a few spasmodic and isolated strikes. The Spring Offensive of 1972 became a test of U.S. determination to resume the

The Cessna A-37 was a good bombing platform for support of ground forces. Following the cease fire, ground-to-air missiles were introduced into South Vietnam from the North and A-37s were prime targets. These Dragonflys of the 526th Fighter Squadron stand ready at Binh Thuy AB. *RG 342-107614 USAF.*

An F-5A from one of the 23rd Tactical Wing squadrons at Bien Hoa AB in April 1970 stands on alert in a revetment. Although this F-5 is equipped with M-82 low drag bombs for ground attack, some stood alert for air defense after the USAF withdrew their F-102 interceptors from Da Nang. *RG 342-KE40774 USAF.*

bombing. If the U.S. failed to react, more aggressive campaigns could be undertaken within South Vietnam, leading to a final military victory. The decision to resume the bombing set the stage for enforcing a settlement on North Vietnam.

Aircraft from airfields on Guam and in Thailand inflicted the heaviest attacks on the Hanoi area of North Vietnam. B-52s, F-4s, F-105s and, for a time, F-111s formed the major attack force against the heartland of the north. The bombing operations were greater than those during the 1966-1968 campaign, in that most all significant targets, including the mining of Haiphong, were to be attacked. From 1 May 1972 the air campaign increased in intensity as the North Vietnamese became more difficult in negotiations. When the negotiations broke down in December, U.S. President Nixon called for a full scale air offensive to convince the North Vietnamese that their homeland was truly going to be destroyed if they did not reach a cease-fire agreement. Most senior military leaders agreed that the December air campaign forced a cease-fire and an agreement to end the war. Many senior political officials were of the same opinion. Just one month later, the cease-fire went into effect on 27 January 1973.

From the time of the cease-fire to the fall of South Vietnam, there was a great change in the overall military situation. This was not only due to the lack of direct support by U.S. forces, but also to the end of replacements and other supplies. What happened to the VNAF in its final years became a major concern, and the center of a study by the USAF for future reference.[20]

The cease-fire agreement brought an end to the American's advisory capacity in Vietnam. In its place, as part of the agreement, the Americans had a Defense Attache Office (DAO) that occupied the former offices of the MACV at Tan Son Nhut Air Base. Small field offices were located in Da Nang, Pleiku, Qui Nhon, Nha Trang, Bien Hoa, Long Binh, Nha Be, Dong Tam, Binh Thuy, and Can Tho. The technical assistance provided by the military and senior civilian officials of the DAO and by the contractors was essential

The FAC in the Cessna Bird Dogs were no longer safe from heavy ground fire after the cease-fire, as in previous years. In certain areas they were forced above 10,000 ft (3048 m) for observation duties and controlling air strikes. Shown here is an O-1 from the 112th Observation Squadron, Bien Hoa. *RG 342-K44802 USAF.*

A VNAF pilot runs to his F-5A in response to ARVN troops in enemy contact. F-5s were maintained on ready-alert at Bien Hoa for this type of support. The personal equipment he is wearing includes partial-pressure G-suit, inflatable flotation vest, survival vest, and gun holster with web belt. *RG 342-104386 USAF.*

to the RVNAF, but because of the cease-fire agreement, the South Vietnamese could not be advised by the Americans in any way on military operations, tactics, or techniques of employment. Its mission was to report on operational matters, such as violations of the cease-fire, and to produce intelligence information on which subsequent decisions concerning the Military Assistance Program and American interests in Southeast Asia could be based.

It was through this DAO that the American/South Vietnamese relationships were maintained, and it was primarily from this source that information from within RVN was obtained. The RVNAF apparently freely shared statistics with the DAO but, as pointed out earlier, the accuracy of some of these claims is questionable. Since this book draws heavily upon post-American influence information conveyed to the DAO and found in their reports, coupled with the DAO's observations at the time, it remains the only relatively complete coverage of this period, and does aid immeasurably in detailing the final history of the South Vietnamese Air Force.

The A-1 Skyraider remained in service until the final days, even though they were worn out and no match for the SA-7 heat seeking missiles. This A-1H of the 520th at Binh Thuy AB has an almost new-looking appearance, since it was photographed in October 1966. It is loaded with napalm-filled tanks. *RG 342- KE23748 USAF.*

Following the Cease Fire

A vital issue to the preservation of the cease-fire was the implicit assumption that if the North Vietnamese elected to initiate a major campaign in South Vietnam, the U.S. would not respond with local air support of South Vietnamese troops, but would launch a total air offensive against North Vietnam, with no respect for any target which supported that nation's will to fight. Thus, the preservation of an uneasy cease-fire rested solely on this threat.

However, it became obsolete with the passage in the U.S. Congress of the Cooper-Church Amendment the previous August. The Amendment restrained the President from authorizing forces to go into Vietnam, Cambodia, and Laos. This could only be construed as the complete disengagement of the U.S. from the Vietnam War. Forces maintained in Thailand as a visible deterrent to North Vietnam lost their value with the passage of the Amendment. With so much discussion in respect to the war and the lack of support for any U.S. military action, it was evident that Congress had no intention of permitting the President to resume the bombing, irrespective of North Vietnamese activities.

From the Spring Offensive of 1972 it was apparent that the South Vietnamese Army (ARVN) would not be able to defend itself against the North Vietnamese Army without continuous and effective air support, mainly supplied by the United States. This was demonstrated in previous battles at Pleiku, An Loc, and Quang Tri; places which would have fallen had it not been for air support. The ARVN relied heavily on air support, and generally would not initiate a major attack unless it was assured. In the absence of the USAF this air support was provided solely by VNAF.

In sharp contrast with other aircraft in well maintained condition, this Skyraider of the 516th Fighter Squadron shows the signs of war weariness. It was about this time in October 1966 that the SEA camouflage scheme was being applied. *Courtesy of Neal Schweider.*

The basic concept surrounding the expansion of VNAF was its ability to provide close air support to the ARVN when conditions permitted. For this reason, the VNAF was given unsophisticated aircraft incapable of operating in a SAM environment augmented with heavy concentrations of radar-directed AAA fire. From U.S. experience over North Vietnam and in the 1972 offensive, it was obvious that there was a requirement for high performance, ECM-equipped aircraft capable of operating under such conditions. To conduct effective close air support missions, these defenses had to be neutralized. In the 1972 Offensive U.S. F-4 Phantom IIs and A-7 Corsair IIs with supporting forces dealt with these targets. During the cease fire, the VNAF was left with a force that was geared to a level of combat similar to the 1968 Tet offensive. It was assumed that further blatant cease-fire violations would result in USAF intervention. Further, it was assumed that, as the VNAF continued to mature, more sophisticated equipment would be introduced into the force.

Another cease-fire consideration was a continuous level of funding, both military and economic. Adequate funding would be needed for up to five years, perhaps longer, if South Vietnam was to become viable and self-sufficient. Without funding, the RVNAF would be unable to cope with continuous engagements of even a limited nature. With the cease-fire, supply lines to South Vietnam would not be intercepted. It was not considered feasible to provide VNAF with the sophisticated equipment needed to operate against the supply routes from the North that fed through neighboring Laos. This would require equipping the VNAF with the highly sophisticated AC-130, more complicated and advanced fighters like the F-4 and A-7, ECM equipment, airborne command posts, laser-guided weapons, and other types of hardware used by U.S. forces which, at the time, were beyond the operating capability of the VNAF. Further, the USAF averaged about 200 sorties a day during the dry season over these supply routes. It was completely impractical to structure the VNAF to both patrol external communications lines *and* simultaneously provide close air support for its army. Therefore, it was apparent that, in the absence of U.S. air power, there was no way to prevent the North Vietnamese from building up logistics stock in and adjacent to South Vietnam sufficient to support various levels of activity.

The decision to equip the VNAF with A-37s and F-5s with simple systems was taken because it was felt that, if the VNAF was given sophisticated aircraft, there would be a temptation to initiate

The revetment area of the 516th FS at Da Nang in 1968 shows another form of aircraft marking. In this case, the letters "VNAF" are used in lieu of the usual flag painted on the rudder. Note the random use of the national insignia on the side of the fuselage.

The number of Bell UH-1 "Hueys" nearly doubled the quantity of any other aircraft in the VNAF inventory. This UH-1H, 69-15618, has the insignia of the "Rampant Elephant" painted on its nose, symbolic of the 215th Helicopter Squadron based at Nha Trang, yet photographed at Phu Cat, both bases in II Corps. *Courtesy of Norman E. Taylor.*

fighter operations against North Vietnam. This would expand the war to a point where North Vietnam would have no option but to mount a large scale campaign to take over all of South Vietnam. So, by not providing the VNAF with sophisticated aircraft, the potential for keeping the fighting at a relatively low level was enhanced, and the outlook for a political settlement would be increased.

During negotiations for a cease-fire, President Thieu adamantly opposed the idea of leaving 135,000 North Vietnamese troops in South Vietnam and considered this issue paramount to the future of South Vietnam. With such a force, the potential for continuing state of conflict existed. He therefore argued that a fundamental point in the cease-fire would be the withdrawal of North Vietnamese forces and verification of that action.

The deadlock on this issue was reflected in the large amount of equipment that was put into South Vietnam just prior to the cease-fire. The large number of aircraft given to the VNAF was completely beyond its capability to maintain. It was hoped that, with considerable contractor support over a period of time, the VNAF would be able to handle such a large force. From the onset, it was understood that the VNAF would find it difficult to operate a force of over 2,000 aircraft. Only the most optimistic thought it likely that the VNAF could manage such a force over the next few years.

The Fleeting Moments of Peace

Negotiators had hardly left the table after signing the Cease-Fire Agreement when the North Vietnamese began preparing for the eventual military conquest of South Vietnam. They began to move south until severely threatened by the superior strength of the South Vietnamese, strategic reserves being methodically brought to these areas of heavy resistance. Anti-aircraft defenses, no longer needed

The VNAF lacked good aerial reconnaissance capability of their own. Aircraft like this RF-5A were sophisticated far beyond what was required and what the VNAF could support. Ten had been supplied to the VNAF, and six were lost prior to the final offensive. *RG 342-107846 USAF.*

Sikorsky H-43 Choctaw helicopters were VNAF's initial main carrier for vertical envelopment operations. Shown here in 1964 are H-34s of the 213th Helicopter Squadron based at Da Nang,. *RG 342-93248 USAF.*

Cessna-built aircraft dominated in various models the fixed wing aircraft used during the Vietnam war. Shown here is a U-17 Skywagon used to supplement O-1s in FAC duties, training, and liaison use. The red rudder on this U-17 shows it to have been assigned to the 122nd Observation Squadron at Binh Thuy AB, 1971. *RG 342- KE48754 USAF.*

Sheltered by this steel revetment, this Cessna A-37 Dragonfly awaits skin repair to be made to the upper fin leading edge, possibly caused by ground fire. This Dragonfly carried the markings of the 524th Fighter Squadron that was based at Nha Trang AB, 1970. *Courtesy of Norman E. Taylor via Roger Besecker.*

to cope with the aerial assaults formerly experienced in the North Vietnamese heartland, could be used to defend against troops now pouring into South Vietnam. Jet airfields were developed in the lower areas of North Vietnam as a counter-threat to the VNAF. The former air base and stronghold at Khe Sanh, in the northwestern part of South Vietnam—once so heavily defended by the Americans in 1968—was enlarged for limited jet operations by enemy forces.

North Vietnamese regular troops infiltrated at an increasing rate. Since they would gain superiority over the ARVN outposts, the plan was to cut the roads to these outposts and then overrun them. Since the cease-fire the North Vietnamese had occupied more than 100 outposts and forced the ARVN to abandon at least another 100. All of these operations took place in preparation for the final offensive, which appeared to be scheduled for 1976, but there was sufficient flexibility therein to permit a rapid exploitation if condi-

This flight of three Dragonflys begin their attack against a known ground target. Although their bombs have been expended, their nose firing mini-guns remain a lethal weapon. These A-37s are part of the 74th Tactical Wing based at Binh Thuy AB in IV Corps. *RG 342-105934 USAF.*

These Hueys from the 217th Helicopter Squadron are on a mission in the area of Can Tho in 1970. They carry an unusual example of subdued colors used for distinctive unit markings on these UH-1Ds. This consists of a dark stylized star over a lighter, irregular colored background. *RG 111-SC 655137 U.S. Army.*

tions permitted. The North Vietnamese proceeded with the knowledge that the U.S. was out of the Vietnam War for good.

Apart from the remarkable increase in NVA antiaircraft strength in South Vietnam, the gravest threat to VNAF aircraft was the SA-7 hand-held heat-seeking missile. From the cease-fire until the end of the following June 1973, there were 22 reported SA-7 attacks on VNAF aircraft, with eight aircraft and their crew lost: one A-37; one F-5A; three A-1s; two UH-1s; and one CH-47. These losses were serious, with a rate slightly better than one out of three. Defense was limited to watching for the telltale flash, often seen from the air, followed by a characteristic smoke and vapor trail, at which time, if detected, the pilot would take evasive action.

By the summer and early autumn of 1974 the strategy of attempting to hold far-flung outposts in South Vietnam was no longer feasible. The North Vietnamese had introduced SA-2s at Khe Sanh and Quang Tri, and SA-7s were now reported in all four corps areas. These defenses grew at an alarming rate, and VNAF losses continued to grow. Eventually some 20,000 anti-aircraft defense troops made their way into South Vietnam. North Vietnam ground forces in the South were taking over control of the air.

Setbacks and Cutbacks

The problems facing the VNAF were more than just the freedom to operate in its own airspace, although this was an increasingly more serious problem, especially in the northern section of the RVN. In the fiscal year 1974, which began on 1 July 1973, U.S. support for the RVNAF was drastically cut. Congress' determination to further reduce military aid came as an additional blow to the VNAF and RVNAF. Despite U.S. promises made to Thieu in January 1973, materiel aid to the South Vietnamese armed forces was not delivered in quantities sufficient to maintain effectiveness. More importantly, the requested financial aid, so essential to a country badly crippled from the effects of more than a decade of severe fighting, was progressively cut by American politicians intent upon prevent-

Northrop F-5A Freedom Fighters and later "E" model TIGER IIs were the VNAF's only jet fighters. Since there was no air opposition, they were used for air-to-ground attack, yet on standby for possible air intercepts. Ground crew of the 522nd Fighter Squadron at Bien Hoa AB manually push the airplane into the revetment protection. 1970. *RG 342-93323 USAF.*

Three ship formation of Northrop F-5As Freedom Fighters of the 522nd Fighter Squadron head for their target while carrying M-82 low drag bombs on under-wing stations. Their lightweight coupled with two J85 jet engines and afterburner gave remarkable performance. *RG 342-107694 USAF.*

ing renewed involvement at any level in Southeast Asia. Instead of receiving the expected 1.6 billion dollars for their war effort, only 700 million dollars was appropriated by Congress, and all requests for additional aid were refused. As so aptly described by one observer, this amounted to slow unilateral disarmament of a country still engaged in a major war.

This cut occurred while the VNAF was in the middle of replacing the F-5A with F-5Es on a one-to-one basis. The Es were far more effective, in that they could provide the air defense capability apparently needed since the withdrawal of U.S. air support. The replacement program, calling for approximately 300 F-5Es, was abruptly terminated after only 100 aircraft had been replaced, because of their high cost. 220 million dollars had already been spent on the purchase of the F-5Es—which included the cost of ammunition and ordnance already in the pipeline—packaging, crating, handling, and transportation. Thus, the remaining 480 million dollars was to cover the rest of the RVNAF expenses.

The VNAF's most basic problem was shared with all of the RVNAF. Its personnel were not paid a wage comparable with inflation. In a country which had been at war since birth, and a major war at that for the past 10 years, military service for the individual was long term. Unlike their former American counterparts, who rotated in and out on one-year tours of duty, the South Vietnamese were in the war for the duration.

The U.S. Defense Attache at the time described the situation very clearly in this manner: When a Major General's pay could only buy two bags of rice a month, meaning that he was not able to feed his family rice, let alone meat, vegetables, and fish sauce, or clothe them and educate his children, then things had to be *truly* grim for those in the lower ranks. In fact, limited physical ability through hunger was reportedly commonplace, even among flying personnel.

How then did the military personnel and their families get along? They took on second jobs after normal military duty hours,

This very colorful U-17 gathers speed on the Ban Me Thuot runway for the return flight to Saigon. The 314th Special Missions Squadron had several U-17s used for courier services. *Courtesy of Rob Mignard via Bob Chenoweth.*

The ramps are deserted of personnel because of the rain shower that has just passed. Douglas A-1s remain in the protection of their revetments with canopies closed, yet still ready for scramble if called upon. These are Skyraiders of the 23rd Tactical Wing at Bien Hoa AB. *Courtesy of Terry Love.*

their families worked, they received help from relatives, and many pilfered what was at hand for resale. Seen in this light, it was not how corrupt a person became, but how honest he remained.

The root of the problem was that military pay was not included in military aid, by Vietnamese law. This meant that the U.S. military aid previously described was not used toward military pay; otherwise, the soldiers would have seen themselves as mercenaries, which to them would have been embarrassing. Pay came direct from the Vietnamese Government, the rates of pay having been set many years ago, and although raised in 1974, inflation had already consumed the increase. Without exception, Vietnamese commanders would have preferred payment in kind—food for their troop—to that in inflated money. Monetary pay could have been used to provide the other necessities of life.

Congressional cuts in military aid also affected VNAF facilities. Nearly abandoned were: the great base at Cam Ranh Bay, the two Tuy Hoas, and Chu Lai—all now transitional airstrips. Hue Phu Bai and Ban Me Thuot were for light service only, with no aircraft permanently assigned. Living conditions at all the bases showed signs of lack of maintenance; repair materials were in short supply, and water systems at several of the bases were barely adequate. Air conditioning for facilities containing electronic gear were, too often, considered a creature comfort, with resulting high failure rates of electronic components and excessive down times. The overall result was that bases deteriorated at a more rapid rate than normal.

Part of this problem lay in the VNAF's Joint General Staff. As described earlier, there were no VNAF personnel at this level of command, making the body a misnomer from the outset. Priorities often favored the ARVN and, as a. consequence, all planning was directed towards the ground conflict. In Vietnam, a military unit's power was based on its current political significance. In its heyday,

Some days are worse than others. This F-5A of the 522nd Fighter Squadron at Bien Hoa was hit by a heat seeking missle, but did not receive a lethal hit, as was the norm. Strikes of this nature brought down many VNAF aircraft.

This was the workhorse of fixed-wing airlift throughout the Vietnamese War. These Douglas C-47s could carry heavy loads into and out of difficult airstrips. These colors and markings are typical of the C-47 fleet. The insignia of the 415th TS is seen on the nose in this picture, taken 14 December 1970 at Tan Son Nhut. *Courtesy of Norman E. Taylor.*

Utility type aircraft saw heavy usage throughout the war. The nose cowling of this Cessna U-17A was obviously replaced, as seen by the mismatch in the black anti-glare tail stripes and unusual markings The slot in the baggage door is for leaflet drops. Photographed at Tan Son Nhut 15 December 1970. *Courtesy of Norman E. Taylor.*

the VNAF was the power base for Marshal Ky. On one occasion, VNAF aircraft had attacked the Presidential Palace and prevented a coup by threatening to bomb a column of insurgent troops, who promptly returned to their base. The VNAF's actions did nothing to endear them to the Army, hence, they were one of the first on President Thieu's list as being politically reliable and aligned to Ky's cause. Consequently, in many ways, by design or otherwise, the VNAF's activities were limited.

The Commander of the VNAF at this time was Lt Gen Tran-van-Minh, who was appointed in 1967, and retained the position to the very end. He was a competent man, reportedly chosen for his reliability, and was well respected throughout the VNAF and the RVNAF. In Vietnamese practice, Marshal Ky could not regress to Commander of VNAF, having been Premier of his country. Instead, by the prerequisites that accompanied his former position, he resided at Tan Son Nhut, among friends still loyal to him that often sought his advice.

Changes in the way the VNAF was deployed occurred during this period. While VNAF had always been controlled by the Army, the situation became even more distinct. This had always been with regard to its organizational structure, but with the USAF presence in TACC [*see* Chapter 5], a major share of the daily sorties throughout the country had been allotted through TACC. With USAF influence gone, decentralized control became more evident. Even though the Corps were technically under the direction of the Joint General Staff, Corps commanders reported directly to the President and were responsive to the JGS only when they considered it desirable. Each individual Corps commander considered VNAF

The personality of this former U.S. Army Cessna O-1A is evident by the skin lines of worn paint. Note the twin-tube smoke rocket launcher under the wing. This Bird Dog of the 116th Observation Squadron was photographed at Binh Thuy in August 1967.

These Sikorsky H-34s were indispensable for vertical envelopment operations in the mid-1960s until replaced by the UH-1 Hueys. The Choctaw helicopters could carry from 12 to 18 troops. Photographed 21 March 1965, this H-34 belongs to the 217th Helicopter Squadron, which operated in IV Corps. *Courtesy of Ted Koppel.*

At Quang Ngai in the Autumn 1970, this Bell UH-1H patiently waits for its next mission. On the nose is the insignia of the 213th Helicopter Squadron. *Courtesy of George Pfromm.*

Random dive headings were used. After pull off climbing turns were made, and the aircraft spent a minimum of time under 5,000 feet with constant jinking. Ordnance was principally slick bombs: Mk-81, -82, and M-117. CBU-24 and 2.75 HVARs were also used. For a while in 1972, the deadly CBU-55s were used by A-37s (as well as A-1s) while the supply lasted. Usually four pylons were devoted to carrying ordnance and two pylons for fuel tanks.

The F-5s consistently bombed fast, high, and often from level flight; aided by an unsophisticated bomb/gun sight. This combination gave them a poor reputation among ground commanders for ineffective bombing on pin-point targets.

For most of these air strike missions, the previous method of USAF and VNAF FACs in the O-1 Bird Dog directing attacks was still recognized as the best. For deeper strikes, however, the flight leader of the fighters was responsible for complete operational control of the attack. The O-1s were also used extensively for visual reconnaissance, but often had to fly too high to be very effective. Cessna O-2As were used in the mountainous regions of I and II units as being his own and not to be used by other Corps commanders. This detrimental arrangement, contrary to USAF doctrine learned through hard experience, prevailed throughout the war, even during the final offensive of 1975. In this aspect, the VNAF could almost be defined as the Vietnamese Army Air Corps.

There was also another effect of corps area control. Because of the cutback in military aid, POL and ammunition were high among the critical elements. Since their management was an Army function, it was the Corps commander who determined how they should be allocated to his units. Each commander had a different method, being independent of the adjacent Corps area. This had a marked effect upon air transport schedules, and often aircraft parts were not received because of loading priorities.

Throughout its life history the VNAF was predominantly a ground support force, dictated by the prevailing tactical situation. There was no question of the VNAF undertaking air combat duties because, until now, the problem had never arisen. There was little effort directed toward cutting enemy supply lines, probably because the U.S.-taught method and uncertain success were both considered to be an unprofitable utilization of expensive ordnance. Strategic bombing was out of the question.

To cope with more sophisticated enemy AAA and the SA-7 missiles, the VNAF did not have the essential ECM or RHAW capability. However, the U.S. Government had already decided against this; though a policy reversal was not necessary, the financial, retrofit, logistic, and training aspects made ECM capability for the VNAF impractical.

Yet, the VNAF continued with air-to-ground support; A-37 Dragonflys being the favorite, having a good weight-to-thrust ratio and short turning radius to work steeply and close in without spending much time at the lower altitudes where light AAA was a problem. Tactics emphasized the effect of surprise and were designed to avert the attention of the gunners on the ground. Strike formations usually had four or more aircraft when simultaneous strikes were possible against nearby targets. The approach to the target initiated with a dive from a relatively high altitude, 10,000 feet and above.

A Bell UH-1D/H of the "Rampant Elephant" squadron is in readiness at Nha Trang. This was the home of the 215th Helicopter Squadron when equipped with UH-1s to replace H-34s. *Courtesy of Donald Mohr.*

Corps after the beginning of 1973. However, the VNAF did not feel that their advantages were worth the increased upkeep, so when support cutbacks occurred, the O-2s were grounded.

For night and bad weather, the A-37s were often used with the AN/TPB-1 BOBS (Beacon-Only Bombing System), a ground based radar bombing system. The A-1s, also beacon equipped, could fly BOBS by day, but were unable to get above the heavy flak (larger than 37 mm). F-5Es were BOBS beacon-equipped but, being dedicated to air defense, they seldom exercised that capability. The earlier F-5As were not 0beacon equipped.

The remaining ground attack aircraft for VNAF were the gunships. These were the AC-47 Spookys—now called "Hoa Long"—of the 817th Attack Squadron at Nha Trang, and the AC-119G and K models of the 819th and 821st Attack Squadrons, respectively, both stationed at Tan Son Nhut. The 821st positioned a detachment of about eight Stinger gunships at Da Nang for base defense. The AC-47s and AC-119Gs, being equipped with 7.63 mm miniguns only, were under-gunned for most engagements with the NVA. The AC-119K Stinger, having the 20 mm M-61, was still able to hold its own, though was often used above its effective altitude. Gunships doubled as flare ships, and were kept on ground alert in case of attack at one of the remote outposts. However, as a rule, the VNAF normally did not conduct visual night attacks with fighters under flares, as was often done by the USAF.

The Vietnamese viewed air defense within their own forces as an appurtenance of a modern sovereign state, but without any true tactical use. Its was dropped as a priority following financial budget restraints. As a result, air defense training was almost halted.

Air defense was controlled by the same organization that controlled tactical air. The airspace to be defended was divided into two sectors: the north being monitored by *Panama* at Da Nang, and *Peacock* at Pleiku; the southern being monitored by *Pyramid* at Ban Me Thuot, *Paris* at Saigon, and *Paddy* at Binh Thuy. The air battle would normally be controlled from the TACC at Tan Son Nhut, but could also be done independently by northern and southern sectors.

Within the limitation of resources, the mechanics of VNAF air defense were considered to be fairly workable. Both the F-5As and A-37s stood air defense alert, and F-5Es were just beginning to come into operational duty when the drastic cutbacks came. In comparison with expected intruders at the time, the F-5E was superior to the MiG-17 and competitive with both the MiG-19 and -21 in air-to-air combat. The A-37 would be used against enemy aircraft under 10,000 feet and 200 knots. They performed most of the live intercepts against various unidentified aircraft that flew without proper clearance, usually prop-driven transports and helicopters. On average, one live intercept was made every month or so on unidentifiable targets. However, there was never an actual engagement with enemy aircraft.

The Joint General Staff appreciated the value of air transport. Over the years they had often seen how troops could be deployed and redeployed, changing a losing ground situation to a winning one. In fact, air transport was used as their substitute for a strategic reserve of forces. The VNAF transport fleet consisted of C-130s, C-119s, C-47s, C-7s, CH-47s, and UH-1s.

The C-130s of the 435th and 437th Transport Squadrons at Tan Son Nhut were the backbone of the fleet and very professionally run. Although the VNAF was only able to keep about 13 or 14 at best of their 25 available aircraft in commission, they maintained the lowest accident rate by aircraft type. The C-119s were to be used for coastal patrol by what was to be the 720th Reconnaissance Squadron, but required modification with suitable radar. Expense precluded this, so the VNAF used them to supplement the C-130s. The few remaining C-47 transports were now used principally to carry VIP parties throughout the country. The C-7As proved almost impossible to maintain. They suffered from engine problems, lack of spare parts, corrosion, and some structural cracks. Owing to budget cuts, most were kept inactive and stored at Pleiku, Da Nang, and Tan Son Nhut, about 20 percent being kept for training and short missions.

The U.S. Army transferred 700 UH-1 Huey helicopters to the VNAF. These proved very difficult to maintain, with only 300-350

A number of Douglas C-47s of the 415th Transport Squadron remained without camouflage throughout the war. These were mostly passenger carrying configurations, and used in the true sense as passenger transports. This unit of the 33rd Tactical Wing was stationed at Tan Son Nhut.

The insignia of the 524th Fighter Squadron adorns the tail of this A-37 Dragonfly. Tail codes were not used on these aircraft, instead using distinctive colors and designs for recognition. *Courtesy of Ralph B Young.*

in commission during 1974. The Huey was much respected by ground commanders—however, by 1974 it was used principally for movement of supplies to remote outposts. The four squadrons of more complex CH-47s proved far more difficult to maintain than the UH-1s.

Combat movement of troops by helicopters was limited by the infrequent insertion and extraction of Long Range Patrols into enemy territory. By now, patrols were being made to walk to their objective, and supply cache systems were being emplaced to sustain longer period of operations in enemy territory. Gone were the ever-present large-scale heliborne operations of earlier years, although a nominal capability remained. One reason for this was the density of enemy defenses, low serviceability rate, and the helicopter's relatively short range, slow speed, and limited payload. Given the number of UH-1s and the types of missions they performed, they sustained more battle damage than any other type of VNAF aircraft.

During late 1974 the last of the VNAF's helicopter squadrons was formed, the 259th. This was strictly a medevac unit, which relieved the other helicopter squadrons of this specialized and hazardous, but essential duty. Its mission was as important to the ARVN ground soldier as search and rescue was to a downed airman. The 259th was divided into eight detachments, each with eight to 12 Hueys, which were then assigned at major air bases throughout South Vietnam.

Because of operational cutbacks and maintenance problems, the VNAF placed into flyable storage all their A-1, T-37, T-41, U-6, C-7, and O-2 aircraft. As a result, up to 10 of the VNAF's 66 flying squadrons were grounded by June 1974 through lack of logistic support. For the first time, the VNAF had a surplus of pilots. Squadrons without aircraft for the most part remained manned, assigning base duties to their personnel while awaiting reassignment to other units. Those with grounded aircraft maintained, at least, a cadre to keep them in flyable condition by doing preflights and turning the tires. Morale hit bottom in the grounded units. The only consolation was, however, that the operational readiness rate for these units increased, whereby the VNAF's capability was increased.

All flight training was brought to a halt, even though the VNAF had the capability to fully train its pilots. Following the Vietnamization program, and before this curtailment, undergraduate pilot training (UPT) began in the T-41 at Nha Trang, followed by 180 hours in the T-37 "Tweety Bird" at Phan Rang. When these aircraft were grounded for economic reasons, UPT reverted to the U-17, followed by the A-37, until the entire training program was stopped in August/ September 1974.

The Struggle to Survive

South Vietnam military leaders met with President Thieu at Da Nang in late 1974 to review the military situation and discuss future strategy. As a result, it was decided that withdrawal from the Central Highlands would be necessary. The defense line needed to be shortened to concentrate forces in the face of an increasing threat. In addition, military aid from the U.S. was uncertain, and under strenuous attack in the Congress; at best, only a fraction of the required aid could be expected. Strict conservation of supplies, ammunition, equipment, and especially fuel, was implemented.

Neither Lt Gen Tran-van-Minh, the VNAF commander, nor any of his field commanders were involved in the consultations. One consequence of being inadequately informed was when the commander of the 6th Air Division at Pleiku, Brig Gen Pham-ngoc-Sang, was given only 48 hours' notice to evacuate his aircraft and personnel from the base and city, this decision having been made by the JGS three months before! There was scant close air support during the withdrawal, because VNAF airmen became involved in evacuation operations and in arranging for their families to reach safety. Although air support was available from adjacent Corps areas, the military structure that existed left each Corps commander to draw upon his own resources. Another decision of the Da Nang meeting necessitated a reduction of just over one-half of the VNAF's planned flying hours to conserve fuel.

Included in these discussions was the concern that the RVNAF losses, including those of VNAF and the Navy, were not replaced, as was the U.S. commitment to do so on a one-for-one basis. Although surpluses existed in some categories on the cease-fire date, and all lost equipment did not require replacement, the almost complete lack of high-frequency replacement parts hindered tactical operations, particularly those of the VNAF. Specifically, VNAF pilots were taking such extreme measures to conserve their aircraft that bombing and strafing missions were ineffective. The VNAF lost 260 aircraft from the cease-fire date to September 1974 (including 66 transferred back to the USAF), and had received only eight O-1s as replacements. Saigon looked to Washington to replace these aircraft, as well as its dwindling stocks of spare parts, aviation fuel, and ammunition under the terms of the cease-fire, but no replacements came.

VNAF AIRCRAFT STATUS AT 30 SEPTEMBER 1974
(Source: Report of Defense Attache Office, Saigon, Jul-Sep 74)
Author's note: Presumably this status pertains only to those actions that relate to the Enhance and Enhance Plus aircraft.

This is a familiar view to members of the 524th Fighter Squadron at Nha Trang. Pilots are about to start engines with these Douglas A-1s, an "H" in the foreground and an "E" beyond. Picture taken in 1966. *Courtesy of Robert Lutes.*

AIRCRAFT TYPE	AUTHORIZED	RECEIVED BY 28 JAN 73	POSSESSED	ATTRITED	OTHER LOSSES
A-1	72	79	69	10	7
A-37	240	248	229	19	8
C/AC 119G/K	36	66	56	2	9*
C-130	32	32	32		
O-1	165	239	188	16	48**
O-2	35	35	32	3	1
T-37	21	24	24		
U-6	8	10	9	1	
U-17	58	85	84	1	1
C-123		19			19***
C-7	48	56	54	2	1
T-41	18	24	24		2
CH-47	64	70	65	5	1
UH-1	842	859	790	69	32
F-5A/B/E/RF	154	151	131	20	6
C-47 All	66	76	66	6	6#

Legend: * Eight aircraft transferred from VNAF to USAF.
** Thirty-five aircraft transferred from VNAF to USAF.
*** Nineteen aircraft transferred from VNAF to USAF.
# Four aircraft transferred from VNAF to USAF.

As North Vietnam deployed ground air defense forces into South Vietnam, the VNAF became less capable of striking. By March 1975 the North Vietnamese had SA-2 coverage as far south as Quang Tri. Khe Sanh, a major supply and staging area, was protected by SA-2s. All of the border area around Kontum, Pleiku, and the "Parrot's Beak" in III Corps was protected by radar-directed AAA and SA-7s. The VNAF lost 28 aircraft to SAMs while flying within their own country from 28 January 1973 to 31 December 1974.

As a result of these heavy losses, it was decided to limit the VNAF flights above Hue, west of Highway One, which paralleled the coast a few miles inland. This area was the most heavily defended by the North Vietnamese. It was not known if the VNAF was restricted from this area because of its losses, or in view of the fact that the area was now held by the North Vietnamese and, in conducting an attack, they would effectively be attacking North Vietnam, which would result in retaliatory action. The effect of this policy, however, neutralized the effectiveness of the VNAF against hard targets, such as troops, tanks, artillery, vehicles, and supplies.

To counter the sophisticated antiaircraft systems ECM equipment was essential. The VNAF did not have this equipment, and could not function effectively in such defended areas. The enemy had, in essence, a secure position from which to stage, prepare, and launch forces in all of the four military regions. Even if the VNAF had ECM, it is debatable whether it could have sustained operations in these high threat areas with such low performing aircraft.

Air superiority has always been a dominant force in any war. The North Vietnamese Air Force had never wanted to achieve air superiority during the conflict. Nevertheless, North Vietnam's ground-based antiaircraft weaponry denied South Vietnam air superiority. As a result, the VNAF was not able to sustain attacks on enemy concentrations prior to North Vietnam's final drive across all of South Vietnam.

One of the major lessons learned from the 1968 and 1972 offensives was that troops should be airlifted to those areas under heaviest attack. The timely movement of troops and support provided a flexibility to ground force commanders that was otherwise denied them. In both offensives supply lines were cut, and supply by air was the only way of supporting many of the isolated forces. Without air support, these forces would have been overrun through lack of reinforcements, ammunition, and food. On the eve of the 1975 Offensive, which brought the final blow to the forces of South Vietnam, only a fraction of the former airlift force remained—only nine C-130s being available on any given day. This was due to fuel leaks and structural problems common to the C-130A, even prior to their transfer to the VNAF. Because of limited tactical flexibility, increased intelligence and thorough planning became fundamental to RVNAF success. However, neither had been achieved by the eve of the final offensive.

The VNAF lost four of its RF-5s prior to the final offensive. SAM defenses precluded the use of these aircraft over significant target areas in much of the country. Furthermore, the camera installation was not capable of providing the details required for air-ground operations. The nose of the RF-5 was designed around cameras too small to be effective at the speeds and altitudes required. Further, the aircraft was too technical for such a small air force. Also, the VNAF's reconnaissance cycle was too slow, and processing equipment not of the latest type. The lumbering EC/RC-47 Gooney Birds suffered from the opposite malady: they took beautiful pictures, but could not survive over target areas because of AAA and SAMs. The consequence of these restrictions was that timely

By December 1970, when this picture was taken of this Douglas A-1H, many she ters of this type had been built as a result of frequent rocket and mortar attacks against airfields. These Skyraiders of the 518th Fighter Squadron were normally located at nearby Bien Hoa. *Courtesy of Norman E. Taylor.*

and vital intelligence information regarding the disposition and location of North Vietnamese forces was not always available. The reconnaissance force was not designed to function in the hostile environment that developed in South Vietnam. Some VNAF reconnaissance was done with hand-held Leica cameras from observation O-1 Bird Dogs flying at about 10,000-12,000 feet.

It was estimated that the VNAF had approximately 390 fighters, a mixture of A-37s and F-5s, of which 90 percent were reported operational in January 1975. Based upon USAF experience with A-37s in Vietnam, an acceptable lower level of 70 percent would give a force of 273 aircraft available with which VNAF should still have been able to generate a sortie rate of at least two sorties per day, per aircraft.

The explanation was simple: the VNAF had the aircraft, but not the fuel. It was estimated that the VNAF had only been allocated half its requirement from South Vietnam's reduced supplies. As a result, the December rate was less than half a sortie per aircraft. The overall total of 4346 sorties reflects the severity of the North Vietnamese threat. During the 1972 Spring Offensive, the fighter force averaged about 504 sorties per day without maximum effort.

Helicopters were less effective when compared to the 1972 Offensive. With the build-up of SA-7s and AAA, helicopters could not operate in the areas where North Vietnamese troops were deployed. Helicopter assaults for restoring lost positions in an SA-7 and concentrated AAA environment were not feasible. As a consequence, much of the mobility that the U.S. Army had provided by helicopters in the 1968 period was reduced in the 1972 Offensive. Yet 24 squadrons of the VNAF were equipped with helicopters. At the time of the cease-fire the VNAF had 929 and, by the end of December, they had lost 154. Also in that two-year period, nearly 300 fixed-wing aircraft were lost, both totals accounting for nearly a fifth of the VNAF's inventory. The changing character of the air environment from passive to hostile neutralized the development of helicopters, except when circumstances dictated; as seen in the 1972 Easter Offensive and the Israeli War of October 1973.

VNAF LOSSES TO ENEMY GUNNERS, JAN 73 - JUN 74
(Source: Report of Defense Attache Office, Saigon, Apr-Jun 74)

Aircraft Type	*Weapon*	*System*
	AAA	SA-7
AC-47	1	-
RC-47	1	-
C-47	-	-
AC-119K	-	1
A-1	0	5
A-37	3	5
F-5	7	1
O-1	7	0
O-2	1	-
UH-1	46	3
CH-47	1	2
Total	67	17

During the 18 month period shown above 84 VNAF aircraft were shot down. According to the DAO report, the enemy's record was considered somewhat poor, given the number of VNAF air operations and the number of shoot-down attempts. While U.S. involvement was relatively small, three U.S. aircraft and one civil aircraft had been shot down, along with one manned and two unmanned U.S. fighters, and two civil aircraft that had been hit. Up to this point, the enemy had not employed radar-controlled or heavy AAA against the VNAF. On the other hand, they had prohibited VNAF operations over major enemy complexes and forced the VNAF to higher altitudes, limiting the effectiveness of its air strikes, logistical resupply, and reconnaissance flights.

One of the most detailed and timely sources of information for the targeting of tactical air strikes was provided by the Forward Air Controller in the O-1 Bird Dog. When U.S. forces were deployed in South Vietnam, FACs literally covered the entire country, with relative immunity to ground fire, at a very low altitude, where the ground action could be seen. By the time of the 1972 Offensive, FACs were being forced out of critical areas by defenses. With the onset of the 1975 Offensive the air situation was such that FACs were not able to operate where there were North Vietnamese troops

As VNAF continued to expand in size with many squadrons added, unit insignia standardized in design according to type of squadron. This insignia on an A-37 is that of fighter squadrons, with their only difference being in their identifying squadron number. This A-37 photographed in May 1975 had escaped to Thailand. *Courtesy of Stephan W. Daniels.*

in contact. On the eve of the Offensive the FAC was not up to the task. It would have been necessary to use FACs in F-4 Phantom IIs to bring targets under attack in the high threat areas, as was done in the 1972 offensive and in North Vietnam.

Some sorties, flown by the three squadrons of A-37s at Binh Thuy, were above 10,000 feet, in support of ground operations in III Corps. These were mostly ineffective, and brought considerable criticism of the VNAF from both U.S. and ARVN forces. The VNAF conducted a large number of these strikes under radar control, since they did not feel they could withstand the losses to SA-7s. In I, II, and IV Corps, strikes were conducted at operational altitudes under 10,000 feet, except when weather was bad, in which case ground radar was used. The possible consequence of VNAF losses seemed justified when it came to the need for close air support for troops in contact, and therefore the altitude restriction was lifted for the Binh Thuy squadrons.

The exchange of intelligence between the VNAF and the Joint General Staff was not satisfactory, nor had it been for many years. This was a hangover from the earlier days when the higher ranking officers for the VNAF were taken from the ARVN staff and ground operations were given priority. Therefore, VNAF intelligence requirements were considered satisfied if the information was in the

Tan Son Nhut Air Base as photographed by an RB-57E in May 1968. View faces east, with the city of Saigon in the background. *Courtesy of Gerry Reponen.*

hands of the Corps commanders. Since these ground commanders had such absolute control, and since VNAF units did not operate independently of the Corps areas, there was no need for the VNAF to have the same relationship with the upper echelon of the Joint General Staff. Air operations suffered because of this inadequate intelligence relationship. The full range of VNAF capability became arbitrarily restricted to the span of concern of the Corps commander.

On the eve of the 1975 Offensive, command and control was totally inadequate to cope with the threat. If versatility was ever needed, it was at this time in order to move the other flexible firepower available—airpower—from area to area rapidly, to counter the local superiority of the enemy. Centralized air control, the most fundamental principle of decisive air operations, was totally absent, whereas, during the 1968 Tet Offensive, the VNAF missions were directed from the Tactical Air Control Center at Tan Son Nhut in conjunction with U.S. units. VNAF Headquarters had no identifiable authority for the employment of their total air resources. The VNAF was divided up into small packets, as had been done in the early days of World War II by the air forces, and as a consequence was improperly employed by Corps commanders, whose vision was limited to the situation in their Corps area.

9

The Final Days

Following the cease-fire in January 1973, the North Vietnamese Army was uninhibited in strength build-up. American airpower no longer attacked the lines of supply to the south. By late 1974 a total of 19 North Vietnamese Army divisions were fully manned and equipped, and 12 of them were actually in South Vietnam. A total of 5 ARVN divisions, including Marine and Airborne, were concentrated in the northern Corps area to face the strongest line of the enemy, leaving the rest of the country sparsely defended and the central provinces vulnerable to attack.

To the Vietnamese people the inevitable was approaching. It was only a matter of time before the North Vietnamese controlled all of South Vietnam. To some strategists, it appeared that this would be in 1976. Throughout it all, there was still hope for the safety of their country, for a number of options remained open. The Vietnamese Air Force was still very much in evidence and, although very much restricted in its former ways of fighting, it was carrying the war to the enemy.

While the VNAF's fighter aircraft were supporting the ground situation, transports continued with the resupply of bases and outposts to the best of their ability with their limited numbers. They too were threatened by the intense antiaircraft brought into South Vietnam by the NVA. Since the only means of resupply was usually by air, new tactics for high altitude drops were developed.

The Joint General Staff depended upon the C-130A of the VNAF as their major airlift support aircraft. In the final days they were crucial; some carried as many as 350 refugees, while 200 was considered the maximum allowable. The VNAF had two squadrons of C-130s, but only five to nine were normally in commission per squadron. *RG 342-102960 USAF*

This Lockheed C-130A, 60-482, waits to be loaded with cargo for a drop-mission of supplies for the Tong Le Chan ARVN camp near the Cambodian border. The JGS depended heavily on this air transport capability during critical ground operations. *Courtesy of Pham Quang Khiem.*

The Versatile Herky

It was becoming more and more difficult to air-drop supplies to ARVN outposts in areas in which the North Vietnamese were present. The accuracy of the AAA and SA-7 were taking a heavy toll of combat air support cargo drops in many areas. The only recourse was to fly higher, out of range, but in so doing, accuracy of the air drops was sacrificed.

A solution to this situation was a plan to make the drop from 9,000 to 10,000 ft (2743 to 3048 m) with a delayed opening parachute that would deploy at 2000 ft (610 m). This would provide minimum time for the cargo to be in the air and to be affected by the wind. It was critical that all cargo dropped by air must land in a confined area so that it could be safely recovered. Before chancing drops of critical supplies the system had to be tested by the VNAF crews first. Recognizing that anything dropped during these tests could fall into enemy hands, something that would not be of value had to be used for the simulated cargo load. The object selected was ice. This could be used to represent the weight and ballistic effect of a cargo package and was totally expendable. Should the enemy recover the parachute, they would be baffled as to what the parachute carried to the ground in the first place once the trace of ice had melted.

Lockheed C-130As of the 435th and 437th were used for these air drops. Not many of these airplanes were available for missions, since about four or five of these Hercules were all that each of the two squadrons could have in commission at one time. Leaving Tan Son Nhut, the airplanes would climb to altitude while en route to their drop zone. Nearing the drop area, ground radar would give the pilot headings to fly, which would also be corrected for wind so that the airplane would track directly across the drop area. Having been given the true air speed of the aircraft by the pilot, the radar controller would compute the trajectory and give the count down as to when the load should leave the open rear door. On command, the load was quickly pulled out by deploying a drogue chute. Repeated passes would then be made, or the aircraft would proceed on to another outpost needing to be resupplied, as part of the preplanned mission. Multiple drops were possible because of the sizable load that the Hercules could carry. Since these drops were fully radar-controlled, dropping through cloud layers on totally obscured drop zones (DZ) presented no problems.

In some situations, it was not uncommon that the two opposing forces at these outposts would work out an arrangement whereby the enemy would not shoot at the ARVN when they recovered their supplies from the DZ, as long as the ARVN did not fire in return when the enemy retrieved the supplies that dropped outside the DZ.

The C-130s, and all VNAF aircraft, became targets for the enemy's heat seeking SA-7 when flying below 10,000 ft (3048 m). To confirm a firing, an aircrew might catch sight of the starting flash, the smoke from the engine, and its telltale vapor trail. Time would run out fast, and evasive action had to be taken immediately. In the case of the C-130s, high energy flares were carried in a specially attached box under the tail. Each crew member's station had what they called a "panic-button" that, when pushed, would discharge one of these flares. When a flare was dropped, while a rocket was tracking the airplane the rocket's path was often diverted to the greater heat source of the flare, and would thus burst a harmless distance from the airplane. Consequently, the first person on board, sighting the telltale trail of a missile, would eject a flare, and at the same time the pilot would bank sharply to break the track of the rocket.

With neither the B-52 Superfortresses nor the heavy fighter bombers of the U.S. forces participating in the conflict against the North Vietnamese, all that remained to carry the war to the enemy were the lightweight A-37s and F-5s of the VNAF. In their low-level attacks in any area in which the North Vietnamese were in force, they were very vulnerable to the intensive antiaircraft weapons the enemy had in place. What then could be substituted for the high-flying, area coverage bombing of the B-52?

Below and following: On the last day of the war, April 30, 1975, a "borrowed" Cessna O-1 from the 124th Observation Squadron, which departed from TSN, appeared over the aircraft carrier *USS Midway*. On a third try by the pilot, a note written on an airways chart of South Vietnam was dropped from the plane and successfully recovered. It read "Can you move these helicopter to the other side, I can land on your runway, I can fly 1 hour more, we have enough time to move. Please rescue me. Major Ly-Bung, Wife and 5 child." Flight deck crews of the *Midway* moved the helicopters aside, and the Major from the 114th at Nha Trang, now abandoned, landed the two-seat O-1 on the carrier, sans tail hook, with room to spare. The Navy crew on the deck erupted with applause. The Major's family was safe, and the VNAF had its first carrier pilot. This O-1 is in the Naval Aviation Museum, Pensacola, Florida. *U.S. Navy.*

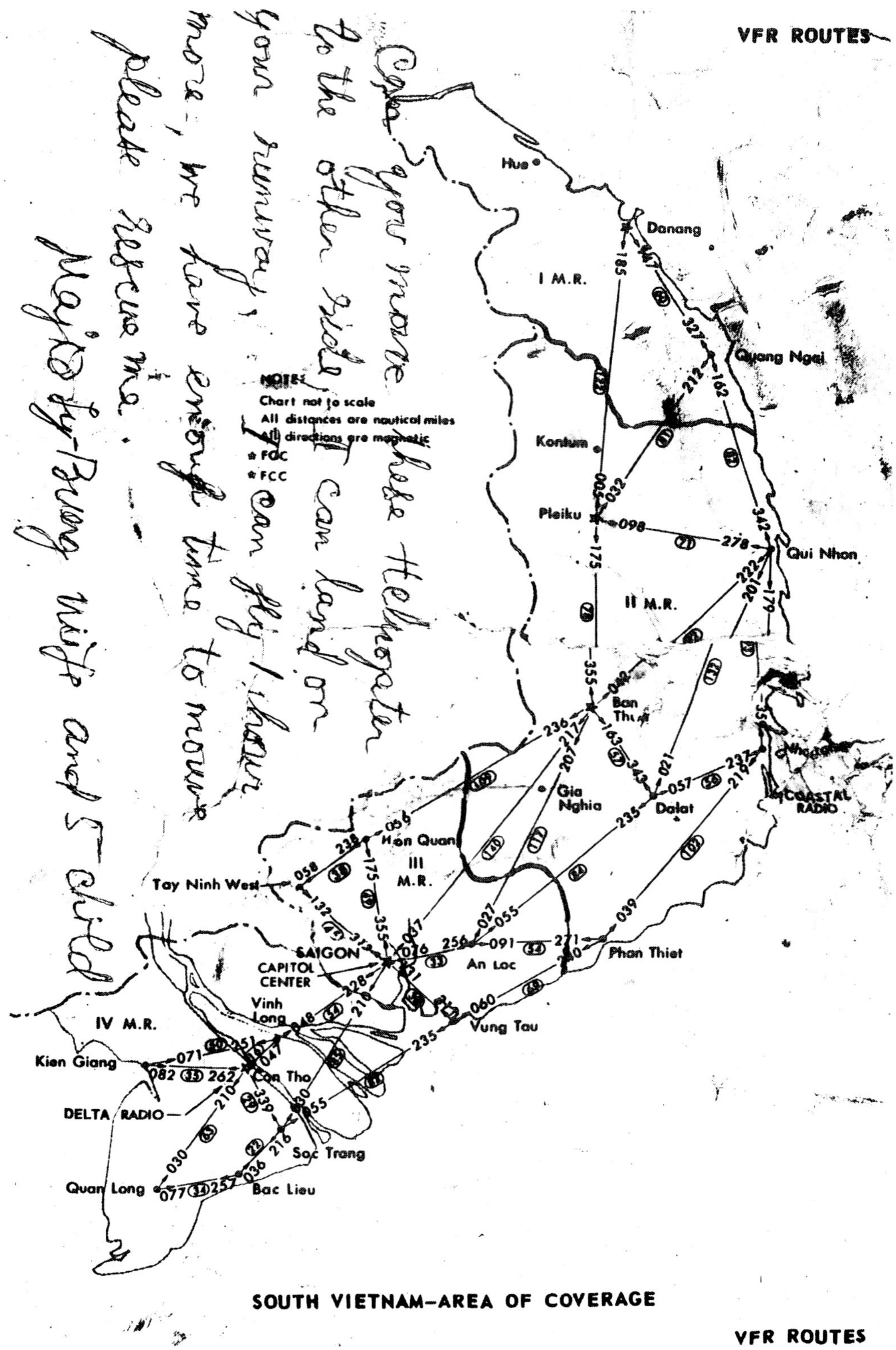

Since the high level resupply drops with C-130s were very effective, why not deliver fire bombs in the same manner? An adaptation of this aerial resupply technique was called BANISH BEACH, which involved a ground radar-controlled, airborne extraction of parachute-retarded pallets of 55 gallon oil drums, filled with napalm or even waste oil and gasoline. The drums burst on impact and the mixture was ignited over an area about 1300 ft (396 m) long by 700 ft (213 m) wide for a typical drop. Later drogue chutes were not needed; they were simply rolled out the rear door of the Herky.

In November 1974 a tremendous explosion that could be heard for miles occurred above an enemy supply concentration. This led the North Vietnamese to believe that American B-52s were back in the combat area; it made newspaper coverage to that effect. The blast area alone covered a circle 150 meters in diameter, leveling trees like toothpicks, and leaving nothing but bare ground. In fact, the blast was caused by a VNAF C-130 modified for the task, carrying a 15,000 lb (6804 kg) general purpose bomb called DAISY CUTTER, left over from the B-36 days, which were rolled out of the tail gate as the ground radar controller gave the familiar "ready, ready, now" command over this target. The Hercules had turned "bomber" once again, causing quite a "bang." The Vietnamese had been provided with 17 of these bombs by the Americans, and all but two were dropped.

It was not just these blockbusters that were used. The 250 lb (113 kg) bombs were easier to handle in getting them rolled out the door at the precise moment. For drops with these bombs, 16 to 24 were carried—a sizable load for any bomber, short of the B-52. The Herky was a valuable asset to the VNAF, despite their small number of serviceable aircraft.

The Tidal Wave

By December 1974 and January 1975 the ground situation had deteriorated drastically. The enemy had stored enough supplies within South Vietnam itself to support an all out offensive. Since freedom of the air no longer belonged to the VNAF in the northern part of I

Corps, action there was relatively light, allowing free reign by communist troops. The railroad between Da Nang and Hue had been cut. The airfield at Hue Phu Bai had been closed because of heavy shelling. In II Corps heavy rains had reduced fighting on both sides. The enemy had an estimated three divisions in the area and more than 360 antiaircraft guns. Since weather was limiting air action, most of the sorties were flown at altitude by A-37s under the drop control of ground radar. A helicopter operation was attempted against Trung Nghia, west of Kontum City, but enemy ground fire forced it to be withdrawn. The VNAF's A-37s supported the operation, but enemy ground fire was too heavy for them also.

Similar situations prevailed in III and IV Corps. Air activity was highly restrictive, and the enemy continued to pour in supplies to sustain an all-out offensive. Supply lines were unhindered across the adjacent borders outside South Vietnam, from IV Corps in the south, all the way to Hanoi in the north. The threat of U.S. resumption of bombing was almost non-existent as a result of the Cooper-Church Amendment. The loss of peripheral areas, particularly Phuoc Long Province, just north of Saigon, had a major psychological effect on the outlook of South Vietnam's political and military leaders.

The country could not be more vulnerable to attack. The plan of the NVA was to cut the country in half at its midpoint. In early March 1975 the inevitable attack was launched, first by cutting the main highway connecting Qui Nhon on the coast with Pleiku in the western highlands. This set up the capture of the important centrally located city of Ban Me Thuot, the capital of Darlac Province. On the night of 9 March more than 4000 rounds hit the city in advance of the tank and infantry assault. By day break, more than one-half of the city was in enemy hands, and before the day was out both airfields were lost. The VNAF's 6th Air Division, principally the 532nd Fighter Squadron with A-37s, flew more than 200 sorties in support of the ARVN, but the North Vietnamese continued to advance. By the 14th, the entire city was in enemy hands, a devastating loss.

Faced with a grave situation, President Thieu made the decision to pull back immediately from Pleiku and Kontum. Convinced that his country was about to be split in half, with a substantial part of the Army cut off in the northern provinces, he ordered a radical redeployment. From this soldiers, their families, and civilians alike interpreted the move as a prelude to Communist occupation, and as a result, there began a process of rapid and uncontrollable disintegration throughout the Central Highlands. What was to have been an orderly withdrawal to reposition military forces turned into panic and filled the roads with refugees, blocking reinforcements from moving to the fighting area.

The only way to safety now for those left behind was by foot or any vehicle available. Because of the interdiction of Highway 19 by the NVA, the main route to Qui Nhon, the column of ARVN and refugees was shifted to an undeveloped road. The VNAF attempted to provide air support to this column from Phu Cat but to little avail. The North Vietnamese directed artillery against the refugees, irrespective of whether they were civilian or military. The VNAF made attempts to drop some supplies to those along the way, but there was no evidence to indicate that an air strike effort was made against the enemy artillery and ambush sites.

The fact that the Command and Reporting Post, code-named *Peacock*, had been partially destroyed, significantly reduced the control of any air operations in the Central Highlands. Lacking this control, there was never any indication that an emergency plan was put into operation to use airpower from other Corps areas to help stabilize the retreat. Once the retreat began, it was a rout all the way to the coast. Estimations are that only about 25 percent of those that began the trek reached the coast.

Left behind at Pleiku were 64 aircraft, 36 of these in flyable storage. No attempt had been made to fly these aircraft out because of time needed to put them in commission. They included a full squadron of A-1 Skyraiders, numerous C-7As, a few Cessna O-2s, and an assortment of other types.

U.S. Marines searched the Vietnamese as they arrived from helicopters on board the *USS Blue Ridge* amphibious command ship. Considering that some of the VC may have posed as VNAF crew members and gone unnoticed, all weapons were confiscated and thrown into the sea for security reasons. *RG 428-K108281 USN*

With the situation in the Pleiku area unraveling, an effort was to be made to hold the enemy at bay in I Corps to the north. A strategy for the defense of Da Nang and the air base there was developed as three North Vietnamese divisions were pressing forward and threatening the high ground west of Hue. In a few days' time at least 15 hamlets had been overrun. As the refugees and RF and PF troops began to move in opposite directions, the roads became clogged and panic again erupted.

On the night of 27 March Gen Vo-xuan-Lanh, Deputy Commander of VNAF, flew into Da Nang to assess the situation there. Seeing what was about to happen, he told Brig Gen Nguyen-duc-Khanh, the 1st Air Division Commander there, to get all of his flyable aircraft off the airfield. Ground attacks by the enemy were expected momentarily, and these aircraft were vital to the VNAF. Again, in order to retain VNAF ground support personnel their evacuation was essential. Beginning that night, eight C-130s began airlifting their people from Da Nang to Tan Son Nhut, Saigon. Copilot on one of these C-130s was Lt Pham-quang-Khiem, who tells this story.

"We were the first to land at Da Nang for this evacuation. This was about 8 o'clock at night," as best Khiem remembers. "As soon as we parked, there was a group of people that immediately assembled at the rear of our aircraft: Marines, Army, civilians, as well as members and families of VNAF. I could guess they numbered about 200. We had to off-load boxes containing helicopter rotor blades, but I assured the people that once these were taken off, we could take all of them to Saigon. I recall to this day how intent they all were to my every word. They remained calm and seemingly patient for the long wait for the K-loader vehicle to arrive to remove the cargo from inside our aircraft.

At about 10 o'clock the K-loader arrived and routinely removed the boxes. When the last container was removed, I never saw a wave of people move so quickly in all my life! In what was hardly more than a second it seemed, the airplane was totally filled—I mean totally. This was the load master's responsibility from here on, so I went into the cockpit through the side door with Capt Nguyen-van-Chuan, and we started the engines. As we taxied out, the load master called on the intercom to say that he could not close the ramp because of the people that were sitting and standing on it as part of the floor. I told him to go ahead and raise it with them on it. 'No way, Lieutenant—I only have one foot inside the cabin myself!'

I looked at Captain Chuan, waiting to hear his solution to the problem. Chuan was a quiet man—didn't say much, but I could tell he had a plan. He eased up on the brakes to allow the airplane to speed up a bit. Then suddenly, he applied the breaks very heavily. We rolled again, followed by almost a sudden stop, and a feeling that the weight in the cabin had shifted! 'The ramp is closed, sir, ready for takeoff back here,' were the reassuring words heard from the loadmaster over the intercom.

Now a helicopter was hovering in front of our nose, seemingly attempting to make us stop. We did not, for it became obvious that the pilot was wanting us to take his family, who were on the helicopter, along with us. We had no room.

No sooner had the helicopter moved away than a three tone camouflage truck pulled in front of us and abruptly stopped on the taxiway. The driver jumped out, and with great deliberation pointed a M-16 rifle at the cockpit, giving the appearance that he would fire at us without hesitation. He then motioned that he too wanted to ride with us. As if we had rehearsed it, both Chuan and I gave the thumbs-up ok signal to the man, and motioned for him to meet us at the end of the runway. He seemed satisfied, put his gun down, hastily got into the truck and sped away to the takeoff end of runway 18. We were free to taxi once again. But when we reached the takeoff end of the runway, we did not even hesitate to stop or get tower clearance for takeoff. Further threats by this crazed man were not needed, especially since we had no more room anyway. Chuan took to the runway, gave it the power, and we took off.

For those that made it to safety in those final hours, when the mass exodus began, they could not help but wonder what would be the next move, over which they had little control. These thoughts are expressed on the faces of these helicopter crew members and their families that made it to safety aboard the *USS Blue Ridge*. *RG 428- K108205 USN*

When we leveled at 21,000 feet (6,400 m) on our way to Saigon, I unstrapped and went to the cabin door. What I saw was unbelievable. The cabin was a compressed mass of humanity. Only those up front were seated; all others were standing, unable to sit, as tightly as the proverbial sardine—with no exaggeration. People were wedged along the sides, hanging like spiders from the overhead static lines, and even cramped in the tail cone of the aircraft with the flight control cables, where no one goes except for ground maintenance. I could not hold back the tears as I gazed at this deplorable situation that my own people were in. In the seat below me, I spotted an old man, heavily furrowed face, who surprisingly had a very happy expression. He was cuddling something in his lap that was wrapped in a towel. Puzzled, I finally got a glimpse of what it was that he was holding. The head of a sewing machine, probably his only worldly possession that remained as a future means to his livelihood.

As our passengers got off the airplane at Tan Son Nhut the load master made the usual count for the record. The best he could figure, there were about 350 people on board, and probably more that he missed counting. For the record, we entered the maximum allowable count; 200 passengers."

Da Nang Air Base came under continuous artillery fire the 28th and 29th. Most of the evacuation of some 130 aircraft were done under these adverse conditions. Approximately 180 aircraft, including 33 A-37s, were abandoned because of the intense artillery fire, confusion, and breakdown of airfield security. The base was under anyone's control.

The rapid disintegration of the situation in I Corps rendered useless any plans for the defense of the Da Nang area. The repositioning of troops from the Quang Tri area near the North Vietnamese border back to Da Nang caused fearful civilians to flee southward. As soldiers no longer with their units and civilians passed through Hue, the stream became a torrent of panic-stricken people, all seeking haven at Da Nang Air Base to the south.

The mass of refugees streaming into Da Nang made an effective defense of the area almost impossible. Aircraft that were still operational departed under shellfire. Left in revetment were two squadrons of C-7As wrapped in their storage paper, yet so vitally needed for this evacuation. One VNAF AC-119, on temporary duty at Da Nang from Tan Son Nhut, was piloted by Capt Vinh-Pho. Following his departure from Da Nang during this mass exodus, he reported that he had to taxi over about 100 dead bodies on the ramp to make it to the runway. There was no other way. People were climbing aboard anything with the hope of escape. Other pilots told of seeing a UH-1 helicopter on the maintenance ramp fully packed with people waiting for the flight crew, not realizing that the craft did not have rotor blades.

Perhaps it was too late in this deteriorating situation to have held Da Nang, but concentrated use of airpower against the exposed elements of the North Vietnamese forces may have made a fight for Da Nang rational. It would have brought a delaying action to allow the establishment of a new defense line further south. But the chaotic situation disrupted leadership, and hastily brought poor morale, poor discipline, and disintegration of unit integrity among all branches of military forces. This demoralization spread throughout the rest of South Vietnam and was a major factor in the near complete disintegration of the remaining forces.

With the fall of Da Nang, one coastal city after another fell in rapid order. Chu Lai was given up in disorder on 26 March. Some heroic fights were waged by small ARVN units resisting the NVA troops that were now pushing south on Highway One, or those coming out of the highlands. The NVA reserve divisions were not being moved south as rapidly as they could be deployed. When the offensive opened, the NVA had about 13 divisions in South Vietnam. By this time, it appeared that all of the NVA reserves would be committed to secure a military victory. More than 19 divisions were eventually deployed, numbering some 325,000 troops.

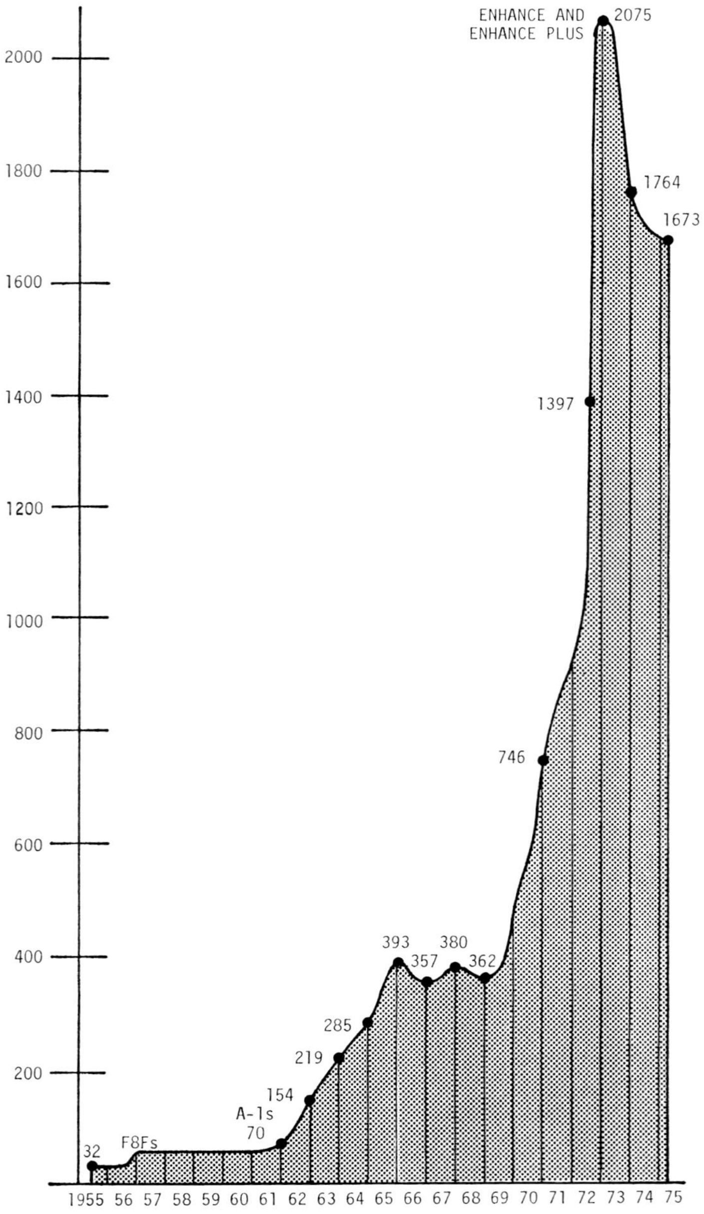

Number of VNAF aircraft by year.

The major coastal city of Qui Nhon fell on 31 March. In a desperate effort to stem the tide, A-37s based at Phu Cat and Phan Rang flew an all-out effort. These A-37s of the 82nd and 92nd Tactical Wings were credited for waging the best fight of the war. Pilots in some cases loaded their own aircraft. The VNAF troops fought as soldiers in defending the airfield at Phu Cat after the ARVN was moved off the base. Targets struck by these units were so close to the airfield that pilots hardly had time to get the gear up before dropping their bombs. As the area became untenable, the Dragonflys had to be evacuated to Bien Hoa and Phan Rang.

An attack of a very different nature took place on 8 April 1975. A VNAF A-37 made a surprise attack by bombing the Presidential Palace in Saigon. President Thieu, left unhurt, was the obvious target of the attack. A VC radio broadcast announced that the pilot, Nguyen-thanh-Trung, was a Communist agent, yet many believed that the attack was part of a coup effort by former Prime Minister Ky and VNAF officers, attempting to unseat Thieu. All those accused vehemently denied the charges, yet the incident increased Thieu's distrust for the Air Force, which he knew retained its loyalty to their former leader, Ky. It was this rivalry between these two powerful men that was primarily blamed for VNAF's inability to gain status within the Vietnamese Army-dominated military hierarchy.

As the war came to its final days, the lack of firm command and control of the VNAF forces became more critical. The VNAF did not have airborne command posts, as the USAF so effectively used in C-130s, in orbit over the combat area. Instead, the loss of VNAF's ground stations like the Combat Reporting Center (CRC) at Da Nang; *Panama*, the Combat Reporting Point (CRP) at Pleiku; *Peacock*, and one at Ban Me Thuot; *Pyramid*, rendered the Tactical Air Control System non-effective for all practical purposes. Only the CRC at Tan Son Nhut remained, but its function was not intended to exercise direct air control of strikes. There were only a few Forward Air Controllers left to conduct any type of coordinated strike, and most of the strikes were conducted without control, and only as the pilots felt it best to make their attacks.

The Wing Commander at Phan Rang, Col Le-van-Thao, fought on with forces under his command for two days after ARVN forces had left the area. Airborne troops were sent in to attempt to hold the airfield, but the defenders were finally overwhelmed on 16 April 1975, and Phan Rang was lost. The last of the 6th Air Division abandoned the airfield with the remaining flyable airplanes, leaving four AC-119s and two A-37s to the enemy.

With the loss of the two northern corps areas—literally half of the country—the Joint General Staff began the day-to-day allocation of sorties between the III and IV Corps Commanders. For the first time a few sorties (20) were reserved to the VNAF Tactical Air Command Center at Tan Son Nhut to be used against targets of its own choice. From about 1-19 April the VNAF averaged about 180 fighter sorties per day. These were allocated by JGS, which sent 100 to III Corps, 60 to IV Corps, and left the reserved 20 for the TACC. Almost all of these sorties were flown against defensive positions at Phan Rang, Phan Thiet, and Xuan Loc, the latter being a most strategic entry to the Saigon area. However, there is no evidence to indicate an attempt was made to interdict the enemy, which was then moving as rapidly as possible, bumper to bumper, down coastal Highway One toward Saigon. Tanks and artillery pieces were reported lined up for miles. Again, the pattern of employment of strike aircraft did not change through this final campaign. One of the main factors was the disruption of the intelligence network, coupled with the lack of serviceable reconnaissance aircraft with which to gather much of this intelligence information. Most of the control of air strikes had to be passed to the hands of ground commanders.

The last ditch effort in defense of Saigon was Xuan Loc, a provincial capital 38 miles northeast of Saigon on the main artery, Highway One. This was not the best position for defense, but South Vietnamese units held out for more than two weeks against superior North Vietnamese forces and a continuous barrage of mortar and artillery. South Vietnamese defenders at Xuan Loc seemed determined to demonstrate that they could fight, despite the poor performance of their comrades at Hue and Da Nang.

If Xuan Loc fell, Bien Hoa would be indefensible, along with its airfield, depot, and arsenal. Thus, VNAF flew more than 600 sorties in support of ARVN in this vital defense. As the enemy flanked Xuan Loc and came within artillery range of Bien Hoa, all operational aircraft were flown to Tan Son Nhut and Binh Thuy, further to the south. In spite of the heavy antiaircraft fire, the VNAF provided effective close air support.

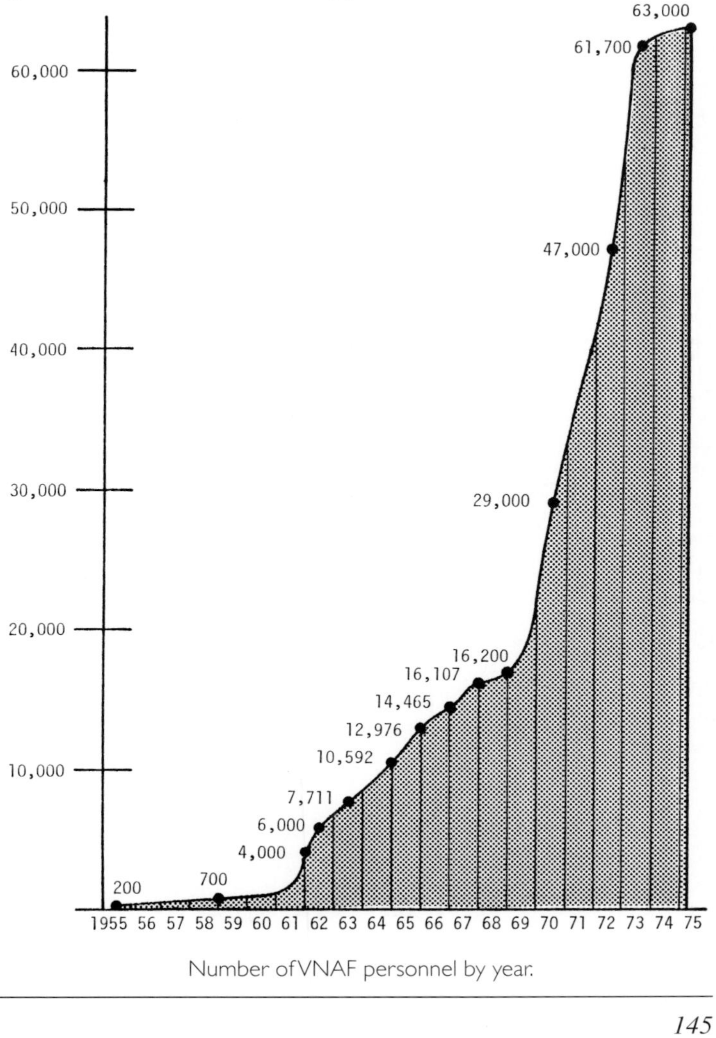

Number of VNAF personnel by year.

By 21 April Xuan Loc lay in ruins and had to be evacuated. President Thieu resigned that same day under heavy political pressure, handing control of the Government to Gen Duong-van-Minh ("Big Minh"), a moderate with whom it was hoped the North Vietnamese would negotiate a coalition government, but the enemy would not. The Communists had momentum and were winning, and it was they that did not need to compromise.

At the close of the Xuan Loc struggle, the VNAF had 1492 aircraft, of which 976 were operationally ready, 135 unserviceable, and 381 lost or abandoned. The fighter force consisted of 169 A-37s and 109 F-5s. Of this force 92 A-37s and 93 F-5s were operational. In spite of the evacuations, shellings, and aircraft out of commission for one reason or another, the VNAF still had an operationally ready fighter force of approximately 180 aircraft, as compared to 392 aircraft at the time of the cease-fire in January 1973.[21]

For all practical purposes, the battle was over with the loss of Xuan Loc, which fell on 22 April. Enemy forces moved toward Saigon, their final objective for so many years. They only slowed outside the city long enough to regroup for the final push. Before this took place a devastating incident occurred that shook VNAF morale and added a new perspective to the air war at the very end.

Early in the evening on the 28th, a flight of three A-37s piloted by VNAF pilots forced into enemy service bombed Tan Son Nhut Air Base. The attack began innocently enough when the tower called to this unidentified flight of Dragonflys east of the field who were beginning to enter an unusual landing pattern. "A-37s east of Tan Son Nhut, identify yourself," came from the tower operator. After a brief hesitation, "We are American built aircraft," came the reply, as the airplanes approached the field. There was no need for further transmissions, for by now they were releasing their bombs and strafing the flight line in a single pass before turning northward. Six 250 lb (113 kg) bombs exploded on the flight line, damaging three AC-119s and several C-47 transports. VNAF F-5s scrambled to intercept them, but the attackers escaped. The airfield remained operational, and the blow was more damaging psychologically than materially, although most Saigonese thought it was an attempted *coup d'etat* rather than an enemy action. It was the first time airpower had been used against the South, and it added further emphasis that the end was near.

North Vietnamese soldiers, tanks, and artillery tightened their stranglehold on Saigon in the last week of April. Shortly after midnight on 29 April, newly-emplaced North Vietnamese 130 mm guns opened up on Tan Son Nhut, destroying several aircraft. The air battle was nearly finished, except for the air crew of an AC-119 gunship that continued patrolling the airfield perimeter all through the night. It landed to rearm and refuel and took off again just before daybreak. Onlookers, anxious to be evacuated aboard any type of transportation, watched the loan gunship as it laid down a sheet of fire on the North Vietnamese troops advancing on the eastern end of the airfield. The episode ended violently at 7:00 AM when the gunship was hit by an SA-7 and plummeted to the ground in flames. A defending A-l Skyraider and its pilot met the same fate a few hours later.

Soon after dawn, the shelling and the practically uncontrollable crowds forced the closing of Tan Son Nhut Airport. Only helicopters were able to operate from obscure locations on the field and around Saigon itself.

On 30 April 1975 the NVA entered the city, forcing President Minh to surrender the city and the country unconditionally. South Vietnam ceased to exist. With its passing, so ended the South Vietnamese Air Force, a military arm having a gallant history that existed for 20 years minus three months—yet experienced not a moment of peace.

Epilogue

During the closing 18 hours of the war, a fleet of 71 helicopters—comprising USMC/USAF H-53s and H-46s—shuttled to and from U.S. ships lying offshore. This was Operation Frequent Wind, the largest evacuation by helicopter ever mounted. They evacuated a total of 5595 South Vietnamese, 1373 Americans, and 85 foreign nationals, as well as 989 members of the U.S. Marine Corps who were sent to oversee the operation.

Before the Communists took complete control, large numbers of former South Vietnamese Air Force personnel flew themselves and their families to U.S. bases in Thailand, or used helicopters to reach U.S. aircraft carriers off the coast. The scene at Tan Son Nhut was grim, as soldiers and refugees fought to board South Vietnamese aircraft. In the confusion, many fell or were pushed off the loading ramps as the aircraft taxied out to takeoff.

As the aircraft and helicopters passed over Saigon on their way eastward to the open sea, those on board could see masses of panic-stricken people trying to force their way aboard crowded boats headed down the Saigon River. To the northeast great ammunition dumps were blown up, and raging fires could be seen in the distance. Like a covey of birds fleeing from a hunter, the South Vietnamese helicopters headed for U.S. carriers which were lying a few miles off shore. Among these was the helicopter carrier *USS Okinawa*, and the aircraft carriers *USS Hancock* and the *USS Midway,* sent to aid the evacuation of Americans from Vietnam. The commitment of VNAF helicopters was totally unplanned. Unceremoniously, each landed at their own discretion and, once unloaded, most were dumped into the sea to make room for more. When there was no more room, others ditched at sea, hoping to be rescued by the adjacent ships. Some leaped from the helicopters, hoping their fall would be cushioned by the sea below.

Of the 130,000 refugees that fled Vietnam by various means in the spring of 1975, most began new lives in the United States, but several thousand settled elsewhere. At least 1500, many of them men whose families had been left behind, returned to Vietnam.

Flight deck personnel on the attack aircraft carrier *USS Midway* stand around a group of Vietnamese evacuees that have just arrived from their fallen country aboard this Bell UH-1. The VNAF helicopters came at random, about 30 in all, and were either ditched or made a deck landing. *RG 428-K108943 USN*

Crewmen of the amphibious command ship *USS Blue Ridge* push a VNAF UH-1 off the deck into the sea to make room for more to land. Helicopter landing space for U.S. helicopters engaged in the evacuation operation had to be maintained as well. Fifteen UH-1s went to the *Blue Ridge*. *RG 428-K108263 USN.*

Maintaining the *esprit de corps* of VNAF that once prevailed in South Vietnam, former members have joined together in comradeship in the United States in the form of chapters of the Vietnamese Air Force Association. The largest of these organizations are located in San Jose and Orange County, California, and Houston, Texas.

According to USAF sources that recorded the numbers of VNAF aircraft that escaped from South Vietnam between 29 April and the surrender, about 132 aircraft were flown to U Tapao, Thailand. Of these, 25 were F-5s, including 22 F-5E models, along with one reconnaissance version, and 27 A-37 Dragonflys. Only nine of the C-130A Hercules were able to be evacuated to Thailand, while one made it to Singapore in early April. The Hercules were flown to Guam and later reached the United States for USAF service. Also to reach Thailand were 45 Bell UH-1 helicopters, while 12 were recovered when they were landed on carrier decks. Eighteen were counted as having crashed at sea. Three Boeing-Vertol CH-47s and one Cessna O-1 Bird Dog were included in these carrier landings.

The pilot of this VNAF UH-1 deliberately ditched near the *USS Blue Ridge* when landing space was not available on its deck. One of the ship's boats stands by to pick up those on board. *RG 428N-711647 USN*

Once the spinning rotor blade of the helicopter struck the water when ditching it often quickly capsized, and many of those on board could be trapped inside. This rescue boat moves toward one person swimming in the water that may have jumped clear before landing. *RG 428-K108295 USN.*

A dispute soon emerged over rightful ownership of the aircraft that escaped to bases in Thailand, a figure of 142 according to Thai sources. The victors in Vietnam claimed ownership, while the U.S. expressed their right of ownership, since they were leased through the Military Assistance Program to the South Vietnamese Government, which no longer existed. The Thai government wished to remain neutral, and in so doing restrained the removal of these aircraft. However, at the same time this controversy was taking place, the U.S. carrier *Midway* made its scheduled departure, and roughly 70 aircraft that were already loaded on board went with the ship. Left behind in Thailand were 72 U.S.-built South Vietnamese aircraft, along with 97 Cambodian aircraft to which the U.S. also had title under the foreign Military Assistance Program. The Vietnamese aircraft included 16 C-47s in a mix of electronic warfare, reconnaissance, and transport configurations, 11 A-1E and G model Skyraiders, 6 C-7A Caribou transports, 3 AC-119 gunships, 14 Cessna U-17 Skywagons, 12 UH-1 Hueys, and 3 O-1 Bird Dogs.

Of the less than 200 aircraft that were saved from what was once the world's fourth largest air force, more than 1100 aircraft had to be left behind in Vietnam. Included in this number were 87

What this VNAF helicopter pilot's intention was in jumping from so high is unknown, but his death on impact is certain. Height above water is difficult to judge. He may have seen other "Hueys" ditch and immediately break-up and capsize. RG *428N-711643 USN.*

Steam continues to spew from this ditched UH-1 as the sea water reaches the hot turbine engine. At least two from on board can be seen together in the water as a boat from the *USS Blue Ridge* rushes to their rescue. *RG 428-K108306 USN.*

An F-5E that escaped to Thailand is lifted by a sling to a barge and then taken to the *USS Midway*. Nearly 100 aircraft were removed from Thailand by this aircraft carrier and taken initially to Guam. This loading took place between 1-7 May 1975. *Courtesy of Stephen W. Daniels.*

F-5s, of which 27 were the newer F-5Es. Dragonflys numbered 95 left in the country, while the enemy took control of 26 A-1 Skyraiders. There were 38 Douglas C-47s abandoned, including AC-47 gunships. Fourteen C-130s were left behind, and it was later disclosed that the enemy operated about three of these, after repairs, until spare parts ran out. Fairchild AC-119 gunships left in South Vietnam came to 37, plus an additional 8 C-119 of the transport variety. Thirty-three C-7A Caribous that were in storage by the VNAF were also lost. It was reported that at least two ex-VNAF F-5s were disassembled and shipped to the Soviet Union for evaluation purposes.

The greatest number of lost aircraft were 434 Bell UH-1 helicopters and 114 Cessna O-1 Bird Dogs. Of the larger helicopters, 32 Boeing Vertol CH-47 Chinooks were left to the enemy. The USAF also reported that approximately 72 other aircraft were left behind in Vietnam, among which were many Cessnas, such as U-17As, O-2As, T-37s, T-41s, and de Havilland U-6 Beavers. It is very prob-

Three F-5Es and one F-5A nestle on a barge to be taken to the *USS Midway* at Thailand. Loading was first done by USAF helicopter until after one was dropped into the sea and one on the ramp; then the rest were lifted by crane and barged. *Courtesy of Stephen W. Daniels.*

The F-5E Tiger IIs were the most critical aircraft being evacuated, because of being new equipment and the potential usefulness to the enemy. Some were left behind and later flew with (North) Vietnamese markings. This F-5A, 10268, is being barged to the *USS Midway*. *Courtesy of Stephen W. Daniels.*

The final F-5E is brought aboard just before darkness settles in. The ship left immediately after the last aircraft was placed aboard. *Courtesy of Stephen W. Daniels.*

Note that the Vietnamese flag on the fin, and possibly the national insignia on the wings and fuselage sides, may have been removed like that of the the F-5s. The red and white polka dots of the 546th Fighter Squadron remained. *Courtesy of Stephen W. Daniels.*

able that most were operational but not sustainable at the time of the takeover, and of little use to the enemy, or they would have been flown out by those evacuating the country. The severe lack of aviation fuel was the primary factor, aside from those cannibalized for parts.

As the war in Southeast Asia continued after the fall of Saigon, spreading to Cambodia, Laos, and the borders of Thailand, airpower was not used as a decisive factor in campaigns. In fact, its use was minimal, if at all. Consequently, the capture of the U.S.-manufactured aircraft of the South Vietnamese Air Force was not a factor in the continuing spread of Communist forces other than the loss of expensive equipment. It was interesting to note that during the 10th anniversary celebration of the end of the war in Saigon, now renamed Ho Chi Minh City, that about three Northrop F-5s with (North) Vietnamese markings participated in the flypast with Soviet MiG fighters.

Some of the VNAF aircraft that evaded or were evacuated from Southeast Asia were offloaded at Guam to await further transport. Seen here are A-37s, UH-1s, CH-47s, and the lone O-1 (far end, center), all from the *USS Midway*. Tents housed Vietnamese refugees as part of Operation New Life. *RG 428-K1 20203 USN.*

Appendix A: Aircraft of VNAF

VNAF Aircraft Described
(By type and sequence in which they are described)

Fighters/Attack:
Grumman F8F-1B Bearcat
Douglas A-1 Skyraider
North American T-28 Trojan
Northrop F-5 Freedom Fighter/Tiger II
Cessna A-37 Dragonfly

Bombers:
Martin B-57B Canberra

Transports:
Marcel Dassault MD-315 Flamant
Beech D18S
Aero Commander
Douglas C-47 Skytrain
Douglas DC-6B
Fairchild C-119 Flying Boxcar
Fairchild C-123K Provider
Lockheed C-130A Hercules
De Havilland C-7A Caribou

Liaison/Observation:
Morane-Saulnier 500 Criquet
Republic RC-3 Seabee
Cessna O-1 Bird Dog
Cessna O-2A Skymaster
Cessna U-17A Skywagon
De Havilland U-6A Beaver

Trainers:
North American T-6G Texan
Cessna T-41D Mescalero
Cessna T-37 "Tweety Bird"
Pazmany PL-2

Helicopters:
Bell H-13 Sioux
Sud-Est Alouette II/III
Sikorsky H-19 Chickasaw
Sikorsky H-34 Chactaw
Bell UH-1 Iroquois
Boeing-Vertol CH-47 Chinook

Source for statistical information where available:
Air Force Almanac, September 1968
Air Force and Space Digest

F8F-1B Bearcat
Low-wing single-engine carrier based fighter designed for the U.S. Navy. The bearcats went into service in the closing months of World War II, and therefore were too late for combat. When U.S. involvement in Korea began, the Bearcats again did not see combat, since they could not deliver the heavy ordnance loads of the Corsairs in ground attack missions. Being superfluous to Navy requirements in Korean operations the equivalent of two squadrons of Bearcats were transferred to the French when the U.S. decided to assist their cause in Indochina. When France withdrew under the Geneva agreement, they turned over 22 of the surviving Bearcats to South Vietnam, serving with that country's 1st Fighter Squadron at Bien Hoa AB beginning 1 June 1956. Some sources say others followed, which may have been three, and would account for the quantity of 25 aircraft given in other sources. The Bearcats remained VNAF's only ordnance carrying aircraft until U.S. supplied AD-6s (A-1s) and T-28s arrived in late 1960/61, after which time the F8Fs were retired. *Manufacturer*: Grumman Aircraft Corp. *Power plant*: Pratt & Whitney R-2800-34W, 28-cylinder air-cooled engine, 24,000 hp. *Dimensions:* span 35 ft 6 in (10.8 m), length 27 ft 6 in (8.4 m), height 13 ft 8 in (4.16 m) *Speed:* 376 knots (695 km/h; 434 mph). *Ceiling:* 38,900 ft (11,856 m). *Range:* 1,140 mi (1,834 km). *Armament*: 4 x 20 mm cannon, 2 x 1,000 lb (4,536 kg) bombs, or 4 x 5 in. rockets. *Crew*: 1. *Maximum gross takeoff weight*: 12,447 lb (5,646 kg) *Using squadron*: 1st Fighter Squadron.

A-1 Skyraider
Close-support aircraft, originally produced for shipboard duty for the U.S. Navy and Marine Corps. Production began at the end of World War II. As Navy and Marine usage was phasing out, about 22 to 25 A-1Hs (then designated AD-6) were sent to VNAF beginning in September 1960 to replace the F8F Bearcats of the 1st Fighter Squadron. Since USAF advisors were training VNAF crews in this Navy aircraft, the Air Force acquired substantial numbers of surplus Navy A-1s to equip their Air Commando squadrons being trained at Hurlburt AFB, Florida, and subsequently deployed to

Vietnam. This led to additional A-1s for VNAF being supplied through MAP by the USAF, and eventually formed seven squadrons. Aircraft were not renumbered with AF serials, but retained Navy Bureau Numbers with the first digit "1" deleted. The A-1H (AD-6) single seat model was used in the greatest number, while the two place A-1E (AD-5) was modified with dual control for the second crew member to be used as tactical trainers, as well as retaining their combat capability. These were used by VNAF in small quantities, as were a few A-1G (AD-5N) and A-1J (AD-7) single seat models. *Manufacturer*: Douglas Aircraft Co. *Power plant*: Wright R-3350-26WA air-cooled radial engine, 2,700 hp. *Dimensions:* span 50 ft 9 in (15.5 m), length 39 ft (11.89 m), height 15 ft 8 in (4.77 m). *Speed:* 317 kts (585 km; 365 mph) maximum. *Ceiling*: about 25,000 ft (7,620 m) *Range:* beyond 2,700 mi (4,345 km) *Bomb load*: 8,000 lb (3,628 kg) on wing bomb racks. *Armament:* 4 x 20 mm cannon. *Crew*: 1. *Maximum gross takeoff weight*: 25,000 lb (11,340 kg). *Using squadrons:* 514th, 516th, 518th, 520th, 522th, 524th, and 530th Fighter Squadrons.

T-28 Trojan

Counterinsurgency fighter developed from former USAF trainer. Higher powered engine with three blade propeller replaced earlier types. Undercarriage was strengthened, and crew armor was provided. Three under-wing pylons on each wing could carry a variety of armament. Introduced into South Vietnam by USAF special air warfare forces in 1960 for tactical training of VNAF personnel. Seventy were eventually transferred to VNAF between 1961 and 1962. Initial equipment for 2nd Fighter Squadron formed at Nha Trang AB in December 1961, and moved in February 1964 to Da Nang AB. By January 1964, 29 Trojans remained in VNAF and were phased out by April 1965, the last of which were 18 reconnaissance versions; RT-28C, stationed at Tan Son Nhut. While the T-28s were in service, two names had been applied. When T-28As were converted to the fighter-bomber role for MDAP use they were renamed Nomad from Trojan, as the trainer model was called. As the airplanes were further modified into the T-28D attack aircraft, these retained the earlier name of Trojan, as well. As time went on, official USAF records show that all models of the T-28 carried the name Trojan. *Manufacturer*: North American Aviation. *Power plant*: Wright R-1820-56S radial air-cooled engine, 426 hp. *Dimensions:* span 40 ft 7 in (12.43 m), length 33 ft (10 m), height 12 ft 8 in (3.85 m). *Speed*: 200 knots (370 km/h; 230 mph). *Ceiling*: above 16,500 ft (5,029 m). *Range:* beyond 1,400 mi (2,253 km). *Armament:* 2 x .50 cal machine guns, 1,800 lb (728 kg) of ordnance, rockets, bombs, incendijel. *Crew:* 2. *Maximum gross takeoff weight:* 9,000 lb (4,082 kg). *Using squadron*: 2nd Fighter Squadron, 314th Special Mission Squadron, 716th Reconnaissance Squadron (RT-28C).

F-5 Freedom Fighter/Tiger II

Lightweight supersonic all-purpose fighter, developed primarily to be furnished to U.S. allies under military assistance program (MAP), which included VNAF. It was developed from the USAF T-38 Talon jet trainer. Twelve Freedom Fighters were diverted from MAP contracts and tested under operational conditions by USAF in Vietnam (Project Skoshi Tiger) in 1966 by the 10th Fighter Squadron, Commando (FCS), to determine the airplane's desired configuration. The 522nd Fighter Squadron at Tan Son Nhut was moved to Bien Hoa to become the first within VNAF to be equipped as of 1 June 1967. By 1974 there were four squadrons with 72 F-5A Freedom Fighters, plus 36 in storage, and three squadrons of F-5E Tiger IIs. Four models reached VNAF service; F-5A was single-seater; F-5B accommodated 2-man crew for training or combat missions; F-5E was basically a VFR day-night fighter having limited all-weather capability, with emphasis on maneuverability rather than speed; and the RF-5A reconnaissance version, of which seven were delivered. *Manufacturer:* Northrop Aircraft Corp. [Data in brackets pertains to F-5E] *Power plant:* 2 General Electric J85-13 turbojets, 4,080 lb (1,850 kg) thrust with afterburner, [J85-21A, 5,000 lb (2,268 kg) with a/b] *Dimensions:* span 26 ft 5 in (8.05 m) [26 ft 8 in (8.12 m)], length 43 ft 11 in (13.14 m) [48 ft 2 in (14.67 m)], height 13 ft (3.96 m) [13 ft 4 in (4.06 m)]. *Speed:* up to Mach 1.63 at 36,000 ft (10,972 m). *Ceiling:* over 55,000 ft (16,764 m). *Range:* combat, 400 mi (644 km), ferry, 2,100 mi (3,380 km) with external tanks. *Armament:* 2 x M39 20 mm cannon in nose, and up to 7,000 lb (3,175 m) of mixed ordnance on four under-wing attachments and one centerline station. *Crew:* F-5A, E, RF-5A, 1; F-5B, 2. *Maximum gross takeoff weight:* 19,000 lb (8,618 kg) [24,676 lb (11,193 kg)]. *Using squadrons:* 522nd, 536th, 538th, 540th, 542nd, and 544th Fighter Squadrons.

A-37 Dragonfly

Close-support attack aircraft developed from the USAF T-37B basic jet trainer. The conflict in SEA inspired the creation of this armed counterinsurgency (COIN) aircraft, which was able to operate from short, unimproved airstrips if required. Engines employed in the tactical version produced more than twice the thrust as the trainer model. USAF Dragonflys were first deployed to Bien Hoa and Pleiku AB in August 1967 under the "Combat Dragon" evaluation program. In November 1968 the first A-37s were delivered to VNAF, eventually in sufficient quantities to equip 10 VNAF squadrons, along with many spare aircraft. A mix of A-37As may have been included with the majority of A-37Bs. The main difference in the two is that the latter were equipped with in-flight refueling and stressed for 6 Gs, compared to 5 Gs for the A-37A. *Manufacturer:* Cessna Aircraft Co. *Power plant:* 2 General Electric J85s, 2,400 lb (1,088 kg) thrust in A-37A, 2,700 lb (1,225 kg) in A-37B. *Dimensions:* span including tip-tanks 35 ft 10| in (10,92 m), length without fuel prob 28 ft 3 in (8.61 m), height 8 ft 10 in (2.70 m). Speed: 312 knots (577 km/h 360 mph). *Ceiling:* 36,000 ft (10,973 m). *Range:* over 650 mi (1,046 km). *Armament/payload:* one nose-mounted GAU-2B/A 7.62 mm Minigun; eight wing pylons able to carry various combinations of rockets and bombs. *Crew:* 1 - 2. *Maximum gross takeoff weight:* 12,000 lb (5,443 kg). *Using squadrons:* 516th, 520th, 524th, 526th, 528th, 532nd, 534th, 546th, 548th, and 550th Fighter Squadrons.

B-57B Canberra

Twin-engine light jet bomber based on the British designed English Electric Canberra. American built Canberras were delivered to USAF bomber and reconnaissance units starting in mid-1950s.

Only two USAF bomber squadrons remained when American forces became openly involved in SEA in 1964. These two squadrons and a reconnaissance unit that acquired RB-57Es operated Canberras continually through the conflict in SEA until 1972. In August 1964 four B-57s were theoretically transferred to VNAF, and operated with the USAF B-57 squadron assigned at Da Nang AB. These VNAF airplanes were frequently interchanged with those of the active USAF bomber squadron for maintenance management. These were flown with USAF crews exclusively until VNAF crews were trained and assumed these duties. By April 1966 VNAF use of B-57s ended, and the airplanes reverted to USAF. *Manufacturer:* Martin Aircraft Co. *Power plant:* 2 Wright J65 engines, 7,200 lb (3,266) thrust, *Dimensions:* 64 ft (19.5 m), length 65 ft 6 in (19.96 m), height 16 ft (4.87 m). *Speed:* 420 knots (777 km/h; 485 mph). *Ceiling:* above 56,000 ft (17,068 m). *Range:* 2,000 mi (3,218 km). *Bomb Load:* up to 8,000 lb (3,628 kg) of mixed weapons in bomb bay and on eight wing pylons. *Armament:* 8 wing mounted .50 cal machine guns or 4 x 20 mm cannon. *Crew:* 2. *Maximum gross take-off weight:* 55,000 lb (24,948 kg). *Using squadrons:* 615th Flight assigned to the USAF 8th and 13th Bombardment Squadrons on an in-country rotational basis.

Marcel Dassault MD-315 Flamant

Twin-engine light transport with large twin-tail and retractable tricycle landing gear. Beginning in July 1950, 72 of these French-built Dassault MD-315s were flown by the French Armee de l'Air in Indochina. The Flamants were in three versions; the MD-315A were for liaison duties; MD-315B were transports able to carry up to 16 troops (as in Vietnam, when within weight limitations); and the MD-315C, a ground support version with external bomb racks and a bombardier's position in the nose. Vietnamese crews returning from flight training in France and North Africa became operational in the Flamant in the spring of 1954, and Flamants were assigned in small numbers to provide limited air support to ground troops, mostly to release enemy pressure on some isolated outposts when directed by the Air Department. However, by the end of 1955, after the fall of Diem Bien Phu, the MD-315 Flamants were returned to the French authorities. Manufacturer: Dassault Aircraft. *Power plant:* 2 S.N.E.C.M.A.-Renault 12S 02-201 air-cooled inline engines, 580 hp. *Dimensions:* span 67 ft 10 in (20.67 m), length 41 ft 0 in (12.5 m), height 14 ft 9 in (4.5 m). *Speed:* 204 knots (378 km/h; 236 mph). *Ceiling:* 26,240 ft (7,998 m). *Range:* 755 mi (1,215 km). *Payload:* 6 to 10 passengers, (normal). *Crew:* 2. *Maximum gross takeoff weight:* 12,760 lb (5,788 kg). *Using squadrons:* ELA (Esquadrille of Liaison, meaning Combat Liaison Tactical Squadron) before the forming of VNAF.

Beech D-18S

Twin-engine, twin-tail utility transport, of which the first of its type flew in January 1937. This versatile all metal aircraft was used in vast numbers during World War II by the USAAF as the C-45, and by the U.S. Navy as the JRB for twin-engine pilot trainer, navigation, photographic and bombardment trainer, as well as for light transport duties. Retired from the USAF in 1964, the U.S. Navy used them through the 1960s, including Navy service in Vietnam. Over 30 of the world's air forces used this light transport, including VNAF. Three or more are known to have been exported to Vietnam around 1954 by Fleetway, Inc., of Burbank, California. They served VNAF in communications and liaison duties until the 1960s, when they were phased out in favor of other aircraft for performing their mission. *Manufacturer:* Beech Aircraft Corp. *Power plant:* Pratt & Whitney R-985-AN-3 air-cooled radial engine, 450 hp. *Dimensions:* span 47 ft 8 in (14,526 m), length 34 ft 3 in (10.43 m), height 9 ft 8 in (2.94 m). *Speed:* 186 knots (345 km/h; 215 mph). *Ceiling:* 20,000 ft (6,096 m). *Range:* 700 mi (1,126 km). *Payload:* 6 - 8 passengers. *Crew:* 1 - 2. *Maximum gross takeoff weight:* 7,850 lb (3,560 kg). *Using squadron:* 312th Special Mission Squadron.

Aero Commander

Twin-engine high-wing general aviation aircraft with tricycle retractable landing gear. Neither the year that this single aircraft arrived in Vietnam, nor the model type can be determined. It was based at Tan Son Nhut, and served as a lightweight VIP transport. President Diem used it occasionally, but said it was too noisy, while President Ky, as a pilot, utilized it more. Colors were lavender and white. It carried no identifying numbers, but had the name *Trieu-Minh* on the nose. Description given is for the Model 560A. *Manufacturer:* Aero Commander. *Power plant:* 2 Lycoming GO-480-D1A 6-cylinder air-cooled engines, 280 hp. *Dimensions:* span 44 ft 1 in (13.43 m), length 35 ft 5 in (10.8 m), height 14 ft 9 in (4.5 m). *Speed:* 179 knots (301 km/h; 206 mph). *Range:* 1,080 mi (1,738 km). *Payload:* 5 - 6 passengers. *Crew:* 1. *Maximum gross takeoff weight:* 6,000 lb (2,721 kg). *Using squadron:* 312th, later 314th Special Mission Squadron.

C-47 Skytrain

Military version of the famed twin-engine Douglas DC-3 commercial transport that first flew in 1935. In all, Douglas built more than 10,000 Gooney Birds. This World War II Military transport was regarded as being obsolete by 1950 by the USAF, yet it served that air force continually until the mid-1970s. Used throughout the life of VNAF as its primary general-purpose transport. Late modifications brought about the AC-47, nicknamed "Puff the Magic Dragon," "Spooky," and "*Hoa Long* (Fire Dragon)"; they carried 2 x 7.62 mm Miniguns for close support missions in Vietnam, mostly for base defense at night. Other models included EC and RC-47s for special reconnaissance missions, as well as VC-47 V.I.P. transports. *Manufacturer:* Douglas Aircraft Co. *Power plant:* 2 Pratt & Whitney R-1830-90D air-cooled radial engines, 1,200 hp. *Dimensions:* span 95 ft (28.95 m), length 64 ft 4 in (19.6 m), height 16 ft 10 in (5.13 m). *Speed:* 161 knots (296 km/h; 185 mph). *Ceiling:* 23,000 ft (7,010 m). *Range:* 2,125 mi (3,420 km). *Payload:* 7,500 lb (3,035 kg) or 28 troops. *Crew:* 3, 7 in AC-47. *Maximum gross takeoff weight:* 33,000 lb (14,969 kg). *Using squadrons:* 312th and 314th Special Mission Squadrons, 413th (1st), 415th (2nd), and 417th Transport Squadrons, 716th and 718th Reconnaissance Squadrons, and 817th Attack Squadron.

Douglas DC-6B

Four-engine pressurized cabin commercial airliner of the immediate post World War II variety. Used as a VIP transport, it is known to have carried Prime Minister Ky, President Thieu, and other officials in the Vietnamese government. It is said to have been purchased from Pan American Airways, but former U.S. registry is not known. Vietnamese registration was XVFCK. Maintained by 314th Special Air Missions Squadron at Tan Son Nhut. *Manufacturer:* Douglas Aircraft Co. *Power plant:* 4 Pratt & Whitney R-2800-CB17 18-cylinder air-cooled radial engines, 2,500 hp. *Dimensions:* span 117 ft 6 in (54.10 m), length 105 ft 7 in (32.24 m), height 17 ft 3 in (5.25 m). *Speed:* 313 knots (578 km/h; 360 mph). *Ceiling:* 29,000 ft (8,839 m). *Range:* 4,910 mi (7,901 km). *Payload:* 28,188 lb (12,786 kg). *Crew:* 3. *Maximum gross takeoff weight:* 106,000 lb (48,082 kg). *Using squadron:* 314th Special Mission Squadron.

C-119 Flying Boxcar

Twin-boom, twin-engine troop carrier, this type made a reappearance in the war in Southeast Asia when assigned to VNAF beginning in March 1968. Sixteen C-119s replaced C-47s in the 413th Transport Squadron at Tan Son Nhut. By 1971 their number increased to 25. The 720th Reconnaissance Squadron was formed with RC-119s for night surveillance coastal patrol by using special sensing equipment, but this equipment was not acquired, and therefore the airplanes were used only as transports. In a new combat career as AC-119 gun ships they augmented, then replaced AC-47 Snoopys. Two versions included the AC-119G with 4 x 7.62 mm Miniguns and AC-119K with two auxiliary jet engines, and armed with a 2 x 20 mm Gatling cannon in addition to 7.62 mm guns. VNAF acquired 36 to 40 of these gun ships beginning in March 1972. *Manufacturer:* Fairchild Hiller Corp. *Power plant:* 2 Wright R-3350-85 turbo compound air-cooled engines, 3,500 hp.; AC-119K was supplemented with 2 J85-17 General Electric turbojets, 2,850 lb (1,293 kg) thrust. *Dimensions:* span 109 ft 4 in (33.32 m), length 86 ft 6 in (26.36 m), height 26 ft 2 in (7.97 m). *Speed:* 162 knots (300 km/h; 185 mph) cruise. *Ceiling:* 30,000 ft (9,144 m). *Range:* 2,000 mi (3,218 km) with 10,000 lb (4,536 kg) payload. *Payload:* 30,000 lb (13,608 kg). *Crew:* 3 - 5, plus armament crews in AC versions. *Maximum gross takeoff weight:* 73,000 lb (33,113 kg); AC-119K, 77,000 lb (34,927 kg). *Using squadrons:* 413th Transport Squadron, 720th Reconnaissance Squadron, 819th, and 821st Attack Squadrons.

C-123K Provider

Jet-assisted twin-engine transport used for cargo and troop-carrier. First flown in 1954, its true potential was not appreciated until they served the USAF in large numbers in Vietnam to support ground forces. Added thrust provided by a pair of General Electric J85 turbojet engines suspended from the wings outboard of standard piston engines to reduce takeoff roll with faster climb to avoid enemy small-arms fire, and enable it to carry one-third heavier payload. High tail assembly and squat landing gear permitted tail-ramp loading for combat equipment. The first Providers to serve in Vietnam were the earlier version without auxiliary jet engines, the C-123B for USAF Operation Mule Team. In 1964 three were lent to VNAF for clandestine missions with the 83rd SOG for two years. The first of three VNAF squadrons of 16 C-123Ks each was formed in May 1971, all of which were stationed at Tan Son Nhut. Ten were lost during their VNAF service, four of which were the result of ground fire. Beginning in early 1973 C-123Ks were replaced by two C-130 squadrons. *Manufacturer:* Fairchild Hiller Corp. Power plant: 2 Pratt & Whitney R-2800-99W air-cooled radial engines, 2,500 hp.; 2 G.E. J85 auxiliary engines, 2,850 lb (1,293 kg) thrust. *Dimensions:* span 110 ft (33.52 m), length 76 ft 3 in (23.24 m), height 34 ft 1 in (10.38 m), *Speed:* 212 knots (394 km/h; 245 mph). *Ceiling:* above 25,000 ft (7,620 m). *Range:* beyond 1,000 mi (1,609 km). *Payload:* 24,000 lb (10,886 kg). *Crew:* 2 - 4. *Maximum gross takeoff weight:* about 60,000 lb (27,216 kg). *Using squadrons:* 421st, 423rd, and 425th Transport Squadrons, and 83rd SOG. (C-123B).

C-130A Hercules

Combat support four-engine transport, initially used in SEA beginning in early 1960s by USAF for intra-theater personnel and cargo hauling. During the final two years of the war, starting in January 1973, VNAF had two C-130A squadrons with 16 aircraft each from USAF resources. Most of the VNAF C-130 missions were airlifting personnel and cargo from Tan Son Nhut to northern MR 1. Due to lack of materiel support, in commission rate often was as low as 2 to 5 aircraft per squadron, per day. In the summer of 1974 some VNAF C-130s flew bombing missions, dropping full loads of 96 fused 55 gal. drums of napalm on enemy concentrations. Fifteen 1,500 lb (6,804 kg) bombs were also dropped by VNAF C-130s. As the enemy advanced southward, the Hercules were used extensively in the evacuation of northern cities, carrying as many as 350 refugees in one plane—150 allowable capacity. Enemy ground fire caused the two VNAF C-130 losses. A number were reclaimed by USAF in the final days of the war. Shortly before the capture of Tan Son Nhut on 29 April 1975, only 10 of the 16 C-130s there were flyable. Seven escaped to U Tapau, Thailand, and one with a defecting crew made it to Singapore four weeks earlier. The North Vietnamese commandeered the rest and operated two or three for a short period. *Manufacturer:* Lockheed-George Co. *Power plant:* 4 Allison T56-7 propjet engines, 4,050 shp each. *Dimensions:* span 132 ft 7 in (40.47 m), length 97 ft 9 in (29.79 m), height 38 ft 4 in (11.68 m). *Speed:* 312 knots (578 km/h; 360 mph). *Ceiling:* above 30,000 ft (9,144 m). *Range:* with 25,000 lb (11,340 kg) payload, 3,700 mi (5,954 km) without pylon tanks. *Payload:* 45,000 lb (20,412 kg). *Crew:* 5. *Maximum gross takeoff weight:* 155,000 lb (70,308 kg). *Using squadrons:* 435th and 437th Transport Squadrons.

C-7A Caribou

Canadian-built STOL tactical twin-engine transport designed as a result of mutual needs for the U.S. and Canadian armies. First flown on July 30, 1958, and initially carried the U.S. Army designation CV-2B. Employed principally by U.S. forces in Vietnam where it supplemented C-123s and C-130s, landing on dirt runways barely 1,000 ft (304 m) long. Transferred from U.S. Army to USAF in

January 1967. Served several air forces throughout Southeast Asia, as well as other parts of the world. First assigned to VNAF from USAF squadrons in Vietnam in late 1971 and formed the 427th Transport Squadron. Two more squadrons followed. By June 1974 nearly all C-7As were placed in storage at Da Nang and Pleiku because of parts shortages and difficulty to maintain. *Manufacturer:* De Havilland Aircraft of Canada Ltd. *Power plant:* 2 Pratt & Whitney R-2000 air-cooled radial engines, 1,450 hp. *Dimensions:* span 95 ft 7 in (29.2 m), length 72 ft 7 in (22.19 m), height 31 ft 9 in (9.67 m). *Speed:* 156 knots (289 km/h; 180 mph). *Ceiling:* 24,000 ft (7,315 m). *Range:* 240 mi (385 km) full payload, 1,300 mi (2,092 km) ferry. *Payload:* 32 troops or 5,000 lb (2,268 kg) cargo. *Crew:* 3. *Maximum gross takeoff weight:* 28,500 lb (12,927 kg). *Using squadrons:* 427th, 429th, and 431st Transport Squadrons.

M.S.500 Criquet

Single-engine high-wing monoplane with metal and wood structure covered with fabric. STOL features were among the earliest to be used on production aircraft. First flown as the German-built Fieseler Fi-156 Storch in 1936, it was designed to meet the *Reichsluftfahrtministerium* specifications for a small army cooperation monoplane. World War II production was transferred to the German-controlled Morane-Saulnier factory at Pateaux, France, which continued production of this 3-seat general-purpose aircraft after France's liberation. This French produced model was the M.S.500 Criquet, which served the post-war French Air Force. Many Criquets were transferred to the Vietnamese Army beginning in October 1953 through 1955, particularly when the French began their departure from Southeast Asia. Initially these were the principal aircraft in greatest number to serve the VNAF when it was first formed. *Manufacturer:* Morane-Saulnier. *Power plant:* Argus As 10c, 8-cylinder air-cooled engine, 240 hp. *Dimensions:* span 46 ft 9 in (14.24 m), length 32 ft 6 in (9.9 m), height 9 ft 10 in (2.99 m). *Speed:* 95 knots (175 km/h; 109 mph). *Ceiling:* 15,090 ft (4,600 m). *Range:* 236 mi (380 km). *Payload:* 3 persons. *Crew:* 1. *Maximum gross takeoff weight:* 2,910 lb (1,320 kg). *Using squadrons:* 1st and 2nd GAO and Air Training Center.

Republic RC-3 Seabee

Single-engine pusher type, all-metal high-wing amphibian with retractable conventional landing gear. Placed in quantity production in mid-1946, the RC-3 Seabee was designed as a simple, low-cost civil and general aviation aircraft. In the early 1950s three or more Seabees were assigned to the Vietnamese Air Department with prospects of supporting maritime requirements in maintaining coastal, inland waterway counterinsurgency patrols. They may have assisted custom officials or internal security authorities operating against smugglers, or those engaged in illegal activities. Very little has been reported of their activities, length of service, or fate of the aircraft. Two were assigned to the 312th Special Mission Squadron at Tan Son Nhut, and one is known to have been stationed at Nha Trang, in which some of the early pilots received training. It is most likely that because of these Seabees, the 600-series of squadron identifying numbers were set aside for amphibian or seaplane squadrons, yet was never used. *Manufacturer:* Republic Aviation Corp. *Power plant:* Franklin 6A8-215-B8F 6-cylinder air-cooled engine, 215 hp. *Dimensions:* span 37 ft 8 in (11.47 m), length 27 ft 11 in (8.51 m), height 9 ft 7 in (2.98 m). *Speed:* 104 knots (192 km/h; 120 mph). *Ceiling:* 12,000 ft (3,658 m). *Range:* 560 mi (900 km). *Payload:* 3 passengers. *Crew:* 1. *Maximum gross takeoff weight:* 3,000 lb (1,360 kg). *Using squadron:* 312th Special Mission Squadron, and Air Training Center.

O-1 Bird Dog

Single-engine all-metal observation aircraft used for air liaison and forward air controller (FAC) duties. One of the earliest U.S. supplied aircraft of VNAF beginning in 1954. Known originally as the L-19, it entered U.S. Army service in large numbers beginning in 1950. A total of 3,381 were built by Cessna, with others being license manufactured by Fuji Heavy Industries for the Japanese Ground Self-Defense Force. Designation changed to O-1 in 1962. Many were reassigned from the U.S. Army to the USAF when combat requirements in Vietnam specified that an Air Force FAC would direct air strikes on close-support missions. Additional O-1s augmented VNAF as departing U.S. forces transferred their Bird Dogs to these observation squadrons for continuation of reconnaissance and FAC duties. O-1s were the most often seen fixed wing aircraft in Vietnam through the entire period of the war. *Manufacturer:* Cessna Aircraft Co. *Power plant:* Continental 0-470 6-cylinder air-cooled engine, 213 hp. *Dimensions:* span 36 ft (10.97 m), length 25 ft 10 in (7.87 m), height 7 ft 4 in (2.23 m). *Speed:* 92 knots (168 km/h; 105 mph). *Ceiling:* 18,500 ft (5,638 m). *Range:* 530 mi (853 km). *Armament:* Target-marking rockets, some U.S. Army O-1s carried .50 cal machine guns. *Crew:* 1. *Maximum gross takeoff weight:* 2,400 lb (1,088 kg). *Using squadrons:* 110th, 112th, 114th, 116th, 118th, 120th, 122th, and 124th Observation Squadrons.

O-2A Skymaster

Twin-engine twin-tail push-pull aircraft, off-the-shelf version of the Cessna 337 Super Skymaster. This USAF O-2A augmented O-1 Bird Dog FAC aircraft in Vietnam beginning in 1967. Because of twin-engine reliability, they were used initially in the remote areas of I Corps and out-of-country missions. A modified door on the right side had a lower window to improve visibility for the pilot seated on the left side of this two seat side-by-side aircraft that was normally flown solo. Rear seats of the standard 337 were not installed. With the withdrawal of U.S. forces in South Vietnam in the early 1970s, VNAF observation squadrons received 35 0-2As, augmenting two squadrons in MR 1 and possibly others. Eventually placed in storage in June 1974 to ease VNAF maintenance load. *Manufacturer:* Cessna Aircraft Co. *Power plant:* 2 Continental IO-360-D 6-cylinder air-cooled engines, 210 hp. each. *Dimensions:* span 38 ft (11.58 m), length 29 ft 9 in (9.06 m), height 9 ft 4 in (2.84 m). *Speed:* 156 knots (288 km/h; 180 mph). *Ceiling:* 20,500 ft (6,248 m). *Range:* 1,000 mi (1,610 km). *Armament:* 4 wing stations which normally carried 14 smoke marking rockets and/or parachute flares. *Payload:* 3 passengers (by adding 2 rear seats) or equivalent cargo. *Crew:* 1. *Maximum gross takeoff weight:* 4,300 lb (1,950 kg). *Using squadrons:* 110th and 120th Observation Squadrons.

U-17A and B Skywagon

General-purpose light utility aircraft and flight trainer, procured by the USAF for VNAF and other countries under the Military Assistance Program. This was the military adaptation of the Cessna 185E (U-17A) and A185E (U-17B) Skywagon. Deliveries to South Vietnam began in 1962 for multi-use: FAC aircraft to supplement O-1s, light transport, psychological warfare, courier, and flight training. Requiring a crew of one, its cabin could accommodate up to six persons. Very similar to the earlier Cessna 180H. Nearly 100 U-17s were delivered to VNAF. *Manufacturer:* Cessna Aircraft Co., *Power plant:* U-17A, Continental IO-470-F 6-cylinder air-cooled engine, 260 hp.; U-17B, IO-520-D, 300 hp. *Dimensions:* span 36 ft 2 in (11.02 m), length 25 ft 9 in (7.84 m), height 7 ft 9 in (2.36 m). *Speed:* 147 knots (272 km/h; 170 mph). *Ceiling:* 17,500 ft (5,334 m). *Range:* 850 mi (1,367 km). *Payload:* 5 passengers, or 1,500 lb (680 kg) cargo. *Crew:* 1. *Maximum gross takeoff weight:* 3,200 lb (1,451 kg). *Using squadrons:* 110th, 112th, 114th, 116th, 118th, 120th, 122nd, and 124th Observation Squadrons, plus one for 83rd SOG and one or more for 314th Special Mission Squadron.

U-6A Beaver

Single-engined, high-wing monoplane used primarily for liaison-administrative duties. Produced in Canada as the DHC–2 for many users, the U.S. Army began taking deliveries in 1947, while limited numbers were also acquired by the USAF. The first of the U-6As were assigned to the VNAF in 1958, their number eventually reaching 17. Duties of the VNAF's Beavers included psychological warfare leaflet drops and loudspeaker broadcasting. *Manufacturer:* de Havilland Aircraft of Canada Ltd. *Power plant:* Pratt & Whitney R-985-AN-3 air-cooled radial engine, 450 hp. *Dimensions:* span 48 ft (14.63 m), length 30 ft 4 in (9.24 m), height 10 ft 5 in (3.17 m). *Speed:* 156 knots (288 km/h; 180 mph). Ceiling: 20,000 ft (6096 m). Range: 600 mi (965 km). *Payload:* 7 passengers or 1000 lb (453 kg). *Crew:* 1. *Maximum gross take-off weight:* 4820 lb (2186 kg). *Used by:* 314th Special Missions Squadron and 716th Reconnaissance Squadron.

T-6G Texan

Single-engined, low-wing monoplane, a basic trainer with conventional retractable landing gear. A development of earlier North American "basic combat" trainers, the AT-6, as it was first called, was accepted as an Advanced Trainer by the USAAF and the U.S. Navy in 1940. The AT-6/SNJ was the most widely-used trainer of its type throughout World War II. They were also used by many other Allied air forces during the war, and as a standard trainer for many years to follow. Many were used in the FAC role by the USAF during the Korean War when they were then called "mosquito missions." Texans were remanufactured in 1949 as T-6Gs, of which 55 were sent to the VNAF from 1954 until 1956 for use as training aircraft at the Air Training Center at Nha Trang. They were withdrawn from Vietnam when all VNAF flight training was conducted in the United States. *Manufacturer:* North American Aviation Inc. *Power plant:* Pratt & Whitney R-1340 air-cooled radial engine, 600 hp. *Dimensions:* span 42 ft (12.8 m), length 29 ft (8.83 m), height 11 ft 9 in (3.58 m). *Speed:* 182 knots (337 km/h; 210 mph). *Ceiling:* 24,200 ft (7376 m). *Range:* 629 mi (1012 km). *Crew:* 2. *Maximum gross take-off weight:* 5155 lb (2338 kg). *Used by:* Air Training Center.

T-41D Mescalero

Single-engined, side-by-side, all-metal, light primary trainer with fixed tricycle landing gear, with a constant-speed propeller. Off-the-shelf military version of Cessna 172E. USAF deliveries began in 1964 for use in a preliminary flight screening program for Air Force pilot candidates. When VNAF pilot training returned from the United States to Vietnam, 22 T-41Ds were sent to the Air Training Center at Nha Trang for use in flight training, and later moved to Phan Rang. The T-41D was the MAP version of the T-41B, having a 28-volt electrical system and simplified equipment. *Manufacturer:* Cessna Aircraft Company. Power-plant: Continental IO-360-D 6-cylinder air-cooled engine, 210 hp. *Dimensions:* span 36 ft 2 in (11.02 m), length 26 ft 6 in (8.07 m), height 8 ft 11 in (2.72 m). *Speed:* 114 knots (210 km/h; 135 mph). *Ceiling:* 13,000 ft (3962 m). *Range:* 720 mi (1158 km). *Crew:* 2, Maximum gross take-off weight: 2300 lb (1043 kg). *Used by:* Air Training Center.

T-37 "Tweety Bird"

Primary jet trainer, featuring side-by-side seating for student and instructor. First introduced as a USAF trainer in 1955 to replace the aging T-33s in the Air Training Command. When the training of VNAF pilots was again conducted in Vietnam, several T-37s were sent there late in the war to be used as transitional trainers for advancement to the A-37s and F-5s. They operated from Phan Rang after that base was turned over to the VNAF in 1971 and used, in part, by the Air Training Center, headquartered at Nha Trang. *Manufacturer:* Cessna Aircraft Co. *Power plant:* 2 Continental J69-T25 turbojets, 1025 lb thrust each. *Dimensions:* span 33 ft 10 in (10.31 m), length 29 ft 4 in (8.94 m), height 9 ft 5 in (2.87 m). *Speed:* 304 knots (562 im/h; 350 mph). Ceiling: 35,000 ft (10,668 m). *Range:* over 650 mi (1046 km). *Crew:* 2. *Maximum gross take-off weight:* 6600 lb (2993 kg). *Used by:* Air Training Center.

Pazmany PL-2

Home-built, all-metal, low-wing, two-seat side-by-side monoplane, featuring tricycle landing gear and aerobatic capability. The construction of this aircraft was a cooperative project within the VNAF. The fuselage was constructed at the Air Logistics Command Depot at Bien Hoa, the wing and control surfaces at Tan Son Nhut, and the tail surfaces were built at Da Nang. Final assembly was made at Tan Son Nhut, and the first flight took place there on 1 July 1971, the VNAF's Air Force Day. It was most successful. Up to this point, the VNAF had intended to build just one aircraft, but with its success, 10 more were planned but did not materialize. They were to be used as a VNAF primary trainer. The structure was stressed to a +6G limit for safety and aerobatics. The fibreglass wing tip tanks had a capacity of 12.5 gallons each. This tip tank arrangement increased effective aspect ratios for improved climb and ceiling. The absence of fuel in the vicinity of the fuselage was a safety feature in case of an accident. *Manufacturer:* VNAF. *Power plant:* Lycoming O-235C-1 4-cylinder air-cooled engine, 108 hp. *Dimensions:* span

28 ft 6 in (8.68 m), length 19 ft 4 in (5.89 m), height 7 ft 8 in (2.33 m). *Speed:* 133 knots (245 km/h; 153 mph). *Ceiling:* 22,000 ft (6705 m). *Range:* 380 mi (611 kn). *Crew:* 2. *Maximum gross take-off weight:* 1900 lb (862 kg). *Used by:* Not assigned.

H-13 Sioux
Single-rotor, two-bladed helicopter with anti-torque tail rotor. Open lattice tail boom with distinctive plexiglass bubble-type canopy. Known collectively as the Bell Model 47, it was produced in many variations and configurations. Used by the armed forces of more than 30 nations, plus innumerable civil organizations. Production span was one of the longest; 1946-1973. Introduced into the VNAF in April 1956 at Tan Son Nhut, an initial small fleet was manned by four pilots and 20 enlisted men. A second H-13 helicopter squadron was later established at Da Nang in October 1961. *Manufacture:* Bell Helicopter Co. *Power plant:* Lycoming O-435 6-cylinder air-cooled engine, 240 hp. *Dimensions:* Main rotor diameter 35 ft 1 in (10.69 m), fuselage length 27 ft 4 in (8.33 m), height 9 ft 6 in (2.89 m). *Speed:* 87 knots (160 km/h; 100 mph). *Ceiling:* 13,200 ft (4023 m). *Range:* 300 mi (483 km). *Payload:* 2 troops. *Crew:*1. *Maximum gross take-off weight:* 2450 lb (1111 kg). *Used by:* 1st and 2nd Helicopter Squadrons.

Alouette II and III
French-built, single-rotor, three-bladed helicopter with anti-torque tail rotor. The fuselage of the Alouette III was constructed of welded-steel tubes with semi-monocoque tail section, and was completely enclosed, in contrast to the open fuselage of the Alouette II. Both had "wasp's head" cockpits, extensively glazed and a light metal frame. The skids of the Alouette II were replaced with a tricycle landing gear on the later model. First flight of the II was 12 March 1955, and 28 February 1959 for the III. The presence of these French-made helicopters in South Vietnam is barely recorded. Two Alouette IIs and three Alouette IIIs were used for VIP, liaison, and limited evacuation duties, operating from Tan Son Nhut for an undetermined period between 1955 until 1963. *Manufacturer:* Sud-Est. [Specifications for Alouette II, SE 3130 precede Alouette III, SA 316B, the latter shown in brackets [].] *Power plants:* Turbomeca Artouste IIC6 turboshaft 530 shp, derated to 360 shp. [IIIB, 870 shp, derated to 570 shp.] *Dimensions:* Main rotor diameter 33 ft 5-1/2 in (10.21 m) [36 ft 2 in (11.02 m)], fuselage length 31 ft 10 in (9.7 m) [35 ft 11 in (10.94 m)], height 9 ft 0 in (2.74 m) [9 ft 10 in (2.99 m)]. *Speed:* 100 knots (184 km/h; 115 mph) [113 knot (209 km/h; 130 mph)]. *Ceiling:* 7050 ft (2149 m) [10,500 ft (3200 m)]. *Range:* 350 mi (563 m) [298 mi (480 m)]. *Payload:* 4 troops [6]. *Crew:* 1. *Maximum gross take-off weight:* 3630 lb (1646 kg) [4960 lb (2250 kg)]. *Used by:* 312th special Missions Squadron.

H-19 Chickasaw
Single-rotor, three-bladed utility helicopter, with anti-torque tail rotor at the end of a high-set boom. Crew compartment was above and forward of the cabin. Landing gear was of the wheeled quadricycle variety. Known commercially as the Sikorsky S-55, it was built for military and civil customers over a 10 year production period, following its first flight in November 1949. The Chickasaw first saw combat in Korea with the U.S. Army as a troop transport and medical evacuation helicopter. Approximately 10 or less H-19Bs were introduced into the VNAF in March 1958 for air evacuation and rescue duties. After a brief service with the VNAF they were replaced by H-34s in 1962. *Manufacturer:* Sikorsky Aircraft Co. *Power plant:* Wright R-1300-3 air-cooled radial engine, 800 hp. *Dimensions:* Main rotor diameter 53 ft 0 in (16.25 m), fuselage length 42 ft 3 in (12.87 m), height 13 ft 4 in (4.06 m). *Speed:* 97 knots (180 km/h; 112 mph). *Ceiling:* 10,500 ft (3200 m). *Range:* 360 mi (580 km). *Payload:* 10 troops or 6 litters with medical attendant. *Crew:* 2. *Maximum gross take-off weight:* 7900 lb (3583 kg). *Used by:* 1st Helicopter Squadron.

H-34 Choctaw
Combat airlift and support helicopter. Single engine, with main rotor having four blades that fold against fuselage for compact storage. Tail section pivots on Navy version to shorten overall length when at rest. Two main landing gear and one tail wheel are not retractable. Engine is mounted behind large clam shell doors in nose of fuselage to allow complete accessibility from ground level. The first of this type flew on 8 March 1954. From 1962-1969 the H-34 was the primary helicopter for combat troop and airlift support. About 230 were supplied to the VNAF over a seven year period. These were transferred from the U.S. Army as the CH-34C Choctaw; from the U.S. Marines as the UH-34D Seahorse, and from the U.S. Navy as the UH-34G Seabat. Civilian versions were known as S-58. *Manufacturer:* Sikorsky Aircraft Co. *Power plant:* Wright R-1820-84, air-cooled radial engine, 1525 hp. *Dimensions:* main rotor diameter 56 ft (17.06 m), fuselage length 46 ft 9 in (14.25 m), height 15 ft 11 in (4.85 m). *Range:*182 mi (293 km). *Payload:* 12-18 passengers, or 8 stretchers. *Crew:* 1-2. *Maximum gross take-off weight:* 13,600 lb (6169 kg). *Used by:* 211th, 213th, 217th, and 219th Helicopter Squadrons.

UH-1D and H Iroquois
Single-engined, skid-equipped utility helicopter with a single two-bladed, all-metal rotor and a two-bladed, anti-torque tail rotor mounted on the left side of the tail boom. The fuselage was of all-metal, semi-monocoque construction. The first production variant, the HU-1A Iroquois, was delivered to the U.S. Army on 30 June 1959. In 1962 the designation became UH-1, but was always better known by its nickname "Huey," derived from the pre-1962 designation HU. These helicopters were introduced into the Vietnam War by the U.S. Army as a replacement for the H-34. They served as gunships, casualty evacuation, search and rescue, vertical envelopment/attack transports, and general utility aircraft. Transfers to the VNAF from U.S. Army units in Vietnam began in 1966, eventually equipping 21 squadrons. *Manufacturer:* Bell Helicopter Co. *Power plant:* 1 Lycoming T53-L-13 turboshaft 1400 shp. *Dimensions:* Main rotor diameter 48 ft (14.63 m), fuselage length 44 ft 7 in (13.65 m), height 13 ft 5 in 94.09m). *Speed:* 113 knots (208 km/h; 130 mph. *Ceiling:* 13,700 ft (4176 m). *Range:* 357 mi (575 km). *Payload:* 13 troops, plus 2 x .50 cal or 7.62 mm flexible MG. *Crew:* 1. *Maximum gross take-off weight:* 9500 lb (4310 kg). *Used by:* 211th, 213th, 215th, 217th, 219th, 221st 223rd, 225th, 227th, 229th, 231st, 133rd, 235th ,

239th, 243rd, 245th, 251st, 253rd, 255th, 257th, and 259th Helicopter Squadrons.

CH-47 Chinook

Twin-turbine, tandem-rotor transport helicopter selected by the U.S. Army in 1959 as a medium-lift transport. First flight was 21 September 1961. Fuselage was almost a rectangular box, having a square cross-section of all-metal, semi-monocoque construction. A large ramp permitted the loading of light vehicles and troops into the cabin from the tail. Dual turboshaft power plants were mounted on the sides of the rear rotor pylon. These powered two interconnecting, contra-rotating, three-bladed tandem rotors. Landing gear was a non-retractable, wheeled quadricycle configuration. The Chinook was credited for the recovery of hundreds of downed aircraft during the Vietnam War. The VNAF received its first squadron of CH-47s, which formed the 237th HS, on 30 September 1970, when U.S. Army units began leaving Vietnam. Eventually, CH-47s equipped four VNAF squadrons, one in each of the four Military Regions, for medium-lift duties. *Manufacturer:* Boeing-Vertol, *Power plant:* 2 Lycoming T55-L-11A turboshaft 3750 shp each. *Dimensions:* Rotor diameter 60 ft (18.29 m), length 99 ft (30.17 m), height 18 ft 8 in (5.68 m). *Speed:* 164 knots (304 km/h; 189 mph). *Ceiling:* 15,000 ft (4572 m). *Range:* 230 mi (370 km). *Payload:* 44 troops or 24 stretchers, or 28,000 lb (12,700 kg) externally slung cargo. *Crew:* 3. *Maximum gross take-off weight:* 33,000 lb (14,969 kg). Used by: 237th, 241st, 247th, and 249th Helicopter Squadrons.

Schedule of Aircraft Supplied to VNAF

The following list of aircraft supplied to VNAF was taken from the *Arms Trade Registers: The Arms Trade With The Third World,* by the Stockholm International Peace Research Institute, published in the U.S. by MIT Press in 1975. They note that the content of this listing came from various unnamed sources, and therefore its completeness and accuracy must be treated accordingly.

Some omissions are apparent, such as the M.S. 500s that were transferred from the French Air Force, Republic Seabees, 56 Bell H-13s, T-37s and others. This list has value, however, for it provides a reference to time periods and quantities of aircraft supplied to VNAF. The purpose for the parenthesis was not given.

Year	*Quantity*	*Aircraft Type*	*Country*
1954	(20)	Cessna L-19	USA
1954	16	Douglas C-47	France
1954	4	Fletcher FD-25	Japan
(1954)	(10)	Beech 18	USA
1954-56	(25)	Grumman F8F	France
1954-56	55	North American T-6	USA
1956	16	Douglas C-47	(USA)
1958	(5)	Sikorsky H-19	USA
1958-59	2	De Havilland DHC-2 U-6	Canada
1960	2	Bell 47G	USA
1960-62	70	North American T-28	USA
1961	4*	Douglas B-26	USA
(1961)	(15)	Bell UH-1	USA
1961-62	150	Douglas A-1E and A-1H	USA
1961-62	5	De Havilland DHC-4	Canada
1962	(5)	Sikorsky H-19	USA
1962-63	(20)	Douglas C-47	USA
(1962-63)	25	Cessna 185	USA
1962-64	80	Sikorsky H-34	USA
1963	(6)*	Douglas B-26K	USA
1964-65	(40)	Cessna O-1	USA
(1964-65)	7	De Havilland DHC-2 U-6	(USA)
(1965-67)	25	Douglas C-47	USA
1966	4	Martin B-57B	USA
1966	1	Douglas DC-6	USA
1966-67	48	Cessna O-1	USA
1967	17	Northrop F-5A	USA
1967	2	Northrop F-5B	USA
1968	16	Fairchild C-119G	USA
1969	60	Cessna A-37	USA
1969-70	150	Bell UH-1H	USA
1970	16	Fairchild AC-119G	USA
1970	20	Vertol CH-47	USA
1970-71	48	Fairchild C-123K	USA
1970-72	104	Cessna A-37	USA
1971	200	Bell UH-1H	USA
1971	1	Pazmany PL-2	USA
1971-72	30	Vertol CH-47	USA
1972	20	Douglas A-1	USA
1972	20	Northrop F-5	USA
1972	30	Northrop F-5	Iran (loan)
1972	70	Northrop F-5	Korea, China (loan)
1972	90	Cessna A-37	USA
1972	549	Bell UH-1H	USA
1972	20	Fairchild C-119K	USA
1972	32	Lockheed C-130A	USA
1972	(5)	Douglas EC-47	USA
1972	20	Vertol CH-47	USA
1972	126	Northrop F-5E (on order, include 28 F-5F)	USA

(* Known not to have been assigned.)

VNAF Aircraft as of 30 September 1969

(Source: Air Force History Office)

Aircraft Type	*Quantity Received*	*Losses*
A-1 (all types)	242	183
A-37	55	1
F-5A	23	5
F-5B	2	0
H-34	193	163
UH-1H	85	0
O-1A	177	97
U-6A	15	6
U-17A	82	15
C-47D	61	20
AC-47	19	4
RC-47	3	0
EC-47	1	0
C-119G	19	1

VNAF Aircraft as of 31 March 1972
(Source: Journal of Military Assistance #118)

Aircraft Type	*Quantity Received*	*Losses*
A-1 (all types)	289	217
A-1E	(11 possessed)	
A-1G	(8 possessed)	
A-1H	(52 possessed)	
A-1J	(1 possessed)	
A-37B	118	10
F-5A	29	9
F-5B	2	0
RF-5A	6	1
UH-1H	765	142
CH-34C	94	92
UH-34D	56	52
UH-34G	81	64
CH-47A	26	1
O-1A	146	107
O-1E	55	16
O-1G	211	17
U-6A	17	7
U-17A	68	36
U-17B	26	6
C-47D	64	42
RC-47D	3	0
EC-47D	2	0
VC-47D	6	0
AC-47D	22	7
C-123K	51	3
T-41D	22	1
C-7A	22	0
AC-119G	24	0
C-119G	22	6

Aircraft Serial Numbers:
Numbers listed here (see below) come from a variety of sources (occasionally conflicting), ranging from visual sightings to official records. Because of the fluid ownership of these aircraft, it is impossible to use serial numbered aircraft for arriving at totals for any given date. Specifically numbered aircraft intending to be transferred to VNAF may have been diverted or canceled. Others having served VNAF may have been transferred back to USAF and U.S. Navy inventories, yet are counted as once being a VNAF aircraft, distorting any total count at any given time.

Special note about A-1 Skyraiders:
One USAF Aircraft System Manager Report for A-1s covering deliveries up to 1972 showed a total of 329 Skyraiders sent to the VNAF inventory (296 listed here): 240 from the Navy, and 89 from the USAF. Of those from the Air Force, 31 were A-1Es, five were A-1E5s, 47 were A-1Hs, and six were A-1Js in the standard Air Force configuration. (The unusual designation of A-1E5 pertained to the 19 USAF modified EA-1Es to a near standard A-1E configuration given the A-1E5 designation.)

Adjustments made in the following A-1 listing from the original *Flying Dragons* are found in the *A-1 Skyraider in Vietnam* by Wayne Mutza.

VNAF A-1 Inventory as of 30 December 1973:

	Gain	Combat Loss	Accident Loss	Returned	On Hand
A-1E	31	11	0	0	20
A-1E5	5	2	0	0	3
A-1G	46	25	2	11	8
A-1H	233	161	29	6	37
A-1J	14	11	1	0	2
Total	329	210	32	17	70

A-1E (AD-5) USN BuNos.
132415
132425
132428 pA
132433
132437 kWc
132444
132448
132455
132474
132638
132643
132647
132652
132653
132655
132657
132663
132665
132666
132667
132668
132669
132670
132673
132675
132683
132686
133858
133860
133861
133862
133866
133872
133875
133876
133878
133879
133882
133885
133891
133892
133896
133897
133898
133899
133906
133914
133915
133919
133920
133922
133927

A-1E5 (EA-1Es Modified)
135177
135185
135206
135215
139577
others

A-1G (AD-5N) USN BuNos.
132481
132482 Wa
132485 We
132487 kWb
132488
132494 kWe
132497 kWb
132498
132503 Wj
132508
132510
132514
132524
132528 Pa
132542 kWc
132551 kWd
132557
132559 kWd
132560
132562
132575
132576
132582
132587
132598
132602
132605
132612 pD
132614
132616 pB
132618
132619 wG
132620 pG
132624
132626
132627 pC
132628 wE
132629 KWe
132630 WG
132635 vWc
132636 Kwc
134976
134981
134987
134997
135036
135037
135038
135042
135043
135047 KWF, wK

A-1H (AD-6) USN BuNos.
134469
134472
134473 A
134479 E
134482 O
134483 KS
134484 O
134488 U
134493
134494
134497 G
134498 K
134499
134500 KC
134505 B
134507 Kb
134511
134514 H
134517
134519 J
134520 R
134522 Vg
134525
134526
134528
134531
134534
134535
134536
134539
134540
134546
134549
134550
134553
134555 C
134557 vE
134561 KQ
134565 U
134569 O
134570
134575
134580
134585 J/Q
134589
134590 H
134592
134595 J
134598
134600 Vq
134602
134605 J, L
134607 LQ
134609
134610
134613
134616
134620
134631 vU
134632
134634
134636 G
135223 UE
135224 A
135226 X
135228 X
135229 C
135237 Y, Yx
135243
135245
135256 C
135257
135258
135260 LJ, H
135276
135278
135279
135281 KA
135283
135286 KL
135288 Z
135289 Z, D
135292
135293
135295
135298 UG
135308 P
135310 KL
135311
135322
135325
135332
135334
135335
135339 A, D
135340 KJ, LR
135343
135352 LT
135355 C
135367
135373
135374
135376 S

135384
135386
135387 R
135392 US
135399 KE
135402
135406
137493 Z, vH, LH
137498
137499 vH
137502
137505 KI, vB
137506 F
137513 KN
137514
137517 P
137519 Vp
136522
137524
137526
137531
137532 Kp
137535
137537
137540 M
137541
137551 B
137553
137554
137558 KO
137560 KX
137564 Y, KH
137567
137569 vA
137570
137571
137574
137577
137586
137587 KJ
137588
137593
137595
137596
137597
137599 KE
137609 KM
137610
137619
137622
137624
137625
139606 KB
139607 T
139608
139609 KP
139610
139612 KN
139616
139618 KS
139619
139622 KG
139624
139626
139629 E
139634
139638
139640
139643 X
139649
139653
139656 KR
139661 G
139662
139663
139664 LI
139665
139667
139673
139674 KM, vV
139676 A
139685
139686
139689 L
139690 UA
139691
139703 N
139705
139706
139707 LM
139711 Vf
139714
139715
139718 B
139723 zK, KF
139730
139733
139737 UL
139744 U, UL
139746 KY
139749
139753
139757 UT
139758 vS
139762
139764
139765
139769 K
139770
139771 KT, LP
139775
139778
139779
139785
139788
139791
139796
139797 UL
139798
139802 LU, UB
139803
139808
139810
139812
139814 vY

A-lJ (AD-7) USN BuNos.
142014
142016
142021
142028
142034
142045 LC
142046 LB
142054
142056 Wa
142058
142060
142064 Lp
142079

F8F-1 and -1B USN BuNos.
095255 I
095338 E
121484 D
121510 G

T-28D *USN BuNos*
(Former T-28Bs)
138267
138344 LL
138365
138374
140040 LT

(Former T-28Cs)
140449 A
140456 B
140457 C
140549
140556 J
140579 ML
146244 MO

F-5A AF Serial Nos.
* Skoshi Tiger aircraft
63-08382/387
63-08389/391
63-08393/396
63-08398/404
63-08406/408
63-08428
63-08431
63-08434
63-08436
64-13306
64-13309
64-13311
64-13312
64-13314 *
64-13315 *
64-13318
64-13326
64-13329/331
64-13332 *
64-13357/359
65-10482
65-10489
65-10493/497
65-10513 *
65-10514 *
65-10515 *
65-10516
65-10518 *
65-10521/522
65-10523 *
65-10524
65-10526/534
65-10536/538
65-10543/544
65-10546 *
65-10547 *
65-10553/555
65-10556 *
65-10557
65-10558 *
65-10559 *
65-10560 *
65-10586
66-09130 *
66-09131
66-09139 *
66-09140
66-09143/145
66-09147
66-09155
66-09170/172
66-09174/175
66-09178/179
66-09180/181
66-09183
66-09185/190
66-09193/195
66-09200/202
66-09204/206
66-14457
66-14459/463
67-21153
66-21154
67-21159
67-21160
67-21162
67-21168/172
67-21175
67-21184
67-21186/187
67-21212/214
71-00266/275

RF-5A AF Serial Nos.
69-7151
69-7160
69-7161
69-7162
69-7163
70-1616
71-0279
71-1037
71-1038

F-5B AF Serial No.s
65-10586 *
65-13074 *
66-09231 *
66-09232 *
73-01606
73-01608

F-5E AF Serial No.s
* 21 recovered on
aircraft carrier at
fall of SVN.
72-01386 *
73-00846 *
73-00847 *
73-00848/854
73-00855 *
73-00856/857
73-00858 *
73-00859/864
73-00865 *
73-00866 *
73-00867
73-00868 *
73-00869
73-00871
73-00872 *
73-00873/878
73-00879 *
73-00880
73-00881 *
73-00882 *
73-00883 *
73-00885 *
73-00892
73-00896 *
73-00897 *
73-00898
73-00899 *
73-00900 *
73-00901
73-00902
73-01628
73-01635 *
73-01636 *
73-01637/639
73-01640 *

A-37A AF Serial No.
67-14507

A-37B AF Serial Nos.
67-14777/789
67-14791
67-14793/822
67-22487/491
68-07913/926
68-07928
68-07931/934
68-07936/939
68-07944
68-07946/947
68-07959/961
68-07964
68-07974/777
68-l0779/810
68-10814/817
68-10820/823
68-10827
69-06334/338
69-06340/347
69-06350
69-06353/354
69-06357/358
69-06360/363
69-06365
69-06373/374
69-06376/377
69-06382

69-06390/392
69-06394/395
69-06399/413
69-06418
69-06431
69-06433/435
69-06437
69-06439/440
69-06444/446
70-01277/278
70-01280
70-01285/287
70-01295/297
71-00790/815
71-00817/850
71-00852/854
71-00857
71-00864/866

B-57B AF Serial Nos.
52-1532 P
52-1541 M
52-1545
52-1567
53-3878 W
53-3928
53-3929
Others were assigned, but generally not more than 4 at any one time.

C-47 AF Serial Nos.
42-92836
42-92839 EA
42-100666 EM, EC
43-15718
43-16164 O
43-18184 Q
43-48058 ?C
43-48151 EG
43-48213 ES
43-48465 EF
43-48476 EQ
43-48415 NI
43-48491 EY
43-48586 NF, CG
43-48816 ES
43-48874 A, EO
43-48879 EG
43-48937 NS
43-49095 EK
43-49113 EN
43-49114 ET
43-49210 EC
43-49257 CH
43-49345 EB
43-49495 EZ
43-49497 EJ
43-49524 M
43-49783 ET
43-49925 EF

44-76302 CL
44-76417 CI
44-76418 EB
44-76502 EL
44-76643 EC
44-76686 CE
44-77012 ER
45-0264 MB
45-0722
45-0882 MC
45-0945 MC

EC-47D AF Serial Nos.
42-10898
42-23520
42-93161
42-93166
42-93735
42-100513
42-100950
42-100984
43-15112
43-15668
43-15979
43-15980
43-16055
43-16123
43-48801 HE
43-49009
43-49013
43-49029 MF
43-49126
43-49703
43-49865
43-49905 MA
43-76524
44-76668
45-00925
503 HF
913 HC

AC-47D AF Serial Nos.
43-16065 H-
43-48701 K-
43-48929
43-49211 KS
43-49517
44-76606 H-

C-119G AF Serial Nos.
53-03157
53-03161 NG
53-03202
53-03218 NB
53-03220
53-07873
53-08124
53-08133

AC-119G AF Serial No.
53-03170

AC-119K AF Serial No.
52-5864
52-5889
52-5910
52-5911
52-5926
52-5940
52-5945
52-9982
53-8121
53-8148
53-3154
53-3187
53-3197
53-3211
53-7830
53-7831
53-7839
53-7850
53.7851
53-7877
53-7879
53-7883
53-8145

C-123K AF Serial Nos.
54-00559 RF
54-00576 RO
54-00577
54-00578 RD
54-00579 X-
54-00584 RA
54-00587 RD
54-00590 XD
54-00591
54-00592
54-00599 QM
54-00601 RC
54-00608
54-00620 R-
54-00624 XD
54-00625

54-00626 XC
54-00627 QL
54-00632 XH
54-00634 QF
54-00637
54-00645 QP
54-00651 X-
54-00654 QA
54-00660 QE
54-00662 XB
54-00670 XE
54-00673 RP
54-00678 RB
54-00682 QJ
54-00684 Q
54-00686 QK
54-00687 XQ
54-00690 XG
54-00696 Q-
54-00697
54-00699 RK
54-04506 XK
54-04508 RL
54-04509 QO
54-04510 XF
54-04511 RQ
54-04514 QD
54-04523 QA
54-04525 XL
54-04536 QN
54-04542 QS
54-04548 QR
54-04553 RE
54-04554 XA
54-04561 XO
54-04564 QC
54-04565 QH
54-04566 RG
54-04569 RJ
55-04568 R-
56-04359
56-04360 QB
56-04363 XJ
56-04365
56-04377 XP
56-04384 R-
56-04387 XI
56-04396
57-06289 RM
57-06290 RH

C-130A AF Serial Nos.
54-01631
54-01634
54-01640
55-00001
55-00002
55-00005
55-00006
55-00008
55-00012
55-00013
55-00016
54-00017
55-00027
55-00034
55-00045
55-00048
56-00472
56-00476
56-00479
56-00480
56-00481
56-00482 HCK
56-00483
56-00489
56-00492
56-00495
56-00500
56-00505
56-00518 HCM
56-00519 HCP
56-00521
56-00524
56-00532
56-00542
56-00543
56-00545
57-00460 HCF
57-00465
57-00472

C-7A AF Serial Nos.
60-03762
60-05431
60-05442 P-
61-02384
61-02397
61-02402
61-02404
61-02407 P-
61-02595
61-02597
61-02598
62-04144
62-04147
62-04150
62-04153/157
62-04159
62-04162
62-04163
62-04166
62-04168
62-04171/172
62-04174
62-04178
62-04181 P-
62-04183
62-04192
62-04195
62-12583
63-09722
63-09726
63-09727
63-09729/731
63-09734/735
63-09738/744
63-09748
63-09752
63-09755
63-09763

O-1 AF Serial Nos.
50-01638
51-01548
51-01916
51-04543
51-04567
51-04803
51-04831
51-04955
51-04991
51-05012
51-05057
51-05099
51-06967
51-07309
51-07401
51-07426
51-07437
51-07476
51-12209
51-11916
51-11959
51-11961
51-11999 B
51-12007
51-12161 BN
51-12165
51-12220 DK
51-12224
51-12236 DP
51-12264 DQ
51-12272
51-12322

51-12368
51-12472 BD
51-12492 DC, BH
51-12503 DJ
51-12519
51-12639
51-12692 DE
51-12697 E
51-12701 BL
51-12704 DA
51-12715 D
51-12792 DC, BE
51-12799 DO
51-12819
51-12829 DM, BE
51-12830 DN
51-12875 BK
51-12900
51-12903
51-14981 FDD
51-16869
53-08037 DA
53-08041
56-02504 DN
56-02528
56-02546
56-02553
51-02596
56-02605
56-02642 N
56-04172

O-2A AF Serial Nos.
67-21381
68-10843
68-10845/847
68-10850
68-10855/856
68-10859/861
68-10863
68-10973
68-10988
68-10991
68-10994
68-10996
68-11007/011
68-11019
68-11021
68-11023/025
68-11035
68-11037
68-11039
68-11043
68-11060
68-11062
68-11066
68-11069

U-6A AF Serial Nos.
51-16534 MT
51-16862 MM
52-06120 MR
52-06127 MS
53-06168 MO
53-08166 MN
56-00363 MP

U-17A AF Serial Nos.
63-13018
63-13020 WF
63-13-21 WC
63-13024
63-13029
63-13030
63-13035
63-13036 XG
63-13313
65-10837 XC
65-10839
56-10845 YF
65-12908 YH
66-13310 YB
66-13311
66-13312
67-14497
67-14500 XR

U-17B AF Serial Nos.
67-22525
67-22527
67-22529
67-22530 YD
68-08939 XN
69-07309/311
69-07310 YB
71-01422/425
71-01427/442
71-01444/448
71-01450

T-41D AF Serial Nos.
70-01594

CH-34A AF Serial Nos.
(From US Army)
53-04494
53-04498
53-04511 JF
54-00891 JE
54-00921
54-00328
54-03883
54-05795
54-05796

CH-34C
(From US Army)
63-13190/210

SH-34G USN BuNos.
131589
137851
138462
138467
138471
138488
139029
139034
140134
140136
141175
141590
143886
143888
143901
143904
143905
143907
143916
149377

UH-34D USN BuNos.
143983
144639
145782
145795
148060
148076
148335
150247

UH-1B AF Serial Nos.
62-02054
62-02060

UH-1H AF Serial Nos.
65-15899
65-16058
66-16309
66-16340
66-16371
66-16438
66-16452
66-16496
66-16503

66-16534
66-16549
66-16562/563
66-16569
66-16574
66-16581
66-16608
66-16651
66-16698
66-16727
66-16730
66-16739
66-16796
66-16813
66-16838
66-16841
66-16852
66-17065
66-17116
67-11700
67-17188
67-17276
67-17278
67-17284
67-17314
67-17346
67-17360
67-17383
67-17385
67-17392
67-17394
67-17430
67-17438
67-17444
67-17507/509
67-17555
67-18567
67-17730/731
67-17742
67-17761
67-17787
67-17829/830
67-17851
67-17881
67-19504
68-15052
68-15134
68-15218
68-15242
68-15247
68-15257
68-15298
68-15315
68-15353
68-15358
68-15384
68-15398
68-15428/429
68-15467
68-15479
68-15504
68-15507
68-15509
68-15542
68-15545/546
68-15575
68-15603/604
68-15709
68-15711
68-15717
68-15731/732
68-15773
68-16078
68-16090
68-16146
68-16161
68-16186
68-16188
68-16207
68-16219
68-16231
68-16255
68-16260
68-16280
68-16287
68-16317
68-16366
68-16377
68-16379
68-16390
68-16393
68-16422
68-16424
68-16442
68-16444
68-16464
68-16493
68-16506
68-16533
68-16535
68-16539/541
68-16551
68-16555
68-16570
68-16580
68-16653
68-16721
69-15028
69-15032
69-15049
69-15054
69-15061
69-15071
69-15109
69-15133
69-15169
69-15182
69-15196
69-15201
69-15206
69-15214
69-15222
69-15274
69-15279
69-15280
69-15285
69-15289
69-15295
69-15317
69-15369
69-15373
69-15377
69-15382
69-15388
69-15391
69-15393
69-15400
69-15407
69-15409/410
69-15413
69-15426/427
69-15430
69-15431/433
69-15437
69-15444/445
69-15451
69-15456
69-15465
69-15468
69-15470/471
69-15504
69-15511 RE
69-15513 PG
69-15516
69-15519 RM
69-15520
69-15522/523
69-15527
69-15535/536
69-15538
69-15543
69-15546
69-15549
69-15554/556
69-15562

69-15574
69-15576
69-15612
69-15618
69-15626
69-15635
69-15638
69-15640
69-15644
69-15663
69-15667
69-15670
69-15685
69-15689
69-15694
69-15696
69-15698
69-15712
69-15714
69-15720
69-15737
69-15744
69-15757
69-15761
69-15765
69-15768/769
69-15774/776
69-15778
69-15780
69-15786
69-15806
69-15809
69-15812
69-15825
69-15832
69-15890
69-15892
69-15895
69-15897
69-15900
69-15904
69-15906/907
69-15955/956
69-15958
69-16650
69-16659/664
69-16666
69-16670
69-16693
69-16704/707
69-16714
69-16718
69-16721
69-16724/726
69-16732
69-17222
69-25741
70-15705
70-15713/717
70-15721/722
70-15725
70-15729
70-15737
70-15740
70-15748
70-15751
70-15756
70-15777
70-15781
70-15786
70-15793
70-15800
70-15801
70-15803/804
70-15806
70-15808
70-15813/814
70-15816
70-15831
70-15840
70-15842
70-15868
70-15874
70-15921/922
70-15924

CH-47A AF Serial Nos.
65-7968
65-7970
65-7972
65-7974/975
65-7985/987
65-7996/998
65-8006
65-8016
65-8025
65-13160
66-00066
66-00078/082
66-00085
66-00094
66-00098/100
66-00105
66-00110
66-00117
66-00125
66-19003/004
66-19026/027
66-19034/035
66-19042
66-19065
66-19070
66-19078/079
66-19082/083
66-19085/086
66-19092

Appendix B: Aircraft Colors and Markings

National Insignia

The South Vietnamese national insignia was as varied in its design and construction as were the many types of aircraft on which it was applied. It is difficult to recognize which of the many designs encountered was considered the true and official format at any particular time. The directives or formal description for insignia layout are not available, and may never have existed. Therefore, the designs shown here have been developed from a close study of a large number of photographs that document their use. The letters used to identify each design type have been assigned by the author. One factor that prevailed, however, was the consistent use of orange-yellow and red that appeared in the flag of the Republic of Vietnam.

When military aircraft were assigned to the VNAF on gaining its independence from the French Air Force in the early 1950s, its small inventory carried a roundel in line with French practice. The colors, however, were different from that of the French. The Vietnamese insignia was described as an orange-yellow circle background with three concentric red bands superimposed upon it. (*see* illustration of Type A Insignia). These bands were symbolic of the three red stripes on the national flag. An insignia of the flag appeared on the rudder of all Vietnamese aircraft, a practice that was followed until the end of the war, 20 years later.

When the United States assumed responsibility for the Military Assistance Program for Vietnam the Vietnamese national insignia took on a completely different format. This was one that matched very closely the design of the U.S. national insignia, for reasons unknown, though it eased the change of markings when aircraft were reassigned between the two air forces.

When the new star and bar insignia was first observed in wide usage on VNAF aircraft (Type B); its likeness to the American insignia varied, since the bar was located on the center line of the circle and not its relationship to the horizontal alignment with the star. It is possible that the earlier orange-yellow was replaced at this point with the international standard yellow, used for the field background. Borders for the circle and the bars were insignia red, contrary to the U.S. insignia blue.

The next observed design was the Type C, which had the same proportions of the standard U.S. insignia, including the above-center for the bar. This was introduced at the time USAF counter-insurgency forces, called "Jungle Jim," began using T-28s and B-26s for combat training Vietnamese aircrews at Bien Hoa. This made the conversion from the U.S. to the Vietnamese insignia simple. The blue border was replaced with red and was carried completely around the blue field. Yellow replaced the white bars. This insignia design was used throughout the war on various aircraft, including the O-1, A-1, and C-123.

The Type D insignia was first seen when a large order of Douglas A-1 Skyraiders was supplied to the VNAF in 1960. This design differed in having a longer bar, which was determined by where the "R": dimension was begun. This format reappeared on the 1968 deliveries of C-119s to the VNAF.

A close match to the Type D insignia was the Type E. The only difference here was that the height of the bar was increased and made to be of equal size vertically on both sides of the horizontal center line. This wider bar design first became popular on many VNAF A-1s, and was later applied to Cessna A-37 Dragonflys.

The most radical change in the star-and-bar design came with the doubling in width of the red border of the insignia. This is illustrated on both Type F and G, their basic difference in design being the size of the horizontal bars. Type F was predominately used on VNAF's large fleet of C-47s, and the Type G was used almost exclusively on U-17 Skywagons.

Other changes in design proportions have been noted, but those shown here were the most dominant. In the early years of the VNAF, this insignia appeared on the left and right wing tips, top and bottom, as well as on both sides of the fuselage. As the VNAF grew, the top right and lower left insignia were not used, which was the custom on U.S. military aircraft. The VNAF aircraft that eventually used the Southeast Asia camouflage scheme utilized the miniaturized national insignia with a blue circle diameter of 15 in (38 cm). It was not unusual at times to see some A-1s and O-1s without insignia at all.

Along with the use of the star-and-bar insignia was a segment of the South Vietnamese flag painted on the rudder. This was a vertical yellow rectangle with three horizontal red stripes. The irregularity in size, shape, and proportions when applied to the VNAF aircraft exceeds the imagination, and therefore, only a few of the formats are illustrated here.

In time the orange cast to the yellow that was distinctively used in the Vietnamese flag gave way to the U.S. Orange-Yellow, which was more yellow. The following gloss colors can be found in the U.S. Federal Standard color catalog 595b, which best describes the standard colors used for the VNAF insignia for non-camouflaged aircraft. For camouflaged aircraft, these colors would have a matt finish, having a 3 instead of a 1 prefix to the 595b color number.

Red	11136
White	17875
Blue	15044*
Orange-Yellow	13432 (early use)
Orange-Yellow	13538 (later use)

*Some blues used for insignia were as light as 15080.

Camouflage and Exterior Colors

As the war in Southeast Asia gained momentum in the early to mid-1960s an array of new camouflage schemes began to appear. Until that time the small variety of aircraft operated by the VNAF retained the colors in which they were received from the French. Morane-Saulnier 500 Criquets, for instance, retained their olive green French camouflage, which may have approximated the U.S. Federal Standard 595b 34096, as sampled from the original paint on the SM-500 in the National Air and Space Museum in Washington, D.C. The VNAF fighter-bomber force of Grumman F8F Bearcats acquired from the French were in their original U.S. Navy Glossy Sea Blue, Federal Standard 595b 15042, until that paint was removed and the aircraft operated in their bare metal. When the Americans began supplying the VNAF with C-47s these, along with the French-acquired transports, operated in their natural aluminum or silver painted finish.

Among the earliest American supplied equipment for VNAF were the Cessna L-19 Bird Dogs to replace the aging Criquets. These were U.S. Army aircraft, and their brown olive drab exteriors were apparent in a wide range of variations well into the 1960s. Darker shades of green were also used, and in the previous years it was possible that some paint acquired from the French for Criquet maintenance was used on some L-19s.

Douglas A-1 Skyraiders were acquired in 1960 from the U.S. Navy and retained their Light Gull Gray (36440) with White (17875) under surfaces, as well as flight control surfaces, then the standard Navy coloring. Subsequent Skyraiders were supplied by the USAF in overall Gray (36373) beginning around 1962. This had become the standard for all USAF aircraft not otherwise operating in their

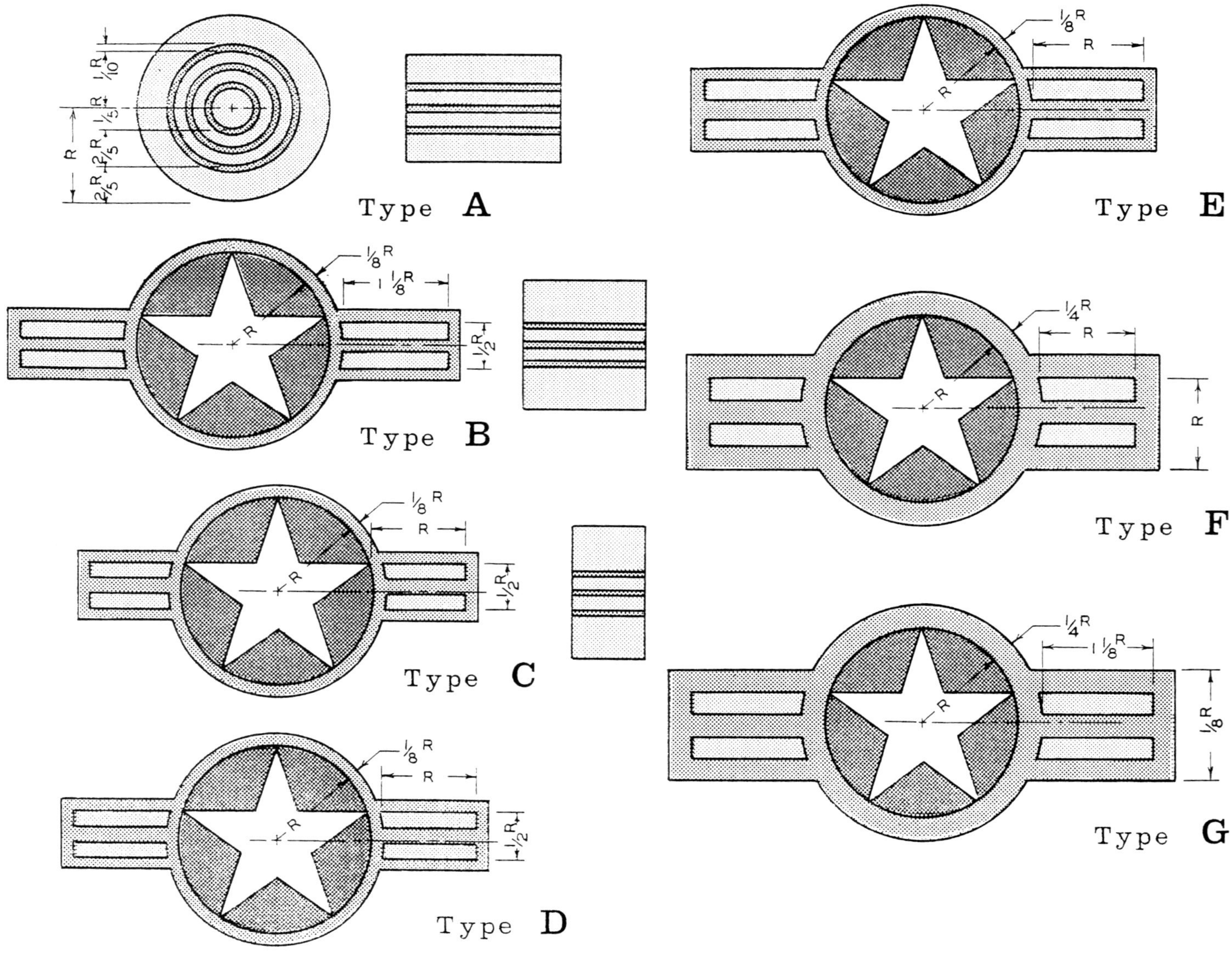

Design configurations for Vietnamese National Insignia.

The earliest form of Vietnamese national insignia consisted of an orange-yellow circle with three red concentric bands. This early tail marking design on MS 500s was larger than what developed in the years that followed. *Courtesy of J. Lebourg*

natural metal finish. T-28Ds sent to Vietnam for both USAF and VNAF use were painted this standard overall Gray.

The Douglas Skyraider was one of the earliest aircraft to operate in the disruptive-pattern type camouflage in Southeast Asia. In 1965 the 83rd Special Operations Group acquired A-1s for their 522nd Fighter Squadron painted with this type of camouflage, which had been developed exclusively for this unit. Patterns varied with each aircraft, but for the majority, the two upper colors were approximately Brown (30166) and Green (34108). The overall White or Gray lower surface (depending upon source of aircraft) was left unchanged. The aircrafts' black serial numbers, which appeared on the fin, were masked over during the camouflage painting, which left as a final form a gray rectangular background for the numbers.

Presumably, these Skyraiders had been acquired from various units who camouflaged them prior to their transfer. This would account for the variations in colors and inconsistent patterns; one aircraft's camouflage scheme consisted of Medium Gray, Green (34148), and Dark Olive (34052), while another had an upper surface of Purple- Brown (30206) and Dark Gray (36559), with Green (34108) across the tail. These colors are only estimates, based upon memory and color photography. Some aircraft retained this paint scheme as late as 1968, perhaps longer.

By mid to late-1966, gray painted Douglas A-1s were changed to the new standard USAF disruptive-pattern camouflage, the application of which was precisely as described in USAF T.O. 1-1-4. It became popularly known as the "SEA camouflage," and appeared on all USAF tactical aircraft deployed in South Vietnam, beginning around 1965, and, in time, on all USAF aircraft worldwide. The camouflage consisted of Dark Green (34079), Green Olive Drab (34102), and Tan (30219) for the upper and side surfaces, and Gray (36622) for the lower surfaces. It remained the camouflage scheme for all tactical fixed-wing VNAF aircraft (as well as USAF) for the remainder of the war. This included all cargo type aircraft, with the exception of some C-47s, particularly those used as VIP transports by the 314th Special Mission Squadron—and general personnel carriers. Transport gunships also used this scheme, but had black (17038) under surfaces for night missions.

Between 1968 and the early 1970s Cessna O-1s underwent a color change. As an increasing number left USAF units for VNAF use in Gray (36373) finish it was decided to paint the existing Olive Drab O-1s in the same color. The newly repainted O-1s began appearing in light grays ranging from approximately 36373 to 36628, with variations to nearly 37772. White (37875) upper wing and tail surfaces (or selected portions when Olive Drab was the general

Reasons for the departure from the orange circular VNAF insignia are not fully known, but as French influence faded, the aircraft they left behind received the new bar and star similar to that of the American insignia. This is a very rare photo showing Crickets with this new insignia design. *Courtesy of Marcel Paquelier.*

This awkwardly positioned Douglas A-1E shows clearly an early form of applying the star and bar type insignia on both wings, top and bottom, of the same size as on both sides of the fuselage. This Skyraider of the 518th FS was transferred direct from the U.S. Navy, as evidenced by their practice of having white control surfaces. *Courtesy of David W. Menard.*

finish) were commonplace on VNAF and USAF FAC aircraft after 1965, so that they could more easily be seen from above by the aircraft they were controlling for air strikes.

Except for a few rare cases, Cessna U-17s retained their overall standard Gray (36373) throughout the war, as did the O-2As.

In the earlier years, VNAF helicopters operated in several camouflage colors. Generally, these helicopters retained the basic color in which they were received—either that of the U.S. Army (X34087) or U.S. Marines (34097). A disruptive-pattern camouflage for H-34s was sometimes obtained by using matt black to create a pattern over the existing basic color. Nearly a squadron strength of H-34s were painted in the colors described for the 83rd SOG during the same period. The camouflage color of Olive Drab (X34087) became more consistent throughout the VNAF when former U.S. Army UH-1s and CH-47s became the main helicopter types in use.

VNAF training aircraft also retained the color in which they were received. North American T-6Gs were Orange-Yellow (33538); Cessna T-41s, Gray (36373); and T-37Bs, natural aluminum metal finish.

The war in Southeast Asia saw the use of a countless variety of unique and unusual camouflage and color schemes, often as variable as the imaginations that created them.

Distinctive Unit Markings

When the Vietnamese Air Force began its modernization program in the early 1960s, it seemed destined to become the most colorful air force in the world. Brightly colored fuselage sashes with stylized patterns made each unit easily distinguishable from another. Some of the new units carried these colorful designs on wingtip tanks as well as their rudder. With more than 60 squadrons in existence in the 1970s, there was an abundant variety of colorful aircraft.

This bright decorative array of color for this air force was not fully realized, however. It appeared that the painters were unable to keep pace with the rapid influx of new aircraft into the VNAF inventory, which blossomed from less than 200 aircraft when expansion began in 1960, to over 2000 by the end of the war, excluding those lost through attrition. Photographs now provide the only record of these elaborate markings.

Aside from unit insignia, fuselage bands were the first form of elaborate markings. These appeared as the VNAF began introducing Douglas AD-6 Skyraiders into their fighter squadrons. There were four designs by late 1962, when only one squadron (1st Fighter Squadron) was equipped with Skyraiders. One may assume that these four designs identified each of the four flights that usually make up a squadron. All of these aircraft carried on their nose the insignia of the 1st Fighter Squadron, which later became the 514th Fighter Squadron on 1 January 1963.

Size of the insignia and proportions used in its design varied with nearly every aircraft type. The basic design followed closely to that used by the United States, although the proportions of the bar on this O-1 at Phu Cat in 1971 of an unidentified unit are extremely exaggerated. *Courtesy of Norman E. Taylor.*

The 1st Fighter Squadron, soon redesignated the 514th Fighter Squadron, adopted four distinctive fuselage band designs for their A-1H Skyraiders. This devil in red, over a black band identified Satan Flight, lead by Nguyen-huu-Chan.

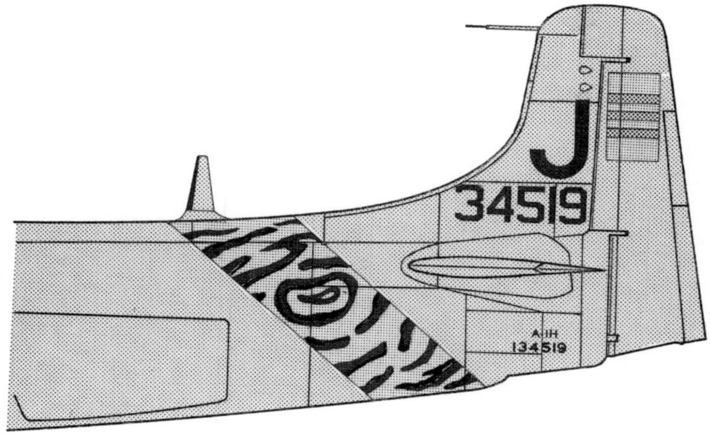

Tiger stripes in orange and black on this A-1H of the 514th Fighter Squadron, marked *Son Vuong* Flight, commanded by Nguyen-huu-Nan. These markings were used from late 1962 to 1963 only, or until such time as the newer band design could be applied.

Squadron Commander Nguyen-quang-Tri had a fuselage band that included all four designs carried on 514th Fighter Squadron aircraft, photographed here in December 1963. Still to be changed was the AD-6 designation under the tail, which became A-1H in September 1962. *Courtesy of E Lundh*

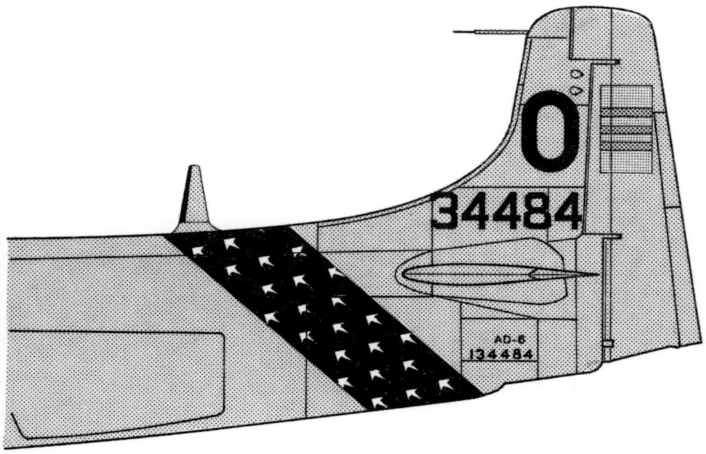

This red band with white stylized arrows is known to have adorned at least one other aircraft in 1964 following the adoption of the yellow and black checkerboard design for aircraft of the newly-formed 23rd Tactical Wing at Bien Hoa.

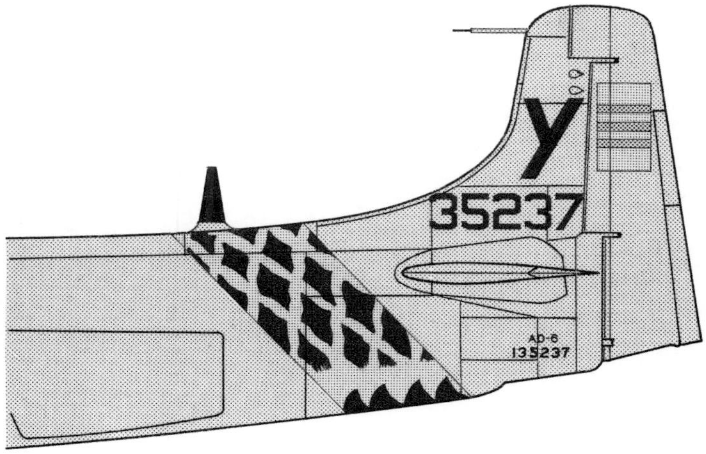

Colors for this band for *Than Phong* Flight of the 514th are thought to be dark blue irregular shapes over orange, with perhaps red tongues of fire at bottom. Flight Commander was To-minh-Chanh. These fuselage bands may have been assigned to flights or squadron sections in the order shown here, based upon descending order of alphabetical tail codes.

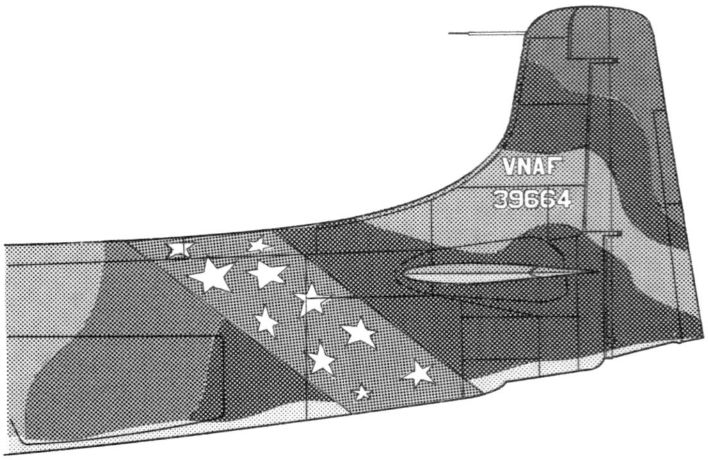

41st Tactical Wing. Fuselage band of dark blue with white stars.

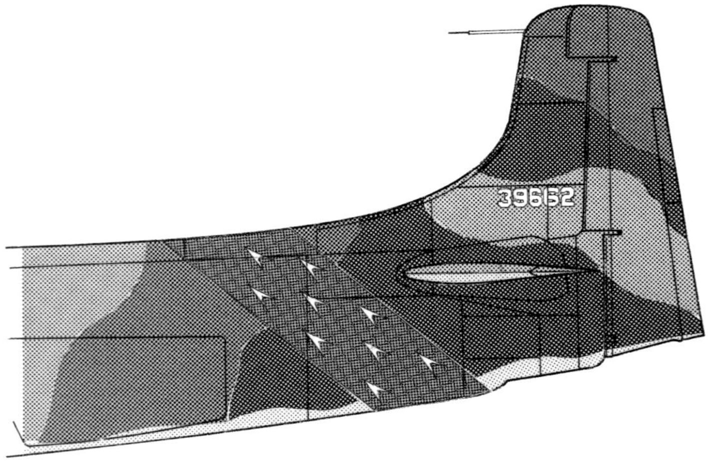

62nd Tactical Wing. Fuselage band of plum, with white stylized arrows. Presumed to be used on A-1s only.

It is possible when existing VNAF units were renumbered in January 1963 that fuselage bands and other distinctive markings were used to identify respective tactical groups, which subsequently became wings. Entirely new designs evolved after this restructuring, and although some of the old markings used by the 514th Fighter Squadron were noted in 1964, or even as late as 1965, it is believed that these were merely carry-overs and due to be changed.

The number of tactical wings increased rapidly when helicopter squadrons were organized into wings, leaving only fixed-wing aircraft in the original wings. This should have brought an abundance of new distinctive unit markings, however, this did not happen. The situation is not clear, but it seems that the designs became base- or even air division-related. The most noticeable sign of this practice was the consistently used stylized star, as well as polkadots, found on Binh Thuy based aircraft, identity between units accomplished by a change in color combinations. Although only three A-37 squadrons were assigned at Binh Thuy, six color and design combinations were noted on these aircraft. Helicopters in its sister wing at Binh Thuy carried this distinctive star and a crescent moon design, but with different color combinations.

Except for the use of the national insignia, there were no regulations for squadron markings. Each squadron's pilots and wing commander selected these markings for approval by the VNAF Headquarters before use.

Distinctive unit markings that can be reasonably identified are listed below. This system, which began in 1963, identified the tactical wing to which the aircraft were assigned. As more wings were formed within the same Corps area the designs remained the same, but in many cases the colors were changed to denote a different tactical wing or squadron within that Corps. The color code numbers given are based upon the Federal Standard FS 595b system, and all colors are approximate.

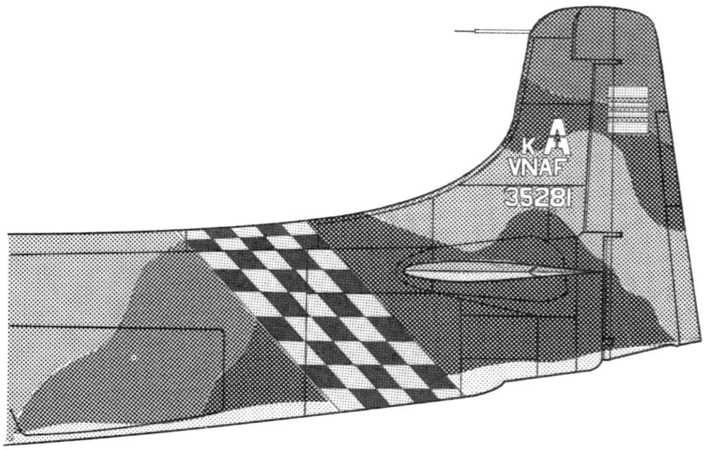

23rd Tactical Wing. Fuselage band of yellow and black checkerboard.

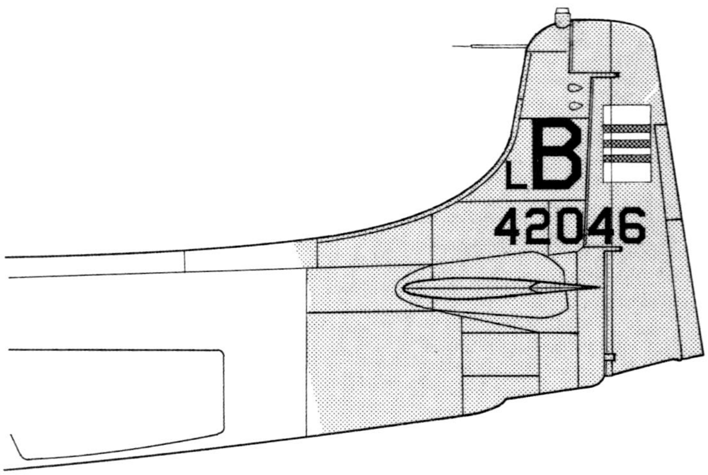

Typical gray aircraft (A-1J) with single-letter squadron identifier L for 516th Fighter Squadron at Da Nang AB.
Squadron letter (L): 9 x 6 x 1-1/2 in. (2 x 15 x 4 cm)
Aircraft letter (B): 24 x 16 x 4 in. (61 x 41 x 10 cm)
Serial Number: 9 x 6 x 1| in. (23 x 15 x 4 cm)

Tail code letters on the multi-place A-1E Skyraiders within the 23rd Tactical Wing at Bien Hoa AB had a unique coding system of their own. All had the large-size letter "W." To differentiate between aircraft, a smaller suffix letter was added, seemingly used in alphabetical sequence. Photos 1 and 2, taken February 1966, show aircraft "A" (32482) with a prefix "K" for the 518th FS, and "B" aircraft, 32487 was without a squadron letter. When the airplane "B" was camouflaged, as shown in photo 3, taken April 1970, it then carried the "K" unit identifier for the 518th FS. Aircraft "C" (32437) is on page (##), and "D" (32559) appears in photo 4, taken in 1970, both with 518th "K" identifiers. *Photos 1 & 2; Courtesy of David W. Menard, 3 & 4, RG 342-KE40780 & KE40778 USAF.*

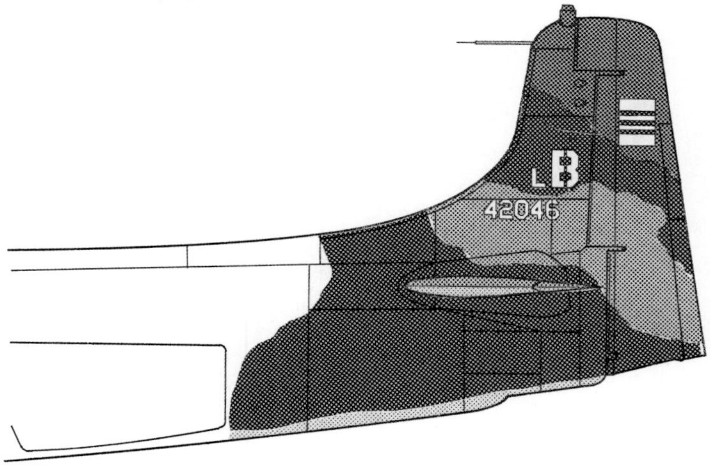

Typical camouflaged aircraft (A-1J) with single-letter squadron identifier L.
Squadron letter (L): 6 × 4 × 1 in. (15 × 10 × 3 cm)
Aircraft letter (B): 12 × 8 × 2 in. (30 × 20 × 5 cm)
Serial Number: 6 × 4 × 1 in. (15 × 10 × 3 cm)

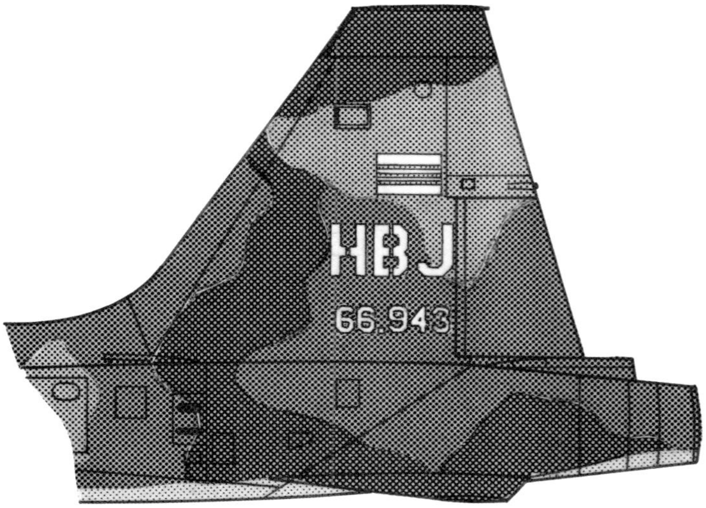

Typical camouflaged aircraft (F-5E) with double-letter squadron identifier HB.
Squadron letter (HB): 12 × 8 × 2 in. (30 × 20 × 5 cm)
Aircraft letter (J): 12 × 8 × 2 in. (30 × 20 × 5 cm
Serial Number: 6 × 4 × 1 in. (15 × 0 × 3 cm)

This style of tail code lettering remained on C-47s throughout the existence of the VNAF, regardless of the source of these aircraft. It was a carryover from the French system of having a ship letter painted over a circle of the squadron color. When French C-47s were transferred to the VNAF, all circles were painted orange-yellow, and a smaller prefix letter to identify the squadron was added. In this case "M" was for the short lived 314th Special Mission Squadron.

	FS 595b	*Aircraft Types*
1st Air Division:		
41st Tactical Wing, Da Nang AB		A-1, A-37, H-34, U-17, O-1
Dark Blue fuselage band	35053 & 35044	
White Stars	37875	
2nd Air Division:		
62nd Tactical Wing, Nha Trang AB		A-1 (524th FS)
Plum fuselage band	37142	
White arrows	37875	
(Later design)		A-37
Dark Blue fuselage band, with 2 parallel rows of:	35044	
White stylized arrows	37875	
Red stylized arrows	31136	
3rd Air Division:		
23rd Tactical Wing, Bien Hoa AB		A-1, F-5. O-1, U-17
63rd Tactical Wing, Bien Hoa AB		
Yellow checkerboard with	33538	
Black	37038	
4th Air Division:		
74th Tactical Wing, Binh Thuy AB		
Green wing tip tanks and rudder with	34108	A-37 (520th FS)
Red stylized stars	31136	
Dark Blue wing tip tanks and rudder with	35044	A-37 (520th FS)
White stylized stars	37875	
Red wing tip tanks and rudder with	31136	A-37 (526th FS)
White stylized stars	37875	
Yellow wing tip tanks and rudder with	33538	A-37 (526th FS)
Black stylized stars	37038	
Dark Blue wing tip tanks and rudder with	35044	A-37 (546th FS)
White polkadots	37875	
Red wing tip tanks and rudder with	31136	A-37 (546th FS)
White polkadots	37875	
Dark Blue wing tip and rudder with	35044	U-17 (116th OS)
White stylized stars	37875	
Red wing tip and rudder	31136	U-17 (122nd OS)
with White stylized stars	37875	
64th Tactical Wing, Can Tho AB		
84th Tactical Wing, Binh Thuy AB		
Dark Blue tail rotor fin with	35044	UH-1 (217th HS)
Yellow stylized stars	33538	
Yellow tail rotor fin with	33538	UH-1 (217th HS)
Black stylized stars	37038	
Red tail rotor fin with	31136	UH-1 (225th HS)
Black stylized stars	37038	
Green tail rotor fin with	34108	UH-1 (227th HS)
White stylized stars	37875	

Yellow tail rotor fin with Black stylized crescent moon	33538 37038	UH-1 (Unidentified.)
Red tail rotor fin with White stylized crescent moon	31136 37875	UH-1 (Unidentified)

Tail Code Identifiers

Tail codes are often used to identify military aircraft of many nations, the larger letters being more easily seen than the serial number; the VNAF may have used this system to a greater extent than other Air Forces, however. Crew assignments in flight scheduling were based exclusively on tail codes, not Air Force serial numbers, which, for instance, was common practice in the USAF. Aircraft maintenance crews also used the same system.

Some air forces used tail codes as radio call signs when aircraft were not on tactical missions. In the VNAF, for example, "Echo Lima" would be a C-47 from the 415th Transport Squadron, and "X-ray Coco" would be a C-123 from the 425th Transport Squadron. The C-130s were an exception, using Herky followed by the last three numbers of the aircraft's serial number.. Tactical missions used the name of the squadron followed by the mission number, such as "Phoenix 12" (English) or "*Phuong-Hoang* 12," (Vietnamese,) identifying the 514th Fighter Squadron.

It is interesting to note that tail codes were used during the execution of flight plans, both domestically or internationally. The letters "XV" (for the Republic of Vietnam, just as "N" for civil aircraft registered in the United States) always prefixed the military code letters; whereas the U.S. used military serial numbers. Although not painted on VNAF aircraft, "XV" formed part of the aircraft's full identification.

The VNAF's tail coding system had a long history in the VNAF. It started as a carry-over from the French system. This was a single letter identifier for the airplane, painted over a color coded circle that identified the squadron to which the aircraft was assigned. This was most apparent on the C-47s, and when these Gooney Birds were transferred to the VNAF these color circles were changed to the national orange-yellow color. To differentiate between aircraft of the two transport squadrons, a small letter "N" eventually preceded the aircraft's identifying tail letter for the 1st Transport Squadron (later becoming the 413th TS), and "E" was used for the 2nd Transport squadron (later becoming the 415th TS).

With the transfer of F8F Bearcats from the French Air Force to the VNAF's 1st Fighter Squadron, the single identifying tail letters were retained. This one letter code system continued with that squadron even after being updated with newer equipment, perhaps by tradition, but as other units were formed, a single letter was assigned to each unit and applied at half the height and in front of the individual aircraft letter, creating the two-letter identifying system. When two types of aircraft were assigned to a unit, each aircraft type often had a different unit identifying letter.

This two letter tail code system worked well as long as there were enough single letter identifiers to go around for the various squadrons. When the further expansion of the VNAF was taking place in the early 1970s it became necessary to use a two letter unit code followed by the ship letter, which then became a three letter tail code. With this system, all letters were of uniform height across the tail. For reasons yet to be learned, A-37 squadrons did not use tail codes, but seemed to rely on more lavishly painted color codes and designs for unit identification.

The accompanying list of assigned unit tail codes is not considered to be complete. There was no common source from which to draw this information other than through the study of photographs and personal recollections of former VNAF members. Far more units existed than are recorded in this listing of known unit code letters. With the rapid addition of new units in the 1970s it is possible that some of these unit identifying letters were never applied to their aircraft, and therefore remain unrecorded through the one remaining source for this information, that being photographs.

Tail Codes and Units Assigned

Squadron Code	*Squadron*	*Aircraft Type*	*Air Base*
None	514 FS	A-1H	Bien Hoa
B	110 OS	O-1	Da Nang
C	314 SM	C-47	Tan Son Nhut

The black tail code identifiers remained unchanged when Douglas A-1s were initially camouflaged. In time, however, these letters were reduced in size and painted white for better contrast, as shown in this 518th Fighter Squadron Skyraider photograph. *RG 342-102114 USAF*

D	112 OS	O-1	Bien Hoa
E	116 OS		Binh Thuy
E	415 TS	C-47	Tan Son Nhut
F	821 AS	AC-119K	Tan Son Nhut
G	110 OS	U-17	Da Nang
H	417 TS	C-47D	Tan Son Nhut
J	213 HS	H-34, UH-1	Da Nang
K	817 AS	AC-47D	Nha Trang
K	518 FS	A-1H	Bien Hoa
L	516 FS	T-28, A-1H	Da Nang
M	716 RS	R/EC-47, U-6	Tan Son Nhut
M	718 RS	EC-47	Tan Son Nhut
N	413 TS	C-47, C-119	Tan Son Nhut
P	516 FS	A-1E	Da Nang
P	429 TS	C-7	Tan Son Nhut
Q	421 TS	C-123K	Tan Son Nhut
R	217 HS	H-34, UH-1	Binh Thuy
R	423 TS	C-123K	Tan Son Nhut
S	1st HS	H-19	Tan Son Nhut
T		UH-1	
U	522 FS	A-1H	Tan Son Nhut
V	520 FS	A-1H	Binh Thuy

W	ATC	U-17	Nha Trang
X	110 OS	U-17	Da Nang
X	425 TS	C-123K	Tan Son Nhut
Y	112 OS	U-17	Bien Hoa
Y	431 TS	C-7	Phu Cat
FF	514 FS *	A-1H	Bien Hoa
FD	124 OS	O-1	Bien Hoa
FK		A-1H	
GZ	437 TS	C-130	Tan Son Nhut
HB		F-5A	Bien Hoa
HC	435 TS	C-130	Tan Son Nhut
HJ	522 FS	F-5	Bien Hoa
HQ	536 FS	F-5	Bien Hoa
HR	819 AS	AC-119	Tan Son Nhut
HR		F-5E	Bien Hoa
HZ		RF-5A	Bien Hoa
kW	518 FS	A-1E	Bien Hoa
PG	419 TS	C-7	Tan Son Nhut
vW	520 FS	A-1E	Binh Thuy

*FFA exists on A-1H with 23rd Tac Wing fuselage band belonging to the National Air and Space Museum. Possible late-war identification given to the 514th that was until then without a tail code.)

Tail Code Size and Format

The following table contains the sizes and tail code letters that were most apparent on VNAF aircraft. Sizes may vary to those given here on various aircraft types. For aircraft not listed, inconsistencies were too numerous, or no information was available.

	Unit Code Letter Size		**Aircraft Code Letter Size**		
Aircraft Type	Single Letter	Double Letter	With Single Unit Letter	With Double Unit Letter	Serial Number Height
A-1 (Gray)	9 in (23 cm)	None	24 in (60 cm)	None	12 in (30 cm)
A-1 (Camou.)	6 in (15 cm)	12 in (30 cm)	6 in (15 cm)		
C-7	21 in (53 cm)	21 in (53 cm)	9 in (23 cm)		
C-47 (Camou.)	8 in (20 cm)	18 in (45 cm)	9 in (23 cm)		
C-123	15 in (38 cm)	24 in (60 cm)	9 in (23 cm)		
C-130		21 in (53 cm)		21 in (53 cm)	9 in (23 cm)
F-5		12 in (30 cm)		12 in (30 cm)	6 in (15 cm)
H-34	6 in (15 cm)		12 in (20 cm)		12 in (30 cm)
O-1	9 in (23 cm)	9 in (23 cm)	12 in (30 cm)	9 in (23 cm)	6 in (15 cm)
U-6	5 in (13 cm)		7 in (28 cm)		6 in (15 cm)
U-17	9 in (23 cm)		12 in (28 cm)		6 in (15 cm)

Letters were generally single stroke Gothic Vertical. Standard width of letters, and numbers were 2/3 of height, except M and W, which were the same width as height. Width of stroke and space between figures should be 1/6 of height.

Douglas A-1 Skyraider VNAF Camouflage

Douglas A-1 Skyraider VNAF Camouflage

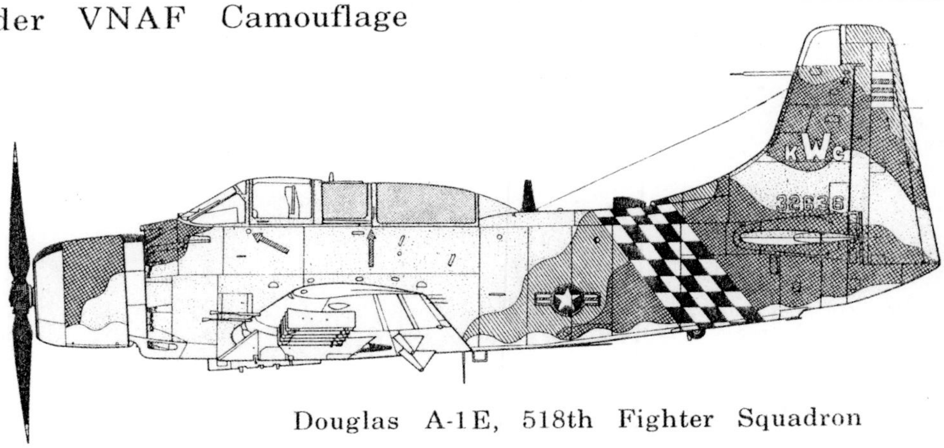

Douglas A-1E, 518th Fighter Squadron

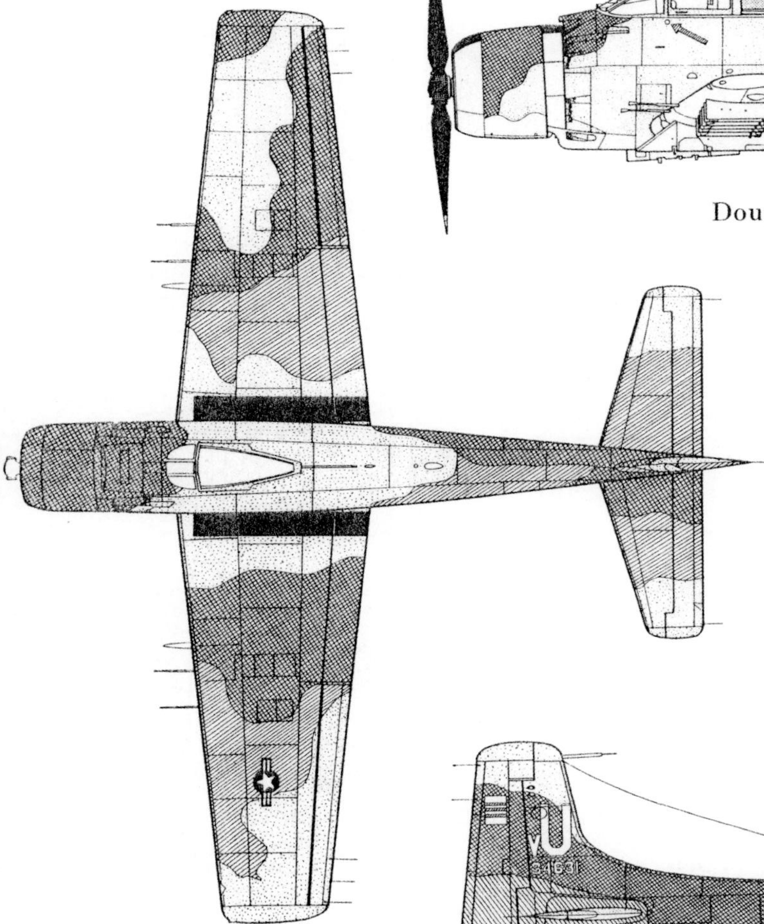

I.A.W. USAF Technical Manual T.O. 1-1-1

Courtesy Koku Fan 7-80.

Douglas A-1H, 520th Fighter Squadron

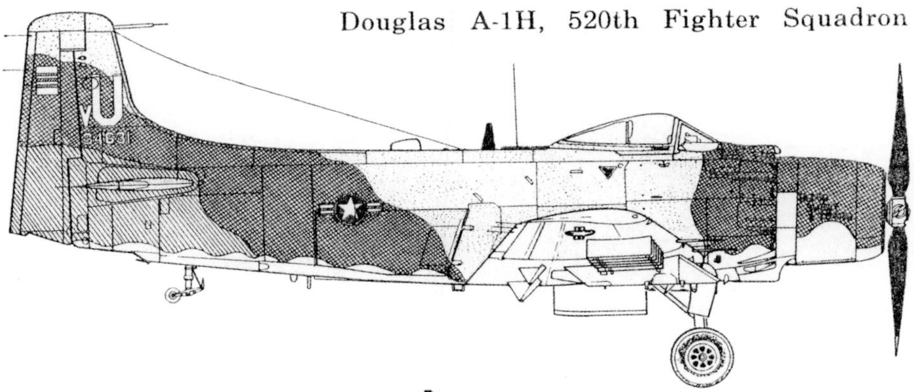

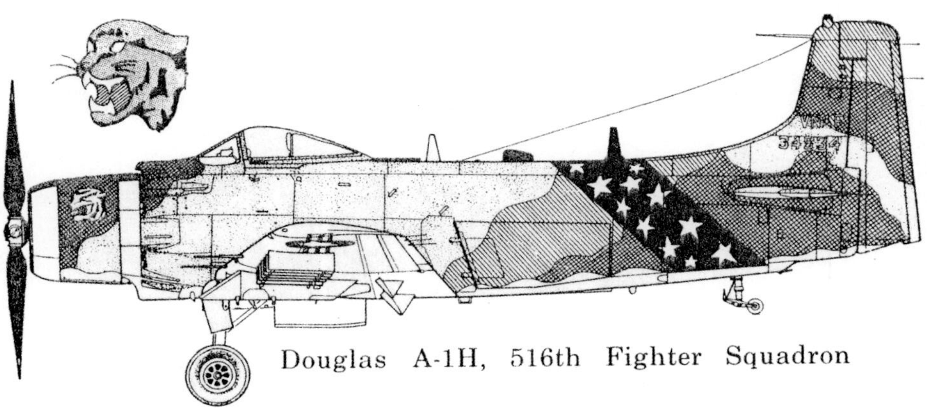

Douglas A-1H, 516th Fighter Squadron

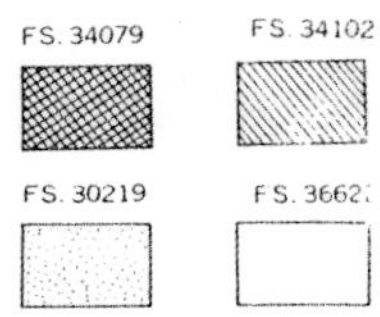

Color Key

The three-color Southeast Asia camouflage scheme was prevalent on military aircraft after the mid-1960s. Note another style of Vietnamese insignia. This de Havilland U-6A Beaver belongs to the 716th Reconnaissance Squadron, a spinoff of the 314th Special Missions Squadron, thus the tail code M. It is configured as a psy war aircraft, with speakers on the left side of the fuselage under the wing. *RG 342- KE44804 USAF.*

Appendix C: Unit Numbering Systems of VNAF

The administration of the early VNAF squadrons was done at the air base headquarters from which they operated. These headquarters soon became numbered groups; the method of base numbering is explained in *Appendix E*

Air Units of Vietnam

As the VNAF continued to expand new groups were established, eventually becoming wings beginning in 1963. The numbering method for these new units followed the same pattern used much earlier, i.e., the first of the two digits being assigned in the sequence in which the wing was established, and the second digit coincided with one of the four Military Regions (Corps Areas) in which it was located.

With two and three tactical wings formed within each Military Region, it was decided to form four Air Divisions in 1970. These carried a single digit number that coincided with the respective MR number. Because of the concentration of military units in the Saigon area, the 5th Air Division was formed at Tan Son Nhut to command the units assigned here. In the final phase of the war the 6th Air Division was formed to command the wings at Pleiku and Phu Cat, while the 3rd concentrated on those at Bien Hoa.

The numbering system used for squadrons was totally different from the foregoing and had no bearing upon assignment location. Squadrons used three digits, which were based on the mission type and formation sequence.

The numbering system began in January 1963 during a period when a major restructuring of VNAF was taking place. The first of these three numbers identified the unit mission, ie, the 500 series signified fighter squadrons, etc. The last two of the three numbers identified the squadron and the sequence in which it was established. Every other number by two was used so that if the first of the three numbers was even, the following two numbers in pair would be odd, and vice versa. The purpose for this has not been determined, but one can be assured that there was good reason. The VNAF squadron mission numbering system was as follows:

100 Observation Squadrons
200 Helicopter Squadrons
300 Special Mission Squadrons
400 Transport Squadrons
500 Fighter Squadrons
600 Amphibian or Seaplane Squadron (None established, Republic Seabees at the time influenced this category.)
700 Reconnaissance Squadrons
800 Transport-type Gunship Squadrons
900 Training Squadrons

Appendix D: Unit Insignia of VNAF

Many of the VNAF's units had a distinctive insignia. The color section on pages 185-190 contain a sampling of these embroidered insignia or color-screened designs, photographed from various collections. The illustrations in the color section are in random order, but are listed here numerically by unit function. The prefix number coincides with the pictured unit insignia. English translations of their Vietnamese mottos are included where appropriate. Both the English and the Vietnamese names given to squadrons were used as their tactical call-signs.

In 1970, all units from air divisions to squadrons underwent a change in insignia in accordance with their role; only the numerals distinguishing each unit were different. Not wishing to give up past traditions, many units kept their earlier designs. Because of this, newer designs were not often seen and therefore not easily collected; some may be lost forever. Where possible, both new and old designs are shown.

1. VNAF Insignia TO-QUOC KHONG GIAN, 'Fatherland - Space'
15. I Air Division BAO-QUOC TRAN-KHONG, 'Protect the Land and Guard the Air'
16. II Air Division
19. III Air Division
20. IV Air Division
23. V Air Division
24. VI Air Division

(Roman numerals were official form of designating air divisions.)

38. 1st Air Division
42. 2nd Air Division
46. 3rd Air Division
86. 4th Air Division
47. 5th Air Division
93. 5th Air Division
96. 6th Air Division

(Arabic numerically-marked air division insignia were non-standard form.)

13. 23nd Tactical Wing, pre-1970
14. 23nd Tactical Wing, post-1970
52. 33nd Tactical Wing, pre-1970
18. 41st Tactical Wing, pre-1970
62. 41st Tactical Wing, post-1970
69. 43rd Tactical Wing, post-1970
49. 51st Tactical Wing, post-1970
74. 53rd Tactical Wing, post-1970
4. 62nd Tactical Wing, pre-1970
22. 72nd Tactical Wing, post-1970
54. 74th Tactical Wing, pre-1970
81. 74th Tactical Wing, post-1970
53. 84th Tactical Wing, post-1970
59. 92nd Tactical Wing, pre-1970
41. 83rd Special Operations Group THAN PHONG, 'Divine Wind'
7. 110th Observation Squadron
29. 112th Observation Squadron THANH-XA, 'Blue Cobra'
103. 114th Observation Squadron
65. 116th Observation Squadron
85. 116th Observation Squadron (subdued)
9. 118th Observation Squadron
2. 122nd Observation Squadron, pre-1970
88. 122nd Observation Squadron, post-1970
78. 211th Helicopter Squadron THAN CHUY, 'Divine Mace'
71. 213th Helicopter Squadron SONG-CHUY, 'Twin Maces'
84. 215th Helicopter Squadron, pre-1970
64. 217th Helicopter Squadron (Gunship) HOA-DIEU, 'Fire Falcon'
68. 217th Helicopter Squadron (Slicks) THAN DIEU, 'Divine Falcon'
112. 221st Helicopter Squadron, post-1970
39. 223rd Helicopter Squadron, post-1970
89. 223rd Helicopter Squadron, post-1970 LOI-DIEN, 'Thunderbird'
66. 227th Helicopter Squadron HAI-AU, 'Sea Gull'
94. 229th Helicopter Squadron
58. 231st Helicopter Squadron
33. 231st Helicopter Squadron 'American Eagle Squadron, VNAF I & M' (Improvement and Modernization Program)
32. 237th Helicopter Squadron
48. 241st Helicopter Squadron PHI DOAN 241, THIEN BANG, 'Flying Squadron 241, Skyhawk'
44. 243rd Helicopter Squadron PHI-DOAN 243, MANH-SU, 'Flying Squadron 243, Strong Lion'
101. 253rd Helicopter Squadron SOI THAN, 'Divine Wolf'
12. 259th Medivac Squadron NHAN AI PHI DOI, 'Charity Flight'
91. 314th Special Missions Squadron THAN-TIEN, 'Divine Arrow'
60. 413th Transport Squadron XICH-LONG, 'Red Dragon'
77. 415th Transport Squadron

82. 415th Transport Squadron
73. 415th Transport Squadron THANH LONG, 'Blue Dragon'
30. 415th Transport Squadron PHI DOAN, 'Flying Squadron'
106. 415th Transport Squadron
107. 417th Transport Squadron LONG MA, 'Dragon Horse'
95. 421st Transport Squadron
110. 423rd Transport Squadron (post-1970)
113. 425th Transport Squadron (post-1970)
36. 429th Transport Squadron SON-LONG, 'Mountain Dragon'
35. 431st Transport Squadron [C-7] PHUONG LONG, 'Perfume Dragon'
70. 435th Transport Squadron *70*
90. 514th Fighter Squadron, pre-1970
17. 514th Fighter Squadron, post-1970 PHUONG HOANG, 'Phoenix'
79. 516th Fighter Squadron, pre-1970 PHI HO, 'Flying Tiger'
102. 518th Fighter Squadron, pre-1970
80. 518th Fighter Squadron, pre-1970 PHI LONG, 'Flying Dragon'
21. 518th Fighter Squadron, post-1970
27. 520th Fighter Squadron, intermediate THAN BAO, 'Divine Bear'
50. 522nd Fighter Squadron, pre-1970 PHI-DOAN 522, 'Flying Squadron 522'
10. 522nd Fighter Squadron, post-1970
3. 524th Fighter Squadron THIEN-LOI, 'Lightning'
99. 528th Fighter Squadron HO-CAP, 'Scorpion'
100. 530th Fighter Squadron
75. 532nd Fighter Squadron
5. 534th Fighter Squadron KIM-NGUU, 'Taurus'
26. 540th Fighter Squadron
25. 546th Fighter Squadron THIEN-SU, 'Angle'
6. 548th Fighter Squadron
51. 716th Electronic Tracking and Aerial Photography Squadron
111. 718th Reconn. Sq. (post-1970)
108 817th Attack Squadron HOA LONG, 'Fire Dragon'
72. 819th Attack Squadron HAC-LONG, 'Black Dragon'
31. 821st Attack Squadron AC-119K, TINH LONG, 'White Dragon'
28. 920th Training Squadron
61. 921st (Unknown)
55. Air Operations Center
45. Control and Reporting Center, 33 Tac. Wing TTKB = TRUNG-TAM KIEM-BAO, 'CRC (Paris Control)'
67. Electronic Security Center AN NINH DIEN TU, 'Security-Electronic'
92. Air Training Center, TTHLKQ, pre-1970 TRUNG-TAM HUAN-LUYEN KHONG-QUAN, 'Air Force Training Center'
56. Air Training Center, TTHLKQ, pre-1970
104. Air Training Center, CC 12, HUAN LUYEN, CC 12, Training'
11. Air Training Center, post-1970 LUYEN-CAN HUAN-CAN, 'Accurate Training, Essential Training'
76. Air Training Center (Early) PHI YEN, 'Flying Swallow' (L-19)
34. Air Training Center (Early) PHI YEN, 'Flying Swallow' (U-17)
96. English School, TRUONG ANH-NGU, TT HL KQ, 'Air Training Center'
97. Training Unit, (at 33rd Wing) HUAN LUYEN, 'Training'
63. Logistics Command KY-TINH TIEP-HAO, 'Quality Inspection, Perfect Supply'
57. Maintenance & Supply Wing, pre-1970 KDKT & TV = Khong-Doan Ky-Thuat & Tiep-Van 'Wing; Maintenance & Supply'
109. 2nd Air Support Center, Bien Hoa
43. Air Medical Center
87. 33rd Wing, Security Group, LD33PT
8. 96th MP Platoon, 953rd Company THAN-DIEU, 'Divine Falcon'
40. Pleiku Base Security 'PK' = PHONG-KHONG
83. (Unidentified) SD2KQ, '2nd Air Force Division' (Helicopter)
114. (Unidentified — part of Air Division) BAO-QUOC TRAN-KHONG, 'Protect the Land and Guard the Air'
37. (Unidentified) XA-VUONG, 'King Cobra'
105. (Unidentified)

Flying Suit Patches

117. 118th Observation Sq. [O-2A] BAC DAU, 'North Star'
119. 241st Helicopter Sq. [CH-47] 'Chinook'
122. 259th Helicopter Squadron
129. UH-1H unit 'Khong Quan Viet Nam' Translates to Vietnamese Air Force.
125. 516th Fighter Squadron PHI HO, 'Flying Tiger'
121. 520th Fighter Squadron THAN BAO, 'Divine Bear'
123. 528th Fighter Squadron HO CAP, 'Scorpion'
120. 534th Fighter Squadron KIM-NGUU, 'Taurus'
115. 546th Fighter Squadron THIEN-SU, 'Angel'
116. F-5 Squadron
124. F-5 Squadron
126. F-5 Squadron
130. F-5 Squadron
127. 819th Attack Squadron Transitioning from USAF 17th SOS
128. 819th Attack Squadron HAC LONG, 'Black Dragon'
118. 821st Attack Squadron
131. C-7A Squadron. Transition Period

VNAF Unit Insignia

1. VNAF Insignia
2. 122nd Observation Sq.
3. 524th Fighter Sq.
4. 62nd Tactical Wing
5. 534th Fighter Sq.
6. 548th Fighter Sq.
7. 110th Observation Sq.
8. 96th MP Platoon
9. 118th Observation Sq.
10. 522nd Fighter Sq.
11. Air Training Center
12. 259th Medivac Sq.
13. 23rd Tactical Wing
14. 23rd Tactical Wing
15. I Air Division
16. II Air Division
17. 514th Fighter Sq.
18. 41st Tactical Wing
19. III Air Division
20. IV Air Division
21. 518th Fighter Sq.
22. 72nd Tactical Wing
23. V Air Division
24. VI Air Division
25. 546th Fighter Sq.
26. 540th Fighter Sq.
27. 520th Fighter Sq.
28. 920th Training Sq.
29. 112th Observation Sq.
30. 415th Transport Sq.
31. 821st Attack Sq.
32. 237th Helicopter Sq.
33. 231th Helicopter Sq.
34. Air Training Ctr. (early)
35. 431th Transport Sq.
36. 429th Transport Sq.
37. (Unknown)
38. 1st Air Division
39. 223nd Helicopter Sq.
40. Pleiku Base Security
41. 83rd Special Operations Gr.
42. 2nd Air Division
43. Air Medical Center
44. 243rd Helicopter Sq.
45. Control & Reporting Center
46. 3rd Air Division
47. 5th Air Division
48. 241st Helicopter Sq.
49. 51st Tactical Wing
50. 522nd Fighter Sq.
51. 716th Electronic Tracking Sq.
52. 33rd Tactical Wing
53. 84th Tactical Wing
54. 74th Tactical Wing
55. Air Operations Center
56. Air Training Center
57. Maint. & Supply Wing
58. 231st Helicopter Sq.
59. 92nd Tactical Wing
60. 413th Transport Sq.
61. (Unidentified)
62. 41st Tactical Wing
63. Logistics Command
64. 217th Helicopter Sq.
65. 116th Observation Sq.
66. 227th Helicopter Sq.
67. Electronic Security Ctr.
68. 217th Helicopter Sq.
69. 43rd Tactical Wing
70. 435th Transport Sq.
71. 213rd Helicopter Sq.
72. 819th Attack Sq.
73. 415th Transport Sq.
74. 53rd Tactical Wing
75. 532nd Fighter Sq.
76. Air Training Center (early)
77. 413th Transport Sq.
78. 211th Helicopter Sq.
79. 516th Fighter Sq.
80. 518th Fighter Sq.
81. 74th Tactical Wing
82. 413th Transport Sq.
83. (Unidentified) SD2KQ
84. 215th Helicopter Sq.
85. 116th Observation Sq.
86. 4th Air Division
87. 33rd Wing, Security Gr.
88. 122nd Observation Sq.
89. 223 Helicopter Sq.
90. 514th Fighter Sq.
91. 314 Special Missions Sq.
92. Air Training Center
93. 5th Air Division
94. 229th Helicopter Sq.
95. 421st Transport Sq.
96. Air Training Center

Ted Koppel Collection

97. (Training Unit, 33rd Wg.)
98. 6th Air Division
99. 528th Fighter Sq.
100. 530th Fighter Sq.
101. 253rd Helicopter Sq.
102. 518th Fighter Sq.
103. 114th Observation Sq.
104. Air Training Center
105. (Unidentified)
106. 415th Transport Sq.
107. 417th Transport Sq.
108. 817th Attack Sq.
109. 2nd Air Support Ctr.
110. 423rd Transport Sq.

Flying Suit Patches

115. A-37 "Angle"
116. F-5 (Transition)
111. 718th Reconn. Sq.
112. 221th Helicopter Sq.
117. 118th Observation Sq.
118. 821st Attack Sq.
113. 425th Transport Sq.
114. (Unidentified)
119. 241st Helicopter Sq.
120. A-37 "Taurus"

J. Foran/C. Kelly Collections

121. 520TH Fighter Sq.
122. 259th Helicopter Sq.
123. 528th Fighter Sq.
124 F-5 squadron
125 516th Fighter Sq.
126. F-5 squadron
127. 819th Attack Sq.
128. 819th Attack Sq.
129. UH-1H KQVN (Sq.)
130. F-5 squadron
131. C-7A squadron
132. UH-1H squadron

Clement Kelly Collection

1. VNAF Insignia

2. 122nd Observation Sq.

3. 524th Fighter Sq.

4. 62nd Tactical Wing

5. 534th Fighter Sq.

6. 548th Fighter Sq.

7. 110th Observation Sq.

8. 96th MP Platoon

9. 118th Observation Sq.

10. 522nd Fighter Sq.

11. Air Training Center

12. 259th Medivac Sq.

13. 23rd Tactical Wing

14. 23rd Tactical Wing

15. I Air Division

16. II Air Division

17. 514th Fighter Sq.

18. 41st Tactical Wing

19. III Air Division

20. IV Air Division

21. 518th Fighter Sq.

22. 72nd Tactical Wing

23. V Air Division

24. VI Air Division

Tom Clinton Collection

25. 546th Fighter Sq.

26. 540th Fighter Sq.

27. 520th Fighter Sq.

28. 920th Training Sq.

29. 112th Observation Sq.

30. 415th Transport Sq.

31. 821st Attack Sq.

32. 237th Helicopter Sq.

33. 231th Helicopter Sq.

34. Air Training Ctr. (early)

35. 431th Transport Sq.

36. 429th Transport Sq.

37. (Unknown)

38. 1st Air Division

39. 223nd Helicopter Sq.

40. Pleiku Base Security

41. 83rd Special Operations Gr.

42. 2nd Air Division

43. Air Medical Center

44. 243rd Helicopter Sq.

45. Control & Reporting Center

46. 3rd Air Division

47. 5th Air Division

48. 241st Helicopter Sq.

Tom Clinton Collection

49. 51st Tactical Wing

50. 522nd Fighter Sq.

51. 716th Electronic Tracking Sq.

52. 33rd Tactical Wing

53. 84th Tactical Wing

54. 74th Tactical Wing

55. Air Operations Center

56. Air Training Center

57. Maint. & Supply Wing

58. 231st Helicopter Sq.

59. 92nd Tactical Wing

60. 413th Transport Sq.

61. (Unidentified)

62. 41st Tactical Wing

63. Logistics Command

64. 217th Helicopter Sq.

65. 116th Observation Sq.

66. 227th Helicopter Sq.

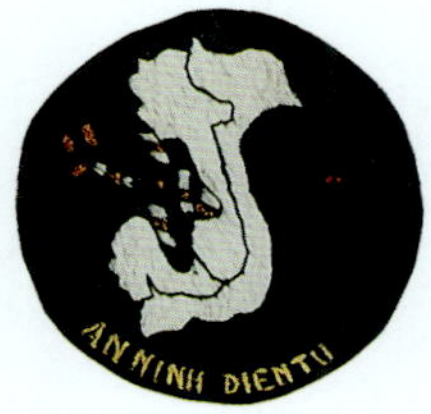

67. Electronic Security Ctr.

68. 217th Helicopter Sq.

69. 43rd Tactical Wing

70. 435th Transport Sq.

71. 213rd Helicopter Sq.

72. 819th Attack Sq.

Tom Clinton Collection

73. 415th Transport Sq.

74. 53rd Tactical Wing

75. 532nd Fighter Sq.

76. Air Training Center (early)

77. 413th Transport Sq.

78. 211th Helicopter Sq.

79. 516th Fighter Sq.

80. 518th Fighter Sq.

81. 74th Tactical Wing

82. 413th Transport Sq.

83. (Unidentified) SD2KQ

84. 215th Helicopter Sq.

85. 116th Observation Sq.

86. 4th Air Division

87. 33rd Wing, Security Gr.

88. 122nd Observation Sq.

89. 223 Helicopter Sq.

90. 514th Fighter Sq.

91. 314 Special Missions Sq.

92. Air Training Center

93. 5th Air Division

94. 229th Helicopter Sq.

95. 421st Transport Sq.

96. Air Training Center

Ted Koppel Collection

97. (Training Unit, 33rd Wg.)

98. 6th Air Division

99. 528th Fighter Sq.

100. 530th Fighter Sq.

101. 253rd Helicopter Sq.

102. 518th Fighter Sq.

103. 114th Observation Sq.

104. Air Training Center

105. (Unidentified)

106. 415th Transport Sq.

107. 417th Transport Sq.

108. 817th Attack Sq.

109. 2nd Air Support Ctr.

110. 423rd Transport Sq.

115. A-37 "Angle"

116. F-5 (Transition)

111. 718th Reconn. Sq.

112. 221th Helicopter Sq.

117. 118th Observation Sq.

118. 821st Attack Sq.

113. 425th Transport Sq.

114. (Unidentified)

119. 241st Helicopter Sq.

120. A-37 "Taurus"

J. Foran/C. Kelly Collection

121. 520TH Fighter Sq.

122. 259th Helicopter Sq.

123. 528th Fighter Sq.

124 F-5 squadron

125 516th Fighter Sq.

126. F-5 squadron

127. 819th Attack Sq.

128. 819th Attack Sq.

129. UH-1H KQVN (Sq.)

130. F-5 squadron

131. C-7A squadron

132. UH-1H squadron

Clement Kelly Collection

Appendix E: Air Bases of South Vietnam

The development of the major tactical air bases in Vietnam was closely related to the organizational structure of the VNAF. As the VNAF expanded with the escalating war, so did the importance of these airfields. They became saturated beyond the point of being able to expand further. Tan Son Nhut and Da Nang Air Bases, for instance, became the most active airports anywhere in the world during the 1960s.

Beginning in 1951, when aircraft were first used as part of Vietnam's military forces, their primary tasks were aerial observation and airlift support within South Vietnam. The country became dotted with small, unimproved airstrips that were basically only suited for light transport and observation aircraft. By 1968 there were 270 identified flight strips throughout all of South Vietnam. Most of these airstrips were adjacent to, if not totally within, villages and towns, since the surrounding areas were not always secure from infiltrators. It was not unusual for the main streets of these villages to be used as airstrips. These airstrips were used by light aircraft and provided the only means of safe travel from village to village for Vietnamese Government personnel. Detachments of VNAF observation and liaison squadrons were scattered throughout the provinces and served the needs of the provincial chiefs, who also controlled military activities within these areas.

In these early days of the VNAF, only a few air bases in South Vietnam could be classed as all-purpose. Included were Bien Hoa, just northeast of Saigon, which served as the VNAF logistical support base; Nha Trang, located on the central east coast, was the VNAF training base; and Tourane—a French-named city and base, now nationally referred to by its Vietnamese name, Da Nang—was the most northerly major air base of South Vietnam. This was used as a logistic support base for that remote part of the country. Tan Son Nhut was primarily a civil airport for the capital city of Saigon, and also supported VNAF activities, mainly as its headquarters base.

In the mid-1950s the VNAF began to grow with the introduction of higher performance aircraft, resulting in the need to improve existing airfields and build new ones. By 1961, as the VNAF organizational structure was expanded, the existing major air bases were given specific identity numbers, as had been the system while under French influence. These designations were:

Air Base 12 Nha Trang
Air Base 23 Bien Hoa
Air Base 33 Tan Son Nhut
Air Base 41 Da Nang
Air Base 62 Pleiku

These numbers were not arbitrary ones, but were quite systematic. The first figure of the two digit numbering system pertained to the sequence in which the airfield was established as a military base, while the second digit identified to which of the four Military Regions it was located. This system was later applied to air group designations.

As the conflict continued, the VNAF was eventually supported by nine major air bases to serve as wing headquarters. Supplementing the five already mentioned were:

Binh Thuy Air Base
Soc Trang Air Base
Phu Cat Air Base
Phan Rang Air Base

In 1972 Can Tho Air Base replaced Soc Trang Air Base, which was turned over to the ARVN.

In addition to the nine major air bases, the VNAF operated from over 100 forward operating locations (FOL) scattered throughout the country.

The following gives the background of each of these major airfields in the sequence in which they were established.

Nha Trang Air Base
This was the only Vietnamese-influenced military air base located in the Republic of Vietnam during the early 1950s. Built by the French in 1949, it was then known as Air Base 194. By mid-1951 Nha Trang was the center for the Air Force Military Training School, and graduated the first 15 student pilot class in March 1952. Before this time, early pilot training for Vietnamese personnel was conducted in French flying schools in France, Algeria, and Morocco.

On 15 December 1952 the training facility was redesignated the Air Instruction Center for VNAF use. Nha Trang was well situated for flight training, not only because of the scarcity of other flying fields, but also for its east central coastal climate and excellent flying weather. This location also had ideal terrain features, which included level ground, mountains to the west, and the sea to the east, all considered good for tactical flight training. The Morane Saulnier MS 500 Criquet, an observation and liaison aircraft obtained from the French, and North American T-6G Texan basic trainers were the early training aircraft at the base.

On 7 July 1955 the training facility at Nha Trang became Tactical Base No. 1, with Major Nguyen-ngoc-Oanh commanding the training facility and Major Vo-Dinh as Base Commander. The two

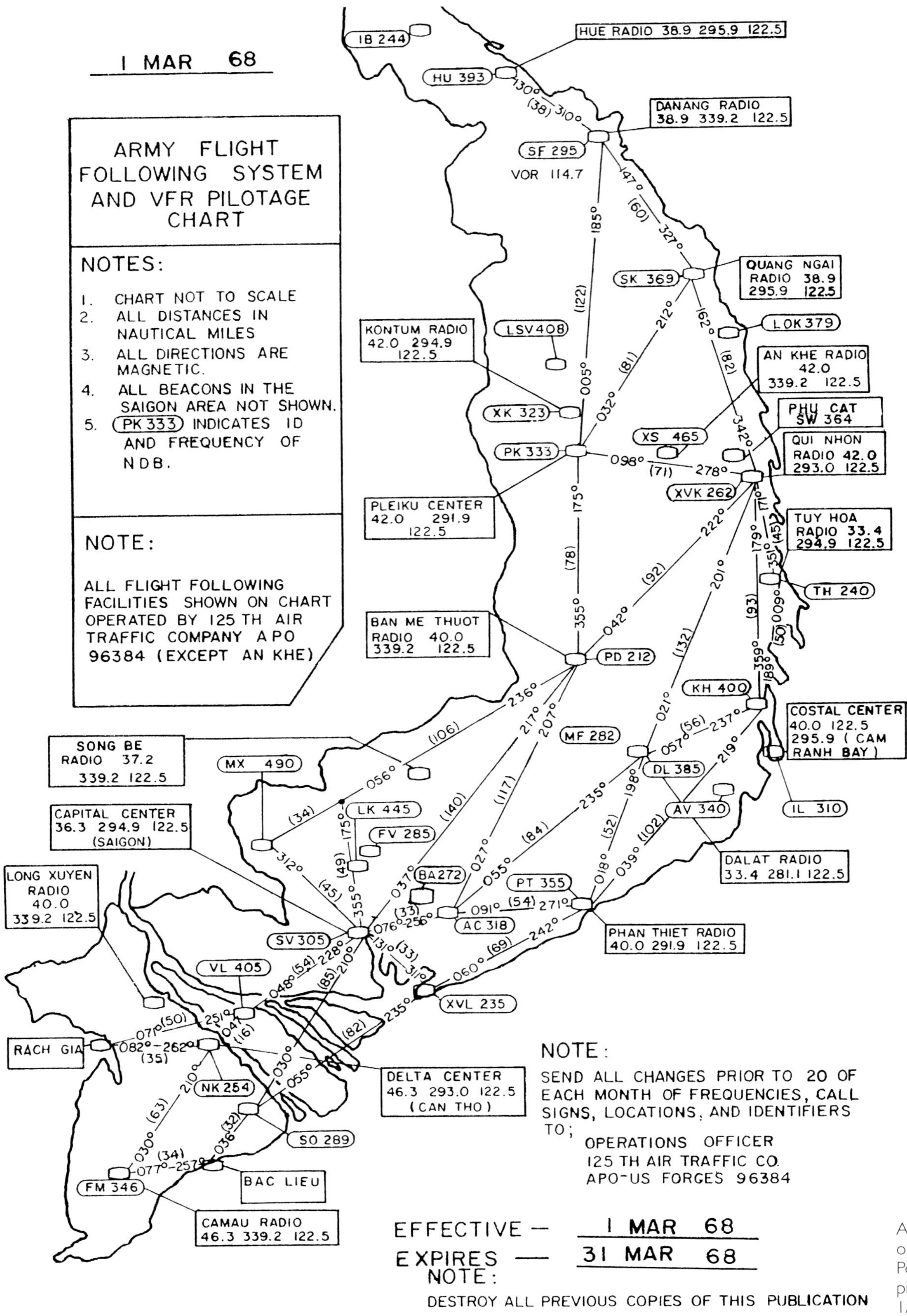

Airways and Distances Map of South Vietnam, 1968. Pocket chart carried by all pilots who flew in-country, 8-1/2" (22 cm) x 13" (33 cm).

elements—base and training—were combined in September 1957, and Nha Trang was designated Air Training Base.

The 2nd Group Artillery Observation (GAO), equipped with MS.500 aircraft, was formed on 1 October 1953 at Nha Trang under French control. The next significant flying unit to be formed there was the 2nd Fighter Squadron in 1961 with T-28 fighter-bombers.

VNAF flight training gradually came under the influence of the U.S. Military Assistance Program. In January 1962 flight training was moved from the Air Training Center at Nha Trang to the United States, leaving only the technical and military schools at the base. By September of that year, the USAF had dispatched a Mobile Training Team to Nha Trang to instruct VNAF personnel in the maintenance of the Cessna U-17 Skywagon in preparation for restarting flight training there. Vietnamese instructors graduated in three classes in July 1963 and gradually replaced USAF personnel.

A Communications and Electronics School was begun at the Center in 1964, and by October 1965 the functions of the Air Training Center and those of combat and support were again separated when the 62nd Wing took over the latter functions when it moved to Nha Trang from Pleiku in January 1965. This became the headquarters base for II Corps when reorganization of VNAF established a tactical air wing in each Corps area.

In the years that followed, the base became totally saturated by USAF joint occupancy, with tactical air units and other VNAF organizations. To alleviate some of the air traffic problems at Nha Trang, the 3,300 ft (1006 m) airstrip at Duc My, 22 miles (35 km) to the north-northwest, became an auxiliary training field to the Air Training Center.

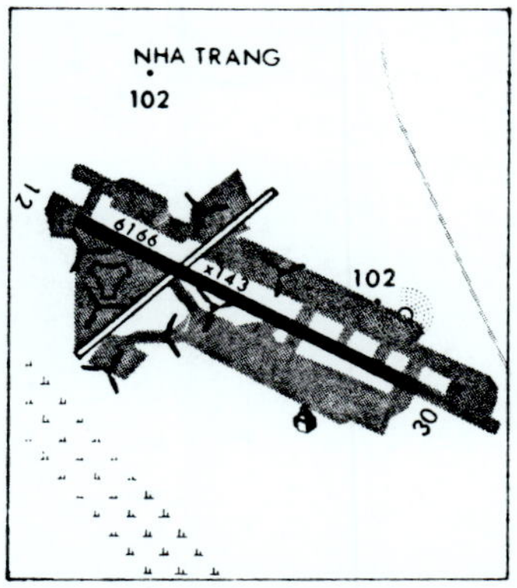

Nha Trang AB as of June 1968.

Nha Trang Air Base was the oldest military flying field in South Vietnam. Primarily a VNAF training base that later became the Headquarters for the 2nd Air Division, its expansion was restricted by the city of Nha Trang, which surrounded it. This view looks down runway 12 to the southeast and the island-sheltered coastline. *RG 342-KKE 19702 USAF*

Bien Hoa Air Base

On 1 June 1955 Bien Hoa Air Base became the VNAF's logistics support base when the French evacuated their main depot at Hanoi. At that time the VNAF was in its final days as an auxiliary air arm under total French control.

Bien Hoa was located on quiet, flat grounds in a rural area 15 miles (24 km) north of Saigon. Not long after it was established as a VNAF base, it took on a tactical role as well as that of a depot. It was here that the 1st Fighter Squadron (later renumbered the 514th FS) was formed on 1 June 1956.

From this point, Bien Hoa became the base of newly formed and continually growing air units. The 23rd Air Group, later to become an Air Wing, and the 3rd Air Division were also stationed there, and the base supported the greatest number of air combat units than any other base throughout South Vietnam. With the influx of USAF tactical air units in the early 1960s, Bien Hoa became a joint operating base for both VNAF and USAF organizations.

Unfortunately, Bien Hoa will be remembered by many as having the two most devastating air base explosions of the war. In the early morning minutes of 1 November 1964, the Viet Cong lobbed more than 60 stand-off mortars on to the flight line, setting ablaze a

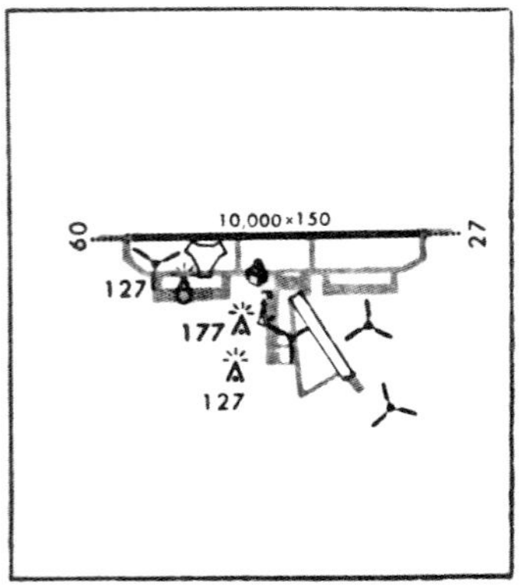

Bien Hoa AB as of June 1968.

Bien Hoa Air Base facing northeast across the ramp of the VNAF's 112th Observation Squadron in the foreground. Note SAC assigned ELINT Lockheed U-2R being towed from hangar (circled). This picture, taken 7 July 1968, shows the newly finished east-west parallel runway.

string of fully-serviced USAF B-57 Canberras. Five were destroyed, four Americans were killed, and 72 others, including VNAF personnel, were wounded. Greater devastation occurred on 16 May 1965 when a flight of American B-57s, preparing for a strike mission with crews on board, erupted in a series of explosions on the Bien Hoa ramp. Ten B-57s, 11 VNAF A-1Hs, and one Navy F-8 Crusader were destroyed. In addition to seven crew members killed, 13 maintenance personnel, along with eight Vietnamese, brought the total to 28 dead and 105 wounded.

As with most of the major air bases in South Vietnam, continuous efforts were made toward enlarging its aircraft support capabilities. Bien Hoa's already lengthened 10,000 ft (3048 m) concrete runway had a similar parallel runway added to it in 1969. Operating facilities continued to grow and included ever-increasing numbers of taxiways and parking ramps with covered aircraft revetments (wonder shelters) and typical open revetments.

With its close proximity to the international airport at Saigon, Bien Hoa was the easiest tactical air base to be reached by visiting reporters, and therefore it received the greatest amount of news and photographic coverage during the war.

Tan Son Nhut

This base was located three miles (5 km) northwest of Saigon, the capital city of South Vietnam. Even before World War II, this airfield was the main airport for French Indochina, of which a part later became Vietnam. It served domestic as well as international flights from this major city. As the war in Southeast Asia escalated, the airport took on a dual role, beginning in 1953, also serving as a military air base. It was not until 1956 that the headquarters for the VNAF was moved from the center of Saigon to this base. Even before that time military aircraft were always in evidence at Tan Son Nhut, mostly C-47s.

By the early 1960s, when the build-up of the VNAF became a reality, air units became more visible on the base. On 4 January 1964 the 33rd Wing was organized at Tan Son Nhut, and the number of air units grew rapidly. In the mid-1960s it was reported as the busiest airport in the world, with a mix of air traffic that approached chaotic proportions. Traffic included international commercial airliners, lightweight liaison aircraft, USAF tactical jets, domestic trans-

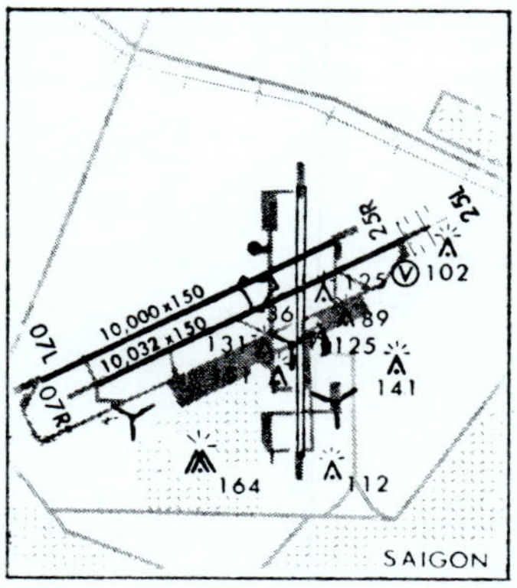

Tan Son Nhut AB as of June 1968.

This striking photo of Tan Son Nhut looks southeast, showing the commercial terminal in the center background. Military operations were in the cluster of buildings and hangars in the center of the photo. Note the many revetments in the center of the field. *Courtesy of Gerry Reponen*

ports of all descriptions, VNAF fighter-bombers, giant C-141s and C-5s of the USAF Military Airlift Command, combat aircraft—some with battle damage and others carrying live ordnance—and covert air operations of Air America, to name but a few. Mixed with these operations was the constant churning of helicopters as they arrived and departed in diverse directions. Reduced runway separation standards had to be accepted, and it was not uncommon to see three aircraft on the runway at one time. This airport moved a million pounds worth of cargo daily.

As a joint VNAF/USAF base with commercial airline activities, saturation point was more than doubled. As an example: by 1966, there were over 24,000 military personnel at Tan Son Nhut and 400 aircraft. The base was originally designed for under 4000 personnel and 75 aircraft during the 1950s. Tactical jets sometimes had to be towed from confined parking areas so that they could be started on the more debris-free taxiway. This always tied up surface aircraft traffic, but it was a necessity. Four-engine aircraft, both jet and reciprocating, were required to taxi with their outboard engines shut down so that they would not be a hazard to objects and people crowding their taxi routes. At night, there seemed to be a greater abundance of illumination flares at Tan Son Nhut than at other major airfields of South Vietnam. This assured better security for the base, but was often a hazard for aircraft landing and taking off.

The airport initially stabilized with two modest, crossed runways, expanding in the 1960s to two 10,000 ft (3048 m) parallel runways in a vain attempt to adequately handle the excessive traffic load.

Two-thirds of Tan Son Nhut was surrounded by the densely-populated suburbs of Saigon, all within easy mortar range of the runway. Fifteen thousand civilian employees wandered around the base, which made security an impossibility. Terrorist bombings and mortar attacks were always a threat to the VNAF Headquarters, the USAF controlling headquarters of 7th Air Force, and radar installations on the base, as well as the large complex of buildings housing VNAF, USAF, and other military personnel.

Da Nang Air Base

Known as Tourane when it was under French influence, this was the most northerly major air base in the Republic of Vietnam. It was located in the northeast coastal area, 85 miles (137 km) south of the Demilitarized Zone, where the 17th Parallel separated the two Vietnams. It is best remembered by the Vietnamese as the strike base from which the VNAF made its first strike into North Vietnam, on 8 February 1965, with a squadron of Douglas A-1s.

It began in November 1957 as Air Force Support Base 4, providing logistics support for that remote part of the country, 400 miles (644 km) north of Saigon. Situated on flat, sandy ground on the south side of the major port city of Da Nang, the area was ideal for an airfield, having unobstructed approaches to its north/south runways. Once little more than a provincial airfield, the base expanded to 2350 acres (951 hectares) with two 10,000 ft (3048 m) asphalt runways with concrete touchdown pads, parallel taxiways, and a heliport. It was under the control of the VNAF's 41st Wing, which was established there on 1 January 1964 as the major Vietnamese air element in I Corps. The base became a joint operating

Da Nang Air Base was a densely-packed military complex that supported VNAF, USAF, U.S. Navy, and U.S. Marine Corps, as well as domestic airlines. It ranked among the busiest in the world. Situated in northern I Corps, it was an important base for the air war over North Vietnam. This is the north end, looking at the east side of this dual-runway air base.

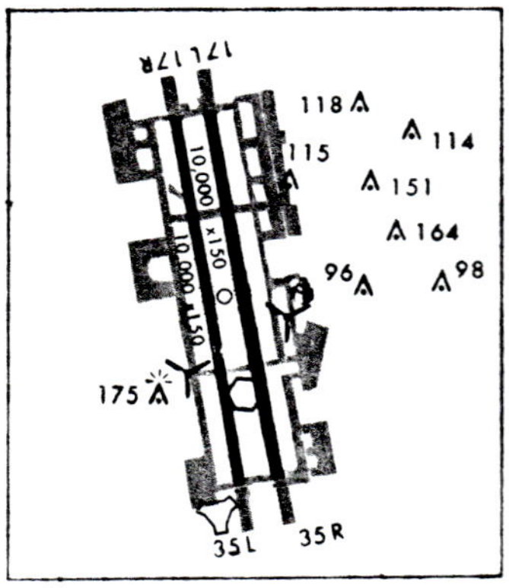

Da Nang AB as of June 1968.

airfield when U.S. Forces came to the aid of the South Vietnamese. As the number of VNAF units at Da Nang continued to increase, so did those of the USAF, and U.S. Marine air units swelled the capacity of the base beyond its limits. Covered and open aircraft revetments were constructed on concrete and asphalt parking aprons. In addition to these permanent assigned combat units, the airfield was an on- and off-loading port for the huge C-141s, C-5s, and contract commercial flights of the Military Airlift Command, as well as a civil terminal for the various domestic airlines.

Da Nang became the world's busiest airport in the single runway category. In the mid-1960s, 1,500 landings and takeoffs were recorded on peak days, besides having two extra traffic patterns for helicopters at the edge of the airstrip. When a parallel runway was added in 1965, Da Nang rivaled Tan Son Nhut as the world's busiest airport. By 1968 an average month saw the number of takeoffs and landings of fixed-wing aircraft exceeding 55,000. With helicopter activities added, the figure approached 67,000. During the winter monsoon at least 4500 of these landings were normally ground-controlled approaches.

For the air war over North Vietnam, Da Nang was considered the most suitable diversionary airfield in case of emergency. Landings of this nature became commonplace for Thailand-based fighter-bombers, reconnaissance aircraft, strike aircraft from the Navy aircraft carriers stationed in the South China Sea, and damaged aircraft of all air units stationed throughout South Vietnam. At Da Nang Air Base, war activities were conducted non-stop.

Pleiku Air Base

This base was located in II Corps, on the western border of South Vietnam, known as the Central Highlands. While all previously described major air bases were situated less than 50 ft (15 m) above sea level in a hot, humid climate, Pleiku's elevation was nearly

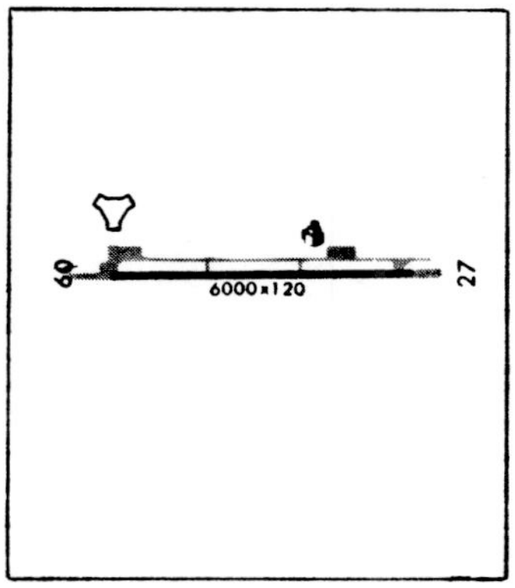

Pleiku AB as of June 1968.

Pleiku Air Base was situated in the Central Highlands in western Vietnam at an altitude of 2,434 ft (742 n). This picture, taken in late 1967, shows several USAF Cessna A-37s in revetments in the foreground, which eventually housed Douglas A-1s of the VNAF's 530th Fighter Squadron. View faces west.

2500 ft (762 m), in a dry, refreshing, crisp atmosphere. The terrain was rolling and sometimes cavernous, having a prairie-like openness, compared to the often dense-vegetated lower level. Natives to the area were known as Montagnards; who were hardy, independent mountain tribesmen still living a Stone Age existence, yet sympathetic and friendly towards the Americans and the South Vietnamese Government.

Pleiku was little more than an undeveloped air strip in December 1962 when it was designated Air Base 62. The 114th Observation Squadron moved to Pleiku from Da Nang the following January, and a detachment of A-1s from Bien Hoa resided there for close air support capability. In March 1964 the tactical elements at Pleiku were formed into the 62nd Tactical Wing.

The 62nd Wing was moved to Nha Trang in January 1965—a base that was also within II Corps—where expansion of its air units could be supported more easily, leaving behind a detachment of support aircraft. Pleiku Air Base was then managed by the 92nd Base Support Group, a maintenance unit, and the base was used as a staging and emergency airfield.

As North Vietnamese infiltration increased within and along the Laotian and Cambodian borders the importance of Pleiku Air Base increased, and base facilities were expanded and improved. The runway was resurfaced and extended to 6000 ft (1829 m), which required extensive ground filling. This base was jointly used for both VNAF and USAF air activities, but never reached the saturation and population proportions of the major air bases of the lowlands.

The mid- to late-1960s saw the formation of the 72nd Tactical Wing at Pleiku with its own squadron of A-1 Skyraiders (530th), along with two helicopter assault squadrons (229th and 235th) and an expansion of the 118th Observation Squadron, which was formed to replace the 114th. The base hosted many tenant organizations of the VNAF, but mostly those of the USAF until their activities were turned over to the VNAF beginning around 1972.

Binh Thuy Air Base

A latecomer as a headquarters base, Binh Thuy was situated 85 miles (137 km) southwest of Saigon in the Mekong Delta, on the southern bank of the Bassoc River, and was the major air base in the IV Corps area.

With the restructuring of the VNAF to coincide with the Corps Area concept, Can Tho airfield served initially as the IV Corps headquarters air base. This airfield was situated nearly in the heart of the city of Can Tho and had no room for expansion. In 1964, construction of Binh Thuy Air Base to replace it was begun a few miles northwest of Can Tho, on paddy fields that had to be drained and filled. It had a single 6000 ft (1829 m) asphalt runway and all necessary support facilities. The headquarters of the 74th Wing at Can Tho was moved to the new base on 1 September 1965. Air units were simultaneously moved to the base, including the 520th Fighter Squadron from Binh Hoa equipped with A-1s; the 217th Helicopter Squadron from Tan Son Nhut with H-34s; and the 116th Observation Squadron formed the year before at Nha Trang. The base was jointly used by the USAF in various capacities with various aircraft. Among these was O-2A transitioning for FAC upgrading to this newly acquired aircraft, for which this author participated.

In the 1970s Binh Thuy became the headquarters for the 4th Air Division, and the 74th Wing had three squadrons of A-37 Dragonflys;

Binh Thuy Air Base was one of the newer airfields of the war. Completed in 1965, it became headquarters for the VNAF 74th and 84th Wings, and later the 4th Air Division. It served USAF units, and was the main air base in the Mekong Delta. This 1967 picture looks to the west across the personnel housing area.

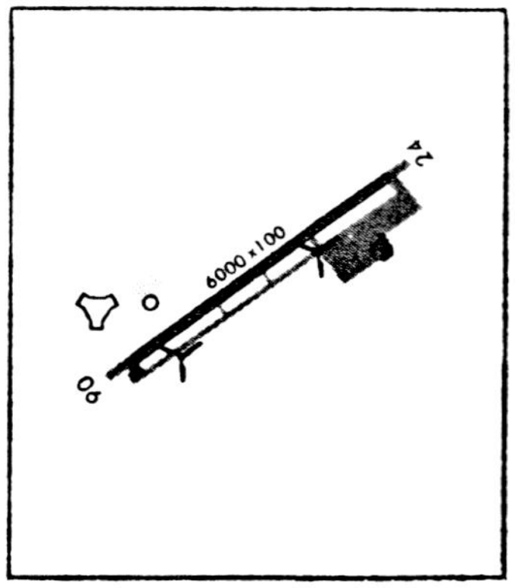

Binh Thuy AB as of June 1968.

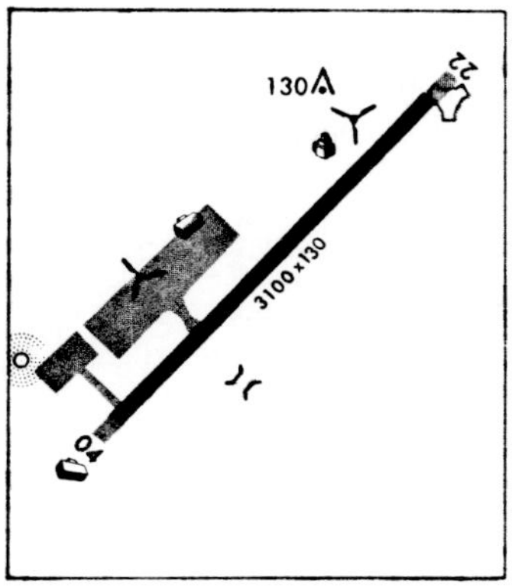

Soc Trang AB as of June 1968.

the 520th, converted from A-1s, and the 526th and 546th Fighter Squadrons. In time a second helicopter wing was formed (64th Tactical Wing) to further the defense of the Delta Region.

Soc Trang Air Base

This base was located in the Mekong Delta, 38 miles (61 km) south-southeast of Binh Thuy Air Base. It was strategically positioned near the mouth of the river, which led through the delta to Phnom Penh, Cambodia. Early in the war, like other airfields in the Delta, its unlighted 3100 ft (945 m) runway needed further development. It was only suitable for daylight operations by T-28s yet, for a while, in mid-1963, it supported a detachment of USAF B-26s, with VNAF observers, for quick response when air support was needed in the Delta. Situated in the IV Corps area, it was part of the 4th Air Division, headquartered at Binh Thuy.

Runway improvements included asphalt resurfacing, adding 60 ft (18 m) overruns—space restrictions prevented runway lengthening. Due to 65 ft (20 m) trees near the southwest end of this short runway, it was advisable to land to the southwest and takeoff to the northeast, winds permitting. Because further development of Soc Trang was impractical it was used for helicopter operations. It accommodated two helicopter squadrons and the 84th Tactical Wing, which was formed there around 1970 and soon moved to Binh Thuy. In 1972 Soc Trang was assigned to the ARVN, and its helicopter squadrons moved—the 211th to Binh Thuy, and the 217th to Can Tho.

Phu Cat Air Base

This tactical air base was located on flat, sandy ground along the coastal highway, 20 miles (32 km) north of Qui Nhon, and due east of Pleiku. It was one of four bases built by the USAF between mid-

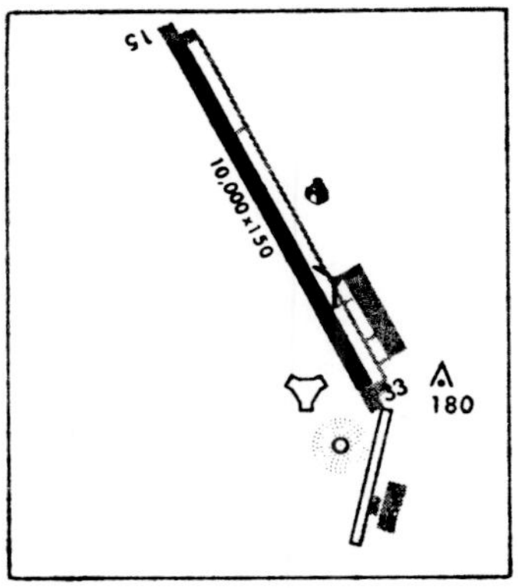

Phu Cat AB as of June 1968.

Phu Cat Air Base after being drenched by the monsoon rains of 1971. Revetments that once housed F-100s became empty between American departures, and the base became headquarters for the VNAF's 82nd Tactical Wing. View faces northwest. *RG 342-KE44876 USAF*

July 1965 and early 1967 for their exclusive use. The new concrete runway was 10,000 (3048 m) x 150 ft (46 m) and had a parallel taxiway. Covered and open aircraft revetments were located on asphalt and AM (aluminum matting) aprons, which housed F-100s, the first tactical aircraft to be stationed at Phu Cat.

Although deliberately built away from heavily populated areas for base security, the unfortunate overlapping of three districts necessitated triple coordination of security operations with local officials. Controlling the dense vegetation that concealed enemy movements and obscured the field of fire was an unending problem. A POL pipeline, laid from the coast to Phu Cat, could not be used because of sabotage and theft.

When the Vietnamization program ended USAF operations at the base the 82nd Tactical Wing, VNAF, established its headquarters there as part of the 6th Air Division. Based at Phu Cat were: the 532rd Fighter Squadron, with A-37s; the 241st and 243rd Helicopter Squadrons, with CH-47s and UH-1s, respectively; and Detachment A of the 259th Helicopter Squadron for medivac duties.

Phan Rang Air Base

Located in the central coastal area, 50 miles (80 km) south of Nha Trang, Phan Rang was a place of many contrasting features. The airfield was located on level, fertile ground that reached about three miles (5 km) to the sea, while the building complex nestled at the base of rugged jungle-clad mountains that extended to the west. Near the entrance to the base were ruins of a fascinating Cham Temple reputedly built in the 12th century, while inside the base was an array of many advanced technologies. To accommodate the expanding war, this air base had been quickly built by the USAF some eight miles (13 km) east of Phan Rang, a city of 24,000 inhabitants. Air operations began at the newly completed Phan Rang Air Base in October 1966 when the USAF's 35th Tactical Fighter Wing moved its F-100s and a squadron of B-57s from Da Nang. The airfield consisted of a 10,000 (3048 m) x 150 ft (46 m) concrete runway with parallel taxiway and covered (Wonder Shelters) and open aircraft revetments, located on asphalt and AM-2 aprons.

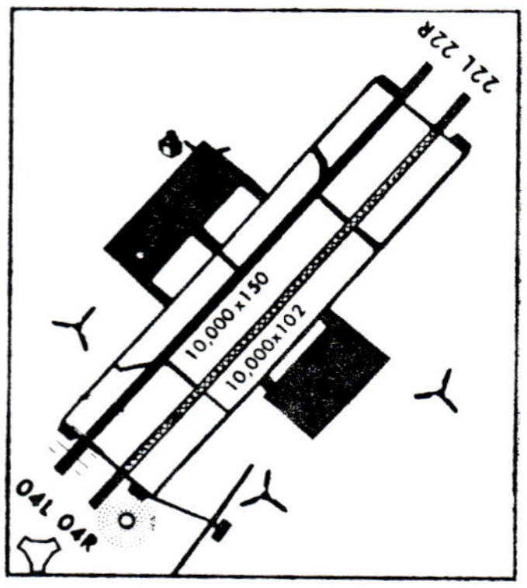

Phan Rang AB as of June 1968.

Phan Rang Air Base was located in the central part of South Vietnam in II Corps, three miles (5 km) from the sea. Construction was completed for air operations in October 1966 for exclusive use by the USAF. With the Vietnamization program, the VNAF 92nd Tactical Wing was formed here in the early 1970s. *RG 342-KKE 33901 USAF*

The 35th sustained continuous air operations there until they moved from Vietnam, together with the RAAF's No. 2 Squadron of Canberras at the end of May 1971. In the closing stages of the war, squadrons from VNAF's 62nd Tactical Wing at Nha Trang moved to Phan Rang. This included the 920th Training Squadron with T-37s and UH-1s. Three A-37 squadrons (524th, 534th, and 548th) operated from Phan Rang Air Base.

These were the larger of the air bases used by the VNAF. Mentioned earlier were the numerous small air strips that dotted South Vietnam that were so vital to communication and secure transportation. Some description of this contrasting type of airfield is worthy of note. Each of these air strips had their own peculiarities. One of these, while being of particular interest to the author, having been stationed and operated daily from there, serves as a good example of that type of flying facility.

This one was located in the once beautiful provincial capital of Hue (pronounced "way"), located 50 miles (80 km) northwest of Da Nang, in the northern section of South Vietnam. It was actually located inside the protective wall of this medieval-style city. This airstrip, initially built in 1940 and later known as Hue Citadel Airport, served Emperor Bao Dai when he governed the central portion of Vietnam, known then as Annam. It was used solely for the Emperor's private airplane which, by description, resembled the four-place Caudron C.620 Simoun low-wing monoplane. The 1,800 ft (549 m) crushed rock strip, with its 600 ft (183 m) grass overrun at the north end, was very serviceable for the liaison aircraft that frequented this strip. In fact, C-123s could squeeze in when needed to deliver aviation fuel and other supplies on those occasions when the enemy blocked the access roads.

The beauty of this once most picturesque of all Vietnamese cities, with its palace and ornate gates strategically placed along the walls, was lost in the description of the many obstacles that obstructed the flight approach to the runway, as listed in the Airdrome Directory for pilots not familiar with the area:

"Approach over 60 ft (18 m) pagoda, 1500 ft (457 m) from runway with 35 ft (11 m) trees at 400 ft (122 m), 25 ft (8 m) wall at 300 ft (91 m), a 200 ft (61 m) water-filled moat at 200 ft (61 m), and a road with a 2 foot (0.6 m) ditch 100 ft (30 m) from runway.'"

This was far from an *unobstructed approach*. When attention could be diverted from the landing, the surroundings were beautiful, with lotus blossoms completely covering the surface of the French-style moat once used to guard this oriental city.

This was not the only landing field in Vietnam having numerous approach obstacles; but the beauty of Hue made up for it.

Air Bases, Airfields, and Airstrips of South Vietnam
(Source: Tactical Aerodrome Directory, 15 June 1968)
The airfields in South Vietnam ranged from all-weather, all-purpose facilities to mere paths, graded sufficiently to accept the lightest liaison aircraft. These medium to small strips were often vital to resupplying fortified outposts and, at times, were the only means of communication with villages. It was in these areas that a number of famous battles of the Vietnam war were fought, but there are few keys to their precise location. Their names have disappeared from updated maps, as the sites themselves have disappeared with the passage of time and, but for histories such as this, would be forgotten. Already, the organization that once maintained the records of these wartime airstrips with their corresponding data has ceased to exist For historical purposes, a list of these airfields and their locations is included here:

Hue Citadel Airport was situated in the heart of Hue city, surrounded by the palace wall and the lotus covered moat. VNAF, U.S. Army, and USAF flight operations were situated in the lower right hand corner. Today this 2400 ft gravel runway is little more than a bicycle or light vehicle path known as *Duong San Bay*.

Name	Corps	Coordinates	RW Length	RW Head	Surface
A Lioi	I	16‘16’N 107‘14’E	2900 ft (884 m)	18/36	Earth
A Ro	I	15‘36’N 107‘29’E	1800 ft (549 m)	07/25	Graded earth
A Shau	I	16‘08’N 107‘20’E	3300 ft (1006 m)	16/34	PSP
An Hiep	IV	10‘02’N 106‘33’E	1500 ft (457 m)	05/23	Sod/clay
An Hoa	I	15‘57’N 108‘05’E	7000 ft (2134 m)	06/24	M8A1
An Khe	II	13‘58’N 108‘40’E	4300 ft (1311 m)	03/21	Concrete
An Khe Golf Course	II	13‘59’N 108‘39’E	3300 ft (1006 m)	16/34	AM-2
An Loc	III	10‘57’N 107‘12’E	3900 ft (1189 m)	09/27	Sod/laterite
An Long	IV	10‘42’N 105‘23’E	3300 ft (1006 m)	10/29	Laterite
An Thinh	I	14‘51’N 108‘53’E	1100 ft (335 m)	13/31	Clay
An Thoi	IV	10‘02’N 104‘02’E	4000 ft (1219 m)	14/32	M8A1
Ba Gi	II	13‘53’N 109‘09’E	1600 ft (488 m)	11/29	Laterite
Ba Gia	I	15‘11’N 108‘39’E	1500 ft (457 m)	10/28	Earth
Ba Long	I	16‘38’N 107‘02’E	1800 ft (549 m)	12/30	Sod
Ba Ngoi	II	11‘53’N 109‘07’E	3600 ft (1097 m)	07/25	Grass
Ba Ria	III	10‘30’N 107‘12’E	1400 ft (427 m)	01/19	Laterite
Ba To	I	14‘45’N 108‘44’E	1400 ft (427 m)	03/21	Earth/laterite
Ba To New	I	14‘45’N 108‘44’E	2400 ft (732 m)	07/25	Earth/gravel
Bac Lieu	IV	09‘18’N 105‘43’E	2000 ft (610 m)	07/25	ASP
Baldy	I	15‘46’N 108‘20’E	2300 ft (701 m)	04/22	Laterite
Ban Don	II	10‘20’N 105‘29’E	3400 ft (1036 m)	08/26	Crushed rock
Ban Me Thuot City	II	12‘41’N 108‘03’E	4400 ft (1341 m)	06/24	ASP/earth
Ban Me Thuot East	II	12‘40’N 108‘07’E	6000 ft (1829 m)	09/27	ASP
Bao Loc	II	11‘34’N 107‘49’E	3500 ft (1067 m)	09/27	M8A1
Boa Loc Plantation	II	11‘33’N 107‘50’E	2000 ft (610 m)	02/20	Clay
Bao Trai	III	10‘54’N 106‘25’E	1300 ft (396 m)	08/26	PSP
Ben Cui	III	11‘16’N 106‘20’E	3200 ft (975 m)	05/23	Laterite
Ben Het	II	14‘41’N 107‘40’E	1500 ft (457 m)	08/26	M8A1
Ben Tranh	IV	10‘25’N 106‘20’E	2000 ft (610 m)	11/29	Laterite
Bien Hoa	III	10‘58’N 106‘49’E	10,000 ft (3048 m)	09/27	Concrete
Binh Ba II	III	10‘37’N 107‘14’E	3500 ft (1067 m)	07/25	Sod
Binh Dai	IV	10‘13’N 106‘41’E	900 ft (274 m)	04/22	Soil cement
Binh Duc	IV	10‘21’N 106‘21’E	1500 ft (457 m)	09/27	Laterite
Binh Gia	III	10‘38’N 107‘15’E	900 ft (274 m)	08/26	Laterite
Binh Hung	IV	08‘53’N 104‘52’E	1300 ft (396 m)	13/31	PSP
Binh Khe	II	13‘57’N 108‘52’E	800 ft (244 m)	04/22	Earth/gravel
Binh Loc	III	11‘01’N 107‘13’E	3900 ft (1189 m)	05/23	Sod
Binh Son	III	10‘47’N 107‘03’E	4500 ft (1371 m)	09/27	Sod
Binh Son	I	15‘17’N 108‘47’E	1000 ft (305 m)	06/24	Clay
Binh Than Thon	IV	10‘54’N 105‘48’E	2300 ft (701 m)	03/21	Sod/clay
Bien Thuy	IV	10‘05’N 105‘43’E	6000 ft (1829 m)	06/24	ASP
Blackhorse	III	10‘49’N 107‘14’E	2300 ft (701 m)	11/29	Laterite
Bong Son	II	14‘25’N 109‘00’E	1700 ft (518 m)	02/20	Laterite
Bu Dop	III	12‘01’N 106‘49’E	2100 ft (640 m)	01/19	Laterite
Bu Glao	II	12‘14’N 107‘16’E	1600 ft (488 m)	16/34	Graded earth
Bu Krak	II	12‘15’N 107‘17’E	1800 ft (549 m)	01/19	Laterite
Bunard	III	11‘39’N 107‘05’E	2900 ft (884 m)	03/21	Laterite
Buon Blech	II	13‘13’N 108‘14’E	3200 ft (975 m)	10/28	M8A1
Buon Brieng	II	13‘09’N 108‘11’E	2100 ft (640 m)	09/27	Clay
Buon Ea Yang	II	12‘41’N 108‘20’E	1500 ft (457 m)	17/35	Sod/laterite
Buon Ha	II	12‘47’N 108‘56’E	1300 ft (396 m)	06/24	Sod
Buon Ho	II	12‘55’N 108‘16’E	1600 ft (488 m)	08/26	Sod
Buon Mi Ga	II	12‘30’N 108‘31’E	1600 ft (488 m)	08/26	Clay
Buon Tsuke	II	12‘18’N 107‘58’E	2400 ft (732 m)	18/36	Sod
Ca Lu	I	16‘42’N 106‘52’E	2300 ft (701 m)	15/33	Laterite/clay
Cai Cai	IV	10‘54’N 105‘33’E	1200 ft (367 m)	01/19	Clay
Cam Lo	I	16‘48’N 107‘00’E	1000 ft (305 m)	09/27	Sod
Cam Rahn AAF	II	11‘54’N 109‘13’E	2900 ft (884 m)	18/36	M8A
Cam Rahn Bay	II	12‘00’N 109‘14’E	10,000 ft (3048 m)	02/20	Concrete

Camp Evans	I	16‘33’N 107‘23’E	2900 ft (884 m)	18/36	Laterite
Can Tho	IV	10‘03’N 105‘46’E	3900 ft (1189 m)	08/26	PSP
Cao Lanh	IV	10‘25’N 105‘39’E	1500 ft (457 m)	07/25	Macadam
Cat	II	13‘28’N 107‘43’E	2300 ft (701 m)	08/26	Earth
Catecka	II	13‘52’N 107‘58’E	4200 ft (1280 m)	07/25	Laterite/sod
Cay Gao	III	11‘05’N 107‘06’E	2600 ft (792 m)	04/22	Earth
Cement Plant	IV	10‘16’N 104‘38’E	1600 ft (488 m)	07/25	Laterite
Chau Duc	IV	10‘42’N 105‘09’E	1700 ft (518 m)	05/23	Clay
Chau Lang	IV	10‘27’N 104‘58’E	1800 ft (549 m)	17/35	Compact earth
Cheo Reo	II	13‘24’N 108‘27’E	3600 ft (1097 m)	06/24	ASP
Chi Linh	III	11‘32’N 106‘46’E	3500 ft (1067 m)	10/28	Laterite
Chon Thanh	III	11‘25’N 106‘37’E	3400 ft (1036 m)	18/36	Laterite
Chu Lai	I	15‘25’N 108‘42’E	8000 ft (24 38 m)	14/32	AM-2
Con Son	IV	08‘44’N 106‘38’E	3700 ft (1128 m)	11/29	ASP
Courtenay	III	10‘46’N 107‘15’E	4100 ft (1250 m)	05/23	Sod
Crystal	II	14‘10’N 109‘03’E	1800 ft (549 m)	17/35	Laterite
Cu Chi AAF	III	10‘59’N 106‘31’E	2900 ft (884 m)	04/22	AM-2
Cu Lao Re Island	I	15‘23’N 109‘09’E	3600 ft (1097 m)	18/36	Sod/sand
Cung Son	II	13‘02’N 108‘59’E	2600 ft (792 m)	09/27	M8A1
Dak Pek	II	15‘05’N 107‘45’E	1600 ft (488 m)	02/20	Earth/cr. rock
Dak Seang	II	14‘50’N 107‘41’E	1400 ft (427 m)	10/28	Clay
Dak To I	II	14‘40’N 107‘49’E	2300 ft (701 m)	12/30	Earth/cr. rock
Dak To II	II	14‘39’N 107‘48’E	4200 ft (1280 m)	10/28	ASP
Dakkir	III	11‘53’N 106‘53’E	2900 ft (884 m)	01/19	Laterite/sod
Dalat/Cam Ly	II	11‘57’N 108‘25’E	4500 ft (1371 m)	10/28	ASP
Dalat/Lien Khuong	II	11‘45’N 108‘23’E	4800 ft (1463 m)	09/27	ASP
Dam Pau	II	11‘48’N 108‘14’E	1700 ft (518 m)	10/28	Sod
Da Nang	I	16‘03’N 108‘12’E	10,000 ft (3048 m)	17/35	ASP/Concrete
Dat Do	III	10‘29’N 107‘16’E	1200 ft (367 m)	17/35	Earth/sod
Dau Tieng	III	11‘17’N 106‘22’E	3100 ft (945 m)	08/26	Laterite
Di An AAF	III	10‘54’N 106‘45’E	2200 ft (671 m)	18/36	Laterite
Dinh Quan	III	11‘12’N 107‘22’E	1200 ft (367 m)	04/22	Laterite
Djamap	III	12‘06’N 107‘09’E	4100 ft (1250 m)	03/21	Laterite/clay
Djiring	II	11‘34’N 108‘07’E	2000 ft (610 m)	18/38	Laterite/sod
Don Phuoc	IV	10‘52’N 105‘28’E	2100 ft (640 m)	13/31	Sod/clay
Dong Ba Thin	II	12‘01’N 109‘12’E	3200 ft (975 m)	14/32	PSP
Dong Bo	III	11‘17’N 107‘10’E	1700 ft (518 m)	12/30	Sod
Dong Ha	I	16‘49’N 107‘05’E	3400 ft (1036 m)	07/25	AM-2
Dong Tam	IV	10‘20’N 106‘18’E	1600 ft (488 m)	17/35	M8A1
Dong Tre	II	13‘18’N 109‘04’E	2500 ft (762 m)	09/27	M8A1
Dong Xoai	III	11‘32’N 106‘53’E	3200 ft (975 m)	07/25	Laterite
Duc Co	II	13‘47’N 107‘38’E	3700 ft (1128 m)	05/23	M8A1
Duc Hoa	III	10‘49’N 106‘27’E	2000 ft (610 m)	05/23	Laterite/PSP
Duc Lap	II	12‘24’N 107‘36’E	2200 ft (671 m)	04/22	Earth
Duc Lao II	II	12‘26’N 107‘41’E	3500 ft (1067 m)	08/26	T-17
Duc My	II	12‘32’N 109‘01’E	2300 ft (701 m)	10/28	Gravel/sand
Duv Pho	I	14‘49’N 108‘58’E	3800 ft (1158 m)	01/19	MX19
Duc Phong	III	11‘48’N 107‘14’E	3100 ft (945 m)	02/20	Laterite
Duc Xuyen	II	12‘11’N 108‘08’E	1900 ft (579 m)	05/23	PSP
Duong Dong	IV	10‘13’N 103‘58’E	3300 ft (1006 m)	07/25	ASP
English	II	14‘28’N 109‘02’E	3600 ft (1097 m)	03/21	M8A1
Gi Lang	I	15‘02’N 108‘28’E	1900 ft (579 m)	04/22	PSP/Laterite
Gia Nghia	II	12‘00’N 107‘41’E	2000 ft (610 m)	04/22	Laterite
Gia Ray	III	10‘57’N 107‘24’E	1700 ft (518 m)	09/27	Laterite/earth
Gia Vuc	I	14‘42’N 108‘34’E	3200 ft (975 m)	18/36	Sod
Giang Tay	II	11‘12’N 108‘23’E	1200 ft (367 m)	09/27	Hard clay
Gio Linh	I	16‘56’N 107‘05’E	1100 ft (335 m)	16/34	Earth
Go Cong	IV	10‘22’N 106‘42’E	1800 ft (549 m)	05/23	Soft ASP
Go Dau Ha	III	11‘04’N 106‘18’E	1300 ft (396 m)	13/31	Earth
Ha Tan	I	15‘51’N 107‘57’E	2600 ft (792 m)	06/24	Sod/clay

Ha Thanh	I	15'06'N 108'34'E	1400 ft (427 m)	08/26	Earth/rock
Ha Tien	IV	10'24'N 104'28'E	2000 ft (610 m)	08/26	Rock
Ha Tien South	IV	10'22'N 104'30'E	1200 ft (367 m)	06/24	Sod/earth
Ham Tan	III	10'42'N 107'44'E	3900 ft (1189 m)	11/29	Laterite
Hammond	II	14'03'N 109'02'E	2700 ft (823 m)	17/35	Sandy clay
Hensel AAF	II	13'51'N 108'03'E	2800 ft (953 m)	09/27	M8A1
Hiep Hoa	III	10'55'N 106'19'E	1900 ft (579 m)	12/30	Laterite/rock
Hoi An	I	15'53'N 108'20'E	1600 ft (488 m)	12/30	PSP/Laterite
Holloway	II	13'59'N 108'02'E	4600 ft (1402 m)	05/23	PSP
Hon Quan	III	11'39'N 106'37'E	1800 ft (549 m)	05/23	Laterite
Hua Duc	I	15'20'N 108'13'E	1600 ft (488 m)	09/27	Earth
Hue Citadel	I	16'28'N 107'34'E	2400 ft (732 m)	12/30	Crushed rock
Hue/Phu Bai	I	16'24'N 107'42'E	5600 ft (1707 m)	9/27	ASP
Joyce	II	14'12'N 109'04'E	1500 ft (457 m)	03/21	Laterite
Kannack	II	14'09'N 108'37'E	1900 ft (579 m)	18/36	Sand/clay
Katum	III	11'40'N 106'13'E	2900 ft (884 m)	16/34	Laterite
Kham Duc	I	15'26'N 107'48'E	4800 ft (1463 m)	04/22	ASP
Khanh Duong	II	12'45'N 108'45'E	1200 ft (367 m)	14/32	Sod
Khanh Duong New	II	12'44'N 108'45'E	3500 ft (1967 m)	15/33	M8A1
Khe Sanh	I	16'39'N 106'44'E	3900 ft (1189 m)	10/28	AM-2
Kien Giang	IV	09'57'N 105'08'E	4000 ft (1219 m)	07/25	Rock/Clay
Kien Long	IV	09'30'N 105'16'E	1800 ft (549 m)	05/23	PSP
Kontum	II	14'21'N 108'01'E	3600 ft (1097 m)	09/27	ASP
Labonte	II	14'19'N 108'58'E	1400 ft (427 m)	18/36	Laterite
Lac Thien	II	12'25'N 108'13'E	1200 ft (367 m)	11/29	PSP
Lai Khe	III	11'12'N 106'37'E	3500 ft (1067 m)	05/23	MX19
Lam Son	III	10'59'N 106'41'E	2300 ft (701 m)	01/19	Laterite
Lao Bao	I	16'35'N 107'22'E	1500 ft (457 m)	12/30	Laterite/sod
Lap Dinh	II	12'06'N 109'09'E	1000 ft (305 m)	09/27	PSP
Loc Ninh	III	11'50'N 106'36'E	3500 ft (1067 m)	02/20	Lateriate
Long Hai	III	10'24'N 107'13'E	2400 ft (732 m)	08/26	M8A1
Long Khot 2	IV	10'55'N 105'50'E	1200 ft (367 m)	06/24	Clay
Long Thanh	III	10'47'N 106'57'E	1800 ft (549 m)	05/23	Laterite/grass
Long Thanh North	III	10'50'N 106'58'E	5000 ft (1524 m)	05/23	ASP
Long Toan	IV	09'39'N 106'30'E	3300 ft (1006 m)	09/27	ASP
Long Xuyen	IV	10'20'N 105'29'E	3400 ft (1036 m)	08/26	Crushed rock
Luong Son	II	11'11'N 108'23'E	2300 ft (701 m)	08/26	Packed clay
Luscombe	III	10'34'N 107'14'E	2800 ft (853 m)	10/28	Laterite
Mahoney AAF	II	14'34'N 109'02'E	1400 ft (427 m)	02/20	Sandy clay
Mai Loc	I	16'44'N 108'58'E	1500 ft (457 m)	18/36	Laterite
Mang Buk	II	14'50'N 108'12'E	2000 ft (610 m)	11/29	Earth/PSP
Marble Mountain	I	16'02'N 108'15'E	4500 ft (1372 m)	17/35	PSP/ASP
M'Drack	II	12'42'N 108'47'E	1700 ft (518 m)	15/33	Clay
Mewal	II	12'52'N 108'06'E	1700 ft (518 m)	12/30	Sod
Minh Long	I	14'56'N 108'43'E	2100 ft (640 m)	03/21	Rock/clay
Minh Thanh	III	11'27'N 106'30'E	4200 ft (1280 m)	04/22	Laterite
Mo Duc	I	14'57'N 108'53'E	1800 ft (547 m)	13/31	Laterite
Moc Hoa	IV	10'46'N 105'56'E	3300 ft (1006 m)	17/35	Laterite
Nam Duong	I	16'54'N 107'00'E	1200 ft (367 m)	05/23	Sod/grass
Nghia Hanh	I	15'03'N 108'47'E	1000 ft (305 m)	18/36	Laterite
Ngok Tavak	I	15'22'N 107'46'E	2000 ft (610 m)	11/29	PSP
Nha Trang	II	12'14'N 109'12'E	6100 ft (1859 m)	12/30	ASP
Nhon Co	II	11'58'N 107'35'E	4300 ft (1311 m)	08/26	Laterite
Ninh Hoa	II	12'30'N 109'09'E	1400 ft (427 m)	11/29	M8A1
Oasis	II	13'48'N 107'53'E	3500 ft (1067 m)	05/23	MX19
Ong Que	III	10'51'N 107'12'E	4200 ft (1280 m)	09/27	Laterite
Phan Rang	II	11'38'N 108'57'E	10,000 ft (3048 m)	04/22	Concrete
Phan Thiet	II	10'54'N 108'04'E	3500 ft (1067 m)	07/25	ASP
Phey Srunh	II	12'02'N 108'09'E	2100 ft (640 m)	18/36	Earth
Pho Trach	I	16'35'N 107'22'E	1500 ft (457 m)	12/30	Laterite/sod

Phu Cat	II	13‘57’N 109‘03’E	10,000 ft (3048 m)	15/33	Concrete
Phu Cat 2	II	13‘58’N 109‘04’E	2600 ft (792 m)	12/30	Laterite
Phu Hiep AAF	II	12‘57’N 109‘23’E	3500 ft (1067 m)	03/21	M8A1
Phu Khuong	III	11‘23’N 106‘14’E	2900 ft (884 m)	06/24	Earth
Phu Loc	IV	09‘25’N 105‘42’E	1700 ft (518 m)	10/28	Laterite
Phu Loi	III	11‘00’N 106‘42’E	2700 ft (823 m)	13/31	ASP
Phu My	III	10‘39’N 107‘03’E	3300 ft (1006 m)	18/36	Crushed rock
Phu Nhon	II	13‘33’N 108‘07’E	3100 ft (945 m)	01/19	T-17
Phu Rieng 1	III	11‘40’N 106‘57’E	2000 ft (610 m)	09/27	Not listed
Phu Tuc	II	13‘12’N 108‘42’E	3600 ft (1097 m)	07/25	T-17
Phuoc Binh	I	15‘43’N 108‘05’E	1700 ft (518 m)	11/29	Graded earth
Phuoc Hoa	III	11‘15’N 106‘45’E	1600 ft (488 m)	08/26	Laterite
Phuoc Vinh	III	11‘18’N 106‘48’E	3600 ft (1097 m)	09/27	Laterite
Plantation	III	10‘58’N 106‘54’E	2000 ft (610 m)	05/23	Laterite
Plateau Gi	II	14‘35’N 108‘17’E	2600 ft (792 m)	07/25	Laterite/PSP
Plei Djereng	II	14‘02’N 107‘39’E	3200 ft (975 m)	18/36	Laterite
Plei Djereng New	II	13‘58’N 107‘39’E	3500 ft (1067 m)	10/28	MX19
Plei Do Lim	II	13‘48’N 108‘07’E	2800 ft (853 m)	09/27	Laterite
Plei Me	II	13‘36’N 107‘55’E	1200 ft (367 m)	09/27	Laterite
Plei Mrong	II	15‘53’N 108‘20’E	1600 ft (488 m)	12/30	Laterite
Pleiku	II	14‘00’N 108‘01’E	6000 ft (1829 m)	09/27	ASP
Pleiku/Nansteph	II	14‘03’N 107‘59’E	1000 ft (305 m)	06/24	Clay
Polei Kleng	II	14‘24’N 107‘48’E	3500 ft (1067 m)	08/26	M8A1
Polei Krong	II	14‘23’N 107‘52’E	1600 ft (488 m)	09/27	Earth
Prek Klok	III	11‘34’N 106‘10’E	2900 ft (884 m)	01/19	M8A1
Quan Loi	III	11‘40’N 106‘40’E	3500 ft (1067 m)	05/23	Laterite
Quan Long	IV	09‘11’N 105‘11’E	3300 ft (1006 m)	09/27	PSP
Quan Long City	IV	09‘10’N 105‘09’E	1900 ft (579 m)	08/26	Gravel
Quang Ngai	I	15‘07’N 108‘46’E	3600 ft (1087 m)	10/28	Earth/ASP
Quang Tri	I	16‘46’N 107‘10’E	3500 ft (1067 m)	14/32	AM-2
Quang Tri 1	I	16‘45’N 107‘11’E	1700 ft (518 m)	18/36	Sod
Quang Tri Lavang	I	16‘44’N 107‘12’E	1900 ft (579 m)	11/29	Laterite
Qui Nhon	II	13‘46’N 109‘14’E	5100 ft (1554 m)	18/36	ASP
Rach Gia City	IV	10‘00’E 106‘06’E	1400 ft (427 m)	05/23	Macadam
Rang Rang	III	11‘20’N 107‘01’E	2200 ft (671 m)	11/29	Laterite
ROK AAF	II	13‘45’N 109‘06’E	2600 ft (792 m)	05/23	PSP
Ruong Ruong	I	16‘07’N 107‘41’E	1600 ft (488 m)	15/33	Gravel
Sadec	IV	10‘17’N 105‘45’E	1600 ft (488 m)	05/23	ASP
Soc Trang	IV	09‘35’N 105‘57’E	3100 ft (945 m)	04/22	ASP
Song Be	III	11‘49’N 106‘58’E	4000 ft (1219 m)	05/23	ASP
Song Be City	III	11‘51’N 107‘00’E	2200 ft (671 m)	18/36	ASP
Song Cau	II	13‘28’N 109‘14’E	2400 ft (732 m)	03/21	Laterite/sand
Song Mao	II	11‘15’N 108‘30’E	3500 ft (1067 m)	09/27	M8A1
Soui Dai	II	14‘00’N 108‘16’E	3500 ft (1067 m)	15/33	Earth
Soui Doi	II	14‘01’N 108‘15’E	1800 ft (547 m)	Unk	Clay
Ta Bat	I	16‘14’N 107‘16’E	1500 ft (457 m)	13/31	Compact clay
Ta Ma	I	14‘54’N 108‘32’E	1900 ft (579 m)	18/36	Sod
Tam Ky	I	15‘32’N 108‘29’E	3900 ft (1189 m)	11/29	ASP
Tam Ky Alternate	I	15‘55’N 108‘29’E	600 ft (183 m)	04/22	Sod
Tan An	III	10‘33’N 106‘24’E	1700 ft (518 m)	10/28	Crushed rock
Tan Son Nhut	III	10‘49’N 106‘39’E	10,000 ft (3048 m)	07/25	Concrete
Tanh Linh	III	11‘05’N 107‘41’E	1900 ft (479 m)	17/35	Laterite
Tay Ninh City	III	11‘19’N 106‘06’E	1900 ft (579 m)	02/20	PSP
Tay Ninh West	III	11‘19’N 106‘04’E	3900 ft (1189 m)	02/20	Laterite
Ten Phuoc	I	15‘29’N 108‘19’E	2100 ft (640 m)	15/33	Clay/gravel
Than Phu	IV	09‘57’N 106‘31’E	1200 ft (367 m)	15/33	Earth
That Son	IV	10‘32’N 105‘01’E	1900 ft (579 m)	08/26	PSP
Thien Giao	II	11‘04’N 108‘08’E	1500 ft (457 m)	18/36	Graded Earth
Thien Ngon	III	11‘36’N 106‘00’E	2400 ft (732 m)	17/35	Laterite
Thoi Hoa	IV	10‘06’N 105‘26’E	1700 ft (518 m)	10/28	Soil/cement

Thuan Hoa	I	15‘08’N 108‘43’E	1500 ft (457 m)	10/28	Laterite
Thuan Loi	III	11‘35’N 106‘53’E	2100 ft (640 m)	02/20	Laterite
Thuong Thoi	IV	10‘49’N 105‘17’E	1400 ft (427 m)	06/24	Earth
Thuy Dong	IV	10‘39’N 106‘10’E	2000 ft (610 m)	07/25	Laterite
Tien Phuoc	I	15‘29’N 108‘19’E	2100 ft (640 m)	15/33	Clay/gravel
Tieu Atar	II	13‘13’N 107‘47’E	1500 ft (457 m)	07/25	Laterite
Tinh Bien	IV	10‘36’N 104‘57’E	2000 ft (610 m)	11/29	ASP
Tonle Cham	II	11‘36’N 106‘29’E	3000 ft (914 m)	14/32	Laterite
Tra Bong	I	15‘15’N 108‘32’E	1000 ft (305 m)	09/27	Earth/gravel
Tra On	IV	09‘58’N 105‘56’E	1300 ft (396 m)	12/30	Grass/clay
Tra Vinh	IV	09‘55’N 106‘20’E	3700 ft (1128 m)	05/23	ASP/crushed rock
Trai Bi	III	11‘29’N 106‘02’E	2700 ft (823 m)	17/35	Laterite
Trang Bang	III	11‘02’N 106‘22’E	1000 ft (305 m)	15/33	Soil cement
Trang Bom	III	10‘57’N 107‘00’E	2600 ft (792 m)	09/27	Sod
Truc Giang	IV	10‘16’N 106‘21’E	3400 ft (1036 m)	09/27	Crushed rock
Trung Lap	III	11‘03’N 106‘28’E	1100 ft (335 m)	03/21	Sod
Tuc Trung	III	11‘05’N 107‘13’E	2900 ft (884 m)	08/26	Grass/clay
Tuy An	II	13‘16’N 109‘15’E	900 ft (274 m)	18/36	Earth
Tuy Hoa	II	13‘03’N 109‘20’E	9500 ft (2896 m)	03/21	Concrete
Tuy Hoa North	II	13‘06’N 109‘18’E	2600 ft (792 m)	16/34	PSP
Van Canh	II	13‘37’N 109‘00’E	3400 ft (1036 m)	03/21	T-17
Van Ninh	II	12‘41’N 109‘14’E	1100 ft (335 m)	03/21	Sod
Van Xa	I	16‘31’N 107‘28’E	1000 ft (305 m)	15/33	Laterite
Vi Thanh	IV	09‘47’N 105‘29’E	2000 ft (610 m)	08/26	Crushed rock/sand
Vi Thanh (Old)	IV	09‘47’N 105‘29’E	2000 ft (610 m)	05/23	Earth
Vinh Chau	IV	09‘19’N 105‘58’E	900 ft (274 m)	07/25	ASP
Vinh Long	IV	10‘15’N 105‘57’E	3500 ft (1067 m)	08/26	M8A1
Vinh Thanh	II	14‘07’N 108‘48’E	1900 ft (479 m)	17/35	ASP
Vo Dat I	III	11‘09’N 107‘30’E	3800 ft (1158 m)	09/27	Earth/laterite
Vung Tau	III	10‘22’N 107‘06’E	4900 ft (1494 m)	18/36	ASP
Xa Tan Rai	II	11‘38’N 107‘50’E	2200 ft (671 m)	07/25	Earth
Xom Cat	III	11‘06’N 106‘58’E	1900 ft (579 m)	16/34	Laterite
Xom Ong Linh	III	11‘05’N 106‘47’E	2000 ft (610 m)	17/35	Sod
Xuan Loc	III	10‘55’N 107‘15’E	3500 ft (1067 m)	10/28	Laterite
Xuyen Moc	III	10‘34’N 107‘26’E	2500 ft (762 m)	12/30	Laterite/sod

Key to types of runway surface:

AM-2: Aluminum Matting
ASP: Asphalt
Laterite: Local red soil containing large amounts of aluminum and ferric hydroxides.
M8A1: Light-duty Steel Matting
MX19: Aluminum Matting
PSP: Pierced Steel Plan
T-17: Coated nylon membrane

Appendix F: Organizational Units of VNAF

This listing is an attempt to record the numbered squadrons, tactical wings, and air divisions that constituted the VNAF. This has been developed from numerous sources of fragmentary information. Although considered numerically complete, the activation and relocation dates are often unknown, or when contradictory, the most logical information in relation to the development of the VNAF has been the choice. No attempt has been made to record the many support units that were part of every tactical wing and separate commands. However, it must be stated that they played an important part in the VNAF's history.

Unit	Headquarters	Activated	Remarks
HQ. VNAF			
Air Department	Saigon	1 July 1951	
	Tan Son Nhut	June 1956	Relocation
Air Force Department	1 July 1956	Name change	
Hq Vietnamese AF		3 Oct 1957	Name change
AIR DIVISIONS			
1st Air Division	Da Nang	Sept 1970	
2nd Air Division	Nha-Trang	July 1970	
3rd Air Division	Bien Hoa	May 1970	
4th Air Division	Binh Thuy	March 1970	Can Tho was annex Hq.
5th Air Division	Tan Son Nhut	January 1971	
6th Air Division	Pleiku		
TACTICAL WINGS			
12th Tac Wing	Nha Trang	Jan 64 to Jan 65	
23rd Tac Wing	Bien Hoa	June 1964	
33rd Tac Wing	Tan Son Nhut	January 4, 1964	
41st Tac Wing	Da Nang	January 1964	As AF Support Base 4 activated Nov. 1957.
43rd Tac Wing	Bien Hoa		
51st Tac Wing	Da Nang		
53rd Tac Wing	Tan Son Nhut		
62nd Tac Wing	Pleiku	March 1964	As Air Base 62, activated Dec 1962.
	Nha Trang	January 1965	Replaced 12th Tac Wing
63rd Tac Wing	Bien Hoa		Regarded as the F-5 Wing
72nd Tac Wing	Pleiku	Early 1965	
74th Tac Wing	Can Tho	April 1, 1964	
		Binh Thuy	
82nd Tac Wing	Phu Cat		
83rd Tac Wing	Tan Son Nhut		
84th Tac Wing	Soc Trang		
92nd Tac Wing	Phan Rang		
GROUPS			
83rd SOG	Tan Son Nhut	1963	Special Operations Group
83rd Tac Group	" " "	1 Jan 1966	Deactivated Jan. 1968.

OBSERVATION SQUADRONS			
1st GAO	Nha Trang	1 Oct 1952	(Group, Artillery Observation)
	Tan Son Nhut	1953	
	Hue Citadel	1954	
	Tan Son Nhut	1955	
	Da Nang	November 1956	
110th Obsn	Da Nang	January 1963	(1st GAO redesignated)
2nd GAO	Nha Trang	1 Oct 1952	(Group, Artillery Observation)
		Tan Son Nhut	October 1959
112th Obsn Sq	Tan Son Nhut	January 1963	(2nd GAO redesignated)
	Bien Hoa	June 1964	
3rd Obsn Sq	Da Nang	December 1961	
114th Obsn Sq	Da Nang	January 1963	(3rd OS redesignated)
	Pleiku	Late 1963	Moved from Da Nang
	Nha Trang	January 1965	Moved from Pleiku
116th Obsn Sq	Nha Trang	June 1964	
		Binh Thuy	Sept 1965
118th Obsn Sq	Pleiku	April 1971	O-1/U-17
120th Obsn Sq	Da Nang	May 1971	O-1/U-17
122nd Obsn Sq	Bien Thuy		
124th Obsn Sq	Bien Hoa	Aug 1972	O-1/U-17
HELICOPTER SQUADRONS			
1st Hel Sq	Tan Son Nhut	April 1956	Established without aircraft.
		June 1957	Activated with H-19s.
211th Hel Sq	Tan Son Nhut	January 1963	Redesignated. H-34s.
	Soc Trang		
	Binh Thuy	UH-1.	
2nd Hel Sq	Da Nang	1 Oct 1961	
213th Hel Sq	January 1963	Redesignated	
215th Hel Sq	Bien Hoa	H-34	
	Nha Trang	UH-1	
217th Hel Sq	Da Nang	1 May1964	H-34
	Tan Son Nhut	July 1964	Moved from Da Nang
	Binh Thuy	December 1965	Moved from TSN
	Can Tho		Moved. Reequipped UH-1
219th Hel Sq	Da Nang		H-34, special operations unit
			UH-1 conversion, 1 Dec 1971
	Nha Trang		Moved
221st Hel Sq	Bien Hoa	Jan 1971	UH-1s from US Army 68th AHC
223rd Hel Sq	Bien Hoa	Sept 1970	UH-1s from US Army 190th AHC
225th Hel Sq	Soc Trang	Oct 1970	UH-1s from US Army 121st AHC
227th Hel Sq	Soc Trang	Nov 1970	UH-1s from US Army 336th AHC
229th Hel Sq	Pleiku	Dec 1970	UH-1s from US Army 189th AHC
231st Hel Sq	Bien Hoa	Mar 1971	UH-1s from US Army 118th AHC
233rd Hel Sq	Da Nang	Jan 1971	UH-1s from US Army 282nd AHC
235th Hel Sq	Pleiku	Feb 1971	UH-1s from US Army 170th AHC at Kontum
237th Hel Sq	Bien Hoa	30 Sept 70	CH-47s from US Army ASHC at Phu Loi
239th Hel Sq	Da Nang	Feb 1972	UH-1
241st Hel Sq	Phu Cat	May 1972	CH-47
243rd Hel Sq	Nha Trang	Nov 1971	UH-1
	Phu Cat		Moved from Nha Trang
245th Hel Sq	Bien Hoa	Dec 1971	UH-1
247th Hel Sq	Da Nang	Dec 1972	CH-47
249th Hel Sq	Can Tho	Dec 1972	CH-47

251st Hel Sq	Bien Hoa		UH-1
253rd Hel Sq	Da Nang		UH-1
255th Hel Sq	Can Tho		UH-1
257th Hel Sq	Da Nang		UH-1
259th Hel Sq	(Multi)		UH-1, Medivac, Det at many bases.

SPECIAL AIR MISSION

312th SM Sq	Nha Trang	1 Aug 1951	
	Tan Son Nhut	1952	Deactivation not recorded.
314th SM Sq	Tan Son Nhut	By 1960s	

TRANSPORT SQUADRONS

1st Transport Sq	Tan Son Nhut	July 1955	C-47
413th Tns Sq		January 1963	Redesignated, C-119G January 1968
2nd Transport Sq	Tan Son Nhut		C-47 Reorganized June 1956, possibly from 312th SM.
415th Tns Sq			Redesignated Jan. 1963. Deactivated 1973
417th Tns Sq	Tan Son Nhut January 1967		Redesignated 817th AS Jun/Aug 1969 when equipped with AC-47s.
419th Tns Sq	Tan Son Nhut	1967	C-47
421st Tns Sq	Tan Son Nhut	May 1971	C-123K. Inactive Jan 1973.
423rd Tns Sq	Tan Son Nhut	July 1971	C-123K. Inactive Jan 1973.
425th Tns Sq	Tan Son Nhut	Dec 1971	C-123K. Inactive Jan 1973.
427th Tns Sq	Phu Cat	March 1972	C-7A
	Da Nang		Moved from Phu Cat
429th Tns Sq	Phu Cat	July 1972	C-7A
	Da Nang		Moved from Phu Cat
	Tan Son Nhut		Moved from Da Nang
431st Tns Sq	Phu Cat	August 1972	C-7A
		Tan Son Nhut	Moved from Phu Cat
433rd Tns Sq			No record.
435th Tns Sq	Tan Son Nhut	January 1973	C-130A.
437th Tns Sq	Tan Son Nhut	January 1973	C-130A.

FIGHTER SQUADRONS

1st Fighter Sq	Bien Hoa	1 June 1956	25 F8F Bearcats. Became 514th FS
2nd Fighter Sq	Nha Trang	December 1961	T-28. Became 516th FS
514th Fighter Sq	Bien Hoa		A-1H. Redesignated 1 Jan 1963.
516th Fighter Sq	Nha Trang		Redesignated Jan. 1963.
	Da Nang		Moved February 1964 A-1Hs by May 1964 A-37s by July 1969
518th Ftr Sq	Bien Hoa	15 Oct 1963	A-1H.
520th Ftr Sq	Bien Hoa	16 June 1964	A-1H.
	Binh Thuy	August 1965	Moved. Converted to A-37.
522nd Ftr Sq	Tan Son Nhut	1Apr 1965	A-1H.
	Bien Hoa	January 1968	Moved. F-5s June 1967.
524th Ftr Sq	Nha Trang	15 Sept 1965	A-37s by March 1969.
	Phan Rang		Move date unknown
526th Ftr Sq	Binh Thuy	1969	A-37
528th Ftr Sq	Da Nang	1 Dec 1970	A-37
530th Ftr Sq	Pleiku	1 Dec 1970	A-1
532nd Ftr Sq	Phu Cat	1 Oct 1972	A-37

	Pleiku		Moved from Phu Cat
534th Ftr Sq	Phan Rang	1 Nov 1972	A-37
536th Ftr Sq	Bien Hoa	December 1972	F-5A First with F-5Es beginning June 10 1974.
538th Ftr Sq	Da Nang		F-5
540th Ftr Sq	Bien Hoa		F-5
542nd Ftr Sq	Bien Hoa		F-5
544th Ftr Sq	Bien Hoa		F-5
546th Ftr Sq	Bien Thuy		A-37
548th Ftr Sq	Phan Rang		A-37
550th Ftr Sq	Da Nang		A-37
RECONNAISSANCE SQUADRONS			
716th Rec Sq	Tan Son Nhut	July 1966	RT-28, EC-47s, U-6s, U-6s, RF-5As.
718th Rec Sq	Tan Son Nhut	Aug 1972	EC-47
720th Rec Sq	Tan Son Nhut	Dec 1972	RC-119Gs used only as transports.
ATTACK SQUADRONS			
817th Atk Sq	Nha Trang	June 1969	AC-47, formerly 417th.
819th Atk Sq	Tan Son Nhut	Sept 1971	AC-119G
821st Att. Sq.	Tan Son Nhut	Dec 1972	AC-119K
TRAINING SQUADRONS			
912th Tng Sq	Nha Trang		T-6G
918th Tng Sq	Nha Trang		T-41
920th Tng Sq	Phan Rang		T-37, UH-1

Appendix G: Commander-in-Chiefs of VNAF

Name	Rank during C in C Period
Tran-van-Ho	Major - Colonel 1955 - 1958
Nguyen-xuan-Vinh	Lt Col - Colonel 1958 - 1962
Huynh-huu-Hien	Colonel 1962 - 1963
Do-khac-Mai	Colonel 1963 (3 mo)
Nguyen-cao-Ky	Colonel - Major Gen 1963 - 1967
Tran-van-Minh	Colonel - Lieut. Gen 1967 - 1975

Appendix H: Ranks and Insignia of the South Vietnamese Air Force

Note: Numbered titles match to the rank illustration. Letters describe color according to the key at end of list.

Vietnamese Title	Translation	USAF Equivalent
OFFICERS		
1. Dai Tuong	Senior General	General
2. Trung Tuong	Intermediate General	Lieutenant General
3. Thieu Toung	Junior General	Major General
4. Chuan Tuong	Sub General	Brigadier General
5. Dai Ta	Senior Grade Superior Officer	Colonel
6. Trung Ta	Intermediate Grade	Lieutenant Colonel
7. Thieu Ta	Junior Grade Superior Officer	Major
8. Dai Uy	Senior Grade Junior Officer	Captain
9. Trung Uy	Intermediate Grade Junior Officer	First Lieutenant
10. Thieu Uy	Junior Grade Junior Officer	Second Lieutenant
11. Sinh Vien Si Quan	Officer Candidate (Pre-1969)	Warrant Officer
12. Sinh Vien Si Quan	Officer Candidate (Post-1969)	Warrant Officer
13. Chuan Uy	Student Officer	Cadet
ENLISTED MEN		
21. Thuong Si Nhat	Master Sergeant (Pre-1969) (n)	Master Sgt. First Class
22. Thuong Si (n)	Master Sergeant (Pre-1969)	Technical Sgt.
23. Thuong Si Nhat	Master Sergeant (Post-1969)(n)	Master Sgt. First Class
24. Thuong Si (n)	Master Sergeant (Post-1969)	Technical Sgt.
25. Trung Si Nhat	Senior Grade NCO	Staff Sergeant-
26. Trung Si (n)	Intermediate Grade NCO	Sergeant
27. Ha Si Nhat (n)	Junior Grade NCO	Senior Airman
28. Ha Si (n)	Low Grade NCO	Airman First Class
29. Binh Nhat	Private First Class	Airman
30. Binh Nhi	Private Second Class	Airman Basic

Key to color descriptions:
(a) Silver stars, all with gold wings and star with silver buttons.
(b) Silver plum blossoms.
(c) Gold plum blossoms.
(d) Gold disc with raised loop in gold.
(e) Gold braid.
(f) Gold disc.
(g) Silver disc.
(h) Silver chevrons and bars.
(i) One silver (upper), two gold chevrons.
(j) Two gold chevrons.
(k) One gold chevron.
(l) White with silver braid.
(m) Black (suppressed visibility)
(n) "Si," the Vietnamese term for "student," is also applied to NCOs.

Ranks and Insignia of the South Vietnamese Air Force

1 (a) 2 (a) 3 (a) 4 (a) 5 (b) 6 (b) 7 (b) 8 (c) 9 (c) 10 (c) 11 (d) 12 (e) 13 (e)

Officer Shoulder Boards (for summer khaki uniform)

21 (f) 22 (g) 23 (h) 24 (h) 25 (h) 26 (h) 27 (i) 28 (j) 29 (k)

Enlisted Men shoulder Boards (for summer khaki uniform)

Cap Insignia, all grades

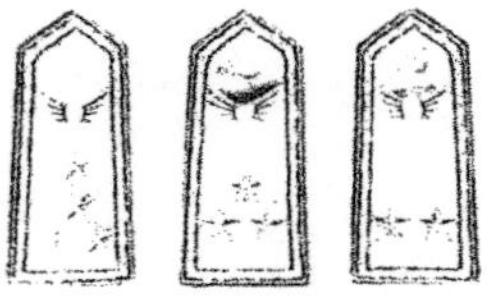

1 2 3

Evening Wear (l)

6 10 13

Ceremonial (e)

4 6 8

Work Uniform (Officers)

24 26 30

Work Uniform (Enlisted)

5 7 9 11(m)

Fatigue Uniform (Officers)

27 28 29

Fatigue Uniform (Enlisted)

James M. Foran Collection

VIETNAMESE MILITARY WINGS

Pilot 1952 - 1953

Aviation Cadet 1952 - 1960

Observer 1952 - 1953

Pilot 1953 - 1960

Observer 1953 - 1954

Radio/Navigator 1953 - 1960

Bombardier 1953 - 1954

Flight Engineer 1953 - 1960

Radio Operator 1953 - 1954

Side facing wings were gold. All others were silver.

J. Foran Collection

Graphics: N.N. Oanh

Appendix I: Vietnamese Military Wings 1960-1975

Senior Pilot

Pilot

Observer

Aviation Cadet

Senior Navigator

Navigator

Radio Operator

Bombardier/Navigator

Flight Engineer
Fixed Wing

Flight Engineer
Helicopter

Gunner

Load Master

Senior Flight Surgeon

Flight Surgeon

Senior Flight Paramedic

Flight Paramedic

(A Angelini Collection)

Appendix J:
Air Viet Nam

On the surface there was a clear distinction between the VNAF and Air Viet Nam, the flag-carrying airline of the Republic of Vietnam, but below the surface there was an air of kinship for which mention must be made regarding this relationship.

Air Viet Nam began operations on 15 October 1951, with an initial fleet of three DC-3s, three DC-4s, and three Bristol Freighters flying daily between Saigon, Hanoi, and Hiphong. Other major cities of Vietnam and Laos were soon added to the airline's network. The fleet was exclusively operated by French crews and service technicians.

This all changed in August 1959, however, when President Diem canceled French contracts and initially replaced them with military flight crews and mechanics taken from the VNAF on a rotational basis. It was common practice for select pilots to be flying combat missions one week and in the uniform of Air Viet Nam the next; then back to combat again. This practice eventually changed, however, and flight crews came from VNAF retirees, some civilian pilots, and transfers directly from VNAF; some others being temporary as the needs dictated. It is because of this personnel crossover that the kinship connection was formed. Operations and maintenance facilities remained completely separate.

In the mid-1960s Air Vietnam extended its air routes beyond the Asian continental shores using, at first, Boeing 707s, shown here on a stop-over at Da Nang. *Courtesy of Pham Quang Khiem.*

Long-standing and upgraded logo of Air Viet Nam.

AIR VIET NAM

Air Vietnam

Air Viet Nam was a part of VNAF to the extent that these civil transports were manned by VNAF pilots. Duties frequently changed from that of flying combat to flying the scheduled Air Viet Nam flights. This DC-3, XV-NIA, prepares for a south takeoff at Da Nang, August 1967. *Courtesy of Nicholas Williams.*

A leased Caravelle of Air Viet Nam awaits passengers at Tan San Nhut Airport in July 1968.

This Boeing 707 of Air Viet Nam boards passengers at Hong Kong's Kai Tak Airport in June 1974. *Courtesy of REG Davies.*

Several Boeing 727s graced the fleet of Air Viet Nam. *Courtesy of Pham Quang Khiem.*

Air Viet Nam doubled its fleet of transports when land transport to many populated centers of the war-torn country was interrupted. For example, between 1961 and 1970 freight/ton mileage increased tenfold, and passenger loads increased 15 times. By 1970 this airline was nearly 83 percent owned by the Republic of Vietnam government.

Although Air Viet Nam had operated services to Laos from its inception, the airline did not become truly international until 1964 when flights were begun to Bangkok, Thailand, via Phnom Penh, Cambodia. Another international service to Kuala Lumpur and Singapore was begun in 1965, and Taipei was added to the international network the following year.

Following the purchase of two Boeing 727s for the international flights, service to Manila was opened in the spring of 1968. By that September the airline inaugurated a major northern through-service—Saigon - Hong Kong - Taipei - Osaka - Tokyo—using the B.727s to expand its international network to a total of 6900 miles (11,000 km).

By 1973 a Boeing 707 was leased and later purchased from Pan American World Airways. This permitted Vietnam's flag carrier to further increase its international services. However, the infamous fuel crisis in late 1973 caused flights to the Philippines to be suspended. Under a pool arrangement with Air France, using the French carrier's Boeing 707 and 747 equipment, Air Viet Nam operated between Saigon and Paris three times weekly.

Inside South Vietnam the company continued to operate its fleet of DC-3s and DC-4s to 19 cities, although this service was reduced following the 1973 cease-fire agreement that made road travel within the country safer and more economical.

Yet Air Viet Nam continued to grow due to the increased demand for international flights. It carried 40 percent more passengers during the spring of 1974 than during the same time the year before. The airline had an optimistic outlook, placing further growth plans upon an influx of tourism with the cease-fire they expected would last. History records what happened, and Air Viet Nam met its demise with that of the nation.

Pilot wings of Air Viet Nam. *Courtesy of Thomas Clinton.*

Boeing 707 in Air Viet Nam's impressive colors by the end of the war.

Glossary

AAA	automatic antiaircraft guns
AB	air base
ACS	air commando squadron
AD	air division
AFB	Air Force Base
AGL	above ground level
AHC	assault helicopter company
ALO	air liaison officer
AOC	Air Operations Command (VNAF)
ASHC	assault support helicopter company
BOBS	Beacon-Only Bombing System
Bogey	Any aircraft the observer cannot identify.
CBU	Cluster Bomb Unit, (Anti-personnel)
CIA	Central Intelligence Agency (US)
COIN	Counterinsurgency
Corps	Used here to generally define Military Regions and Tactical Regions.
DAO	Defense Attache Office
Dirty Thirty	USAF C-47 pilots attached to VNAF (1962-63) An unofficial nickname.
div	division
DMZ	demilitarized zone
DZ	drop zone
ECM	Electronic countermeasure
FAC	forward air control; forward air controller
Farm Gate	Det. 2, 4400th Combat Crew Training Squadron and subsequently USAF air commando activity at Bien Hoa Air Base.
FS	Fighter Squadron
Flaming Dart	United States-Vietnamese Air Force air reprisal strikes against North Vietnam, February 1965.
FOL	forward operations location
FM	frequency modulation
G	gravity
GAO	Group, Artillery Observation
GAU	Gun, Aircraft Unit (followed by a number for type)
ICC	International Control Commission
Jinking	To take jerking evasive action in an aircraft.
Jungle Jim	The 4400th Combat Crew Training Squadron and subsequent USAF air commando activity at Eglin Air Force Base, Florida.
HVAR	High velocity aircraft rocket.
K-loader	a lifter vehicle used to load aircraft and trucks
KIA	killed in action
KQVN	Khong Quan Viet Nam (Vietnamese Air Force)
LOC	line of communication
LZ	landing zone
M-117	750 lb (340 kg) low drag general purpose bomb

MAAG	Military Assistance Advisory Group
MAAGV	Military Assistance Advisory Group, Vietnam
MACV	Military Assistance Command, Vietnam
MAG	Military Advisory Group
MAP	Military Assistance Program
MDAP	Mutual Defense Assistance Program
MK-81	250 lb (113 kg) low drag general purpose bomb
MK-82	500 lb (226 kg) low drag general purpose bomb
MP	Military Police
MR	Military Region that coincides with numbered corps areas. Same as Tactical Region.
napalm	gasoline with substance added to form a jelly like compound for fire bombs
NAS	Naval Air Station
NATO	North Atlantic Treaty Organization
NVA	North Vietnam Army
OJT	on-the-job training
OS	Observation Squadron
PACAF	Pacific Air Forces (USAF)
PF	Popular Force (village level)
POL	Petroleum, oil, lubricants.
PTS	Pilot Training Squadron
RAG	Replacement Air Group (US Navy)
RF	Regional Force (under province chief)
RHAW	Radar Homing and Warning
RVN	Republic of Vietnam
RVNAF	Republic of Vietnam Armed Forces
SA- (SA-7)	surface-to-air type of weapon
SAM	surface-to-air missile
SM	special mission
SEA	Southeast Asia
SEATO	Southeast Asia Treaty Organization
SOG	Special Operations Group
Sortie	Flight of a tactical nature into airspace where enemy action can be expected.
SOS	Special Operations Squadron
SVN	South Vietnam
TR	Tactical Region (Same as Corps Area)
TACS	Tactical Air Control System
TASS	Tactical Air Support Squadron, USAF.
TOCC	Tactical Operations Control Center
TS	Transport Squadron
TSN	Station identifier for Tan Son Nhut Airport
UPT	Undergraduate Pilot Training
US	United States (of America)
USAF	United States Air Force
USMC	United States Marine Corps
USN	United States Navy
VC	Viet Cong
VFR	visual flight rules
Viet Cong	Viet Nam Cong San: Vietnamese communist, usually South Vietnamese communists.
Viet Minh	Initial description of Vietnamese communists. Was later used to indicate ethnic North Vietnamese forces who entered Laos prior to regular North Vietnamese Army troops.
VIP	very important person
VN	Vietnam
VNAF	Vietnamese Air Force (South)
White Whale	Specially configured C-123 for Gen. Westmoreland

Frequently Used Vietnamese Terms and their Meanings

Bảo-Quốc Trấn Không = Protect the Land and Guard the Air

Đòan = Squadron

Hổ = Tiger

Huấn-Luyện = Training

Không-Đòan = Air Wing

Không-Quân = Air Force

Không-Quân Việt-Nam = KQVN Air Force, Vietnam (VNAF)

Long = Dragon

Phi-Đòan = Flying Squadron

Sư-Đòan Không-Quân = Division, Air Force

Thần= Divine

Tổ-Quốc Không-Gian = Fatherland - Space

Trung-Tâm = Center

Trung-Tâm Huấn-Luyện Không-Quân

TTHLKQ = Air Training Center (TTHLKQ came from : Trung-Tâm Huấn-Luyện Không-Quân)

Vietnamese Names and Words

Geographical locations appear in this book in the approved American language format. Listed below are these location names with their Vietnamese spelling.

An-Lộc

An-Nam

Ban-Mê-Thuột.

Biên-Hòa

Bình-Thủy

Cam-ranh

Cần-Thơ

Cao-Bằng

Chợ-Lớn

Chu-Lai

Đà-Nẵng

Điện-Biên-Phủ

Đồng-Đế

Đông-Hà

Hải-Phòng

Hà-Nội

Hồ-chí-Minh City

Huế

Lam-Sơn

Lạng-Sơn

MeKong

Nha-Trang

Phang-Rang

Phan-Thiết

Phát-Diệm

Phú-Bài

Phù-Cát

Qui-Nhơn

Sài-Gòn

Tân-Sơn-Nhứt

Tuy-Hòa

Việt-Nam

Vĩnh-Linh

Vũng-Tàu

Xuân-lộc

Bibliography

The United States Air Force in Southeast Asia 1961-1973, edited by Carl Berger, Office of US Air Force History, Washington, DC 1977.
The Vietnamese Air Force. 1951-1975, USAF Southeast Asia Monograph Series, Volume 3, Monographs 4 and 5, edited by A J C. Lavalle, Office of US Air Force History, Washington, DC 1975.
The United States Air Force in Southeast Asia, The Advisory Years to 1965, by Robert F Futrell, Office of US Air Force History, Washington, DC 1981.
Air Power in Three Wars, by General William W Momyer, USAF (Ret.), Office of US Air Force History, Washington, DC 1978.
Seventh Air Force In Country Tactical Air Operations Handbook, Seventh Air Force Pamphlet No 55-1, 1968.
Vietnam from Cease-Fire to Capitulation, by William E Le Gro, US Army Center of Military History, Washington, DC.
Twenty Years and Twenty Days, by Nguyen Cao Ky, Stein and Day Publishers, New York, 1976.
The Fall of South Vietnam: Statements by Vietnamese Military and Civilian Leaders, by Stephen T Hosmer, Konrad Kellen, Brian M Jenkins, report prepared for Historian, Office of the Secretary of Defense, Rand Corp, 1978. Also Crane-Russak Co, 1980.
Skyraider, The Douglas A-1 'Flying Dump Truck', by Rosario Rausa, The Nautical & Aviation Publishing Company of America, Annapolis, Maryland 1982.
French Air Force In Indochina, Transport and Bombardment, 1945-1954. By Jean-Michel Guhl, Sup Air Publications, Paris 1981.
History of French Military Aviation, by Gen Charles Christienne and Gen Lierre Lissarrague, Charles-Lavauzelle, Paris & Limoges 1978.
B-57 Canberra At War 1964-1972, by Robert C Mikesh, Ian Allan Ltd, London 1980
Martin B-57 Canberra, the Complete Record, by Robert C Mikesh, Schiffer Publishing Ltd, Atglen, Pa. 1995.

Many feature articles, newspaper and magazine stories, and Air force history documents were drawn upon in the course of gathering information for this book. Some of the more important ones are listed below:

'Behind the Headlines in Viet Nam' by Peter T. White, National Geographic, February 1967, 149-193.
Senate Committee on Foreign Relations, 93rd Congress, 2nd Session, December 1974.
Project CHECO Report, 'Organization, Mission and Growth of the Vietnamese Air Force 1949-1968' Headquarters PACAF, 1968.
Corona Harvest, US Policy to Southeast Asia, 1948-1968, 600pp, Air University.
ATC Historical Monograph 'Air Training Command's Support of Forces in Southeast Asia 1961-1973' HQ Air Training Command..
ATC Historical Monograph 'History of Foreign Training in ATC 1941-1976' Hq Air Training Command.

Defense Attache Office, Saigon, RVN, reports on:
'Deputy Chief of Staff, Plans and Operations, Jul-Dec 1972'
'History, Jan 1972-Mar 1973, The New Agencies'.
'History, FY 1973: Contingency withdrawal planning'.
'History, Apr-Jun 1973: DAO mission and functions'.
'Quarterly review and analysis for Apr-Jun 1973'.
'Weekly Status Reports, 14 May 1973 to 30 Sep 1973'.
'History narrative, 1 Apr 1974 to 30 Jun 1974'.
'History narrative, 1 Jul 1974 to 30 Sep 1974'.
'Overview of Working Environment in DAO & VNAF in Sep 1974'.
(All on file in Office of US Air Force History, Washington.)

Although not used directly as source material, the following books, referring to the VNAF, are recommended reading.

Vietnam, The History and the Tactics, consultant editor John Pimlott, Crescent Books, New York, 1982.
The Vietnam Experience, Rain of Fire, Air War, 1969-1973, by John Marrocco, Boston Publishing Company, Boston, Mass, 1984
Air War Over Southeast Asia, Volumes 1, 2, & 3, by Lou Drendel, Squadron/Signal Publications, Carrollton, Texas 1982.
A-1 Skyraider in Vietnam, by Wayne Mutza, Schiffer Publishing Ltd., Atglen PA, 2003.

Notes

1. Unofficial name for the Bell UH-1 helicopter.
2. Ten Aviation Cadets from civilian status, and four Student Officers already commissioned 2nd Lts. from National Academy at Dalat; Nguyen-ngoc-Oanh, Vo-Dinh, Tu-bo-Cam and Nguyen-the-Anh.
3. Among the first were Tran-van-Ho, Nguyen-cao-Ky, Huynh-huu-Hien, and Ha-xuan-Vinh.
4. Short name given to the Revolutionary League for the Independence of Vietnam, made up of communists nationalists and smaller parties in 1941 to resist the Japanese and later the French to win independence for Vietnam. In 1946 the Communists eliminated the nationalists and the Viet Minh were communists only. See glossary.
5. North Atlantic Treaty Organization.
6. Southeast Asia Treaty Organization
7. Army of the Republic of Vietnam (Republic of Vietnam Armed Forces)
8. Joint General Staff (JGS),a Vietnamese Army general staff composed almost entirely of Army officers, the Chairman of which directs the commanders of the Air Force, the Navy, and the Marine Corps, as well as the commanders of the principal field commands, installations and facilities.
9. Presumably, attrition during the preceding five years took the rest. Some sources state that 25 Bearcats were transferred to the VNAF.
10. The USAF book, The Advisory Years to 1965 shows the 1st Helicopter Squadron being formed June 1957 with H-19s.
11. A flying technique where the aircraft is made to lose flying speed and to drop by pointing the nose steeply upward.
12. AVM Nguyen-cao-Ky, as Chairman of the Central Executive Committee, functioned as Prime Minister, yet retained the position of Commander of the VNAF until 1967.
13. One combat mission by a single aircraft flown in airspace where enemy fire may be expected is a sortie.
14. Call-sign of Ky acquired from the 518 Fighter Squadron with which he normally flew.
15. The word *skoshi* means 'small' in Japanese, a word frequently used by many American servicemen who had been stationed in Japan.
16. HQ PACAF, CHECO Report VNAF 1949-1968.
17. Ibid.
18. Biographical Data Sheets, Hq 7AF, USAF Advisory Group, Office of Information.
19. That study was prepared by former Lt Col Charles McDonald and former Maj A.J.C. Lavalle under the leadership of Gen WW Momyer, USAF (Ret.) It is from this detailed study that much of the material in this chapter is extracted in order to convey comprehensive coverage of the VNAF.
20. USAF SEA Monograph 4, page 79.

Index

Countries

General

Aircraft